TO

GEORGE BRYAN, Esꞯ.

THIS WORK IS INSCRIBED,

BY

HIS SINCERE AND

AFFECTIONATE FRIEND,

THOMAS MOORE.

PREFACE

THE FIFTH EDITION.

" **I** seek truth," said an ancient, " by which nobody ever yet was injured; " * — except, sometimes, (he might have added,) those who venture to *tell* it. This penalty, to which the speakers of truth are exposed, I was prepared to encounter when I undertook the following work. By treating my subject with the spirit of a partisan, I might have secured at least the favour of those to whom I devoted myself; while, by an impartial view of the faults, as well as merits, of all parties, I had but little chance of gaining the good-will of any. The latter was, however, the plan that I adopted, and the result has been very much what I expected. The partisans, on all sides, are dissatisfied with my book. The Tory, of course, is shocked by my Whiggism ; —

* Ζητω την αληθειην ὑφ ἡς ἐδεις πωποτε ιβλαβη. Marc. Antonin.

the Whigs are rather displeased at my candour in conceding, that they have sometimes been wrong, and the Tories right; while the Radical, in his patriotic hatred of both parties, is angry with me for allowing any merit to either. In the mean while, the flattering reception which the work has received from the public in general, not only abundantly consoles me for all such criticism, but justifies the independent course which I have taken.

Conscious, however, as I was of approaching my task, with that fairness of spirit which should characterize such a work, in my other qualifications for the undertaking I was far from having the same confidence. My only hope was, that I should be able, by research and care, to make up for my deficiency in political knowledge; and so far, in this respect, has the result repaid my efforts, that — wide as is the range of events, both public and private, to which my work refers, and sifted as it has been by no friendly hands — however angrily my views and opinions may have been questioned, not a single statement that I have advanced has been disproved.

I have been accused, however, of some omissions and inaccuracies, of which the following are the most important : —

1. I have stated that, in the latter years of Mr. Sheridan's life, the Prince Regent offered to bring him into Parliament, but that he declined the offer. On this the writers of articles in the *Westminster* and *Quarterly Reviews* remark, that I *ought* to have known and added the sequel of this transaction — namely, that the Prince Regent presented to Mr. Sheridan the sum (4000*l.*) intended for the purchase of a seat.

2. In giving an account of the imprisonment of Mr. Sheridan, for debt, in the year 1814, I have said that ' arrangements were made for his release by Mr. Whitbread.' In contradiction to this the Quarterly Reviewer asserts, that his liberation was effected by the interposition of the Prince Regent.

3. In detailing the particulars of the 200*l.* transmitted through Mr. Vaughan to Sheridan on his death-bed, I have stated that the gift was respectfully declined by the family. To this the Quarterly Reviewer answers, that the gift was *not* declined by the family; that it was on the

[A] 2

contrary accepted, made use of, and afterwards, 'on suspicions and pride being awakened,' repaid.

In answering these three charges I shall abstain from all reference whatever to the style or temper in which they have been brought forward — anger having little to do with the truth, on either side of the question.

First, then — with respect to the gift of the 4000*l*. — not only had I never heard it stated that such was the sequel of the transaction, but now that it *is* so stated, must beg leave to withhold my belief : — *not* from any doubt of the disposition of the Illustrious Personage in question to perform such an act of kindness towards Sheridan, but because the statement, at variance as it is with my own information, rests solely on the assertion of two anonymous writers, who differ with each other as to the most material points of the case. If, however, these writers (after first settling this difference between themselves) will enable me, by reference to documents or any existing persons, to authenticate the main point of their statement — the gift of the 4000*l*. — I shall be most happy to correct my own omission, and to be made the humble instrument of recording an act of such liberality in these pages.

I come now to the Second Charge. In detailing the particulars of Mr. Sheridan's imprisonment in 1814, I have given a letter addressed by him to Mr. Whitbread, and dated from the spunging-house, in which he says, ' I enclosed you yesterday three different securities, which, had you been disposed to have acted even as a private friend, would have made it certain that you might have done so without the smallest risk. These you discreetly offered to put into the fire, when you found the object of your humane visit satisfied by seeing me safe in prison.'

In the very face of this authentic document, which proves that Mr. Whitbread had ' seen' Sheridan in the spunging-house, and that a day or two elapsed between this visit and the liberation of Sheridan, the Quarterly Reviewer does not hesitate to bring forward his own private version of the circumstance — namely, that ' Mr. Whitbread left the dinner-table, and repaired to the spunging-house the moment Sheridan's note (acquainting him with his arrest) was delivered to him, but that, before he could reach the place

[A] 3

of confinement, the person of Sheridan was already at liberty, in consequence of the unsolicited and instantaneous interference of Sheridan's royal master.'

Such is the random manner in which this writer supports his charges of inaccuracy, and such the vague assertions which the public are called upon, in the very teeth of documentary evidence, to believe.

On the Third point — the offer of 200*l.* through Mr. Vaughan — the Quarterly Reviewer is no less unlucky in his *facts* than on the second. He is pleased to say, that I ought to have applied to certain nameless gentlemen, to whom he himself is indebted for his lights on the subject. I was, however, satisfied with the authority of the two persons between whom the transaction passed,* Mr. Vaughan and Dr. Bain. Mr. Vaughan has been some time dead; but Dr. Bain is (happily for his many friends) still alive,

---

* In the same manner my account of the early love and marriage of Sheridan (which has also been cavilled at by this Reviewer, on the authority of a clumsy forgery in the Gentleman's Magazine) was noted down, in every particular, from the lips of no less competent and trustworthy a witness than the surviving sister of Mr. Sheridan, Mrs. H. Lefanu.

and the following note from him on the subject will, I trust, be a sufficient answer to this *accurate** Reviewer: —

' *Thompson's Hotel, Cavendish-square, April 20, 1826.*

' My dear Sir — The statement which you have given in your Life of my late friend, Mr. Sheridan, that 200*l.* was the sum proffered to me by Mr. Vaughan, and that it was respectfully declined by the family, is perfectly correct.

Believe me, my dear Sir, very faithfully yours,

' A. BAIN.'

' *Thomas Moore, Esq.*
Sloperton Cottage.'

Having thus disposed of objections, which, had I been guided by my own estimate of their importance, I should hardly have thought worthy of the trouble of an answer, I am happy to take this opportunity of declaring, that, whatever I

---

* Among many other proofs of this *accuracy*, I shall select but the following. In speaking of the Translation of Aristænetus, by Sheridan and Halhed, the Reviewer gravely accuses me of ' having, for the first time, printed some specimens of a performance, which its juvenile authors could get no bookseller to publish.' It is hardly necessary to add, (what every one but this well-informed critic knows,) that the Translation of Aristænetus *was* published by a very respectable bookseller, and that copies of it are by no means rare.

[A] 4

may still presume to think of the conduct pursued towards Mr. Sheridan, I have never meant
to impute to the Illustrious Personage, concerned
in these transactions, any general want of that
munificence which should belong to his high
station.   On the contrary, I have heard more
than one instance of the private generosity of
that Personage (far better authenticated than
any that these awkward apologists have brought
forward) which would render me not slow in be-
lieving any similar acts of kindness attributed to
him.   As little could I have meant to doubt the
readiness of the Whig friends of Sheridan to
assist him, while he made one of their circle, on
any occasions when he may have required their
aid; though, in justice to him, I must repeat
that such appeals were far from frequent.   The
strong remarks which I hazarded, and which
have produced — naturally enough, perhaps —
so much irritation, apply solely to the last few
months of Sheridan's life, and to the neglect
with which he was left to die, in the hands of
bailiffs, by those, of whose society he had been,
through life, the light and ornament.   To this
neglect — which, however excusable in the few
whom his conduct in 1812 had injured, can be

but little defended in the many, whom that conduct but remotely affected, and admits of no vindication whatever in the quarter, for which that sacrifice of character was made — to this neglect alone my remarks applied, and I see no reason whatever to retract or soften them. The occasion called for a strong lesson to the great and prosperous, which if I had shrunk from giving, through either fear or partiality, though I might thereby have better consulted my ease and interest, I certainly should not have been upon such good terms with my own conscience as I feel at present.

Among a few inadvertencies, which I had not before an opportunity of correcting, I beg to direct the attention of the reader to the following : —

In the list of persons present at the funeral of Mr. Sheridan, the name of Lord Jersey was erroneously included — that nobleman having declined attending on the occasion. It ought also to have been mentioned, as some extenuation of the inconsistency of many who crowded to that funeral, that Mrs. Sheridan wrote letters to most of them, requesting their attendance.

I had said, (vol. ii. p. 446.) " he appears but rarely to have had recourse to pecuniary assistance from friends." To the few whom I have mentioned as ministering in this way to his comfort, I have much pleasure in adding the Duke of Bedford, who, about a year before his death, lent him 200*l.*

In an anecdote related of Mr. Sheridan and Lord Edward Fitzgerald, (vol. ii. p. 189.) the accidental omission of the few words, " on his leaving the room,": afforded an opening, unluckily, for an attack upon the memory of Sheridan, (*Westminster Review*, No. VIII.) as remarkable for its malice, as for the total ignorance of Sheridan's character, which it exhibited. These words, omitted by mistake in transcribing; are now restored.

Since the foregoing Preface was written, I have been furnished with some information on the subject of the Royal gift to Sheridan, which, though I am unable to verify it by any documentary evidence, comes from a quarter in which I am disposed to place considerable confidence. By the account thus communicated to me, both my own original impression and the statement opposed to it are, in some degree, reconciled; as it appears that though the Royal Personage did actually bestow this gift, yet, through the fault of the agent to whom the money was entrusted, Sheridan never received it.

The sum in question (3000*l.* or 4000*l.*, my informant is uncertain which,) was, it seems, transmitted, for the purpose of purchasing a seat for Sheridan, through the hands of the late Lord Hastings, and was by him entrusted to Mr. Cockrell, an attorney, who professed to have the means of effecting the object desired. When Sheridan, as I have stated, declined accepting a seat on such terms, the Prince generously ordered that the money intended for the purchase should be given to him; but the person to whom it was confided, having (says my authority) " under unwarrantable pretences" detained it in his hands, the benevolent intentions of the Royal donor were frustrated. There is said to be a letter extant from the nobleman employed in the transaction, which would prove the circumstances to be as I have stated them; but, though I have taken some pains to procure this document, my efforts, I am sorry to say, have not been successful.

From the same quarter I have been favoured with some explanation on the subject of a charge brought against the late Mr. Whitbread, in a letter, (vol. ii. p. 442) which has been thought to bear hard on the memory of that gentleman. In that letter Sheridan says, " If you had not forcibly withheld from me the twelve thousand pounds, in consequence of a threatening letter from a miserable swindler, whose claim you, in particular, knew to be a lie, I should at least have been out of the reach of this state of miserable insult." The explanation given of the transaction here alluded to, is, in the words of my authority, as follows: — " Mr. Whitbread, having been furnished by the Treasurer of the

theatre and Mr. Burgess with a list or statement of the *bonâ fide* debts due from that concern, made his arrangements with the creditors
and proprietors accordingly; and whatever was
due to Mr. Sheridan would have been paid to
him upon the faith of the list so delivered. —
Mr. Taylor, of the Opera House, however, advanced a claim upon Mr. Whitbread for the
payment of upwards of 20,000*l.*, which he pretended was due to him from the proprietors of
the late theatre, and threatened to file a bill in
Chancery to obtain an injunction to restrain the
expenditure of the subscription money until he
was paid. — Such an unexpected claim alarmed
Mr. Whitbread, and he was advised by counsel
not to pay the proprietors any money until it
was disposed of. After a most strict investigation, however, the claim turned out to be
nothing more than an impudent attempt to obtain a large sum of money, although not a shilling
of it was due: but not the slightest blame ought
to be imputed to Mr. Whitbread on this account;
— he and the Committee were, by the Act of
Parliament, responsible for the distribution of
the subscription money to the creditors of the
theatre, according to the list delivered; and if

Taylor's claim had been proved, the Committee, of which Mr. Whitbread was the chairman, would have been liable for the money they might have paid to Mr. Sheridan, after the notice of that claim."

The author of an article in the last number of the Edinburgh Review, in noticing the extracts from the foregoing Preface which appeared in some of the newspapers, remarks on " the too great asperity with which (as it appears to him,) I still speak of the neglect that Sheridan experienced in his last sickness from most of his former associates." It is possible, though such is not my own impression, that my feelings on this point may have carried me too far. In order, therefore, that my future readers may be in possession of the reasons, on which a more favourable view of the conduct of these persons is founded, I give the following extract from the article alluded to : —

" The circumstances of palliation are suggested by Mr. Moore's own narrative. Sheridan had behaved inexcusably to the most distinguished of his former associates in 1812, and had, from that period, naturally lived in a state of alienation from their society. The actual urgency of his distress, it is admitted, was not known till it was too late materially to relieve them, although it was no sooner divulged than inquiries and offers of service flowed in, in abundance: and as to the splendid mustering, even of his alienated friends, at the funeral, the fact that they were expressly written to, and requested to attend, by Mrs. Sheridan, really seems to afford the most satisfactory explanation, and to convert what might otherwise appear to be mere selfish ostentation, into an act of kindness and propriety."

CONTENTS

OF

THE FIRST VOLUME.

broke through all the indolence and indifference of his character.

Harrow, at this time, possessed some peculiar advantages, of which a youth like Sheridan might have powerfully availed himself. At the head of the school was Doctor Robert Sumner, a man of fine talents, but, unfortunately, one of those, who have passed away without leaving any trace behind, except in the admiring recollection of their contemporaries. His taste is said to have been of a purity almost perfect, combining what are seldom seen together, that critical judgment which is alive to the errors of genius, with the warm sensibility that deeply feels its beauties. At the same period, the distinguished scholar, Dr. Parr, who, to the massy erudition of a former age, joined all the free and enlightened intelligence of the present, was one of the under masters of the school ; and both he and Dr. Sumner endeavoured, by every method they could devise, to awaken in Sheridan a consciousness of those powers, which, under all the disadvantages of indolence and carelessness, it was manifest to them that he possessed. But remonstrance and encouragement were equally thrown away upon the good-humoured but immovable indifference of their pupil; and though there exist among Mr. Sheridan's papers some curious proofs of a degree of industry in study for which few have ever given him credit, they are probably but the desultory efforts of a later period of his life, to recover the loss of that first precious time, whose susceptibility of instruction, as well as of pleasure, never comes again.

One of the most valuable acquisitions he derived from Harrow was that friendship, which lasted throughout his life, with Dr. Parr, — which mutual admiration very early began, and the "*idem sentire de re publica*" of course not a little strengthened.

As this learned and estimable man has, within the last few weeks, left a void in the world which will not be easily filled up, I feel that it would be unjust to my readers not to give, in his own words, the particulars of Sheridan's school-days, with which he had the kindness to favour me, and to which his name gives an authenticity and interest too valuable on such a subject to be withheld :—

"DEAR SIR,   Hatton, August 3. 1818.
"With the aid of a scribe I sit down to fulfil my promise about Mr. Sheridan. There was little in his boyhood worth communication. He was inferior to many of his school-fellows in the ordinary business of a school, and I do not remember any one instance in which he distinguished himself by Latin or English composition,

in prose or verse. * Nathaniel Halhed, one of
his school-fellows, wrote well in Latin and Greek.
Richard Archdall, another school-fellow, ex-
celled in English verse. Richard Sheridan aspired to no rivalry with either of them. He was
at the uppermost part of the fifth form, but he
never reached the sixth, and, if I mistake not,
he had no opportunity of attending the most
difficult and the most honourable of school business, when the Greek plays were taught — and
it was the custom at Harrow to teach these at
least every year. He went through his lessons
in Horace, and Virgil, and Homer well enough
for a time. But, in the absence of the upper
master, Doctor Sumner, it once fell in my way
to instruct the two upper forms, and upon calling up Dick Sheridan, I found him not only
slovenly in construing, but unusually defective
in his Greek grammar. Knowing him to be a
clever fellow, I did not fail to probe and to teaze
him. I stated his case with great good-humour
to the upper master, who was one of the best
tempered men in the world; and it was agreed
between us, that Richard should be called oftener
and worked more severely. The varlet was not
suffered to stand up in his place; but was sum-

---

* It will be seen, however, though Dr. Parr was not aware
of the circumstance, that Sheridan did try his talent at English verse before he left Harrow.

moned to take his station near the master's table, where the voice of no prompter could reach him; and, in this defenceless condition he was so harrassed, that he at last gathered up some grammatical rules, and prepared himself for his lessons. While this tormenting process was inflicted upon him, I now and then upbraided him. But you will take notice that he did not incur any corporal punishment for his idleness: his industry was just sufficient to protect him from disgrace. All the while Sumner and I saw in him vestiges of a superior intellect. His eye, his countenance, his general manner, were striking. His answers to any common question were prompt and acute. We knew the esteem, and even admiration, which, somehow or other, all his school-fellows felt for him. He was mischievous enough, but his pranks were accompanied by a sort of vivacity and cheerfulness, which delighted Sumner and myself. I had much talk with him about his apple-loft, for the supply of which all the gardens in the neighbourhood were taxed, and some of the lower boys were employed to furnish it. I threatened, but without asperity, to trace the depredators, through his associates, up to their leader. He with perfect good-humour set me at defiance, and I never could bring the charge home to him. All boys and all masters were pleased with him. I often praised him as a lad of great talents, —

often exhorted him to use them well; but my exhortations were fruitless. I take for granted that his taste was silently improved, and that he knew well the little which he did know. He was removed from school too soon by his father, who was the intimate friend of Sumner, and whom I often met at his house. Sumner had a fine voice, fine ear, fine taste, and, therefore, pronunciation was frequently the favourite subject between him and Tom Sheridan. I was present at many of their discussions and disputes, and sometimes took a very active part in them, — but Richard was not present. The father, you know, was a wrong-headed, whimsical man, and, perhaps, his scanty circumstances were one of the reasons which prevented him from sending Richard to the University. He must have been aware, as Sumner and I were, that Richard's mind was not cast in any ordinary mould. I ought to have told you that Richard, when a boy, was a great reader of English poetry; but his exercises afforded no proof of his proficiency. In truth, he, as a boy, was quite careless about literary fame. I should suppose that his father, without any regular system, polished his taste, and supplied his memory with anecdotes about our best writers in our Augustan age. The grandfather, you know, lived familiarly with Swift. I have heard of him, as an excellent scholar. His boys in Ireland once performed a Greek play, and when Sir William Jones and I were talking over this event, I determined to make the experiment in England. I selected some of my best boys, and they performed the Œdipus Tyrannus, and the Trachinians of Sophocles. I wrote some Greek Iambics to vindicate myself from the imputation of singularity, and grieved I am that I did not keep a copy of them. Milton, you may remember, recommends what I attempted.

" I saw much of Sheridan's father after the death of Sumner, and after my own removal from Harrow to Stanmer. I respected him, — he really liked me, and did me some important services, — but I never met him and Richard together. I often enquired about Richard, and, from the father's answers, found they were not upon good terms, — but neither he nor I ever spoke of his son's talents but in terms of the highest praise."

In a subsequent letter Dr. Parr says, " I referred you to a passage in The Gentleman's Magazine, where I am represented as discovering and encouraging in Richard Sheridan those intellectual powers, which had not been discovered and encouraged by Sumner. But the statement is incorrect. We both of us discovered talents, which neither of us could bring into action while Sheridan was a schopl-boy. He gave us few op-

portunities of praise in the course of his school-
business, and yet he was well aware that we
thought highly of him, and anxiously wished more
to be done by him than he was disposed to do.

" I once or twice met his mother, — she was
quite celestial.   Both her virtues and her genius
were highly esteemed by Robert Sumner.   I
know not whether Tom Sheridan found Richard
tractable in the art of speaking, — and, upon such
a subject, indolence or indifference would have
been resented by the father as crimes quite inexpiable. One of Richard's sisters now and then
visited Harrow, and well do I remember that, in
the house where I lodged, she triumphantly repeated Dryden's Ode upon St. Cecilia's Day,
according to the instruction given to her by her
father.   Take a sample : —

> " ' *None* but the brave,
> None but the *brave*,
> None *but* the brave deserve the fair.'

Whatever may have been the zeal or the proficiency of the sister, naughty Richard, like Gallio,
seemed to care nought for these things.

" In the later periods of his life Richard did
not cast behind him classical reading. He spoke
copiously and powerfully about Cicero. He had
read, and he had understood the four orations
of Demosthenes read and taught in our public

schools. He was at home in Virgil and in Horace. I cannot speak positively about Homer, — but I am very sure that he read the Iliad now and then ; *not* as a professed scholar would do, critically, but with all the strong sympathies of a poet reading a poet. * Richard did not, and could not forget what he once knew, but his path to knowledge was his own, — his steps were noiseless, — his progress was scarcely felt by himself, — his movements were rapid but irregular.

"Let me assure you that Richard, when a boy, was by no means vicious. The sources of his infirmities were a scanty and precarious allowance from the father; the want of a regular plan for some profession ; and, above all, the act of throwing him upon the town, when he ought to have been pursuing his studies at the University. He would have done little among mathematicians at Cambridge; — he would have been a rake, or an idler, or a trifler, at Dublin; — but I am inclined to think that at Oxford he would have become an excellent scholar.

" I have now told you all that I know, and it amounts to very little. I am very solicitous for

* It was not one of the least of the triumphs of Sheridan's talent, to have been able to persuade so acute a scholar as Dr. Parr, that the extent of his classical acquirements was so great as is here represented, and to have thus impressed with the idea of his remembering so much, the person who best knew how little he had learned.

justice to be done to Robert Sumner. He is one of the six or seven persons among my own acquaintance, whose taste I am accustomed to consider perfect, and, were he living, his admiration   *   *   *   *   *

  *   *   *   *   *" †

During the greater part of Richard's stay at Harrow, his father had been compelled by the embarrassment of his affairs to reside with the remainder of the family in France, and it was at Blois, in the September of 1766, that Mrs. Sheridan died — leaving behind her that best kind of fame, which results from a life of usefulness and purity, and which it requires not the aid of art or eloquence to blazon. She appears to have been one of those rare women, who, united to men of more pretensions but less real intellect than themselves, meekly conceal this superiority even from their own hearts, and pass their lives, without a remonstrance or murmur, in gently endeavouring to repair those evils, which the indiscretion or vanity of their partners has brought upon them.

As a supplement to the interesting communication of Doctor Parr, I shall here subjoin an extract from a letter, which the eldest sister of Sheridan, Mrs. E. Lefanu, wrote a few months

† The remainder of the letter relates to other subjects.

after his death to Mrs. Sheridan, in consequence of a wish expressed by the latter that Mrs. Lefanu would communicate such particulars as she remembered of his early days. It will show, too, the feeling which his natural good qualities, in spite of the errors by which they were obscured and weakened, kept alive to the last, in the hearts of those connected with him, — that sort of retrospective affection, which, when those whom we have loved become altered, whether in mind or person, brings the recollection of what they once were, to mingle with and soften our impression of what they are.

After giving an account of the residence of the family in France, she continues : — " We returned to England, when I may say I first became acquainted with my brother — for faint and imperfect were my recollections of him, as might be expected from my age. I saw him ; and my childish attachment revived with double force. He was handsome, not merely in the eyes of a partial sister, but generally allowed to be so. His cheeks had the glow of health, his eyes, — the finest in the world, — the brilliancy of genius, and were soft as a tender and affectionate heart could render them. The same playful fancy, the same sterling and innoxious wit, that was shown afterwards in his writings, cheered and delighted the family-circle. I admired — I almost adored

him. I would most willingly have sacrificed my
life for him, as I, in some measure, proved to him
at Bath, where we resided for some time, and
where events that you must have heard of engaged him in a duel. My father's displeasure
threatened to involve me in the denunciations
against him, for committing what he considered
as a crime. Yet I risked every thing, and in the
event was made happy by obtaining forgiveness for
my brother. * * * * You may perceive, dear sister,
that very little indeed have I to say on a subject
so near your heart, and near mine also. That
for years I lost sight of a brother whom I loved
with unabated affection—a love that neither absence or neglect could chill—I always consider
as a great misfortune."

On his leaving Harrow, where he continued
till near his eighteenth year, he was brought home
by his father, who, with the elder son, Charles,
had lately returned from France, and taken a
house in London. Here the two brothers for some
time received private tuition from Mr. Lewis
Kerr, an Irish gentleman, who had formerly practised as a physician, but having, by loss of health,
been obliged to give up his profession, supported
himself by giving lessons in Latin and Mathe-
matics. They attended also the fencing and
riding-schools of Mr. Angelo, and received instructions from their father in English grammar

and oratory. Of this advantage, however, it is probable, only the elder son availed himself, as Richard, who seems to have been determined to owe all his excellence to nature alone, was found as impracticable a pupil at home as at school. But, however inattentive to his studies he may have been at Harrow, it appears, from one of the letters of his school-fellow, Mr. Halhed, that, in poetry, which is usually the first exercise, in which these young athletæ of intellect try their strength, he had already distinguished himself, — and, in conjunction with his friend Halhed, had translated the seventh Idyl, and many of the lesser poems of Theocritus. This literary partnership was resumed soon after their departure from Harrow. In the year 1770, when Halhed was at Oxford, and Sheridan residing with his father at Bath, they entered into a correspondence (of which, unluckily, only Halhed's share remains), and, with all the hope and spirit of young adventurers, began and prosecuted a variety of works together, of which none but their translation of Aristænetus ever saw the light.

There is something in the alliance between these boys peculiarly interesting. Their united ages, as Halhed boasts in one of his letters, did not amount to thirty-eight. They were both abounding in wit and spirits, and as sanguine as the consciousness of talent and youth could make them; both inspired with a taste for pleasure, and thrown upon their own resources for the means of gratifying it; both carelessly embarking, without rivalry or reserve, their venture of fame in the same bottom, and both, as Halhed discovered at last, passionately in love with the same woman.

It would have given me great pleasure to have been enabled to enliven my pages, with even a few extracts from that portion of their correspondence, which, as I have just mentioned, has fallen into my hands. There is in the letters of Mr. Halhed a fresh youthfulness of style, and an unaffected vivacity of thought, which I question whether even his witty correspondent could have surpassed. As I do not, however, feel authorized to lay these letters before the world, I must only avail myself of the aid which their contents supply, towards tracing the progress of his literary partnership with Sheridan, and throwing light on a period so full of interest in the life of the latter.

Their first joint production was a farce, or rather play, in three acts, called " Jupiter," written in imitation of the burletta of Midas, whose popularity seems to have tempted into its wake a number of these musical parodies upon heathen fable. The amour of Jupiter with *Major* Amphitryon's wife, and *Sir Richard* Ixion's

VOL. I.   c

courtship of Juno, who substitutes *Miss Peggy Nubilis* in her place, form the subject of this ludicrous little drama, of which Halhed furnished the burlesque scenes, — while the form of a rehearsal, into which the whole is thrown, and which, as an anticipation of " The Critic " is highly curious, was suggested and managed entirely by Sheridan. The following extracts will give some idea of the humour of this trifle ; and in the character of Simile the reader will at once discover a sort of dim and shadowy pre-existence of Puff : —

" *Simile.* Sir, you are very ignorant on the subject, —it is the method most in vogue.

" *O'Cul.* What ! to make the music first, and then make the sense to it afterwards !

" *Sim.* Just so.

" *Monop.* What Mr. Simile says is very true, gentlemen ; and there is nothing surprising in it, if we consider now the general method of writing *plays* to *scenes*.

" *O'Cul.* Writing *plays* to *scenes !* — Oh, you are joking.

" *Monop.* Not I, upon my word. Mr. Simile knows that I have frequently a complete set of scenes from Italy, and then I have nothing to do but to get some ingenious hand to write a play to them.

" *Sim.* I am your witness, sir. Gentlemen, you perceive you know nothing about these matters.

" *O'Cul.* Why, Mr. Simile, I don't pretend to know much relating to these affairs, but what I think is this, that in this method, according to your principles, you must often commit blunders.

" *Sim.* Blunders ! to be sure I must, but I always could get myself out of them again. Why, I'll tell you an instance of it.—You must know I was once a journeyman sonnet-writer to Signor Squallini. Now, his method, when seized with the *furor harmonicus* was constantly to make me sit by his side, while he was thrumming on his harpsichord, in order to make extempore verses to whatever air he should beat out to his liking. I remember, one morning, as he was in this situation, *thrum, thrum, thrum,* (*moving his fingers as if beating on the harpsichord,*) striking out something prodigiously great, as he thought,—' Hah !' said he,—' hah ! Mr. Simile, *thrum, thrum, thrum,* by gar here is vary fine, — *thrum, thrum, thrum,* write me some words directly.' — I durst not interrupt him to ask on what subject, so instantly began to describe a fine morning.

" ' Calm was the land and calm the seas,
    And calm the heaven's dome serene,
  Hush'd was the gale and hush'd the breeze,
    And not a vapour to be seen."

I sang it to his notes.—' Hah ! upon my vord vary pritt, — *thrum, thrum, thrum,* — stay, stay, — *thrum, thrum.* — Hoa ! upon my vord, here it must be an adagio,— *thrum, thrum,* — oh ! let it be an *Ode to Melancholy.*'

" *Monop.* The Devil !—there you were puzzled sure.

" *Sim.* Not in the least, — I brought in a *cloud* in the next stanza, and matters, you see, came about at once.

" *Monop.* An excellent transition.

" *O'Cul.* Vastly ingenious indeed.

" *Sim.* Was it not? hey ! it required a little command, — a little presence of mind, — but I believe we had better proceed.

" *Monop.* The sooner the better, — come, gentlemen, resume your seats.

" *Sim.* Now for it. Draw up the curtain, and (*looking at his book*) enter Sir Richard Ixion, — but stay, — zounds, Sir Richard ought to over-hear Jupiter and his wife quarrelling, — but, never mind, — these accidents have spoiled the division of my piece. — So enter, Sir Richard, and look as cunning as if you had overheard them. Now for it, gentlemen, — you can't be too attentive.

" *Enter* Sir RICHARD IXION, *completely dressed with bag, sword, &c.*

" *Ix.* 'Fore George, at logger-heads, — a lucky minute,
'Pon honour, I may make my market in it.
Dem it, my air, address, and mien must touch her,
Now out of sorts with him, — less God than butcher.
O rat the fellow, — where can all his sense lie,
To gallify the lady so immensely ?
Ah ! *le grand bête qu'il est !* — how rude the bear is !
The world to two-pence he was ne'er at *Paris.*
Perdition stap my vitals, — now or never
I'll niggle snugly into Juno's favour.
Let's see — (*looking in a glass*) my face, — toll loll —
    'twill work upon her,
My person — oh, immense, upon my honour.
My eyes, — oh fie, — the naughty glass it flatters, —
Courage, — Ixion flogs the world to tatters. [*Exit Ixion.*

" *Sim.* There is a fine gentleman for you, — in the very pink of the mode, with not a single article about him his own, — his words pilfered from magazines, his address from French valets, and his clothes not paid for.

" *Macd.* But pray, Mr. Simile, how did Ixion get into heaven?

" *Sim.* Why, sir, what's that to any body?—perhaps by Salmoneus's Brazen Bridge, or the Giant's Mountain, or the Tower of Babel, or on Theobald's bull-dogs, or — who the devil cares how? — he is there, and that's enough.

*   *   *   *

" *Sim.* Now for a Phœnix of a song.

" *Song by* JUPITER.

" You dogs, I'm Jupiter Imperial,
   King, Emperor, and Pope ætherial,
    Master of th' Ordnance of the sky. —

" *Sim.* Z——ds, where's the ordnance? Have you forgot the pistol? (*to the* Orchestra.)

" *Orchestra.* (*to some one behind the scenes.*) Tom, are not you prepared.

" *Tom.* (*from behind the scenes.*) Yes, sir, but I flash'd in the pan a little out of time, and had I staid to prime, I should have shot a bar too late.

" *Sim.* Oh then, Jupiter, begin the song again. — We must not lose our ordnance.

" You dogs, I'm Jupiter Imperial,
   King, Emperor, and Pope ætherial,
    Master of th' Ordnance of the sky; &c. &c.
[*Here a pistol or cracker is fired from behind the scenes.*

" *Sim.* This hint I took from Handel.—Well, how do you think we go on?

" *O'Cul.* With vast spirit, — the plot begins to thicken.

"*Sim.* Thicken! aye, — 'twill be as thick as the calf of your leg presently. Well, now for the real, original patentee Amphitryon. What, ho, Amphitryon! Amphitryon! — 'tis Simile calls. — Why, where the devil is he?

"*Enter* SERVANT.

"*Monop.* Tom, where is Amphitryon?

"*Sim.* Zounds, he's not arrested too, is he?

"*Serv.* No, sir, but there was but *one black eye* in the house, and he is waiting to get it from Jupiter.

"*Sim.* To get a black eye from Jupiter, — oh, this will never do. Why, when they meet, they ought to match like two beef-eaters."

According to their original plan for the conclusion of this farce, all things were at last to be compromised between Jupiter and Juno; Amphitryon was to be comforted in the birth of so mighty a son; Ixion, for his presumption, instead of being fixed to a *torturing* wheel, was to have been fixed to a vagrant monotroche, as knife-grinder, and a grand chorus of deities intermixed with " knives, scissors, pen-knives to grind," (set to music as nearly as possible to the natural cry,) would have concluded the whole.

That habit of dilatoriness, which is too often attendant upon genius, and which is for ever making it, like the pistol in the scene just quoted, " shoot a bar too late," was, through life, remarkable in the character of Mr. Sheridan, — and we have here an early instance of its influence over him. Though it was in August, 1770, that he received the sketch of this piece from his friend, and though they both looked forward most sanguinely to its success, as likely to realize many a dream of fame and profit, it was not till the month of May in the subsequent year, as appears by a letter from Mr. Ker to Sheridan, that the probability of the arrival of the manuscript was announced to Mr. Foote. " I have dispatched a card, as from H. H., at Owen's Coffee-house, to Mr. Foote, to inform him that he may expect to see your dramatic piece about the 25th instant."

Their hopes and fears in this theatrical speculation are very naturally and lively expressed throughout Halhed's letters, sometimes with a degree of humorous pathos, which is interesting as characteristic of both the writers : — " the thoughts," he says, " of 200*l.* shared between us are enough to bring the tears into one's eyes." Sometimes, he sets more moderate limits to their ambition, and hopes that they will, at least, get the freedom of the play-house by it. But at all times he chides, with good-humoured impatience, the tardiness of his fellow-labourer in applying to the managers. Fears are expressed that Foote may have made other engagements, — and that a piece, called " Dido," on the same mythological plan, which had lately been produced with but little success, might prove an obstacle to the reception of theirs. At Drury Lane, too, they had little hopes of a favourable hearing, as Dibdin was one of the principal butts of their ridicule.

The summer season, however, was suffered to pass away without an effort; and in October, 1771, we find Mr. Halhed flattering himself with hopes from a negotiation with Mr. Garrick. It does not appear, however, that Sheridan ever actually presented this piece to any of the managers; and, indeed, it is probable, from the following fragment of a scene found among his papers, that he soon abandoned the groundwork of Halhed altogether, and transferred his plan of a rehearsal to some other subject, of his own invention, and, therefore, more worthy of his wit. It will be perceived that the puffing author was here intended to be a Scotchman.

" *M.* Sir, I have read your comedy, and I think it has infinite merit; but, pray, don't you think it rather grave?

" *S.* Sir, you say true; it *is* a grave comedy. I follow the opinion of Longinus, who says comedy ought always to be sentimental. Sir, I value a sentiment of six lines in my piece no more than a nabob does a rupee. I hate those dirty, paltry equivocations, which go by the name of puns, and pieces of wit. No, sir, it ever was my opinion that the stage should be a place of rational entertainment; instead of which, I am very

sorry to say, most people go there for their diversion:
accordingly, I have formed my comedy so that it is no
laughing, giggling piece of work. He must be a very
light man that shall discompose his muscles from the
beginning to the end.

" *M.* But don't you think it may be too grave?

" *S.* O never fear; and as for hissing, mon, they might
as well hiss the common prayer-book: for there is the
viciousness of vice and the virtuousness of virtue in every
third line.

" *M.* I confess there is a great deal of moral in it;
but, sir, I should imagine if you tried your hand at
tragedy ——

" *S.* No, mon, there you are out, and I'll relate to you
what put me first on writing a comedy. You must know
I had composed a very fine tragedy about the valiant
Bruce. I showed it my Laird of Mackintosh, and he
was a very candid mon, and he said my genius did not
lie in tragedy: I took the hint, and, as soon as I got
home, began my comedy."

We have here some of the very thoughts and
words, that afterwards contributed to the fortune
of Puff; and it is amusing to observe how long
this subject was played with by the current of
Sheridan's fancy, till at last, like " a stone of
lustre from the brook," it came forth with all
that smoothness and polish, which it wears in his
inimitable farce, The Critic. Thus it is, too,
and but little to the glory of what are called our
years of discretion, that the life of the *man* is
chiefly employed in giving effect to the wishes
and plans of the *boy*.

Another of their projects was a periodical Miscellany, the idea of which originated with Sheridan, and whose first embryo movements we trace in a letter to him from Mr. Lewis Ker, who undertook with much good nature the negotiation of the young authors' literary concerns in London. The letter is dated 30th of October, 1770.—" As to your intended periodical paper, if it meets with success, there is no doubt of profit accruing, as I have already engaged a publisher of established reputation to undertake it for the account of the authors. But I am to indemnify him in case it should not sell, and to advance part of the first expense, all which I can do without applying to Mr. Ewart." —" I would be glad to know what stock of papers you have already written, as there ought to be ten or a dozen at least finished before you print any, in order to have time to prepare the subsequent numbers, and ensure a continuance of the work. As to the coffee-houses, you must not depend on their taking it in at first, except you go on the plan of The Tatler, and give the news of the week. For the first two or three weeks the expense of advertising will certainly prevent any profit being made. But when that is over, if a thousand are sold weekly, you may reckon on receiving 5l. clear. One paper a week will do

better than two. Pray say no more as to our
accounts."

The title intended by Sheridan for this paper
was, " Hernan's Miscellany," to which his friend
Halhed objected, and suggested " The Reformer," as a newer and more significant name.
But, though Halhed appears to have sought
among his Oxford friends, for an auxiliary or
two in their weekly labours, this meditated Miscellany never proceeded beyond the first number, which was written by Sheridan, and which I
have found among his papers. It is too diffuse
and pointless to be given entire ; but an extract
or two from it will not be unwelcome, to those
who love to trace even the first, feeblest begin-
nings of genius.

" HERNAN'S MISCELLANY.

" No. I.

" ' I will sit down and write for the good of the people
— for (said I to myself, pulling off my spectacles, and
drinking up the remainder of my six-pen'worth) it cannot
be but people must be sick of these same rascally politics.
All last winter nothing but — God defend me ! 'tis tiresome to think of it.' I immediately flung the pamphlet
down on the table, and taking my hat and cane walked
out of the coffee-house.

" I kept up as smart a pace as I could all the way
home, for I felt myself full of something, and enjoyed my
own thoughts so much, that I was afraid of digesting them,

lest any should escape me. At last I knocked at my own door — ' So!' said I to the maid who opened it, (for I never would keep a man ; not, but that I could afford it, —however, the reason is not material now,) ' So!' said I, with an unusual smile upon my face, and immediately sent for a quire of paper and half a hundred of pens — the only thing I had absolutely determined on in my way from the coffee-house. I had now got seated in my arm-chair, — I am an infirm old man, and I live on a second floor, — when I began to ruminate on my project. The first thing that occurred to me (and certainly a very natural one) was to examine my common-place book. So I went to my desk, and took out my old faithful red-leather companion, who had long discharged the office of treasurer to all my best hints and memorandums : but, how was I surprised, when one of the first things that struck my eyes was the following memorandum, legibly written, and on one of my best sheets of vellum : — ' Mem. — *Oct.* 20*th*, 1769, *left the Grecian, after having read*——'*s Poems, with a determined resolution to write a Periodical Paper, in order to reform the vitiated taste of the age ; but, coming home and finding my fire out, and my maid gone abroad, was obliged to defer the execution of my plan to another opportunity.*' Now, though this event had absolutely slipped my memory, I now recollected it perfectly, — ay, so my fire *was* out indeed, and my maid *did* go abroad sure enough. — ' Good Heavens!' said I, ' how great events depend upon little circumstances!' However, I looked upon this as a memento for me no longer to trifle away my time and resolution ; and thus I began to reason, — I mean, I *would* have reasoned, had I not been interrupted by a noise of some one coming up stairs. By the alternate thump upon the steps, I soon discovered it must be my old and intimate friend Rudliche. *   *

*   *   *   *   *

"But, to return, in walked Rudliche.— 'So, Fred.' — 'So, Bob.' — 'Were you at the Grecian to-day?' — 'I just stepped in.' — 'Well, any news?' — 'No, no, there was no news.' Now, as Bob and I saw one another almost every day, we seldom abounded in conversation; so, having settled one material point, he sat in his usual posture, looking at the fire and beating the dust out of his wooden leg, when I perceived he was going to touch upon *the* other subject; but, having by chance cast his eye on my face, and finding (I suppose) something extraordinary in my countenance, he immediately dropped all concern for the weather, and putting his hand into his pocket, (as if he meant to find what he was going to say, under pretence of feeling for his tobacco-box,) 'Hernan! (he began) why, man, you look for all the world as if you had been thinking of something.' — 'Yes,' replied I, smiling, (that is, not actually smiling, but with a conscious something in my face,) 'I have, indeed, been thinking a little.'— 'What, is't a secret?' —'Oh, nothing very material.' Here ensued a pause, which I employed in considering whether I should reveal my scheme to Bob; and Bob in trying to disengage his thumb from the string of his cane, as if he were preparing to take his leave. This latter action, with the great desire I had of disburthening myself, made me instantly resolve to lay my whole plan before him. 'Bob,' said I, (he immediately quitted his thumb,) 'you remarked that I looked as if I had been thinking of something, — your remark is just, and I'll tell you the subject of my thought. You know, Bob, that I always had a strong passion for literature: — you have often seen my collection of books, not very large, indeed, however I believe I have read every volume of it twice over, (excepting ———'s *Divine Legation of Moses*, and

Bath his share of the work, and in the following month we find Sheridan preparing, with the assistance of a Greek grammar, to complete the task. " The 29th ult. (says Mr. Ker, in a letter to him from London, dated Dec. 4. 1770,) I was favoured with yours, and have since been hunting for Aristænetus, whom I found this day, and therefore send to you, together with a Greek grammar. I might have dispatched at the same time some numbers of the Dictionary, but not having got the two last numbers, was not willing to send any without the whole of what is published, and still less willing to delay Aristænetus's journey by waiting for them." The work alluded to here is the Dictionary of Arts and Sciences, to which Sheridan had subscribed, with the view, no doubt, of informing himself upon subjects of which he was as yet wholly ignorant; having left school, like most other young men at his age, as little furnished with the knowledge that is wanted in the world, as a person would be for the demands of a market, who went into it with nothing but a few ancient coins in his pocket.

The passion, however, that now began to take possession of his heart was little favourable to his advancement in any serious studies; and it may easily be imagined that, in the neighbourhood of Miss Linley, the Arts and Sciences were

suffered to sleep quietly on their shelves. Even
the translation of Aristænetus, though a task
more suited, from its amatory nature, to the
existing temperature of his heart, was proceeded
in but slowly; and it appears from one of Halhed's letters, that this impatient ally was already
counting upon the *spolia opima* of the campaign,
before Sheridan had fairly brought his Greek
grammar into the field. The great object of
the former was a visit to Bath; and he had set
his heart still more anxiously upon it, after a
second meeting with Miss Linley at Oxford.
But the profits expected from their literary undertakings were the only means to which he
looked for the realizing of this dream; and he
accordingly implores his friend, with the most
comic piteousness, to drive the farce on the stage
by main force, and to make Aristænetus sell
whether he will or not. In the November of
this year we find them discussing the propriety
of prefixing their names to the work — Sheridan
evidently not disinclined to venture, but Halhed
recommending that they should wait to hear
how " Sumner and the wise few of their acquaintance" would talk of the book, before they
risked any thing more than their initials. In
answer to Sheridan's enquiries as to the extent
of sale they may expect in Oxford, he confesses

that, after three coffee-houses had bought one a-piece, not two more would be sold.

That poverty is the best nurse of talent has long been a most humiliating truism ; and the fountain of the Muses, bursting from a barren rock, is but too apt an emblem of the hard source, from which much of the genius of this world has issued. How strongly the young translators of Aristænetus were under the influence of this sort of inspiration, appears from every paragraph of Halhed's letters, and might easily, indeed, be concluded of Sheridan, from the very limited circumstances of his father — who had nothing beside the pension of 200*l.* a year, conferred upon him in consideration of his literary merits, and the little profits he derived from his lectures in Bath, to support with decency himself and his family. The prospects of Halhed were much more golden, but he was far too gay and mercurial to be prudent ; and from the very scanty supplies which his father allowed him, had quite as little of " le superflu, chose si nécessaire," as his friend. But whatever were his other desires and pursuits, a visit to Bath, — to that place which contained the two persons he most valued in friendship and in love, — was the grand object of all his financial speculations ; and among other ways and means that, in the delay of the expected resources from

Aristænetus, presented themselves, was an exhibition of 20*l.* a-year, which the college had lately given him, and with five pounds of which he thought he might venture " adire Corinthum."

Though Sheridan had informed his friend that the translation was put to press some time in March, 1771, it does not appear to have been given into the hands of Wilkie, the publisher, till the beginning of May, when Mr. Ker writes thus to Bath : — " Your Aristænetus is in the hands of Mr. Wilkie, in St. Paul's Church-yard, and to put you out of suspense at once, will certainly make his appearance about the 1st of June next, in the form of a neat volume, price 3*s.* or 3*s.* 6*d.*, as may best suit his size, &c., which cannot be more nearly determined at present. I have undertaken the task of correcting for the press . . . . Some of the Epistles that I have perused seem to me elegant and poetical ; in others I could not observe equal beauty, and here and there I could wish there were some little amendment. You will pardon this liberty I take, and set it down to the account of old-fashioned friendship." Mr. Ker, to judge from his letters, (which, in addition to their other laudable points, are dated with a precision truly exemplary,) was a very kind, useful, and sensible person, and in the sober hue of his intellect exhibited a striking contrast, to the sparkling vivacity of the two sanguine and impatient young wits, whose affairs he so good-naturedly undertook to negociate.

At length in August, 1771, Aristænetus made its appearance — contrary to the advice of the bookseller, and of Mr. Ker, who represented to Sheridan the unpropitiousness of the season, particularly for a first experiment in authorship, and advised the postponement of the publication till October. But the translators were too eager for the rich harvest of emolument they had promised themselves, and too full of that pleasing but often fatal delusion — that calenture, under the influence of which young voyagers to the shores of Fame imagine they already see her green fields and groves in the treacherous waves around them — to listen to the suggestions of mere calculating men of business. The first account they heard of the reception of the work was flattering enough to prolong awhile this dream of vanity. "It begins (writes Mr. Ker, in about a fortnight after the publication,) to make some noise, and is fathered on Mr. Johnson, author of the English Dictionary, &c. See to-day's Gazetteer. The critics are admirable in discovering a concealed author by his style, manner, &c."

Their disappointment at the ultimate failure of the book was proportioned, we may suppose, to the sanguineness of their first expectations. But the reluctance, with which an author yields to the sad certainty of being unread, is apparent in the eagerness with which Halhed avails himself of every encouragement for a rally of his hopes. The Critical Reviewers, it seems, had given the work a tolerable character, and quoted the first Epistle. * The Weekly Review in the Public Ledger had also spoken well of it, and cited a specimen. The Oxford Magazine had transcribed two whole Epistles, without mentioning from whence they were taken. Every body, he says, seems to have read the book, and one of those *hawking booksellers* who attend the coffee-houses assured him it was written by Dr. Armstrong, author of the Œconomy of Love. On the strength of all this he recommends that another volume of the Epistles should be published immediately — being of opinion that the readers of the first volume

* In one of the Reviews I have seen it is thus spoken of: — " No such writer as Aristænetus ever existed in the classic æra ; nor did even the unhappy schools, after the destruction of the Eastern empire, produce such a writer. It was left to the latter times of monkish imposition to give such trash as this, on which the translator has ill spent his time. We have been as idly employed in reading it, and our readers will in proportion lose their time in perusing this article."

would be sure to purchase the second, and that the publication of the second would put it in the heads of others to buy the first. Under a sentence containing one of these sanguine anticipations, there is written, in Sheridan's hand, the word " Quixote!"

They were never, of course, called upon for the second part, and, whether we consider the merits of the original or of the translation, the world has but little to˙ regret in the loss. Aristænetus is one of those weak, florid sophists, who flourished in the decline and degradation of antient literature, and strewed their gaudy flowers of rhetoric over the dead muse of Greece. He is evidently of a much later period than Alciphron, to whom he is also very inferior in purity of diction, variety of subject, and playfulness of irony. But neither of them ever deserved to be wakened from that sleep, in which the commentaries of Bergler, De Pauw, and a few more such industrious scholars have shrouded them.

The translators of Aristænetus, in rendering his flowery prose into verse, might have found a precedent and model for their task in Ben Jonson, whose popular song, " Drink to me only with thine eyes," is, as Mr. Cumberland first remarked, but a piece of fanciful mosaic, collected out of the love-letters of the sophist

Philostratus.   But many of the narrations in
Aristænetus are incapable of being elevated
into poetry ; and, unluckily, these familiar parts
seem chiefly to have fallen to the department of
Halhed, who was far less gifted than his coad-
jutor with that artist-like touch, which polishes
away the mark of vulgarity, and gives an air of
elegance even to poverty.   As the volume is
not in many hands, the following extract from
one of the Epistles may be acceptable — as well
from the singularity of the scene described, as
from the specimen it affords of the merits of the
translation :

" Listen — another pleasure I display,
That help'd delightfully the time away.
From distant vales, where bubbles from its source
A crystal rill, they dug a winding course :
See ! thro' the grove a narrow lake extends,
Crosses each plot, to each plantation bends ;
And while the fount in new meanders glides,
The forest brightens with refreshing tides.
Tow'rds us they taught the new-born stream to flow,
Tow'rds us it crept, irresolute and slow :
Scarce had the infant current trickled by,
When lo ! a wondrous fleet attracts our eye ;
Laden with draughts might greet a monarch's tongue,
The mimic navigation swam along.
Hasten, ye ship-like goblets, down the vale,
* Your freight a flagon, and a leaf your sail.

    " * In the original, this luxurious image is pursued so
far that the very leaf, which is represented as the sail of the

O may no envious rush thy course impede,
Or floating apple stop thy tide-borne speed.
" His mildest breath a gentle zephyr gave ;
The little vessels trimly stemm'd the wave :
Their precious merchandise to land they bore,
And one by one resign'd the balmy store.
Stretch but a hand, we boarded them, and quaft
With native luxury the temper'd draught.
For where they loaded the nectareous fleet,
The goblet glow'd with too intense a heat ;
Cool'd by degrees in these convivial ships,
With nicest taste it met our thirsty lips."

As a scholar like Halhed could hardly have been led into the mistake, of supposing τυ Mηδικυ φυτυ φυλλω to mean "a leaf of a medicinal nature." we may, perhaps, from this circumstance, not less than from the superior workmanship of the verses, attribute the whole of this Epistle and notes to Sheridan.

There is another Epistle, the 12th, as evidently from the pen of his friend, the greater part of which is original, and shows, by its raciness and vigour, what difference there is between " the first sprightly runnings " of an author's own mind, and his cold vapid transfusion of the thoughts of another. From stanza 10th to the end is all

---

vessel, is particularized as of a medicinal nature, capable of preventing any ill effects the wine might produce." — *Note by the Translator.*

added by the translator, and all spirited;—though full of a bold, defying libertinism, as unlike as possible to the effeminate lubricity of the poor sophist, upon whom, in a grave, treacherous note, the responsibility of the whole is laid.   But by far the most interesting part of the volume is the last Epistle of the book, " From a Lover resigning his Mistress to his Friend," in which Halhed has contrived to extract from the unmeaningness of the original a direct allusion to his own fate; and, forgetting Aristænetus and his dull personages, thinks only of himself, and Sheridan, and Miss Linley.

" Thee, then, my friend, — if yet a wretch may claim
A last attention by that once dear name, —
Thee I address : — the cause you must approve;
I yield you — what I cannot cease to love.
Be thine the blissful lot, the nymph be thine :
I yield my love, — sure, friendship may be mine.
Yet must no thought of me torment thy breast;
Forget me, if my griefs disturb thy rest,
Whilst still I'll pray that thou may'st never know
The pangs of baffled love, or feel my woe.
But sure to thee, dear, charming — fatal maid !
(For me thou'st charm'd, and me thou hast betray'd,)
This last request I need not recommend —
Forget the lover thou, as he the friend.
Bootless such charge ! for ne'er did pity move
A heart that mock'd the suit of humble love.
Yet, in some thoughtful hour — if such can be,
Where love, Timocrates, is join'd with thee —

In some lone pause of joy, when pleasures pall,
And fancy broods o'er joys it can't recall,
Haply a thought of me, (for thou, my friend,
May'st then have taught that stubborn heart to bend,)
A thought of him, whose passion was not weak,
May dash one transient blush upon her cheek ;
Haply a tear — (for I shall surely then
Be past all power to raise her scorn again —)
Haply, I say, one self-dried tear may fall : —
One tear she'll give, for whom I yielded all !

  *   *   *   *   *   *   *
  *   *   *   *   *   *   *

My life has lost its aim ! — that fatal fair
Was all its object, all its hope or care:
She was the goal, to which my course was bent,
Where every wish, where every thought was sent;
A secret influence darted from her eyes, —
Each look, attraction, and herself the prize.
Concentred there, I liv'd for her alone;
To make her glad and to be blest was one.

  *   *   *   *   *   *   *

Adieu, my friend — nor blame this *sad* adieu,
Though sorrow guides my pen, it blames not you.
Forget me—'tis my pray'r ; nor seek to know
The fate of him whose portion must be woe,
Till the cold earth outstretch her friendly arms,
And Death convince me that he *can* have charms."

But Halhed's was not the only heart, that
sighed hopelessly for the young Maid of Bath,
who appears, indeed, to have spread her gentle
conquests, to an extent almost unparalleled in

the annals of beauty. Her personal charms, the exquisiteness of her musical talents, and the full light of publicity which her profession threw upon both, naturally attracted round her a crowd of admirers, in whom the sympathy of a common pursuit soon kindled into rivalry, till she became at length an object of vanity as well as of love. Her extreme youth, too,— for she was little more than sixteen when Sheridan first met her,— must have removed, even from minds the most fastidious and delicate, that repugnance they might justly have felt to her profession, if she had lived much longer under its tarnishing influence, or lost, by frequent exhibitions before the public, that fine gloss of feminine modesty, for whose absence not all the talents and accomplishments of the whole sex can atone.

She had been, even at this early age, on the point of marriage with Mr. Long, an old gentleman of considerable fortune in Wiltshire, who proved the reality of his attachment to her in a way which few young lovers would be romantic enough to imitate. On her secretly representing to him that she never could be happy as his wife, he generously took upon himself the whole blame of breaking off the alliance, and even indemnified the father, who was proceeding to bring the transaction into court, by settling 3000*l.* upon his daughter. Mr. Sheridan, who owed to this liberal conduct not only the possession of the woman he loved, but the means of supporting her during the first years of their marriage, spoke invariably of Mr. Long, who lived to a very advanced age, with all the kindness and respect which such a disinterested character merited.

It was about the middle of the year 1770 that the Sheridans took up their residence in King's Mead * Street, Bath, where an acquaintance commenced between them and Mr. Linley's family, which the kindred tastes of the young people soon ripened into intimacy. It was not to be expected,— though parents, in general, are as blind to the first approach of these dangers, as they are rigid and unreasonable after they have happened, — that such youthful poets and musicians† should come together, without Love very soon making one of the party. Accordingly, the two brothers became deeply enamoured of Miss Linley. Her heart, however, was not so wholly un-preoccupied, as to yield at once to the

---

* They also lived, during a part of their stay at Bath, in New King Street.

† Dr. Burney, in his Biographical Sketch of Mr. Linley, written for Rees's Cyclopædia, calls the Linley family "a nest of nightingales." The only surviving members of this accomplished family are the Reverend Ozias Linley and my friend Mr. William Linley, whose taste and talent, both in poetry and music, most worthily sustain the reputation of the name that he bears.

passion which her destiny had in store for her. One of those transient preferences, which in early youth are mistaken for love, had already taken lively possession of her imagination; and to this the following lines, written at that time by Mr. Sheridan, allude: —

" *To the Recording Angel.*

Cherub of heaven, that from thy secret stand
  Dost not, the follies of each mortal here,
Oh, if Eliza's steps employ thy hand,
  Blot the sad legend with a mortal tear.
Nor, when she errs, through passions wild extreme,
  Mark then her course, nor heed each trifling wrong;
Nor when her sad attachment is her theme,
  Note down the transports of her erring tongue.
But when she sighs for sorrows not her own,
Let that dear sigh to Mercy's cause be given;
And bear that tear to her Creator's throne,
Which glistens in the eye upraised to Heaven!"

But in love, as in every thing else, the power of a mind like Sheridan's must have made itself felt through all obstacles and difficulties. He was not long in winning the entire affections of the young "Syren,"— though the number and wealth of his rivals, the ambitious views of her father, and the temptations to which she herself was hourly exposed, kept his jealousies and fears perpetually on the watch. He is supposed, indeed, to have been indebted to self-observation, for that portrait of a wayward and morbidly sensitive lover, which he has drawn so strikingly in the character of Falkland.

With a mind in this state of feverish wakefulness, it is remarkable that he should so long have succeeded in concealing his attachment, from the eyes of those most interested in discovering it. Even his brother Charles was for some time wholly unaware of their rivalry, — and went on securely indulging in a passion, which it was hardly possible, with such opportunities of intercourse, to resist, and which survived long after Miss Linley's selection of another had extinguished every hope in his heart but that of seeing her happy. Halhed, too, who at that period corresponded constantly with Sheridan, and confided to him the love with which he also had been inspired by this enchantress, was for a length of time left in the same darkness upon the subject, and without the slightest suspicion that the epidemic had reached his friend — whose only mode of evading the many tender enquiries and messages, with which Halhed's letters abounded, was by referring to answers, which had, by some strange fatality, miscarried, and which we may conclude, without much uncharitableness, had never been written.

Miss Linley went frequently to Oxford, to perform at the oratorios and concerts; and it may easily be imagined that the ancient allegory of the Muses throwing chains over Cupid was here reversed, and the quiet shades of learning not a little disturbed by the splendour of these " angel visits." The letters of Halhed give a lively idea, not only of his own intoxication, but of the sort of contagious delirium, like that at Abdera described by Lucian, with which the young men of Oxford were affected by this beautiful girl. In describing her singing he quotes part of a Latin letter, which he himself had written to a friend upon first hearing her ; and it is a curious proof of the readiness of Sheridan, notwithstanding his own fertility, to avail himself of the thoughts of others, that we find in this extract, word for word, the same extravagant comparison of the effects of music to the process of Egyptian embalmment — " extracting the brain through the ears" — which was afterwards transplanted into the dialogue of the Duenna :—" *Mortuum quendam ante Ægypti medici quam pollincirent cerebella de auribus unco quodam hamo solebant extrahere ; sic de meis auribus non cerebrum, sed cor ipsum exhausit lusciniola, &c. &c.*" He mentions, as the rivals most dreaded by her admirers, Norris, the singer, whose musical talents, it was thought, recommended him to her, and Mr. Watts, a gentleman-commoner, of very large fortune.

While all hearts and tongues were thus occupied about Miss Linley, it is not wonderful that rumours of matrimony and elopement should, from time to time, circulate among her apprehensive admirers ; or that the usual ill-compliment should be paid to her sex of supposing that wealth must be the winner of the prize. It was at one moment currently reported at Oxford that she had gone off to Scotland with a young man of 3000*l.* a-year, and the panic which the intelligence spread is described in one of these letters to Sheridan (who no doubt shared in it) as producing " long-faces" every where. Not only, indeed, among her numerous lovers, but among all who delighted in her public performances, an alarm would naturally be felt at the prospect of her becoming private property ; —

" *Te juga Taygeti, posito te Mænala flebunt*
Venatu, mæstoque diu lugebere Cyntho.
Delphica quinetiam fratris delubra tacebunt." *

Thee, thee, when hurried from our eyes away,
Laconia's hills shall mourn for many a day —
The Arcadian hunter shall forget his chace,
And turn aside, to think upon that face ;
While many an hour Apollo's songless shrine
Shall wait in silence for a voice like thine !

* Claudian De Rapt. Proserp. lib. ii. v. 244.

But, to the honour of her sex, which is, in general, more disinterested than the other, it was found that neither rank nor wealth had influenced her heart in its election; and Halhed, who, like others, had estimated the strength of his rivals by their rent-rolls, discovered at last that his unpretending friend, Sheridan, (whose advances in courtship and in knowledge seem to have been equally noiseless and triumphant,) was the chosen favourite of her, at whose feet so many fortunes lay. Like that Saint, Cecilia, by whose name she was always called, she had long welcomed to her soul a secret visitant *, whose gifts were of a higher and more radiant kind, than the mere wealthy and lordly of this world can proffer. A letter, written by Halhed on the prospect of his departure for India †, alludes so delicately to this discovery, and describes the state of his own heart so mournfully, that I must again, in parting with him and his correspondence, express the strong regret that I feel, at

---

* " The youth, found in her chamber, had in his hand two crowns or wreaths, the one of lilies, the other of roses, which he had brought from Paradise."—*Legend of St. Cecilia.*

† The letter is evidently in answer to one which he had just received from Sheridan, in which Miss Linley had written a few words, expressive of her wishes for his health and happiness. Mr. Halhed sailed for India about the latter end of this year.

not being able to indulge the reader with a perusal of these letters. Not only as a record of the first short flights of Sheridan's genius, but as a picture, from the life, of the various feelings ·of youth, its desires and fears, its feverish hopes and fanciful melancholy, they could not have failed to be read with the deepest interest.

To this period of Mr. Sheridan's life we are indebted for most of those elegant love-verses, which are so well known and so often quoted. The lines, " Uncouth is this moss-covered grotto of stone," were addressed to Miss Linley, after having offended her by one of those lectures upon decorum of conduct, which jealous lovers so frequently inflict upon their mistresses, — and the grotto, immortalized by their quarrel, is supposed to have been in Spring Gardens, then the fashionable place of resort in Bath.

I have elsewhere remarked that the conceit in the following stanza resembles a thought in some verses of Angerianus : —

" And thou, stony grot, in thy arch may'st preserve
　Two lingering drops of the night-fallen dew,
Let them fall on her bosom of snow, and they'll serve
　As tears of my sorrow entrusted to you."

" *At quam per niveam cervicem influxerit humor
　Dicite non roris sed pluvia hæc lacrimæ.*"

Whether Sheridan was likely to have been a

reader of Angerianus is, I think, doubtful — at all events the coincidence is curious.

" Dry be that tear, my gentlest love," is supposed to have been written at a later period; but it was most probably produced at the time of his courtship, for he wrote but few love-verses after his marriage. This song having been hitherto printed incorrectly, I shall give it here, as it is in the copies preserved by his relations.

" Dry be that tear, my gentlest love,*
　　Be hush'd that struggling sigh,
Nor seasons, day, nor fate shall prove
　　More fix'd, more true than I.
Hush'd be that sigh, be dry that tear,
Cease boding doubt, cease anxious fear. —
　　Dry be that tear.

" Ask'st thou how long my love will stay,
　　When all that's new is past ? —
How long, ah Delia, can I say
　　How long my life will last ?
Dry be that tear, be hush'd that sigh,
At least I'll love thee till I die. —
　　Hush'd be that sigh.

" And does that thought affect thee too,
　　The thought of Sylvio's death,
That he who only breath'd for you,
　　Must yield that faithful breath ?

* An Elegy by Halhed, transcribed in one of his letters to Sheridan, begins thus : " Dry be that tear, be hush'd that struggling sigh."

Hush'd be that sigh, be dry that tear,
Nor let us lose our Heaven here. —
    Dry be that tear."

There is in the second stanza here a close resemblance to one of the madrigals of Montreuil,
a French poet, to whom Sir John Moore was
indebted for the point of his well known verses,
" If in that breast, so good so pure." * Mr.
Sheridan, however, knew nothing of French,
and neglected every opportunity of learning it,
till, by a very natural process, his ignorance of
the language grew into hatred of it. Besides,
we have the immediate source from which he
derived the thought of this stanza, in one of the
Essays of Hume, who, being a reader of foreign
literature, most probably found it in Montreuil.†

* " The grief, that on my quiet preys,
    That rends my heart and checks my tongue,
  I fear will last me all my days,
    And feel it will not last me long."
It is thus in Montreuil : —
    " C'est un mal que j'aurai tout le tems de ma vie ;
      Mais je ne l'aurai pas long-tems."
 † Or in an Italian song of Menage, from which Montreuil,
who was accustomed to such thefts, most probably stole it.
The point in the Italian is, as far as I can remember it, ex-
pressed thus : —
        " In van, o Filli, tu chiedi
          Se lungamente durera l'ardore
          *   *   *   *   *
          Chi lo potrebbe dire ?
        Incerta, o Filli, e l'ora del morire."

The passage in Hume (which Sheridan has done little more than versify) is as follows : — " Why so often ask me, *How long my love shall yet endure ?* Alas, my Cælia, can I resolve the question ? *Do I know how long my life shall yet endure ?"* *

The pretty lines, " Mark'd you her cheek of rosy hue ?" were written, not upon Miss Linley, as has been generally stated, but upon Lady Margaret Fordyce, and form part of a poem which he published in 1771, descriptive of the principal beauties of Bath, entitled " Clio's Protest, or the Picture varnished," — being an answer to some verses by Mr. Miles Peter Andrews, called " The Bath Picture," in which Lady Margaret was thus introduced : —

> " Remark too the dimpling, sweet smile
> Lady Marg'ret's fine countenance wears."

The following is the passage in Mr. Sheridan's poem, entire ; and the beauty of the six favourite lines shines out so conspicuously, that we cannot wonder at their having been so soon detached, like ill set gems, from the loose and clumsy workmanship around them : —

> " But, hark ! — did not our bard repeat
> The love-born name of M-rg-r-t ? —

* The Epicurean.

E 3

Attention seizes every ear;
We pant for the description *here :*
' If ever dulness left thy brow,
' *Pindar,*' we say, ' 'twill leave thee now.'
But O ! old Dulness' son anointed
His mother never disappointed ! —
And here we all were left to seek
A dimple in F-rd-ce's cheek !

".And could you really discover,
In gazing those sweet beauties over,
No other charm, no winning grace,
Adorning either mind or face,
But one poor *dimple,* to express
The *quintessence* of *loveliness ?*

" .... Mark'd you her cheek of rosy hue?
Mark'd you her eye of sparkling blue?
That eye, in liquid circles moving;
That cheek abash'd at Man's approving;
The *one,* Love's arrows darting round;
The *other,* blushing at the wound :
Did she not speak, did she not move,
Now *Pallas* — now the Queen of Love !"

There is little else in this poem worth being extracted, though it consists of about four hundred lines; — except, perhaps, his picture of a good country house-wife, which affords an early specimen of that neat pointedness of phrase, which gave his humour, both poetic and dramatic, such a peculiar edge and polish : —

" We see the Dame, in rustic pride,
A bunch of keys to grace her side,
Stalking across the well-swept entry,
To hold her council in the pantry;
Or, with prophetic soul, foretelling
The peas will boil well by the shelling;
Or, bustling in her private closet,
Prepare her lord his morning posset;
And while the hallow'd mixture thickens,
Signing death-warrants for the chickens:
Else, greatly pensive, poring o'er
Accounts her cook had thumb'd before;
One eye cast up upon that *great book*,
Yclep'd *The Family Receipt Book;*
By which she's rul'd in all her courses,
From stewing figs to drenching horses.
— Then pans and pickling skillets rise,
In dreadful lustre, to our eyes,
With store of sweetmeats, rang'd in order,
And *potted nothings* on the border;
While salves and caudle-cups between,
With squalling children, close the scene."

We find here, too, the source of one of those familiar lines, which so many quote without knowing whence they come; — one of those stray fragments, whose parentage is doubtful, but to which (as the law says of illegitimate children) " *pater est populus.*"

" You write with ease, to show your breeding,
But easy writing's curst hard reading."

In the following passage, with more of the
tact of a man of the world than the ardour of a
poet, he dismisses the object nearest his heart
with the mere passing gallantry of a compliment : —

> " O ! should your genius ever rise,
> And make you *Laureate* in the skies,
> I'd hold my life, in twenty years,
> You'd spoil the *music* of the *spheres*.
> — Nay, should the rapture-breathing Nine
> In one celestial concert join,
> Their sovereign's power to rehearse,
> — Were you to furnish them with verse,
> By Jove, I'd fly the heavenly throng,
> Tho' *Phœbus* play'd and *Linley* sung."

On the opening of the New Assembly Rooms
at Bath, which commenced with a ridotto,
Sept. 30. 1771, he wrote a humorous description
of the entertainment, called " An Epistle from
Timothy Screw to his Brother Henry, Waiter
at Almack's," which appeared first in The Bath
Chronicle, and was so eagerly sought after, that
Crutwell, the editor, was induced to publish it
in a separate form. The allusions in this trifle
have, of course, lost their zest by time ; and a
specimen or two of its humour will be all that
is necessary here.

" Two rooms were first opened—the *long* and the *round* one,
(These *Hogstyegon* names only serve to confound one,)
Both splendidly lit with the new chandeliers,
With drops hanging down like the bobs at Peg's ears :
While jewels of *paste* reflected the rays,
And *Bristol-stone* diamonds gave strength to the blaze :
So that it was doubtful, to view the bright clusters,
Which sent the most light out, the ear-rings or lustres.
   *   *   *   *   *   *

Nor less among you was the medley, ye fair !
I believe there *were* some beside quality there :
Miss *Spiggot*, Miss *Brussels*, Miss *Tape*, and Miss *Socket*,
Miss *Trinket*, and aunt, with her leathern pocket,
With good Mrs. *Soaker*, who made her old chin go,
For hours, hobnobbing with Mrs. *Syringo :*
Had *Tib* staid at home, I b'lieve none would have miss'd her,
Or pretty *Peg Runt*, with her tight little sister," &c. &c.

CHAP. II.

DUELS WITH MR. MATHEWS. — MARRIAGE WITH MISS LINLEY.

Towards the close of the year 1771, the elder Mr. Sheridan went to Dublin, to perform at the theatre of that city, — leaving his young and lively family at Bath, with nothing but their hearts and imaginations to direct them.

The following letters, which passed between him and his son Richard during his absence, though possessing little other interest than that of having been written at such a period, will not, perhaps, be unwelcome to the reader : —

" Dublin, Dec. 7th, 1771.

" My dear Richard,

" How could you be so wrong-headed as to commence cold bathing at such a season of the year, and I suppose without any preparation too ? You have paid sufficiently for your folly, but I hope the ill effects of it have been long since over. You and your brother are fond of quacking, a most dangerous disposition with

regard to health. Let slight things pass away
of themselves ; in a case that requires assistance
do nothing without advice. Mr. Crooke is a
very able man in his way. Should a physician
be at any time wanting, apply to Dr. Nesbitt,
and tell him that at leaving Bath I recommended
you all to his care. This indeed I intended to
have mentioned to him, but it slipped my memory. I forgot Mr. Crooke's bill, too, but desire I may have the amount by the next letter.
Pray what is the meaning of my hearing so seldom from Bath ? Six weeks here, and but two
letters ! You were very tardy ; what are your
sisters about ? I shall not easily forgive any
future omissions. I suppose Charles received
my answer to his, and the 20*l.* bill from Whately.
I shall order another to be sent at Christmas
for the rent and other necessaries. I have not
time at present to enter upon the subject of
English authors, &c. but shall write to you upon
that head when I get a little leisure. Nothing
can be conceived in a more deplorable state
than the stage of Dublin. I found two miserable companies opposing and starving each other.
I chose the least bad of them ; and, wretched
as they are, it has had no effect on my nights,
numbers having been turned away every time I
played, and the receipts have been larger than
when I had Barry, his wife, and Mrs. Fitz-

Henry to play with me. However, I shall not be able to continue it long, as there is no possibility of getting up a sufficient number of plays with such poor materials. I purpose to have done the week after next, and apply vigorously to the material point which brought me over. I find all ranks and parties very zealous for forwarding my scheme, and have reason to believe it will be carried in parliament after the recess, without opposition. It was in vain to have attempted it before, for never was party violence * carried to such a height as in this sessions; the House seldom breaking up till eleven or twelve at night. From these contests, the desire of improving in the article of elocution is become very general. There are no less than five persons of rank and fortune now waiting my leisure to become my pupils. Remember me to all friends, particularly to our good landlord and landlady. I am, with love and blessing to you all,

" Your affectionate father,
" THOMAS SHERIDAN.

" P. S. — Tell your sisters I shall send the poplins as soon as I can get an opportunity."

---

* The money-bill brought forward this year under Lord Townshend's administration, encountered violent opposition and was finally rejected.

" Dear Father,

" We have been for some time in hopes of receiving a letter, that we might know that you had acquitted us of neglect in writing. At the same time we imagine that the time is not far when writing will be unnecessary ; and we cannot help wishing to know the posture of the affairs, which, as you have not talked of returning, seem probable to detain you longer than you intended. I am perpetually asked when Mr. Sheridan is to have his patent for the theatre, which all the Irish here take for granted, and I often receive a great deal of information from them on the subject. Yet I cannot help being vexed when I see in the Dublin papers such bustling accounts of the proceedings of your House of Commons, as I remember it was your argument against attempting any thing from parliamentary authority in England. However, the folks here regret you, as one that is to be fixed in another kingdom, and will scarcely believe that you will ever visit Bath at all ; and we are often asked if we have not received the letter which is to call us over.

" I could scarcely have conceived that the winter was so near departing, were I not now writing after dinner by day-light. Indeed the first winter-season is not yet over at Bath. They have balls, concerts, &c. at the rooms, from the old subscription still, and the spring ones are immediately to succeed them. They are likewise going to perform oratorios here. Mr. Linley and his whole family, down to the seven year olds, are to support one set at the new rooms, and a band of singers from London another at the old. Our weather here, or the effects of it, have been so uninviting to all kinds of birds, that there has not been the smallest excuse to take a gun into the fields this winter;—a point more to the regret of Charles than myself.

" We are all now in dolefuls for the Princess Dowager; but as there was no necessity for our being dressed or weeping mourners, we were easily provided. Our acquaintances stand pretty much the same as when you left us,—only that I think in general we are less intimate, by which I believe you will not think us great losers. Indeed, excepting Mr. Wyndham, I have not met with one person with whom I would wish to be intimate; though there was a Mr. Lutterel, (brother to the Colonel,)—who was some months ago introduced to me by an old Harrow acquaintance,—who made me many professions at parting, and wanted me vastly to name some way in which he could be useful to me;

but the relying on *acquaintances*, or *seeking* of friendships, is a fault which I think I shall always have prudence to avoid.

" Lissy begins to be tormented again with the tooth-ache ; — otherwise, we are all well.

" I am, Sir,

Your sincerely dutiful and affectionate son,

" Friday, Feb. 29.   R. B. SHERIDAN.

" I beg you will not judge of my attention to the improvement of my hand-writing by this letter, as I am out of the way of a better pen."

Charles Sheridan, now one-and-twenty, the oldest and gravest of the party, finding his passion for Miss Linley increase every day, and conscious of the imprudence of yielding to it any further, wisely determined to fly from the struggle altogether. Having taken a solemn farewell of her in a letter, which his youngest sister delivered, he withdrew to a farm-house about seven or eight miles from Bath, little suspecting that he left his brother in full possession of that heart, of which he thus reluctantly and hopelessly raised the siege. Nor would this secret perhaps have been discovered for some time, had not another lover, of a less legitimate kind than either, by the alarming importunity of his courtship, made an explanation on all sides necessary.

Captain Mathews, a married man and intimate with Miss Linley's family, presuming upon the innocent familiarity which her youth and his own station permitted between them, had for some time not only rendered her remarkable by his indiscreet attentions in public, but had even persecuted her in private with those unlawful addresses and proposals, which a timid female will sometimes rather endure, than encounter that share of the shame, which may be reflected upon herself by their disclosure. To the threat of self-destruction, often tried with effect in these cases, he is said to have added the still more unmanly menace of ruining her reputation, if he could not undermine her virtue. Terrified by his perseverance, and dreading the consequences of her father's temper, if this violation of his confidence and hospitality were exposed to him, she at length confided her distresses to Richard Sheridan ; who, having consulted with his sister, and, for the first time, disclosed to her the state of his heart with respect to Miss Linley, lost no time in expostulating with Mathews, upon the cruelty, libertinism, and fruitlessness of his pursuit. Such a remonstrance, however, was but little calculated to conciliate the forbearance of this professed man of gallantry, who, it appears by the following allusion to him under the name of Lothario, in a poem

written by Sheridan at the time, still counted
upon the possibility of gaining his object, or, at
least, blighting the fruit which he could not
reach : —

> " Nor spare the flirting *Cassoc'd rogue,*
>   Nor antient Cullin's polish'd brogue ;
>   Nor gay *Lothario's* nobler name,
>   That *Nimrod* to all female fame."

In consequence of this persecution, and an
increasing dislike to her profession, which made
her shrink more and more from the gaze of the
many, in proportion as she became devoted to
the love of one, she adopted, early in 1772, the
romantic resolution of flying secretly to France,
and taking refuge in a convent, — intending,
at the same time to indemnify her father, to
whom she was bound till the age of 21, by the
surrender to him of part of the sum which
Mr. Long had settled upon her.   Sheridan,
who, it is probable, had been the chief adviser
of her flight, was, of course, not slow in offering
to be the partner of it.   His sister, whom he
seems to have persuaded that his conduct in this
affair arose solely from a wish to serve Miss Linley, as a friend, without any design or desire to
take advantage of her elopement, as a lover, not
only assisted them with money out of her little
fund for house expenses, but gave them letters

of introduction to a family with whom she had been acquainted at St. Quentin. On the evening appointed for their departure, — while Mr. Linley, his eldest son, and Miss Maria Linley, were engaged at a concert, from which the young Cecilia herself had been, on a plea of illness, excused, — she was conveyed by Sheridan in a sedan-chair from her father's house in the Crescent, to a post-chaise which waited for them on the London road, and in which she found a woman whom her lover had hired, as a sort of protecting Minerva, to accompany them in their flight.

It will be recollected that Sheridan was at this time little more than twenty, and his companion just entering her eighteenth year. On their arrival in London, with an adroitness which was, at least, very dramatic, he introduced her to an old friend of his family (Mr. Ewart, a respectable brandy-merchant in the city,) as a rich heiress who had consented to elope with him to the Continent ; — in consequence of which the old gentleman, with many commendations of his wisdom, for having given up the imprudent pursuit of Miss Linley, not only accommodated the fugitives with a passage on board a ship, which he had ready to sail from the port of London to Dunkirk, but gave them letters of recommendation to his correspondents at that place, who with the same zeal and dispatch facilitated their journey to Lisle.

On their leaving Dunkirk, as was natural to expect, the chivalrous and disinterested protector degenerated into a mere selfish lover. It was represented by him, with arguments which seemed to appeal to prudence as well as feeling, that, after the step which they had taken, she could not possibly appear in England again but as his wife. He was, therefore, he said, resolved not to deposit her in a convent, till she had consented, by the ceremony of a marriage, to confirm to him that right of protecting her, which he had now but temporarily assumed. It did not, we may suppose, require much eloquence, to convince her heart of the truth of this reasoning; and, accordingly, at a little village, not far from Calais, they were married about the latter end of March, 1772, by a priest well known for his services on such occasions.

They thence immediately proceeded to Lisle, where Miss Linley, as she must still be called, giving up her intention of going on to St. Quentin, procured an apartment in a convent, with the determination of remaining there, till Sheridan should have the means of supporting her as his acknowledged wife. A letter which he wrote to his brother from this place, dated April 15., though it throws but little additional light on the narrative, is too interesting an illustration of it to be omitted here.

" DEAR BROTHER,

" Most probably you will have thought me very inexcusable for not having writ to you. You will be surprised, too, to be told that, except your letter just after we arrived, we have never received one line from Bath. We suppose for certain that there are letters somewhere, in which case we shall have sent to every place almost but the right, whither, I hope, I have now sent also. You will soon see me in England. Every thing on our side has at last succeeded. Miss L—— is now fixing in a convent, where she has been entered some time. This has been a much more difficult point than you could have imagined, and we have, I find, been extremely fortunate. She has been ill, but is now recovered; this, too, has delayed me. We would have wrote, but have been kept in the most tormenting expectation, from day to day, of receiving your letters; but, as every thing is now so happily settled here, I will delay no longer giving you that information, though probably I shall set out for England, without knowing a syllable of what has happened with you. All is well, I hope, and I hope, too, that though you may have been ignorant, for some time of our proceedings, *you* never could have been uneasy lest any thing should tempt me to depart, even in a thought, from the honour and consistency which engaged me at first. I wrote to M——* above a week ago, which I think was necessary and right. I hope he has acted the one proper part which was left him; and, to speak from my *feelings*, I cannot but say that I shall be very happy to find no further disagreeable consequence pursuing him; for, as Brutus says of Cæsar, &c. —if I delay one moment longer, I lose the post.

" I have writ now, too, to Mr. Adams, and should apologize to you for having writ to him first, and lost my time for you. Love to my sisters, Miss L —— to all.

" Ever, Charles, your affec*. Brother,

" R. B. SHERIDAN.

" I need not tell you that we altered quite our route."

The illness of Miss Linley, to which he alludes, and which had been occasioned by fatigue and agitation of mind, came on some days after her retirement to the convent; but an English physician, Dr. Dolman of York, who happened to be resident in Lisle at the time, was called in to attend her; and in order that she might be more

* Mathews.

directly under his care, he and Mrs. Dolman invited her to their house, where she was found by Mr. Linley, on his arrival in pursuit of her. After a few words of private explanation from Sheridan, which had the effect of reconciling him to his truant daughter, Mr. Linley insisted upon her returning with him immediately to England, in order to fulfil some engagements which he had entered into on her account; and, a promise being given that, as soon as these engagements were accomplished, she should be allowed to resume her plan of retirement at Lisle, the whole party set off amicably together for England.

On the first discovery of the elopement, the landlord of the house in which the Sheridans resided had, from a feeling of pity for the situation of the young ladies, — now left without the protection of either father or brother, — gone off, at break of day, to the retreat of Charles Sheridan, and informed him of the event which had just occurred. Poor Charles, wholly ignorant till then of his brother's attachment to Miss Linley, felt all that a man may be supposed to feel, who had but too much reason to think himself betrayed, as well as disappointed. He hastened to Bath, where he found a still more furious lover, Mr. Mathews, enquiring at the house every particular of the affair, and almost avowing, in the impotence of his rage, the unprincipled design which this summary step had frustrated. In the course of their conversation, Charles Sheridan let fall some unguarded expressions of anger against his brother, which this gentleman, who seems to have been eminently qualified for a certain line of characters indispensable in all romances, treasured up in his memory, and, as it will appear, afterwards availed himself of them. For the four or five weeks during which the young couple were absent, he never ceased to haunt the Sheridan family, with enquiries, rumours, and other disturbing visitations; and, at length, urged on by the restlessness of revenge, inserted the following violent advertisement in The Bath Chronicle : —

" Wednesday, April 8th, 1772.

" Mr. Richard S******* having attempted, in a letter left behind him for that purpose, to account for his scandalous method of running away from this place, by insinuations derogating from *my* character, and that of a young lady, innocent as far as relates to *me*, or *my* knowledge ; since which he has neither taken any notice of letters, or even informed his own family of the place where he has hid himself; I can no longer think he deserves the treatment of a gentleman, and therefore shall trouble myself no further about him than, in this public method, to post him as a L***, and a treacherous S********.

" And as I am convinced there have been many malevolent incendiaries concerned in the propagation of this infamous lie, if any of them, unprotected by *age*, *infirmities*, or profession, will dare to acknowledge the part they have acted, and affirm *to* what they have said *of* me, they may depend on receiving the proper reward of their villainy, in the most public manner. The world will be candid enough to judge properly (I make no doubt) of any private abuse on this subject for the future ; as nobody can defend himself from an accusation he is ignorant of.

" THOMAS MATHEWS."

On a remonstrance from Miss Sheridan upon this outrageous proceeding, he did not hesitate to assert that her brother Charles was privy to it ; — a charge which the latter with indignation repelled, and was only prevented by the sudden departure of Mathews to London from calling him to a more serious account for the falsehood.

At this period the party from the Continent arrived ; and as a detail of the circumstances which immediately followed has been found in Mr. Sheridan's own hand-writing, — drawn up hastily, it appears, at the Parade Coffee-house,

Bath, the evening before his second duel with
Mr. Mathews, — it would be little better than
profanation to communicate them in any other
words.

"It has ever been esteemed impertinent to
appeal to the public in concerns entirely private;
but there now and then occurs a *private* incident
which, by being explained, may be productive of
public advantage. This consideration, and the
precedent of a public appeal in this same affair,
are my only apologies for the following lines : —

"Mr. T. Mathews thought himself essentially
injured by Mr. R. Sheridan's having co-operated
in the virtuous efforts of a young lady to escape
the snares of vice and dissimulation. He wrote
several most abusive threats to Mr. S., then in
France. He laboured, with a cruel industry, to
vilify his character in England. He publicly
posted him as a scoundrel and a liar. Mr. S.
answered him from France (hurried and surprized), that he would never sleep in England
till he had thanked him as he deserved.

"Mr. S. arrived in London at 9 o'clock at
night. At 10 he is informed, by Mr. S. Ewart,
that Mr. M. is in town. Mr. S. had sat up at
Canterbury, to keep his idle promise to Mr. M.
— He resolved to call on him that night, as, in
case he had not found him in town, he had

called on Mr. Ewart to accompany him to Bath, being bound by Mr. Linley not to let any thing pass between him and Mr. M. till he had arrived thither. Mr. S. came to Mr. Cochlin's, in Crutched Friars, (where Mr. M. was lodged,) about half after twelve. The key of Mr. C.'s door was lost; Mr. S. was denied admittance. By two o'clock he got in. Mr. M. had been previously down to the door, and told Mr. S. he should be admitted, and had retired to bed again. He dressed, complained of the cold, endeavoured to get heat into him, called Mr. S. his *dear friend*, and forced him to — *sit down*.

" Mr. S. had been informed that Mr. M. had sworn his death; — that Mr. M. had, in numberless companies, produced bills on France, whither he meant to retire, on the completion of his revenge. Mr. M. had warned Mr. Ewart to advise his friend not even to come in his way without a sword, as he could not answer for the consequence.

" Mr. M. had left two letters for Mr. S., in which he declares he is to be met with at *any* hour, and begs Mr. S. will not ' *deprive himself of so much sleep*, or *stand on any ceremony.*' Mr. S. called on him at the hour mentioned. Mr. S. was admitted with the difficulty mentioned. Mr. S. declares that, on Mr. M.'s perceiving that he came to answer *then* to his challenge, he does not remember ever to have seen a *man* behave so perfectly dastardly. Mr. M. detained Mr. S. till seven o'clock the next morning. He (Mr. M.) said he never meant to quarrel with Mr. S. He convinced Mr. S. that his enmity ought to be directed solely against his brother and another gentleman at Bath. Mr. S. went to Bath. ＊ ＊ ＊ ＊ ＊ ＊ ＊ " †

On his arrival in Bath, (whither he travelled with Miss Linley and her father,) Sheridan lost not a moment in ascertaining the falsehood of the charge against his brother. While Charles, however, indignantly denied the flagitious conduct imputed to him by Mathews, he expressed his opinion of the step which Sheridan and Miss Linley had taken, in terms of considerable warmth, which were overheard by some of the family. As soon as the young ladies had retired to bed, the two brothers, without any announcement of their intention, set off post together for London, Sheridan having previously written the following letter to Mr. Wade, the Master of the Ceremonies : —

    " Sir,
    " I ought to apologise to you for troubling

† The remainder of this paper is omitted, as only briefly referring to circumstances, which will be found more minutely detailed in another document.

you again on a subject which should concern so few.

"I find Mr. Mathews's behaviour to have been such that I cannot be satisfied with his *concession*, as a *consequence* of an *explanation* from me. I called on Mr. Mathews last Wednesday night at Mr. Cochlin's, without the smallest expectation of coming to any *verbal* explanation with him. A proposal of a *pacific* meeting the next day was the consequence, which ended in those advertisements and the letter to you. As for Mr. Mathews's honour or *spirit* in this whole affair, I shall only add that a few hours may possibly give some proof of the latter; while, in my own justification I affirm that it was far from being my fault that this point now remains to be determined.

"On discovering Mr. Mathews's *benevolent* interposition in my own family, I have counterordered the advertisements that were agreed on, as I think even an *explanation* would now misbecome me; an agreement to them was the effect more of mere *charity* than *judgment*. As I find it necessary to make *all* my sentiments as public as possible, your declaring this will greatly oblige

"Your very humble Servant,

"R. B. SHERIDAN.

"Sat. 12 o'clock, May 2d, 1772.

"*To William Wade, Esq.*"

On the following day (Sunday) when the young gentlemen did not appear, the alarm of their sisters was not a little increased, by hearing that high words had been exchanged the evening before, and that it was feared a duel between the brothers would be the consequence. Though unable to credit this dreadful surmise, yet full of the various apprehensions which such mystery was calculated to inspire, they had instant recourse to Miss Linley, the fair *Helen* of all this strife, as the person most likely to be acquainted with their brother Richard's designs, and to relieve them from the suspense under which they laboured. She, however, was as ignorant of the transaction as themselves, and their mutual distress being heightened by sympathy, a scene of tears and fainting-fits ensued, of which no less remarkable a person than Doctor Priestley, who lodged in Mr. Linley's house at the time, happened to be a witness.

On the arrival of the brothers in town, Richard Sheridan instantly called Mathews out. His second on the occasion was Mr. Ewart, and the particulars of the duel are thus stated by himself, in a letter which he addressed to Captain Knight, the second of Mathews, soon after the subsequent duel in Bath : —

" Sir,

" On the evening preceding my last meeting with Mr. Mathews, Mr. Barnett * produced a paper to me, written by Mr. Mathews, containing an account of our former meetings in London. As I had before frequently heard of Mr. Mathews's relation of that affair, without interesting myself much in contradicting it, I should certainly have treated this in the same manner, had it not been seemingly authenticated by Mr. Knight's name being subscribed to it. My asserting that the paper contains much misrepresentation, equivocation, and falsity, might make it appear strange that I should apply to you in this manner for information on the subject : but, as it likewise contradicts what I have been told were Mr. Knight's sentiments and assertions on that affair, I think I owe it to his credit, as well as my own justification, first, to be satisfied from himself whether he really subscribed and will support the truth of the account shown by Mr. Mathews. Give me leave previously to relate what *I* have affirmed to have been a real state of our meeting in London, and which I am now ready to support on my honour, or my oath, as the best account I can give of Mr. Mathews's relation is, that it is almost directly opposite to mine.

* The friend of Mathews in the second duel.

" Mr. Ewart accompanied me to Hyde Park, about six in the evening, where we met you and Mr. Mathews, and we walked together to the ring. — Mr. Mathews refusing to make any other acknowledgement than he had done, I observed that we were come to the ground : Mr. Mathews objected to the spot, and appealed to you. — We proceeded to the back of a building on the other side of the ring, the ground was there perfectly level. I called on him, and drew my sword (he having previously declined pistols). Mr. Ewart observed a sentinel on the other side of the building ; we advanced to another part of the Park. I stopped again at a seemingly convenient place : Mr. Mathews objected to the observation of some people at a great distance, and proposed to retire to the Hercules' Pillars till the Park should be clear : we did so. In a little time we returned. — I again drew my sword ; Mr. Mathews again objected to the observation of a person who seemed to watch us. Mr. Ewart observed that the chance was equal, and engaged that no one should stop him, should it be necessary for him to retire to the gate, where we had a chaise and four, which was equally at his service. Mr. Mathews declared that he would not engage while any one was within sight, and proposed to defer it till next morning. I turned to you and said that ' this was trifling work,' that I could not admit of

any delay, and engaged to remove the gentleman (who proved to be an officer, and who, on
my going up to him, and assuring him that any
interposition would be ill timed, politely retired).
Mr. Mathews, in the mean time, had returned
towards the gate; Mr. Ewart and I called to
you, and followed. We returned to the Hercules' Pillars, and went from thence, by agreement, to the Bedford Coffee House, where, the
master being alarmed, you came and conducted
us to Mr. Mathews at the Castle Tavern, Hen-
rietta Street. Mr. Ewart took lights up in his
hand, and almost immediately on our entering
the room we engaged. I struck Mr. Mathews's
point so much out of the line, that I stepped up
and caught hold of his wrist, or the hilt of his
sword, while the point of mine was at his breast.
You ran in and caught hold of my arm, exclaiming, ' *Don't kill him.*' I struggled to disengage
my arm, and said his sword was in my power.
Mr. Mathews called out twice or thrice, ' *I beg
my life.*' — We were parted. You immediately
said, ' *There he has begged his life, and now there
is an end of it;*' and, on Mr. Ewart's saying
that, when his sword was in my power, as I
attempted no more you should not have interfered, you replied that you *were wrong*, but that
you had *done it hastily and to prevent mischief*
— or words to that effect. Mr. Mathews then

hinted that I was rather *obliged to your inter-* CHAP.
position for the advantage; you declared that II.
' *before* you did so, both the swords were in 1772.
Mr. Sheridan's power.' Mr. Mathews still
seemed resolved to give it another turn, and
observed that *he had never quitted his sword.* —
Provoked at this, I then swore (with too much
heat perhaps) that he should either give up his
sword and I would break it, or go to his guard
again. He refused — but, on my persisting, either
gave it into my hand, or flung it on the table, or
the ground (*which,* I will not absolutely affirm).
I broke it, and flung the hilt to the other end of
the room. He exclaimed at this. I took a
mourning sword from Mr. Ewart, and presenting
him with mine, gave my honour that what had
passed should never be mentioned by me, and
he might now right himself again. He replied
that he ' *would never draw a sword against the*
man who had given him his life:' — but, on his
still exclaiming against the indignity of breaking his sword (which he had brought upon himself) Mr. Ewart offered him the pistols, and
some altercation passed between them. Mr.
Mathews said, that he *could never show his face*
if it were known how his sword was broke — that
such a thing had never been done — that it can-
celled all obligations, &c. &c. You seemed to
think it was wrong, and we both proposed, that

if he never misrepresented the affair, it should not be mentioned by us. This was settled. I then asked Mr. Mathews, whether (as he had expressed himself sensible of, and shocked at the injustice and indignity he had done me in his advertisement) it did not occur to him that he owed me another satisfaction; and that, as it was now in his power to do it without discredit, I supposed he would not hesitate. This he absolutely refused, unless conditionally; I insisted on it, and said I would not leave the room till it was settled. After much altercation, and with much ill-grace, he gave the apology, which afterwards appeared. We parted, and I returned immedietely to Bath. I, there, to Colonel Gould, Captain Wade, Mr. Creaser, and others, mentioned the affair to Mr. Mathews's credit — said that chance had given me the advantage, Mr. Mathews had consented to that apology, and mentioned nothing of the sword. Mr. Mathews came down, and in two days I found the whole affair had been stated in a different light, and insinuations given out to the same purpose as in the paper, which has occasioned this trouble. I had *undoubted authority* that these accounts proceeded from Mr. Mathews, and likewise that Mr. Knight had never had any share in them. I then thought I no longer owed Mr. Mathews the compliment to conceal any circumstance, and I related the affair to several gentlemen exactly as above.

" Now, sir, as I have put down nothing in this account but upon the most assured recollection, and, as Mr. Mathews's paper either directly or equivocally contradicts almost every article of it, and as your name is subscribed to that paper, I flatter myself that I have a right to expect your answer to the following questions . — First,

" Is there any falsity or misrepresentation in what I have advanced above?

" With regard to Mr. Mathews's paper — did I, in the Park, seem in the smallest article inclined to enter into conversation with Mr. Mathews? — He insinuates that I did.

" Did Mr. Mathews not *beg his life ?* — He affirms he did not.

" Did I break his sword *without warning ?* — He affirms I did it without warning, on his laying it on the table.

" Did I not offer him mine? — He omits it.

" Did Mr. Mathews give me the apology, as a point of generosity, *on my desisting to demand it ?* — He affirms he did.

" I shall now give my reasons for doubting your having authenticated this paper.

" 1. Because I think it full of falsehood and misrepresentation, and Mr. Knight has the character of a man of truth and honour.

" 2. When you were at Bath, I was informed that you had never expressed any such sentiments.

" 3. I have been told that, in Wales, Mr. Mathews never *told his story* in the presence of Mr. Knight, who had never there insinuated anything to my disadvantage.

" 4. The paper shown me by Mr. Barnett contains (if my memory does not deceive me), three separate sheets of writing-paper. Mr. Knight's evidence is annexed to the last, which contains chiefly a copy of our *first* proposed advertisements, which Mr. Mathews had, in Mr. Knight's presence, agreed should be destroyed as totally void ; and which (in a letter to Colonel Gould, by whom I had insisted on it) he declared upon his honour he knew nothing about, nor should ever make the least use of.

" These, sir, are my reasons for applying to yourself, in preference to any appeal to Mr. Ewart, my second on that occasion, which is what I would wish to avoid. As for Mr Mathews's assertions, I shall never be concerned at them. I have ever avoided any verbal altercation with that gentleman, and he has now secured himself from any other.

" I am your very humble servant,

" R. B. SHERIDAN."

It was not till Tuesday morning that the young ladies at Bath were relieved from their suspense by the return of the two brothers, who entered evidently much fatigued, not having been in bed since they left home, and produced the apology of Mr. Mathews, which was instantly sent to Crutwell for insertion. It was in the following terms : —

" Being convinced that the expressions I made use of to Mr. Sheridan's disadvantage were the effects of passion and misrepresentation, I retract what I have said to that gentleman's disadvantage, and particularly beg his pardon for my advertisement in The Bath Chronicle.

" THOMAS MATHEWS." *

With the odour of this transaction fresh about him, Mr. Mathews retired to his estate in Wales, and, as he might have expected, found himself universally shunned. An apology may be, according to circumstances, either the noblest effort of manliness or the last resource of fear,

* This appeared in The Bath Chronicle of May 7th. In another part of the same paper there is the following paragraph : — " We can with authority contradict the account in The London Evening Post of last night, of a duel between Mr. M—t—ws and Mr. S—r—n, as to the time and event of their meeting, Mr. S. having been at this place on Saturday, and both these gentlemen being here at present."

and it was evident, from the reception which this gentleman experienced every where, that the former, at least, was not the class to which his late retraction had been referred. In this crisis of his character, a Mr. Barnett, who had but lately come to reside in his neighbourhood, observing with pain the mortifications to which he was exposed, and perhaps thinking them, in some degree, unmerited, took upon him to urge earnestly the necessity of a second meeting with Sheridan, as the only means of removing the stigma left by the first; and, with a degree of Irish friendliness, not forgotten in the portrait of Sir Lucius O'Trigger, offered himself to be the bearer of the challenge. The desperation of persons, in Mr. Mathews's circumstances, is in general much more formidable than the most acknowledged valour; and we may easily believe that it was with no ordinary eagerness he accepted the proposal of his new ally, and proceeded with him, full of vengeance, to Bath.

The elder Mr. Sheridan, who had but just returned from Ireland, and had been with some little difficulty induced to forgive his son for the wild achievements he had been engaged in during his absence, was at this time in London, making arrangements for the departure of his favourite, Charles, who, through the interest of Mr. Wheatley, an old friend of the family, had been ap-

pointed Secretary to the Embassy in Sweden.
Miss Linley —wife and no wife — obliged to conceal from the world what her heart would have
been most proud to avow, was also absent from
Bath, being engaged at the Oxford music-meeting. The letter containing the preliminaries of
the challenge was delivered by Mr. Barnett, with
rather unnecessary cruelty, into the hands of
Miss Sheridan, under the pretext, however, that
it was a note of invitation for her brother, and
on the following morning, before it was quite
daylight, the parties met at Kingsdown — Mr.
Mathews, attended by his neighbour Mr. Barnett, and Sheridan by a gentleman of the name
of Paumier, nearly as young as himself, and but
little qualified for a trust of such importance and
delicacy.

The account of the duel, which I shall here
subjoin, was drawn up some months after, by the
second of Mr. Mathews, and deposited in the
hands of Captain Wade, the master of the ceremonies. Though somewhat partially coloured,
and (according to Mr. Sheridan's remarks upon
it, which shall be noticed presently) incorrect in
some particulars, it is, upon the whole, perhaps
as accurate a statement as could be expected,
and received, as appears by the following letter
from Mr. Brereton, (another of Mr. Sheridan's
intimate friends,) all the sanction that Captain

Paumier's concurrence in the truth of its most material facts could furnish.

"Dear Sir,

"In consequence of some reports spread to the disadvantage of Mr. Mathews, it seems he obtained from Mr. Barnett an impartial relation of the last affair with Mr. Sheridan, directed to you. This account Mr. Paumier has seen, and I, at Mr. Mathews's desire, inquired from him if he thought it true and impartial: he says it differs, in a few immaterial circumstances only, from his opinion, and has given me authority to declare this to you.

"I am, dear Sir,
"Your most humble and obedient servant,
"(Signed) WILLIAM BRERETON.
"Bath, Oct. 24. 1772."

Copy of a Paper left by Mr. Barnett in the Hands of Captain William Wade, Master of the Ceremonies at Bath.

"On quitting our chaises at the top of Kingsdown, I entered into a conversation with Captain Paumier, relative to some preliminaries I thought ought to be settled in an affair, which was likely to end very seriously ;— particularly the method of using their pistols, which Mr. Mathews had repeatedly signified his desire to use prior to swords, from a conviction that Mr. Sheridan would run in on him, and an ungentlemanlike scuffle probably be the consequence. This, however, was refused by Mr. Sheridan, declaring he had no pistols : Captain Paumier replied he had a brace (which I know were loaded). — By my advice, Mr. Mathews's were not loaded, as I imagined it was always customary to load on the field, which I mentioned to Captain Paumier at the White Hart, before we went out, and desired he would draw his pistols. He replied, as they were already loaded, and they going on a public road at that time of the morning, he might as well let them remain so till we got to the place appointed, when he would on his honour draw them, which I am convinced he would have done had there been time ; but Mr. Sheridan immediately drew his sword, and, in a vaunting manner, desired Mr. Mathews to draw (their ground was very uneven, and near the post-chaises). — Mr. Mathews drew ; Mr. Sheridan advanced on him at first ; Mr. Mathews in turn advanced fast on Mr. Sheridan ; upon which he retreated, till he very suddenly ran in upon Mr. Mathews, laying himself exceedingly open, and endeavouring to get hold of Mr. Mathews's sword ; Mr. Mathews received him on his point, and, I believe, disengaged his sword from Mr. Sheridan's body, and gave him another wound ;

which I suppose, must have been either against one of his ribs, or his breast-bone, as his sword broke, which I imagine happened from the resistance it met with from one of those parts; but whether it was broke by that, or on the closing, I cannot aver.

" Mr. Mathews, I think, on finding his sword broke, laid hold of Mr. Sheridan's sword-arm, and tripped up his heels : they both fell; Mr. Mathews was uppermost, with the hilt of his sword in his hand, having about six or seven inches of the blade to it, with which I saw him give Mr. Sheridan, as I imagined, a skin-wound or two in the neck; for it could be no more,— the remaining part of the sword being broad and blunt; he also beat him in the face either with his fist or the hilt of his sword. Upon this I turned from them, and asked Captain Paumier if we should not take them up; but I cannot say whether he heard me or not, as there was a good deal of noise; however, he made no reply. I again turned to the combatants, who were much in the same situation : I found Mr. Sheridan's sword was bent, and he slipped his hand up the small part of it, and gave Mr. Mathews a slight wound in the left part of his belly: I that instant turned again to Captain Paumier, and proposed again our taking them up. He in the same moment called out, ' Oh! he is killed,

he is killed!' — I as quick as possible turned
again, and found Mr. Mathews had recovered
the point of his sword, that was before on the
ground, with which he had wounded Mr. Sheridan in the belly : I saw him drawing the point
out of the wound.   By this time Mr. Sheridan's
sword was broke, which he told us. — Captain
Paumier called out to him, ' My dear Sheridan,
beg your life, and I will be yours for ever.'   I
also desired him to ask his life : he replied, ' No,
by God, I won't.'   I then told Captain Paumier
it would not do to wait for those punctilios (or
words to that effect,) and desired he would assist
me in taking them up.   Mr. Mathews most
readily acquiesced first, desiring me to see Mr.
Sheridan was disarmed.   I desired him to give
me the tuck, which he readily did, as did Mr.
Sheridan the broken part of his sword to Captain
Paumier.   Mr. Sheridan and Mr. Mathews both
got up, the former was helped into one of the
chaises, and drove off for Bath, and Mr. Mathews made the best of his way to London.

" The whole of this narrative I declare, on the
word and honour of a gentleman, to be exactly
true ; and that Mr. Mathews discovered as much
genuine, cool, and intrepid resolution as man
could do.

" I think I may be allowed to be an impartial
relater of facts, as my motive for accompanying

Mr. Mathews was no personal friendship, (not having any previous intimacy, or being barely acquainted with him,) but from a great desire of clearing up so ambiguous an affair, without prejudice to either party, — which a stranger was judged the most proper to do, — particularly as Mr. Mathews had been blamed before for taking a relation with him on a similar occasion.

" (Signed)   WILLIAM. BARNETT.*

" October, 1772."

* The following account is given as an " Extract of a letter from Bath," in The St. James's Chronicle, July 4. : " Young Sheridan and Captain Mathews of this town, who lately had a rencontre in a tavern in London, upon account of the maid of Bath, Miss Linley, have had another this morning upon Kingsdown, about four miles hence. Sheridan is much wounded, but whether mortally or not is yet uncertain. Both their swords breaking upon the first lunge, they threw each other down and with the broken pieces hacked at each other rolling upon the ground, the seconds standing by, quiet spectators. Mathews is but slightly wounded, and is since gone off." The Bath Chronicle, on the day after duel, (July 2d,) gives the particulars thus :—" This morning about three o'clock, a second duel was fought with swords, between Captain Mathews and Mr. R. Sheridan, on Kingsdown, near this city, in consequence of their former dispute respecting an amiable young lady, which Mr. M. considered as improperly adjusted ; Mr. S. having, since their first rencontre, declared his sentiments respecting Mr. M. in a manner that the former thought required satisfaction. Mr. Sheridan received three or four wounds in his breast and sides, and now lies very ill. Mr. M. was only slightly wounded, and left this city soon after the affair was over."

The comments which Mr. Sheridan thought it necessary to make upon this narrative have been found in an unfinished state among his papers; and though they do not, as far as they go, disprove any thing material in its statements, (except, perhaps, with respect to the nature of the wounds which he received,) yet, as containing some curious touches of character, and as a document which he himself thought worth preserving, it is here inserted.

" *To William Barnett, Esq.*
"Sir,

" It has always appeared to me so impertinent for individuals to appeal to the public on transactions merely private, that I own the most apparent necessity does not prevent my entering nto such a dispute without an awkward consciousness of its impropriety. Indeed, I am not without some apprehension, that I may have no right to plead your having led the way in my excuse ; as it appears not improbable that some ill-wisher to you, sir, and the cause you have been engaged in, betrayed you first into this *exact narrative,* and then exposed it to the public eye, under pretence of vindicating your friend. However, as it is the opinion of some of my friends, that I ought not to suffer these papers to pass wholly unnoticed, I shall make a few observations on them with that moderation which becomes one who is highly conscious of the impropriety of staking his single assertion against the apparent testimony of three. This, I say, would be an impropriety, as I am supposed to write to those who are not acquainted with the parties. I had some time ago a copy of these papers from Captain Wade, who informed me that they were lodged in his hands, to be made public only by judicial authority. I wrote to you, sir, on the subject, to have from yourself an avowal that the account was yours ; but as I received no answer, I have reason to compliment you with the supposition that you are not the author of it. However, as the name *William Barnett* is subscribed to it, you must accept my apologies for making use of that as the ostensible signature of the writer — Mr. Paumier likewise (the gentleman who went out with me on that occasion in the character of a second) having assented to every thing material in it, I shall suppose the whole account likewise to be his ; and as there are some circumstances which could come from no one but Mr. Mathews, I shall (without meaning to take from its authority) suppose it to be Mr. Mathews's also.

" As it is highly indifferent to me whether the account I am to observe on be considered as accurately true or not, and I believe it is of very

little consequence to any one else, I shall make
those observations just in the same manner as I
conceive any indifferent person of common sense,
who should think it worth his while to peruse
the matter with any degree of attention.   In this
light, the *truth* of the articles which are asserted
under Mr. Barnett's name is what I have no
business to meddle with ; but, if it should appear
that this *accurate narrative* frequently contradicts itself as well as all probability, and that
there are some positive facts against it, which do
not depend upon any one's assertion, I must
repeat that I shall either compliment Mr. Barnett's judgment, in supposing it not his, or his
humanity in proving the *narrative* to partake
of that confusion and uncertainty, which his
well-wishers will plead to have possessed him in
the transaction.   On this account, what I shall
say on the subject need be no further addressed
to you ; and, indeed, it is idle, in my opinion,
to address even the publisher of a newspaper on
a point that can concern so few, and ought to
have been forgotten by them.   This you must
take as my excuse for having neglected the matter so long.

" The first point in Mr. Barnett's narrative
that is of the least consequence to take notice
of, is, where Mr. M. is represented as having repeatedly signified his desire to use pistols prior

to swords, from a conviction that Mr. Sheridan would run in upon him, and an ungentlemanlike scuffle probably be the consequence. This is one of those articles which evidently must be given to Mr. Mathews : for, as Mr. B.'s part is simply to relate a matter of fact, of which he was an eye-witness, he is by no means to answer for Mr. Mathews's *private convictions.* As this insinuation bears an obscure allusion to a past transaction of Mr. M.'s, I doubt not but he will be surprized at my indifference in not taking the trouble even to explain it. However, I cannot forbear to observe here that had I, at the period which this passage alludes to, known what was the theory which Mr. M. held of *gentlemanly scuffle,* I might, possibly, have been so unhappy as to have put it out of his power ever to have brought it into practice.

" Mr. B. now charges me with having cut short a number of pretty preliminaries, concerning which he was treating with Captain Paumier, by drawing my sword, and, in a vaunting manner; desiring Mr. M. to draw. Though I acknowledge (with deference to these gentlemen) the full right of interference which seconds have on such occasions, yet I may remind Mr. B. that he was acquainted with my determination with regard to pistols before we went on the Down, nor could I have expected it to have been proposed.

' Mr. M. drew; Mr. S. advanced, &c. :' — here
let me remind Mr. B. of a circumstance, which
I am convinced his memory will at once acknowledge."

This paper ends here: but in a rougher
draught of the same letter (for he appears to
have studied and corrected it with no common
care) the remarks are continued, in a hand not
very legible, thus : —

" But Mr. B. here represents me as drawing
my sword in a *vaunting* manner. This I take to
be a reflection ; and can only say, that a person's
demeanour is generally regulated by their idea
of their antagonist, and, for what I know, I may
now be writing in a vaunting style. Here let me
remind Mr. B. of an omission, which, I am convinced, nothing but want of recollection could
occasion, yet which is a material point in an exact
account of such an affair, nor does it reflect in
the least on Mr. M. Mr. M. could not possibly
have drawn his sword on my calling to him, as

   *   *   *   *   *   * †

" Mr. B.'s account proceeds, that I ' advanced
first on Mr. M.,' &c. &c. ; ' which, (says Mr. B.)
I imagine, happened from the resistance it met
with from one of those parts ; but whether it was
broke by that, or on the closing, I cannot aver.'

† It is impossible to make any connected sense of the
passage that follows.

How strange is the confusion here! — First, it certainly broke; — whether it broke against rib or no, doubtful; — then, indeed, whether it broke at all, uncertain. * * * * But of all times Mr. B. could not have chosen a worse than this for Mr. M.'s sword to break; for the relating of the action unfortunately carries a contradiction with it; — since if, on closing, Mr. M. received me on his point, it is not possible for him to have made a lunge of such a nature as to break his sword against a rib-bone. But as the time chosen is unfortunate, so is the place on which it is said to have broke, — as Mr. B. might have been informed, by enquiring of the surgeons, that I had no wounds on my breast or rib with the point of a sword, they being the marks of the jagged and blunted part."

He was driven from the ground to the White Hart; where Ditcher and Sharpe, the most eminent surgeons of Bath, attended and dressed his wounds, — and, on the following day, at the request of his sisters, he was carefully removed to his own home. The newspapers, which contained the account of the affair, and even stated that Sheridan's life was in danger, reached the Linleys at Oxford, during the performance, but were anxiously concealed from Miss Linley by her father, who knew that the intelligence would totally disable her from appearing. Some persons, who were witnesses of the performance that day, still talk of the touching effect which her beauty and singing produced upon all present, — aware, as they were, that a heavy calamity had befallen her, of which she herself was perhaps the only one in the assembly ignorant.

In her way back to Bath she was met at some miles from the town by a Mr. Panton, a clergyman, long intimate with the family, who, taking her from her father's chaise into his own, employed the rest of the journey in cautiously breaking to her the particulars of the alarming event that had occurred. Notwithstanding this precaution, her feelings were so taken by surprize, that, in the distress of the moment, she let the secret of her heart escape, and passionately exclaimed, " My husband! my husband!" — demanding to see him, and insisting upon her right as his wife to be near him, and watch over him day and night. Her entreaties, however, could not be complied with ; for the elder Mr. Sheridan, on his return from town, incensed and grieved at the catastrophe to which his son's imprudent passion had led, refused for some time even to see him, and strictly forbade all intercourse between his daughters and the Linley family. But the appealing looks of a brother, lying wounded and unhappy, had more power over their hearts than the commands of a father, and they, accordingly, contrived to communicate intelligence of the lovers to each other.

In the following letter, addressed to him by Charles at this time, we can trace that difference between the dispositions of the brothers, which with every one except their father, rendered Richard, in spite of all his faults, by far the most popular and beloved of the two : —

"DEAR DICK,   London, July 3d, 1772.

" It was with the deepest concern I received the late accounts of you, though it was somewhat softened by the assurance of your not being in the least danger. You cannot conceive the uneasiness it occasioned to my father. Both he and I were resolved to believe the best, and to suppose you safe, but then we neither of us could approve of the cause in which you suffer. All your friends here condemned you. You risked every thing, where you had nothing to gain, to give your antagonist the thing he wished, a chance for recovering his reputation. Your courage was past dispute : — he wanted to get rid of the contemptible opinion he was held in, and you were good-natured enough to let him do it at your expense. It is not now a time to scold, but all your friends were of opinion, you could, with the greatest propriety, have refused to meet him. For my part, I shall suspend my judgment

till better informed, only I cannot forgive your
preferring swords.

"I am exceedingly unhappy at the situation
I leave you in with respect to money matters,
the more so as it is totally out of my power to be
of any use to you. Ewart was greatly vexed at
the manner of your drawing for the last 20*l.* —
I own, I think with some reason.

"As to old Ewart, what you were talking
about is absolutely impossible; he is already surprized at Mr. Linley's long delay, and, indeed,
I think the latter much to blame in this respect.
I did intend to give you some account of myself
since my arrival here, but you cannot conceive
how I have been hurried, — even much pressed
for time at this *present writing*. I must therefore
conclude, with wishing you speedily restored to
health, and that if I could make your purse as
whole as that will shortly be, I hope, it would
make me exceedingly happy.

"I am, dear Dick, yours sincerely,
"C. F. SHERIDAN."

Finding that the suspicion of their marriage,
which Miss Linley's unguarded exclamation had
suggested, was gaining ground in the mind of
both fathers,— who seemed equally determined
to break the tie, if they could arrive at some
positive proof of its existence, — Sheridan wrote

frequently to his young wife, (who passed most of this anxious period with her relations at Wells,) cautioning her against being led into any acknowledgment, which might further the views of the elders against their happiness. Many methods were tried upon both sides, to ensnare them into a confession of this nature; but they eluded every effort, and persisted in attributing the avowal which had escaped from Miss Linley before Mr. Panton and others, to the natural agitation and bewilderment into which her mind was thrown at the instant.

As soon as Sheridan was sufficiently recovered of his wounds *, his father, in order to detach him, as much as possible, from the dangerous recollections which continually presented themselves in Bath, sent him to pass some months at Waltham Abbey, in Essex, under the care of . Mr. and Mrs. Parker of Farm Hill, his most particular friends. In this retirement, where he continued, with but few and short intervals of absence, from August or September, 1772, till the spring of the following year, it is probable that, notwithstanding the ferment in which his heart was kept, he occasionally and desultorily

* The Bath Chronicle of the 9th of July has the following paragraph :— " It is with great pleasure we inform our readers that Mr. Sheridan is declared by his surgeon to be out of danger."

occupied his hours in study. Among other proofs of industry, which his manuscripts exhibit, and which may possibly be referred to this period, is an abstract of the History of England — nearly filling a small quarto volume of more than a hundred pages, closely written. I have also found in his *early* hand-writing (for there was a considerable change in his writing afterwards) a collection of remarks on Sir William Temple's works, which may likewise have been among the fruits of his reading at Waltham Abbey.

These remarks are confined chiefly to verbal criticism, and prove, in many instances, that he had not yet quite formed his taste to that idiomatic English, which was afterwards one of the great charms of his own dramatic style. For instance, he objects to the following phrases : — " Then I *fell* to my task again." — " These things *come*, with time, to be habitual." — " By which these people *come* to be either scattered or destroyed." — " Which alone could pretend to *contest it* with them :" (upon which phrase he remarks, " *It* refers to nothing here :") and the following graceful idiom in some verses by Temple : —

" Thy busy head can find no gentle rest,
For thinking on the' events," &c. &c.

Some of his observations, however, are just and tasteful. Upon the Essay "Of Popular Discontents," after remarking, that "Sir W. T. opens all his Essays with something as foreign to the purpose as possible," he has the following criticism : — " Page 260., ' Represent misfortunes for faults, and *mole-hills* for *mountains*,' — the metaphorical and literal expression too often coupled. P. 262., ' Upon these four wheels the chariot of state may in all appearance drive easy and safe, or at least not be too much *shaken* by the usual *roughness* of ways, unequal *humours* of *men*, or any common accidents,' — another instance of the confusion of the metaphorical and literal expressions."

Among the passages he quotes from Temple's verses, as faulty, is the following : —

" ———— that we may *see*
Thou art indeed the empress of the *sea*."

It is curious enough, that he himself was afterwards guilty of nearly as illicit a rhyme in his song " When 'tis night," and always defended it : —

" But when the fight's *begun*,
Each serving at his *gun*."

Whatever grounds there may be for referring these labours of Sheridan to the period of his retirement at Waltham Abbey, there are certainly but few other intervals in his life that could be selected as likely to have afforded him opportunities of reading. Even here, however, the fears and anxieties that beset him were too many and incessant to leave much leisure for the pursuits of scholarship. However a state of excitement may be favourable to the developement of genius — which is often of the nature of those seas, that become more luminous the more they are agitated, — for a student a far different mood is necessary; and in order to reflect with clearness the images that study presents, the mind should have its surface level and unruffled.

The situation, indeed, of Sheridan was at this time particularly perplexing. He had won the heart, and even hand, of the woman he loved, yet saw his hopes of possessing her farther off than ever. He had twice risked his life against an unworthy antagonist, yet found the vindication of his honour still incomplete, from the misrepresentations of enemies, and the yet more mischievous testimony of friends. He felt within himself all the proud consciousness of genius, yet, thrown on the world without even a profession, looked in vain for a channel through which to direct its energies. Even the precarious hope, which his father's favour held out, had been purchased by an act of duplicity which his conscience could not approve; for he had been induced, with the view, perhaps, of blinding his father's vigilance, not only to promise that he would instantly give up a pursuit so unpleasing to him, but to take " an oath equivocal" that he never would marry Miss Linley.

The pressure of these various anxieties upon so young and so ardent a mind, and their effects in alternately kindling and damping its spirit, could only have been worthily described by him who felt them ; and there still exist some letters which he wrote during this time, to a gentleman well known as one of his earliest and latest friends. I had hoped that such a picture, as these letters must exhibit, of his feelings at that most interesting period of his private life, would not have been lost to the present work. But scruples — over-delicate, perhaps, but respectable, as founded upon a systematic objection to the exposure of *any* papers, received under the seal of private friendship — forbid the publication of these precious documents. The reader must, therefore, be satisfied with the few distant glimpses of their contents, which are afforded by the answers of his correspondent, found among the papers entrusted to me. From these it appears, that through all his letters the same strain of sadness and despondency prevailed, — sometimes breaking out into aspirings of ambition, and sometimes rising into a tone of cheerfulness, which but ill concealed the melancholy under it. It is evident, also, and not a little remarkable, that in none of these overflowings of his confidence had he as yet suffered the secret of his French marriage with Miss Linley to escape; and that his friend accordingly knew but half the wretched peculiarities of his situation. Like most lovers, too, imagining that every one who approached his mistress must be equally intoxicated with her beauty as himself, he seems anxiously to have cautioned his young correspondent (who occasionally saw her at Oxford and at Bath) against the danger that lay in such irresistible charms. From another letter, where the writer refers to some message, which Sheridan had requested him to deliver to Miss Linley, we learn, that she was at this time so strictly watched, as to be unable to achieve — what to an ingenious woman is seldom difficult — an answer to a letter which her lover had contrived to convey to her.

It was at first the intention of the elder Mr. Sheridan to send his daughters, in the course of this autumn, under the care of their brother Richard, to France. But, fearing to entrust them to a guardian, who seemed himself so much in need of direction, he altered his plan, and, about the beginning of October, having formed an engagement for the ensuing winter with the manager of the Dublin Theatre, gave up his house in Bath, and set out with his daughters for Ireland. At the same time Mr. Grenville (afterwards Marquis of Buckingham), who had passed a great part of this and the preceding summer at Bath, for the purpose of receiving instruction from Mr. Sheridan in elocution, went also to Dublin on a short visit, accompanied by Mr. Cleaver, and by his brother Mr. Thomas Grenville — between whom and Richard Sheridan an intimacy had at this period commenced, which continued with uninterrupted cordiality ever after.

Some time previous to the departure of the elder Mr. Sheridan for Ireland, having taken before a magistrate the depositions of the postillions who were witnesses of the duel at Kingsdown, he had earnestly entreated of his son to join him in a prosecution against Mathews, whose conduct on the occasion he and others considered as by no means that of a fair and honourable antagonist. It was in contemplation of a measure of this nature, that the account of the meeting already given was drawn up by Mr. Barnet, and deposited in the hands of Captain Wade. Though Sheridan refused to join in legal proceedings — from an unwillingness, perhaps, to keep Miss Linley's name any longer

afloat upon public conversation — yet this revival of the subject, and the conflicting statements to which it gave rise, produced naturally
in both parties a relapse of angry feelings, which
was very near ending in a third duel between
them. The authenticity given by Captain Paumier's name to a narrative which Sheridan considered false and injurious, was for some time a
source of considerable mortification to him ; and
it must be owned, that the helpless irresolution
of this gentleman during the duel, and his weak
acquiescence in these misrepresentations afterwards, showed him as unfit to be trusted with
the life as with the character of his friend.

How nearly this new train of misunderstanding had led to another explosion, appears from
one of the letters already referred to, written in
December, and directed to Sheridan at the Bedford Coffee-house, Covent Garden, in which the
writer expresses the most friendly and anxious
alarm at the intelligence which he has just received, — implores of Sheridan to moderate his
rage, and reminds him how often he had resolved never to have any concern with Mathews
again. Some explanation, however, took place,
as we collect from a letter dated a few days
later ; and the world was thus spared not only
such an instance of inveteracy, as three duels

between the same two men would have exhibited, but, perhaps, the premature loss of a life
to which we are indebted, for an example as
noble, and a lesson as useful, as ever genius and
its errors have bequeathed to mankind.

The following Lent Miss Linley appeared in
the oratorios at Covent Garden; and Sheridan
who, from the nearness of his retreat to London,
(to use a phrase of his own, repeated in one of
his friend's letters,) " trod upon the heels of
perilous probabilities," though prevented by the
vigilance of her father from a private interview,
had frequent opportunities of seeing her in public. Among many other stratagems which he
contrived, for the purpose of exchanging a few
words with her, he more than once disguised
himself as a hackney-coachman, and drove her
home from the theatre.

It appears, however, that a serious misunderstanding at this time occurred between them, —
originating probably in some of those paroxysms
of jealousy, into which a lover like Sheridan
must have been continually thrown, by the numerous admirers and pursuers of all kinds,
which the beauty and celebrity of his mistress
attracted. Among various alliances invented
for her by the public at this period, it was ru-
moured that she was about to be married to Sir

Thomas Clarges ; and in The Bath Chronicle of
April, 1773, a correspondence is given as authentic between her and " Lord Grosvenor,"
which, though pretty evidently a fabrication,
yet proves the high opinion entertained of the
purity of her character. The correspondence is
thus introduced, in a letter to the editor : —
" The following letters are confidently said to
have passed between Lord G——r, and the
celebrated English syren, Miss L——y. I send
them to you for publication, not with any view
to increase the volume of literary scandal,
which, I am sorry to say, at present needs no
assistance, but with the most laudable intent of
setting an example for our modern belles, by
holding out the character of a young woman,
who, notwithstanding the solicitations of her
profession, and the flattering example of higher
ranks, has added *incorruptible virtue* to a number of the most elegant qualifications."

Whatever may have caused the misunderstanding between her and her lover, a recon-
cilement was with no great difficulty effected,
by the mediation of Sheridan's young friend
Mr. Ewart ; and, at length, after a series of
stratagems and scenes which convinced Mr. Linley that it was impossible much longer to keep
them asunder, he consented to their union, and
on the 13th of April, 1773, they were mar-

ried by license * — Mr. Ewart being at the same time wedded to a young lady with whom he also had eloped clandestinely to France, but was now enabled, by the forgiveness of his father, to complete this double triumph of friendship and love.

A curious instance of the indolence and pro-crastinating habits of Sheridan used to be related by Woodfall, as having occurred about this time. A statement of his conduct in the duels having appeared in one of the Bath papers, so false and calumnious as to require an immediate answer, he called upon Woodfall to request that his paper might be the medium of it. But wish-ing, as he said, that the public should have the whole matter fairly before them, he thought it right that the offensive statement should first be inserted, and in a day or two after be followed by his answer, which would thus come with more relevancy and effect. In compliance with his wish Woodfall lost not a moment, in tran-scribing the calumnious article into his columns — not doubting, of course, that the refutation of it would be furnished with still greater eager-ness. Day after day, however, elapsed, and, notwithstanding frequent applications on the one side, and promises on the other, not a line

* Thus announced in The Gentleman's Magazine : —
" Mr. Sheridan of the Temple to the celebrated Miss Linley of Bath."

of the answer was ever sent by Sheridan, —who, having expended all his activity in assisting the circulation of the poison, had not industry enough left to supply the antidote. Throughout his whole life, indeed, he but too consistently acted upon the principles, which the first Lord Holland used playfully to impress upon his son : — " Never do to-day what you can possibly put off till to-morrow, nor ever do, yourself, what you can get any one else to do for you."

CHAP. III.

CHAP.
III.
———
1773.

A FEW weeks previous to his marriage, Sheridan had been entered a student of the Middle Temple. It was not, however, to be expected that talents like his, so sure of a quick return of fame and emolument, would wait for the distant and dearly-earned emoluments, which a life of labour in this profession promises. Nor, indeed, did his circumstances admit of any such patient speculation. A part of the sum which Mr. Long had settled upon Miss Linley, and occasional assistance from her father (his own having withdrawn all countenance from him), were now the only resources, besides his own talents left him. The celebrity of Mrs. Sheridan as a singer was, it is true, a ready source of wealth; and offers of the most advantageous kind were pressed upon them, by managers of concerts both in town and country. But with a pride and delicacy, which received the tribute of Dr. Johnson's praise, he rejected at once all thoughts of allowing her to re-appear in public; and, instead of profiting by the display of his wife's talents, adopted the manlier resolution of seeking an independence by his own. An engagement had been made for her some months before by her father, to perform at the music-meeting that was to take place at Worcester this summer. But Sheridan, who considered that his own claims upon her had superseded all others, would not suffer her to keep this engagement.

How decided his mind was upon the subject will appear from the following letter, written by him to Mr. Linley about a month after his marriage, and containing some other interesting particulars, that show the temptations with which his pride had, at this time, to struggle: —

" DEAR SIR,   East Burnham, May 12. 1773.

" I purposely deferred writing to you till I should have settled *all* matters in London, and in some degree settled ourselves at our little home. Some unforeseen delays prevented my finishing with Swale till Thursday last, when every thing was concluded. I likewise settled with him for his own account, as he brought it to me, and, for a *friendly* bill, it is pretty decent.

—Yours of the 3d instant did not reach me till yesterday, by reason of its missing us at Morden. As to the principal point it treats of, I had given my answer some days ago to Mr. Isaac of Worcester. He had inclosed a letter to Storace for my wife, in which he dwells much on the nature of the agreement you had made for her eight months ago, and adds, that ' as this is no new application, but a request that you (Mrs. S.) will fulfil a positive engagement, the breach of which would prove of fatal consequence to our Meeting, I hope Mr. Sheridan will think his honour in some degree concerned in fulfilling it.'—Mr. Storace, in order to enforce Mr. Isaac's argument, showed me his letter on the same subject to him, which begins with saying, ' We must have Mrs. Sheridan, somehow or other, if possible!'—the plain English of which is that, if her husband is not willing to let her perform, we will persuade him that he acts *dishonourably* in preventing her from fulfilling a *positive engagement*. This I conceive to be the very worst mode of application that could have been taken; as there really is not common sense in the idea that my *honour* can be concerned in my wife's fulfilling an engagement, which it is impossible she should ever have made.—Nor (as I wrote to Mr. Isaac) can you, who gave the promise, whatever it was, be in the least charged with the breach of it, as your daughter's marriage was an event which must always have been looked to by them as quite as natural a period to your right over her as her death. And, in my opinion, it would have been just as reasonable to have applied to you to fulfil your engagement in the latter case as in the former. As to the *imprudence* of declining this engagement, I do not think, even were we to suppose that my wife should ever on any occasion appear again in public, there would be the least at present. For instance, I have had a gentleman with me from Oxford (where they do not claim the least *right* as from an engagement), who has endeavoured to place the idea of my complimenting the University with Betsey's performance in the strongest light of advantage to me. This he said, on my declining to let her perform on any agreement. He likewise informed me, that he had just left Lord North (the Chancellor), who, he assured me, would look upon it as the highest compliment, and had expressed himself so to him. Now, should it be a point of inclination or convenience to me to break my resolution with regard to Betsey's performing, there surely would be more sense in obliging Lord North (and probably from *his own* application) and the University, than Lord Coventry and Mr. Isaac. For, were she to sing at Worcester, there would not be the least compliment in her performing at Oxford. Indeed, they would have a right to *claim it*—particularly, as that is the mode of application they have chosen from Worcester. I have mentioned the Oxford matter merely as an argument, that I can have no kind of inducement to accept of the proposal from Worcester. And, as I have written fully on the subject to Mr. Isaac, I think there will be no occasion for you to give any further reasons to Lord Coventry — only that I am sorry I cannot accept of his proposal, civilities, &c. &c., and refer him for my motives to Mr. Isaac, as what I have said to you on the subject I mean for you only, and, if more remains to be argued on the subject in general, we must defer it till we meet, which you have given us reason to hope will not be long first.

" As this is a letter of business chiefly, I shall say little of our situation and arrangement of affairs, but that I think we are as happy as those who wish us best could desire. There is but one thing that has the least weight upon me, though it is one I was prepared for. But time, while it strengthens the other blessings we possess, will, I hope, add that to the number. You will know that I speak with regard to my father. Betsey informs me you have written to him again — have you heard from him ?   *   *   *
  *   *   *   *   *   *

" I should hope to hear from you very soon, and I assure you, you shall now find me a very exact correspondent; though I hope you will not give me leave to confirm my character in that respect before we meet.

" As there is with this a letter for Polly and you, I shall only charge you with mine and Betsey's best love to her, mother, and Tom, &c. &c. and believe me your sincere friend, and affectionate son,

" R. B. SHERIDAN."

At East Burnham, from whence this letter is dated, they were now living in a small cottage, to which they had retired immediately on their marriage, and to which they often looked back with a sigh in after times, when they were more prosperous, but less happy. It was during a very short absence from this cottage, that the following lines were written by him : —

" Teach me, kind Hymen, teach — for thou
    Must be my only tutor now —
Teach me some innocent employ,
That shall the hateful thought destroy,
That I this whole long night must pass
In exile from my love's embrace.
Alas, thou hast no wings, oh Time ! *
It was some thoughtless lover's rhyme,

* It will be perceived that the eight following lines are the foundation of the song " What bard, oh Time," in the Duenna.

Who, writing in his Chloe's view,
Paid her the compliment through you.
For had he, if he truly lov'd,
But once the pangs of absence prov'd,
He'd cropt thy wings, and, in their stead,
Have painted thee with heels of lead.
But 'tis the temper of the mind,
Where we thy regulator find.
Still o'er the gay and o'er the young
With unfelt steps you flit along, —
As Virgil's nymph o'er ripen'd corn,
With such etherial haste was borne,
That every stock with upright head,
Denied the pressure of her tread.
But o'er the wretched, oh, how slow!
And heavy sweeps thy scythe of woe !
Oppress'd beneath each stroke they bow,
Thy course engraven on their brow,
A day of absence shall consume
The glow of youth and manhood's bloom,
And one short night of anxious fear
Shall leave the wrinkles of a year.
For me who, when I'm happy, owe
No thanks to fortune that I'm so,
Who long have learn'd to look at one
Dear object, and at one alone,
For all the joy, or all the sorrow,
That gilds the day or threats the morrow,
I never felt thy footsteps light,
But when sweet love did aid thy flight,
And, banish'd from his blest dominion,
I cared not for thy borrow'd pinion.
  " True, she is mine, and, since she's mine,
At trifles I should not repine :

But oh, the miser's real pleasure
Is not in knowing he has treasure ;
He must behold his golden store,
And feel, and count his riches o'er.
Thus I, of one dear gem possest,
And in that treasure only blest,
There every day would seek delight,
And clasp the casket every night."

Towards the winter they went to lodge for a short time with Storace, the intimate friend of Mr. Linley, and in the following year attained that first step of independence, a house to themselves ; — Mr. Linley having kindly supplied the furniture of their new residence, which was in Orchard-Street, Portman-Square. During the summer of 1774, they passed some time at Mr. Canning's and Lord Coventry's ; but, so little did these visits interfere with the literary industry of Sheridan, that, as appears from the following letter written to Mr. Linley in November, he had not only at that time finished his play of the Rivals, but was on the point of " sending a book to the press :"—

" DEAR SIR,   Nov. 17th, 1774.

" If I were to attempt to make as many apologies as my long omission in writing to you requires, I should have no room for any other subject. One excuse only I shall bring forward, which is, that I have been exceedingly employed, and I believe *very profitably*. However, before I explain how, I must ease my mind on a subject, that much more nearly concerns me than any point of business or profit. I must premise to you that Betsey is now very well, before I tell you abruptly that she has encountered another disappointment and consequent indisposition. * * * * However, she is now getting entirely over it, and she shall never take any journey of the kind again. I inform you of this now, that you may not be alarmed by any accounts from some other quarter, which might lead you to fear she was going to have such an illness as last year, of which I assure you, upon my honour, there is not the least apprehension. If I did not write now, Betsey would write herself, and in a day she will make you quite easy on this head.

"I have been very seriously at work on a book, which I am just now sending to the press, and which I think will do me some credit, if it leads to nothing else. However, the profitable affair is of another nature. There will be a *Comedy* of mine in rehearsal at Covent-Garden within a few days. I did not set to work on it till within a few days of my setting out for *Crome*, so you may think I have not, for these last six weeks, been very idle. I have done it at Mr.

Harris's (the manager's) own request; it is now complete in his hands, and preparing for the stage. He, and some of his friends also who have heard it, assure me in the most flattering terms that there is not a doubt of its success. It will be very well played, and Harris tells me that the least shilling I shall get (if it succeeds) will be six hundred pounds. I shall make no secret of it towards the time of representation, that it may not lose any support my friends can give it. I had not written a line of it two months ago, except a scene or two, which I believe you have seen in an odd act of a little farce.

" Mr. Stanley was with me a day or two ago on the subject of the oratorios. I find Mr. Smith has declined, and is retiring to Bath. Mr. Stanley informed me, that on his applying to the King for the continuance of his favour, he was desired by His Majesty to make me an offer of Mr. Smith's situation and partnership in them, and that he should continue his protection, &c. — I declined the matter very civilly and very peremptorily. I should imagine that Mr. Stanley would apply to you ; — I started the subject to him, and said you had twenty Mrs. Sheridans more. However, he said very little : — if he does, and you wish to make an alteration in your system at once, I should think you may stand in Smith's place. I would not listen to him on any other terms, and I should think the King might be made to signify his pleasure for such an arrangement. On this you will reflect, and if any way strikes you that I can move in it, I need not add how happy I shall be in its success.

*   *   *   *   *   *

" I hope you will let me have the pleasure to hear from you soon, as I shall think any delay unfair, — unless you can plead that you are writing an opera, and a folio on music beside. Accept Betsey's love and duty.

" Your sincere and affectionate

" R. B. SHERIDAN."

What the book here alluded to was, I cannot with any accuracy ascertain. Besides a few sketches of plays and poems, of which I shall give some account in a subsequent Chapter, there exist among his papers several fragments of Essays and Letters, all of which — including the unfinished plays and poems — must have been written by him in the interval between 1769, when he left Harrow, and the present year ; though at what precise dates during that period there are no means of judging.

Among these are a few political Letters, evidently designed for the newspapers ; — some of them but half copied out, and probably never sent.   One of this description, which must have been written immediately on his leaving school, is a piece of irony against the Duke of Grafton, giving reasons why that nobleman should not lose his head, and, under the semblance of a defence, exaggerating all the popular charges against him.

The first argument (he says) of the Duke's adversaries " is founded on the regard which ought to be paid to justice, and on the good effects which, they affirm, such an example would have, in suppressing the ambition of any future minister.   But, if I can prove that his ——— might be made a much greater example of by being suffered to live, I think I may without vanity affirm that their whole argument will fall to the ground.   By pursuing the methods which they propose, viz. chopping off his ———'s head, I allow the impression would be stronger at first ; but we should consider how soon that wears off. If, indeed, his ———'s crimes were of such a na- ture, as to entitle his head to a place on Temple- Bar, I should allow some weight to their argu- ment.   But, in the present case, we should reflect how apt mankind are to relent after they have inflicted punishment ; — so that, perhaps, the same men who would have detested the noble lord, while alive and in prosperity, point- ing him as a scare-crow to their children, might,

CHAP.
III.

1774.

after being witnesses to the miserable fate that
had overtaken him, begin in their hearts to pity
him; and from the fickleness so common to
human nature, perhaps, by way of compensation,
acquit him of part of his crimes; insinuate, that
he was dealt hardly with, and thus, by the re-
membrance of their compassion on this occasion,
be led to show more indulgence to any future
offender in the same circumstances." There is
a clearness of thought and style here very remarkable in so young a writer.

In affecting to defend the Duke against the
charge of fickleness and unpunctuality, he says,
" I think I could bring several instances which
should seem to promise the greatest steadiness
and resolution. I have known him make the
Council wait, on the business of the whole nation,
when he has had an appointment to Newmarket.
Surely, this is an instance of the greatest honour;
— and, if we see him so punctual in private ap-
pointments, must we not conclude that he is
infinitely more so in greater matters? Nay, when
W——s * came over, is it not notorious that the
late Lord Mayor went to His Grace on that evening, proposing a scheme which, by securing this
fire-brand, might have put an end to all the
troubles he has caused. But His Grace did not
see him:—no, he was a man of too much honour;
he had *promised* that evening to attend Nancy

* Wilkes.

Parsons to Ranelagh, and he would not disappoint her, but made three thousand people witnesses of his punctuality."

There is another Letter, which happens to be dated (1770), addressed to " Novus," — some writer in Woodfall's Public Advertiser, — and appearing to be one of a series to the same correspondent. From the few political allusions introduced in this letter, (which is occupied chiefly in an attack upon the literary style of " Novus,") we can collect that the object of Sheridan was to defend the new ministry of Lord North, who had, in the beginning of that year, succeeded the Duke of Grafton. Junius was just then in the height of his power and reputation ; and, as, in English literature, one great voice produces a multitude of echoes, it was thought at that time indispensable to every letter-writer in a newspaper, to be a close copyist of the style of Junius : of course, our young political tyro followed this " mould of form" as well as the rest. Thus, in addressing his correspondent — " That gloomy seriousness in your style, — that seeming consciousness of superiority, together with the consideration of the infinite pains it must have cost you to have been so elaborately wrong,— will not suffer me to attribute such numerous errors to any thing but real ignorance, joined with most consummate vanity." The following is a specimen of his acuteness in criticising the absurd style of his adversary : — " You leave it rather dubious whether you were most pleased with the glorious opposition to Charles I., or the dangerous designs of that monarch, which you emphatically call ' the arbitrary projects of a Stuart's nature.' What do you mean by the projects of a man's *nature?* A man's natural disposition may urge him to the commission of some actions ; — Nature may instigate and encourage, but I believe you are the first that ever made her a projector."

It is amusing to observe, that, while he thus criticises the style and language of his correspondent, his own spelling, in every second line, convicts him of deficiency in at least one common branch of literary acquirement : — we find *thing* always spelt *think;* — *whether, where,* and *which* turned into *wether, were,* and *wich ;*—and double *m's* and *s's* almost invariably reduced to " single blessedness." This sign of a neglected education remained with him to a very late period, and, in his hasty writing, or scribbling, would occasionally recur, to the last.

From these Essays for the newspapers it may be seen how early was the bias of his mind towards politics. It was, indeed, the rival of literature in his affections during all the early part of his life, and, at length, — whether luckily for himself or not it is difficult to say, — gained the mastery.

There are also among his manuscripts some commencements of Periodical Papers, under various names, " The Detector," " The Dramatic Censor," &c. ; — none of them, apparently, carried beyond the middle of the first number. But one of the most curious of these youthful productions is a Letter to the Queen, recommending the establishment of an Institution, for the instruction and maintenance of young females in the better classes of life, who, from either the loss of their parents or from poverty, are without the means of being brought up suitably to their station. He refers to the asylum founded by Madame de Maintenon, at St. Cyr, as a model, and proposes that the establishment should be placed under the patronage of Her Majesty, and entitled " The Royal Sanctuary." The reader, however, has to arrive at the practical part of the plan, through long and flowery windings of panegyric, on the beauty, genius, and virtue of women, and their transcendent superiority, in every respect, over men.

. The following sentence will give some idea of the sort of eloquence with which he prefaces this grave proposal to Her Majesty : — " The dispute about the proper sphere of women is idle. That men should have attempted to draw a line for their orbit, shows that God meant them for comets, and above our jurisdiction. With them the enthusiasm of poetry and the idolatry of love is the simple voice of nature." There are, indeed, many passages of this boyish composition, a good deal resembling in their style those ambitious apostrophes, with which he afterwards ornamented his speeches on the trial of Hastings.

He next proceeds to remark to Her Majesty, that in those countries where " man is scarce better than a brute, he shows his degeneracy by his treatment of women," and again falls into metaphor, not very clearly made out : — " The influence that women have over us is as the medium through which the finer Arts act upon us. The incense of our love and respect for them creates the atmosphere of our souls, which corrects and meliorates the beams of knowledge."

The following is in a better style : — " However, in savage countries where the pride of man has not fixed the first dictates of ignorance into law, we see the real effects of nature. The wild Huron shall, to the object of his love, become gentle as his weary rein-deer ; — he shall present to her the spoil of his bow on his knee ; — he shall watch without reward the cave where she sleeps ; — he shall rob the birds for feathers for her hair, and dive for pearls for her neck ; — her look shall be his law, and her beauties his worship!" He then endeavours to prove that, as it is the destiny of man to be ruled by woman, he ought, for his own sake, to render her as fit for that task as possible : — "How can we be better employed than in perfecting that which governs us ? The brighter they are, the more we shall be illumined. Were the minds of all women cultivated by inspiration, men would become wise of course. They are a sort of pentagraphs with which nature writes on the heart of man ; —what *she* delineates on the original map will appear on the copy."

In showing how much less women are able to struggle against adversity than men, he says, — "As for us, we are born in a state of warfare with poverty and distress. The sea of adversity is our natural element, and he that will not buffet with the billows deserves to sink. But you, oh you, by nature formed of gentler kind, can *you* endure the biting storm ? shall you be turned to the nipping blast, and not a door be open to give you shelter ?"

After describing, with evident seriousness, the nature of the institution of Madame de Maintenon, at St. Cyr, he adds the following strange romantic allusion : — "Had such a charity as I have been speaking of existed here, the mild *Parthenia* and my poor *Laura* would not have fallen into untimely graves."

K 2

The practical details of his plan, in which it is equally evident that he means to be serious, exhibit the same flightiness of language and notions. The King, he supposes, would have no objection to " grant Hampton-Court, or some other palace, for the purpose," and " as it is (he continues, still addressing the Queen,) to be immediately under Your Majesty's patronage, so should Your Majesty be the first member of it. Let the constitution of it be like that of a university —Your Majesty, Chancellor ; some of the first ladies in the kingdom sub-chancellors ; whose care it shall be to provide instructors of real merit. The classes are to be distinguished by age, — none by degree. For, as their qualification should be gentility, they are all on a level. The instructors should be women, except for the languages. Latin and Greek should not be learned ; —the frown of pedantry destroys the blush of humility. The practical part of the sciences, as of astronomy, &c. should be taught. In history they would find that there are other passions in man than love. As for novels, there are some I would strongly recommend ; but romances infinitely more. The one is a represent-ation of the effects of the passions as they should be, though extravagant ; the other, as they are. The latter is falsely called nature, and is a pic-ture of depraved and corrupted society ; the other is the glow of nature. I would, therefore, exclude all novels that show human nature depraved: —however well executed, the design will disgust."

He concludes by enumerating the various good effects which the examples of female virtue, sent forth from such an institution, would produce upon the manners and morals of the other sex ; and in describing, among other kinds of coxcombs, the cold, courtly man of the world, uses the following strong figure : —" They are so clipped, and rubbed, and polished, that God's image and inscription is worn from them, and when He calls in his coin, He will no longer know them for his own."

There is still another Essay, or rather a small fragment of an Essay, on the Letters of Lord Chesterfield, which, I am inclined to think, may have formed a part of the rough copy of the book, announced by him to Mr. Linley as ready in the November of this year. Lord Chesterfield's Letters appeared for the first time in 1774, and the sensation they produced was exactly such as would tempt a writer in quest of popular subjects to avail himself of it. As the few pages which I have found, and which contain merely scattered hints of thoughts, are numbered as high as 232, it is possible that the preceding part of the work may have been sufficiently complete to go into the printer's hands, and that there, like so many more of his "unshelled brood," it died without ever taking wing. A few of these memorandums will, I have no doubt, be acceptable to the reader.

" Lord C.'s whole system in no one article calculated to make a great man. — A noble youth should be ignorant of the things, he wishes him to know ; — such a one as he wants would be *too soon* a man.

" Emulation is a dangerous passion to encourage, in some points, in young men ; it is so linked with envy : — if you reproach your son for not surpassing his school-fellows, he will hate those who are before him. — Emulation not to be encouraged even in virtue. True virtue will, like the Athenian, rejoice in being surpassed ; — a friendly emulation cannot exist in two minds ; — one must hate the perfections in which he is eclipsed by the other ; — thus, from hating the quality in his competitor, he loses the respect for it in himself : — a young man by himself better educated than two. — A Roman's emulation was not to excel his countrymen, but to make his country excel : this is the true, the other selfish. — Epaminondas, who reflected on the pleasure his success would give his father, most glorious ; — an emulation for that purpose, true.

" The selfish vanity of the father appears in all these letters — his sending the copy of a letter for his sister.— His object was the praise of his own mode of education. — How much more noble the affection of Morni in Ossian ; ' Oh, that the name of Morni,' &c. &c. *

* " Oh that the name of Morni were forgot among the people ! that the heroes would only say, ' Behold the father

" His frequent directions for constant employment entirely ill founded : — a wise man is formed more by the action of his own thoughts than by continually feeding it. 'Hurry,' he says, 'from play to study; never be doing nothing.'— I say, 'Frequently be unemployed; sit and think.' *There are on every subject but a few leading and fixed ideas; their tracks may be traced by your own genius, as well as by reading :* — a man of deep thought, who shall have accustomed himself to support or attack all he has read, will soon find nothing new : — thought is exercise, and the mind like the body must not be wearied."

These last few sentences contain the secret of Sheridan's confidence in his own powers. His subsequent success bore him out in the opinions he thus early expressed, and might even have persuaded him that it was in consequence, not in spite, of his want of cultivation that he succeeded.

On the 17th of January, 1775, the comedy of The Rivals was brought out at Covent-Garden, and the following was the cast of the characters on the first night : —

Sir Anthony Absolute .	.	*Mr. Shuter.*
Captain Absolute	.	*Mr. Woodward.*
Falkland . . .	.	*Mr. Lewis.*

of Gaul!' " Sheridan applied this, more than thirty years after, in talking of his own son, on the hustings of Westminster, and said that, in like manner, he would ask no greater distinction than for men to point at him and say, " There goes the father of Tom Sheridan."

CHAP. III. 1775.	Acres . . .	.	*Mr. Quick.*
	Sir Lucius O'Trigger .	.	*Mr. Lee.*
	Fag	.	*Mr. Lee Lewis.*
	David . . .	.	*Mr. Dunstal.*
	Coachman . . .	.	*Mr. Fearon.*
	Mrs. Malaprop .	.	*Mrs. Green.*
	Lydia Languish .	.	*Miss Barsanti.*
	Julia . .	.	*Mrs. Bulkley.*
	Lucy . .	.	*Mrs. Lessingham.*

This comedy, as is well known, failed on its first representation, — chiefly from the bad-acting of Mr. Lee in Sir Lucius O'Trigger.   Another actor, however, Mr. Clinch, was substituted in his place, and the play being lightened of this and some other incumbrances, rose at once into that high region of public favour, where it has continued to float so buoyantly and gracefully ever since.

The following extracts from letters written at that time by Miss Linley (afterwards Mrs. Tickell) to her sister, Mrs. Sheridan, though containing nothing remarkable, yet, as warm with the feelings of a moment so interesting in Sheridan's literary life, will be read, perhaps, with some degree of pleasure.   The slightest outline of a celebrated place, taken on the spot, has often a charm beyond the most elaborate picture finished at a distance.

" MY DEAREST ELIZA,   Bath

" We are all in the greatest anxiety about Sheridan's play, — though I do not think there is the least doubt of its succeeding. I was told last night that it was his own story, and therefore called ' The Rivals;' but I do not give any credit to this intelligence.   *   *   *

" I am told he will get at least 700*l.* for his play."

" Bath, January, 1775.

" It is impossible to tell you what pleasure we felt at the receipt of Sheridan's last letter, which confirmed what we had seen in the newspapers of the success of his play. The *knowing ones* were very much disappointed, as they had so very bad an opinion of its success. After the first night we were indeed all very fearful that the audience would go very much prejudiced against it. But now, there can be no doubt of its success, as it has certainly got through more difficulties than any comedy which has not met its doom the first night. I know you have been very busy in writing for Sheridan, — I don't mean *copying,* but *composing :* — it's true, indeed ; — you must not contradict me when I say you wrote the much-admired epilogue to The Rivals. How I long to read it! What makes it more certain is, that my *father* guessed it was *yours* the first time he saw it praised in the paper."

This statement respecting the epilogue would, if true, deprive Sheridan of one of the fairest leaves of his poetic crown. It appears, however, to be but a conjecture hazarded at the moment, and proves only the high idea entertained of Mrs. Sheridan's talents by her own family. The cast of the play at Bath, and its success there and elsewhere, are thus mentioned in these letters of Miss Linley : —

" Bath, February 18. 1775.

" What shall I say of The Rivals ! — a compliment must naturally be expected; but really it goes so far beyond any thing I *can* say in its praise, that I am afraid my modesty must keep me silent. When you and I meet I shall be better able to explain myself, and tell you how much I am delighted with it. We expect to have it *here* very soon : — it is now in rehearsal. You pretty well know the merits of our principal performers : — I'll show you how it is cast.

Sir Anthony	*Mr. Edwin.*
Captain Absolute	*Mr. Didier.*
Falkland	*Mr. Diamond.*

(A new actor of great merit, and a sweet figure.)

Sir Lucius	*Mr. Jackson.*

Acres	.	.	. *Mr. Keasberry.*
Fag	.	.	. *Mr. Brunsdon.*
Mrs. Malaprop	.	.	*Mrs. Wheeler.*
Miss Lydia	.	.	*Miss Wheeler.*

(Literally, a very pretty romantic girl of seventeen.)

Julia	.	.	. *Mrs. Didier.*
Lucy	.	.	. *Mrs. Brett.*

There, Madam, do not you think we shall do your Rivals some justice ? I'm convinced it won't be done better any where out of London. I don't think Mrs. Mattocks can do Julia very well."

" Bath, March 9. 1775.

" You will know by what you see enclosed in this frank my reason for not answering your letter sooner was, that I waited the success of Sheridan's play in Bath ; for, let me tell you, I look upon our theatrical tribunal, though not in *quantity*, in *quality* as good as yours, and I do not believe there was a critic in the whole city that was not there. But, in my life, I never saw any thing go off with such uncommon applause. I must first of all inform you that there was a very full house ; — the play was performed inimitably well ; nor did I hear, for the honour of our Bath actors, one single prompt the whole night ; but I suppose the poor creatures never acted with such shouts of applause in their lives, so that they were incited by that to do their best. They lost many of Malaprop's good sayings by the applause: in short, I never saw or heard any thing like it; — before the actors spoke, they began their clapping. There was a new scene of the N. Parade, painted by Mr. Davis, and a most delightful one it is, I assure you. Every body says,—Bowers in particular,—that yours in town is not so good. Most of the dresses were entirely new, and very handsome. On the whole, I think Sheridan is vastly obliged to poor dear Keasberry for getting it up so well. We only wanted a good Julia to have made it quite complete. You must know that it was entirely out of Mrs. Didier's style of playing: but I never saw better acting than Keasberry's — so all the critics agreed."

" Bath, August 22d, 1775.

" Tell Sheridan his play has been acted at Southampton: — above a hundred people were turned away the first night. They say there never was any thing so universally liked. They have very good success at Bristol, and have played The Rivals several times: — Miss Barsanti, Lydia, and Mrs. Canning, Julia."

To enter into a regular analysis of this lively play, the best comment on which is to be found

in the many smiling faces, that are lighted up
around wherever it appears, is a task of criticism
that will hardly be thought necessary. With
much less wit, it exhibits perhaps more humour
than The School for Scandal, and the dialogue,
though by no means so pointed or sparkling, is,
in this respect, more natural, as coming nearer the
current coin of ordinary conversation; whereas,
the circulating medium of The School for Scandal is diamonds. The characters of The Rivals,
on the contrary, are *not* such as occur very
commonly in the world; and, instead of producing striking effects with natural and obvious
materials, which is the great art and difficulty of
a painter of human life, he has here overcharged
most of his persons with whims and absurdities,
for which the circumstances they are engaged in
afford but a very disproportionate vent. Accordingly, for our insight into their characters,
we are indebted rather to their confessions than
their actions. Lydia Languish, in proclaiming
the extravagance of her own romantic notions,
prepares us for events much more ludicrous and
eccentric, than those in which the plot allows
her to be concerned; and the young lady herself
is scarcely more disappointed than we are, at
the tameness with which her amour concludes.
Among the various ingredients supposed to be
mixed up in the composition of Sir Lucius

O'Trigger, his love of fighting is the only one whose flavour is very strongly brought out ; and the wayward, captious jealousy of Falkland, though so highly coloured in his own representation of it, is productive of no incident answerable to such an announcement ; — the imposture which he practises upon Julia being, perhaps, weakened in its effect, by our recollection of the same device in the Nut-brown Maid and Peregrine Pickle.

The character of Sir Anthony Absolute is, perhaps, the best sustained and most natural of any, and the scenes between him and Captain Absolute are richly, genuinely dramatic. His surprise at the apathy with which his son receives the glowing picture which he draws of the charms of his destined bride, and the effect of the question, " And which is to be mine, sir, — the niece or the aunt ?" are in the truest style of humour. Mrs. Malaprop's mistakes, in what she herself calls " orthodoxy," have been often objected to as improbable from a woman in her rank of life ; but though some of them, it must be owned, are extravagant and farcical, they are almost all amusing, — and the luckiness of her simile, " as headstrong as an *allegory* on the banks of the Nile," will be acknowledged as long as there are writers to be run away with,

by the wilfulness of this truly " headstrong "
species of composition.

Of the faults of Sheridan both in his witty
and serious styles — the occasional effort of the
one, and the too frequent false finery of the other
— some examples may be cited from the dialogue
of this play. Among the former kind is the
following elaborate conceit : —

" *Falk.* Has Lydia changed her mind ? I should
have thought her duty and inclination would now have
pointed to the same object.

" *Abs.* Ay, just as the eyes of a person who squints ;
when her love-eye was fixed on me, t'other — her eye of
duty — was finely obliqued : but when duty bade her
point that the same way, off turned t'other on a swivel,
and secured its retreat with a frown."

This, though ingenious, is far too laboured ; —
and of that false taste by which sometimes, in his
graver style, he was seduced into the display of
second-rate ornament, the following speeches of
Julia afford specimens : —

" Then on the bosom of your wedded Julia, you may
lull your keen regret to slumbering ; while virtuous love,
with a cherub's hand, shall smooth the brow of upbraid-
ing thought, and pluck the thorn from compunction."

Again ; — " When hearts deserving happiness would
unite their fortunes, virtue would crown them with an
unfading garland of modest, hurtless flowers ; but ill-
judging passion will force the gaudier rose into the

wreath, whose thorn offends them when its leaves are dropt."

But, notwithstanding such blemishes, — and it is easy for the microscopic eye of criticism to discover gaps and inequalities in the finest edge of genius, — this play, from the liveliness of its plot, the variety and whimsicality of its characters, and the exquisite humour of its dialogue, is one of the most amusing in the whole range of the drama; and even without the aid of its more splendid successor, The School for Scandal, would have placed Sheridan in the first rank of comic writers.

A copy of The Rivals has fallen into my hands, which once belonged to Tickell, the friend and brother-in-law of Sheridan, and on the margin of which I find written by him in many places his opinion of particular parts of the dialogue.* He has also prefixed to it, as coming from Sheridan, the following humorous dedication, which, I take for granted, has never

* These opinions are generally expressed in two or three words, and are, for the most part, judicious. Upon Mrs. Malaprop's quotation from Shakspeare, " Hesperian curls," &c. he writes, " Overdone — fitter for farce than comedy." Acres's classification of oaths, " This we call the *oath referential*," &c. he pronounces to be " Very good, but above the speaker's capacity." Of Julia's speech, " Oh woman, how true should be your judgment, when your resolution is so weak!" he remarks, " On the contrary, it seems to be of little consequence whether any person's judgment be weak or not, who wants resolution to act according to it."

before met the light, and which the reader will
perceive by the allusions in it to the two Whig
ministries, could not have been written before
the year 1784 : —

" DEDICATION TO IDLENESS.

" MY DEAR FRIEND,

" If it were necessary to make any apology
for this freedom, I know you would think it a
sufficient one, that I shall find it easier to dedi-
cate my play to you than to any other person.
There is likewise a propriety in prefixing your
name to a work begun entirely at your suggestion, and finished under your auspices ; and I
should think myself wanting in gratitude to you,
if I did not take an early opportunity of acknowledging the obligations which I owe you. There
was a time — though it is so long ago that I now
scarcely remember it, and cannot mention it
without compunction — but there was a time,
when the importunity of parents, and the example of a few injudicious young men of my
acquaintance, had almost prevailed on me to
thwart my genius, and prostitute my abilities by
an application to serious pursuits. And if you
had not opened my eyes to the absurdity and
profligacy of such a perversion of the best gifts
of nature, I am by no means clear that I might
not have been a wealthy merchant or an eminent

lawyer at .this very moment. Nor was it only on my first setting out in life that I availed myself of a connection with you, though, perhaps, I never reaped such signal advantages from it as at that critical period. I have frequently since stood in need of your admonitions, and have always found you ready to assist me — though you were frequently brought by your zeal for me into new and awkward situations, and such as you were at first, naturally enough, unwilling to appear in. Amongst innumerable other instances, I cannot omit two, where you afforded me considerable and unexpected relief, and, in fact, converted employments usually attended by dry and disgusting business, into scenes of perpetual merriment and recreation. I allude, as you will easily imagine, to those cheerful hours which I spent in the Secretary of State's office and the Treasury, during all which time you were my inseparable companion, and showed me such a preference over the rest of my colleagues, as excited at once their envy and admiration. Indeed, it was very natural for them to repine at your having taught me a way of doing business, which it was impossible for them to follow — it was both original and inimitable.

" If I were to say here all that I think of your excellences, I might be suspected of flattery ; but I beg leave to refer you for the test of my sincerity to the constant tenor of my life and actions ; and shall conclude with a sentiment of which no one can dispute the truth, nor mistake the application, — that those persons usually deserve most of their friends who expect least of them.

" I am, &c. &c. &c.

" R. B. SHERIDAN."

The celebrity which Sheridan had acquired, as the chivalrous lover of Miss Linley, was, of course, considerably increased by the success of The Rivals ; and, gifted as he and his beautiful wife were with all that forms the magnetism of society, — the power to attract, and the disposition to be attracted, — their life, as may easily be supposed, was one of gaiety both at home and abroad. Though little able to cope with the entertainments of their wealthy acquaintance, her music and the good company which his talents drew around him, were an ample repayment for the more solid hospitalities which they received. Among the families visited by them was that of Mr. Coote (Purden), at whose musical parties Mrs. Sheridan frequently sung, accompanied occasionally by the two little daughters* of Mr. Coote, who were the originals of the

* The charm of her singing, as well as her fondness for children, are interestingly described in a letter to my friend Mr. Rogers, from one of the most tasteful writers of the

L 2

children introduced into Sir Joshua Reynolds's portrait of Mrs. Sheridan as St. Cecilia. It was here that the Duchess of Devonshire first met Sheridan; and, as I have been told, long hesitated as to the propriety of inviting to her house two persons of such equivocal rank in society, as he and his wife were at that time considered. Her Grace was reminded of these scruples some years after, when "the player's son" had become the admiration of the proudest and fairest; and when a house, provided for the Duchess herself at Bath, was left two months unoccupied, in consequence of the social attractions of Sheridan, which prevented a party then assembled at Chatsworth from separating. These are triumphs which, for the sake of all humbly born heirs of genius, deserve to be commemorated.

In gratitude, it is said, to Clinch, the actor, for the seasonable reinforcements which he had brought to The Rivals, Mr. Sheridan produced this year a farce called "St. Patrick's Day, or the Scheming Lieutenant," which was acted on the 2d of May, and had considerable success.

present day :— " Hers was truly ' a voice as of the cherub choir,' and she was always ready to sing without any pressing. She sung here a great deal, and to my infinite delight; but what had a peculiar charm was, that she used to take my daughter, then a child, on her lap, and sing a number of childish songs with such a playfulness of manner, and such a sweetness of look and voice, as was quite enchanting."

Though we must not look for the usual point of Sheridan in this piece, where the hits of pleasantry are performed with the broad end or *mace* of his wit, there is yet a quick circulation of humour through the dialogue, — and laughter, the great end of farce, is abundantly achieved by it. The moralizing of Doctor Rosy, and the dispute between the justice's wife and her daughter, as to the respective merits of militia-men and regulars, are highly comic : —

" Psha, you know, mamma, I hate militia officers; a set of dunghill cocks with spurs on — heroes scratch'd off a church-door. No, give me the bold upright youth, who makes love to-day, and has his head shot off to-morrow. Dear ! to think how the sweet fellows sleep on the ground, and fight in silk stockings and lace ruffles.

" *Mother.* Oh barbarous ! to want a husband that may wed you to-day, and be sent the Lord knows where before night; then in a twelvemonth, perhaps, to have him come like a Colossus, with one leg at New York and the other at Chelsea Hospital."

Sometimes, too, there occurs a phrase or sentence, which might be sworn to, as from the pen of Sheridan, any where. Thus, in the very opening : —

" 1*st Soldier.* I say you are wrong; we should all speak together, each for himself, and all at once, that we may be heard the better.

" *2d Soldier.* Right, Jack, we'll *argue in platoons.*"

Notwithstanding the great success of his first attempts in the drama, we find politics this year renewing its claims upon his attention, and tempting him to enter into the lists with no less an antagonist than Dr. Johnson. That eminent man had just published his pamphlet on the American question, entitled " Taxation no Tyranny ; " — a work, whose pompous sarcasms on the Congress of Philadelphia, when compared with what has happened since, dwindle into puerilities, and show what straws upon the great tide of events are even the mightiest intellects of this world. Some notes and fragments, found among the papers of Mr. Sheridan, prove that he had it in contemplation to answer this pamphlet; and, however inferior he might have been in style to his practised adversary, he would at least have had the advantage of a good cause, and of those durable materials of truth and justice, which outlive the mere workmanship, however splendid, of talent. Such arguments as the following, which Johnson did not scruple to use, are, by the haughtiness of their tone and thought, only fit for the lips of autocrats : —

" When they apply to our compassion, by telling us that they are to be carried from their own country to be tried for certain offences, we are not so ready to pity them, as to advise them not to offend. While they are innocent, they are safe.

" If they are condemned unheard, it is because there is no need of a trial. The crime is manifest and notorious," &c. &c.

It appears from the fragments of the projected answer, that Johnson's pension was one of the points upon which Mr. Sheridan intended to assail him. The prospect of being able to neutralize the effects of his zeal, by exposing the nature of the chief incentive from which it sprung, was so tempting, perhaps, as to overrule any feelings of delicacy, that might otherwise have suggested the illiberality of such an attack. The following are a few of the stray hints for this part of his subject : —

" It is hard when a learned man thinks himself obliged to commence politician. — Such pamphlets will be as trifling and insincere as the venal quit-rent of a birth-day ode. *

" Dr. J.'s other works, his learning and infirmities, fully entitled him to such a mark of distinction. — There was no call on him to become politician. — The easy quit-rent * of refined

---

* On another scrap of paper I find " the miserable quit-rent of an annual pamphlet." It was his custom in composition (as will be seen by many other instances) thus to try the same thought in a variety of forms and combinations, in order to see in which it would yield the greatest produce of wit.

panegyric, and a few grateful rhymes or flowery
dedications to the intermediate benefactor   *

*   *   *   *

" The man of letters is rarely drawn from
obscurity by the inquisitive eye of a sovereign :
— it is enough for Royalty to gild the laurelled
brow, not explore the garret or the cellar. — In
this case, the return will generally be ungrateful
— the patron is most possibly disgraced or in
opposition — if he (the author) follows the dictates of gratitude, he must speak his patron's
language, but he may lose his pension ; but to
be a standing supporter of ministry, is probably
to take advantage of that competence against
his benefactor. When it happens that there is
great experience and political knowledge, this
is more excusable ; but it is truly unfortunate
where the fame of far different abilities adds
weight to the attempts of rashness   *   *

*   *   *   *   * "

He then adds this very striking remark : —
" Men seldom think deeply on subjects on
which they have no choice of opinion : — they
are fearful of encountering obstacles to their
faith (as in religion), and so are content with
the surface."

Dr. Johnson says, in one part of his pamphlet,
— " As all are born the subjects of some state
or other, we may be said to have been all born

consenting to some system of government." On
this Sheridan remarks : — " This is the most
slavish doctrine that ever was inculcated. If by
our birth we gave a tacit bond for our acquiescence in that form of government under which
we were born, there never would have been an
alteration of the first modes of government —
no Revolution in England."

Upon the argument derived from the right of
conquest he observes ; — " This is the worst
doctrine that can be with respect to America.
— If America is ours by conquest, it is the
conquerors who settled there that are to claim
these powers."

He expresses strong indignation at the " arrogance," with which such a man as Montesquieu
is described as " the fanciful Montesquieu," by
" an eleemosynary politician, who writes on the
subject merely because he has been rewarded for
writing otherwise all his lifetime."

In answer to the argument against the claims
of the Americans, founded on the small proportion of the population that is really represented
even in England, he has the following desultory
memorandums : — " In fact, every man in England is represented — every man can influence
people, so as to get a vote, and even if in an
election votes are-divided, each candidate is supposed equally worthy — as in lots — fight Ajax

or Agamemnon.* — This an American cannot do in any way whatever.

" The votes in England are perpetually shifting : — were it an object, few could be excluded. — Wherever there is any one ambitious of assisting the empire, he need not put himself to much inconvenience. — If the Doctor indulged his studies in Cricklade or Old Sarum, he might vote : — the dressing meat, the simplest proof of existence, begets a title. — His pamphlet shows that he thinks he can influence some one ; not an anonymous writer in the paper but contributes his mite to the general tenor of opinion. — At the eve of an election, his Patriot † was meant to influence more than the single voice of a rustic. — Even the mob, in shouting, give votes where there is not corruption."

It is not to be regretted that this pamphlet was left unfinished. Men of a high order of genius, such as Johnson and Sheridan, should never enter into warfare with each other, but, like the gods in Homer, leave the strife to inferior spirits. The publication of this pamphlet would most probably have precluded its author

* He means to compare an election of this sort to the casting of lots between the Grecian chiefs in the 7th book of The Iliad.

† The name of a short pamphlet, published by Dr. Johnson, on the Dissolution of Parliament in 1774.

from the distinction and pleasure which he afterwards enjoyed in the society and conversation
of the eloquent moralist, who, in the following
year, proposed him as a member of the Literary
Club, and always spoke of his character and
genius with praise. Nor was Sheridan wanting
on his part with corresponding tributes ; for, in
a prologue which he wrote about this time to
the play of Sir Thomas Overbury, he thus alludes to Johnson's Life of its unfortunate author : —

> " So pleads the tale, and gives to future times
> The son's misfortunes, and the parent's crimes ;
> There shall his fame, if own'd to night, survive,
> Fix'd by the hand that bids our language live."

CHAP. IV.

CHAP.
IV.
———
1775.

MR. SHERIDAN had now got into a current of dramatic fancy, of whose prosperous flow he continued to avail himself actively. The summer recess was employed in writing The Duenna ; and his father-in-law, Mr. Linley, assisted in selecting and composing the music for it. As every thing connected with the progress of a work, which is destined to be long the delight of English ears, must naturally have a charm for English readers, I feel happy in being enabled to give, from letters written at the time by Mr. Sheridan himself to Mr. Linley, some details relating to their joint adaptation of the music, which, judging from my own feelings, I cannot doubt will be interesting to others.

Mr. Linley was at this time at Bath, and the following letter to him is dated in October, 1775, about a month or five weeks before the opera was brought out : —

" Dear Sir,   c

" We received your songs to-day, with which _
we are exceedingly pleased. I shall profit by
your proposed alterations ; but I'd have you to
know that we are much too chaste in London
to admit such strains as your Bath spring in-
spires. We dare not propose a peep beyond the
ancle on any account : for the critics in the pit
at a new play are much greater prudes than the
ladies in the boxes. Betsey intended to have
troubled you with some music for correction
and I with some stanzas, but an interview with
Harris to-day has put me from the thoughts of
it, and bent me upon a much more important
petition. You may easily suppose it is nothing
else than what I said I would not ask in my
last. But, in short, unless you can give us three
days in town, I fear our opera will stand a chance
to be ruined. Harris is extravagantly sanguine
of its success as to plot and dialogue, which is
to be rehearsed next Wednesday at the theatre.
They will exert themselves to the utmost in the
scenery, &c., but I never saw any one so dis-
concerted as he was at the idea of there being
no one to put them in the right way as to music.
They have no one there whom he has any opinion of — as to Fisher (one of the managers)
he don't choose he should meddle with it. He
entreated me in the most pressing terms to write

instantly to you, and wanted, if he thought it could be any weight, to write himself. Is it impossible to contrive this? couldn't you leave Tom * to superintend the concert for a few days? If you can manage it, you will really do me the greatest service in the world. As to the state of the music, I want but three more airs, but there are some glees and quintets in the last act, that will be inevitably ruined, if we have no one to set the performers at least in the right way. Harris has set his heart so much on my succeeding in this application, that he still flatters himself we may have a rehearsal of the music in Orchard Street to-morrow se'nnight. Every hour's delay is a material injury both to the opera and the theatre, so that if you can come and relieve us from this perplexity, the return of the post must only forerun your arrival; or (what will make us much happier) might it not bring *you*? I shall say nothing at present about the lady ' with the soft look and manner,' because I am full of more than hopes of seeing you. For the same reason I shall delay to speak about G—— † ; only this much I will say, that I am more than ever positive I could make good my part of the matter; but that I still remain an infidel as to G.'s retiring, or parting with his

* Mrs. Sheridan's eldest brother.   † Garrick.

share, though I confess he *seems* to come closer
to the point in naming his price.

" Your ever sincere and affectionate

" R. B. SHERIDAN."

On the opposite leaf of this letter is written, in Mrs. S.'s hand-writing, — " Dearest father, I shall have no spirits or hopes of the opera, unless we see you.

" ELIZA ANN SHERIDAN."

In answer to these pressing demands, Mr. Linley, as appears by the following letter, signified his intention of being in town as soon as the music should be put in rehearsal. In the instructions here given by the poet to the musician, we may perceive that he somewhat apprehended, even in the tasteful hands of Mr. Linley, that predominance of harmony over melody, and of noise over both, which is so fatal to poetry and song, in their perilous alliance with an orchestra. Indeed, those elephants of old, that used to tread down the ranks they were brought to assist, were but a type of the havoc that is sometimes made both of melody and meaning by the overlaying aid of accompaniments.

" DEAR SIR,

" Mr. Harris wishes so much for us to get you to town, that I could not at first convince him that your proposal of not coming till the music was in rehearsal was certainly the best, as you could stay but so short a time. The truth is, that what you mention of my getting a *master* to teach the performers is the very point where the matter sticks, there being no such person as a master among them. Harris is sensible there ought to be such a person; however, at present, every body sings there according to their own ideas, or what chance instruction they can come at. We are, however, to follow your plan in the matter; but can at no rate relinquish the hopes of seeing you in eight or ten days from the date of this; when the music (by the specimen of expedition you have given me) will be advanced as far as you mention. The parts are all writ out and doubled, &c. as we go on, as I have assistance from the theatre with me.

" My intention was to have closed the first act with a song, but I find it is not thought so well. Hence I trust you with one of the inclosed papers; and, at the same time, you must excuse my impertinence in adding an idea of the cast I would wish the music to have; as I think I have heard you say you never heard Leoni *,

* Leoni played Don Carlos.

and I cannot briefly explain to you the character and situation of the persons on the stage with him. The first (a dialogue between Quick and Mrs. Mattocks *), I would wish to be a pert, sprightly air; for, though some of the words mayn't seem suited to it, I should mention that they are neither of them in earnest in what they say. Leoni takes it up seriously, and I want him to show himself advantageously in the six lines, beginning 'Gentle maid.' I should tell you, that he sings nothing well but in a plaintive or pastoral style; and his voice is such as appears to me always to be hurt by much accompaniment. I have observed, too, that he never gets so much applause as when he makes a cadence. Therefore my idea is, that he should make a flourish at 'Shall I grieve thee?' and return to 'Gentle maid,' and so sing that part of the tune again. † After that, the two last lines, sung by the three, with the persons only varied, may get them off with as much spirit as possible. The second act ends with a *slow* glee, therefore I should think the two last lines in question had better be brisk, especially as Quick and Mrs. Mattocks are concerned in it.

* Isaac and Donna Louisa.
† It will be perceived, by a reference to the music of the opera, that Mr. Linley followed these instructions implicitly and successfully.

" The other is a song of Wilson's in the third act. I have written it to your tune, which you put some words to, beginning, ' Prithee, prithee, pretty man ! ' I think it will do vastly well for the words : Don Jerome sings them when he is in particular spirits ; therefore the tune is not too light, though it might seem so by the last stanza — but he does not mean to be grave there, and I like particularly the returning to ' O the days when I was young ! ' We have mislaid the notes, but Tom remembers it. If you don't like it for words, will you give us one ? but it must go back to ' O the days,' and be *funny*. I have not done troubling you yet, but must wait till Monday."

A subsequent letter contains further particulars of their progress.

" DEAR SIR,

" Sunday evening next is fixed for our first musical rehearsal, and I was in great hopes we might have completed the score. The songs you have sent up of ' Banna's Banks,' and ' Deil take the Wars,' I had made words for before they arrived, which answer excessively well ; and this was my reason for wishing for the next in the same manner, as it saves so much time. They are to sing ' Wind, gentle evergreen,' just as you sing it (only with other words), and I wanted only such support from the instruments, or such joining in, as you should think would help to set off and assist the effort. I inclose the words I had made for ' Wind, gentle evergreen,' which will be sung, as a catch, by Mrs. Mattocks, Dubellamy *, and Leoni. I don't mind the words not fitting the notes so well as the original ones. ' How merrily we live,' and ' Let's drink and let's sing,' are to be sung by a company of *friars* over their wine.† The words will be parodied, and the chief effect I expect from them must arise from their being *known*; for the joke will be much less for these jolly fathers to sing any thing new, than to give what the audience are used to annex the idea of jollity to. For the other things Betsy mentioned, I only wish to have them with such accompaniment as you would put to their *present* words, and I shall have got words to my liking for them by the time they reach me.

" My immediate wish at present is to give the performers their parts in the music (which they expect on Sunday night), and for any assistance the orchestra can give to help the effect of the glees, &c., that may be judged of and added at a

* Don Antonio.
† For these was afterwards substituted Mr. Linley's lively glee, " This bottle's the sun of our table."

rehearsal, or, as you say, on enquiring how they
have been done ; though I don't think it follows
that what Dr. Arne's method is must be the best.
If it were possible for Saturday and Sunday's post
to bring us what we asked for in our last letters,
and what I now enclose, we should still go
through it on Sunday, and the performers should
have their parts complete by Monday night. We
have had our rehearsal of the speaking part, and
are to have another on Saturday. I want Dr.
Harrington's catch, but, as the sense must be
the same, I am at a loss how to put other words.
Can't the under part ('A smoky house,' &c.)
be sung by one person and the other two change?
The situation is — Quick and Dubellamy, two
lovers, carrying away Father Paul (Reinold) in
great raptures, to marry them : — the Friar has
before warned them of the ills of a married life,
and they break out into this. The catch is particularly calculated for a stage effect ; but I don't
like to take another person's words, and I don't
see how I can put others, keeping the same idea
(' of seven squalling brats,' &c.) in which the
whole affair lies. However, I shall be glad of
the notes, with Reinold's part, if it is possible, as
I mentioned.*

" I have literally and really not had time to
write the words of any thing more first and then

---

* This idea was afterwards relinquished.

send them to you, and this obliges me to use this apparently awkward way.   *   *

*   *   *   *   *   *

" My father was astonishingly well received on Saturday night in Cato : I think it will not be many days before we are reconciled.

" The inclosed are the words for ' Wind, gentle evergreen ;' a passionate song for Mattocks †, and another for Miss Brown ‡, which solicit to be clothed with melody by you, and are all I want. Mattocks's I could wish to be a broken, passionate affair, and the first two lines may be recitative, or what you please, uncommon. Miss Brown sings hers in a joyful mood : we want her to show in it as much execution as she is capable of, which is pretty well ; and, for variety, we want Mr. Simpson's hautboy to cut a figure, with replying passages, &c., in the way of Fisher's ' *M'ami, il bel idol mio*,' to abet which I have lugged in ' Echo,' who is always

---

† The words of this song, in composing which the directions here given were exactly followed, are to be found in scarce any of the editions of The Duenna. They are as follows : —

" Sharp is the woe that wounds the jealous mind,
   When treachery two fond hearts would rend;
But oh ! how keener far the pang to find
   That traitor in our bosom friend."

‡ " Adieu, thou dreary pile."

allowed to play her part.   I have not a moment
more.   Yours ever sincerely."

The next and last extract I shall give at present is from a letter, dated Nov. 2. 1775, about
three weeks before the first representation of the
opera.

" Our music is now all finished and rehearsing,
but we are greatly impatient to see *you*.   We
hold your coming to be *necessary* beyond con-
ception.   You say you are at our service after
Tuesday next ; then ' I conjure you by that you
do possess,' in which I include all the powers
that preside over harmony, to come next Thursday night (this day se'nnight) and we will fix a
rehearsal for Friday morning.   From what I see
of their rehearsing at present, I am become still
more anxious to see you.

" We have received all your songs, and are
vastly pleased with them.   You misunderstood
me as to the hautboy song ; I had not the least
intention to fix on ' *Bel idol mio.*'   However, I
think it is particularly well adapted, and, I doubt
not, will have a great effect.   *   *   *
*   *   *   *   *"

An allusion which occurs in these letters to
the prospect of a reconciliation with his father

gives me an opportunity of mentioning a circumstance connected with their difference, for the
knowledge of which I am indebted to one of the
persons most interested in remembering it, and
which, as a proof of the natural tendency of
Sheridan's heart to let all its sensibilities flow in
the right channel, ought not to be forgotten.
During the run of one of his pieces, having received information from an old family servant
that his father (who still refused to have any intercourse with him) meant to attend, with his
daughters, at the representation of the piece,
Sheridan took up his station by one of the side
scenes, opposite to the box where they sat, and
there continued, unobserved, to look at them
during the greater part of the night. On his
return home, he was so affected by the various
recollections that came upon him, that he burst
into tears, and, being questioned as to the cause
of his agitation by Mrs. Sheridan, to whom it
was new to see him returning thus saddened
from the scene of his triumph, he owned how
deeply it had gone to his heart, " to think that
there sat his father and his sisters before him,
and yet that he alone was not permitted to go
near them or speak to them."

On the 21st of November, 1775, The Duenna
was performed at Covent Garden, and the following is the original cast of the characters : —

Don Ferdinand	.	.	.	*Mr. Mattocks.*
Isaac Mendoza	.	.	.	*Mr. Quick.*
Don Jerome	.	.	.	*Mr. Wilson.*
Don Antonio	.	.	.	*Mr. Dubellamy.*
Father Paul	.	.	.	*Mr. Mahon.*
Lopez	.	.	.	*Mr. Wewitzer.*
Don Carlos	.	.	.	*Mr. Leoni.*
Francis	.	.	.	*Mr. Fox.*
Lay Brother	.	.	.	*Mr. Baker.*
Donna Louisa	.	.	.	*Mrs. Mattocks.*
Donna Clara	.	.	.	*Miss Brown.*
The Duenna	.	.	.	*Mrs. Green*

The run of this opera has, I believe, no parallel in the annals of the drama. Sixty-three nights was the career of The Beggar's Opera ; but The Duenna was acted no less than seventy-five times during the season, the only intermissions being a few days at Christmas, and the Fridays in every week ; — the latter on account of Leoni, who, being a Jew, could not act on those nights.

In order to counteract this great success of the rival house, Garrick found it necessary to bring forward all the weight of his own best characters ; and even had recourse to the expedient of playing off the mother against the son, by reviving Mrs. Frances Sheridan's comedy of The Discovery, and acting the principal part in it himself. In allusion to the increased fatigue

which this competition with The Duenna brought
upon Garrick, who was then entering on his
sixtieth year, it was said, by an actor of the day,
that " the old woman would be the death of the
old man."

The Duenna is one of the very few operas in
our language, which combines the merits of legitimate comedy with the attractions of poetry
and song; — that divorce between sense and
sound, to which Dr. Brown and others trace the
cessation of the early miracles of music, being
no where more remarkable than in the operas
of the English stage. The " Sovereign of the
willing soul" (as Gray calls Music) always loses
by being made exclusive sovereign, — and the
division of her empire with poetry and wit, as
in the instance of The Duenna, doubles her real
power.

The intrigue of this piece (which is mainly
founded upon an incident borrowed from " The
Country Wife" of Wycherley) is constructed
and managed with considerable adroitness, having just material enough to be wound out into
three acts, without being encumbered by too
much intricacy, or weakened by too much ex-
tension. It does not appear, from the rough
copy in my possession, that any material change
was made in the plan of the work, as it proceeded. Carlos was originally meant to be a

Jew, and is called "Cousin Moses" by Isaac,
in the first sketch of the dialogue; but, possibly,
from the consideration that this would apply too
personally to Leoni, who was to perform the
character, its designation was altered. The
scene in the second act, where Carlos is introduced by Isaac to the Duenna, stood, in its
original state, as follows:—

"*Isaac.*   Moses, sweet coz, I thrive, I prosper.
"*Moses.*   Where is your mistress?
"*Isaac.*   There, you booby, there she stands.
"*Moses.*   Why she's damn'd ugly.
"*Isaac.*   Hush! (*stops his mouth.*)
"*Duenna.*   What is your friend saying, Don?
"*Isaac.*   Oh, ma'am, he's expressing his raptures at
such charms as he never saw before.
"*Moses.*   Aye, such as I never saw before indeed,
(*aside.*)
"*Duenna.*   You are very obliging, gentlemen; but,
I dare say, sir, your friend is no stranger to the influence
of beauty. I doubt not but he is a lover himself.
"*Moses.*   Alas! madam, there is now but one woman
living, whom I have any love for, and truly, ma'am, you
resemble her wonderfully.
"*Duenna.*   Well, sir, I wish she may give you her
hand as speedily as I shall mine to your friend.
"*Moses.*   Me her hand!—O Lord, ma'am—she is
the last woman in the world I could think of marrying.
"*Duenna.*   What then, sir, are you comparing me
to some wanton—some courtezan?
"*Isaac.*   Zounds! he durstn't.

" *Moses.*   O not I, upon my soul.

" *Duenna.*   Yes, he meant some young harlot —
some ——

" *Moses.*   Oh, dear madam, no — it was my mother
I meant, as I hope to be saved.

" *Isaac.*   Oh the blundering villain ! *(aside.)*

" *Duenna.*   How, sir — am I so like your mother?

" *Isaac.*   Stay, dear madam — my friend meant —
that you put him in mind of what his mother was when
a girl — didn't you, Moses?

" *Moses.*   Oh yes, madam, my mother was formerly
a great beauty, a great toast, I assure you;— and when
she married my father about thirty years ago, as you
may perhaps remember, ma'am ——

" *Duenna.*   I, sir !   I remember thirty years ago !

" *Isaac.*   Oh, to be sure not, ma'am — thirty years !
no, no — it was thirty months he said, ma'am — wasn't
it, Moses?

" *Moses.*   Yes, yes, ma'am — thirty months ago, on
her marriage with my father, she was, as I was saying, a
great beauty ; — but catching cold, the year afterwards,
in child-bed of your humble servant ——

" *Duenna.*   Of you, sir ! — and married within these
thirty months !

" *Isaac.*   Oh the devil ! he has made himself out but
a year old ! —Come, Moses, hold your tongue.— You
must excuse him, ma'am — he means to be civil — but
he is a poor simple fellow — an't you, Moses?

" *Moses.*   'Tis true, indeed, ma'am," &c. &c. &c.

The greater part of the humour of Moses
here was afterwards transferred to the character
of Isaac, and it will be perceived that a few of
the points are still retained by him.

The wit of the dialogue, except in one or two instances, is of that accessible kind which lies near the surface — which is produced without effort and may be enjoyed without wonder. He had not yet searched his fancy for those curious fossils of thought, which make The School for Scandal such a rich museum of wit. Of this precious kind, however, is the description of Isaac's neutrality in religion — "like the blank leaf between the Old and New Testament." As an instance, too, of the occasional abuse of this research, which led him to mistake laboured conceits for fancies, may be mentioned the far-fetched comparison of serenaders to Egyptian embalmers, "extracting the brain through the ears." For this, however, his taste, not his invention, is responsible, as we have already seen that the thought was borrowed from a letter of his friend Halhed.

In the speech of Lopez, the servant, with which the opera opens, there are, in the original copy, some humorous points, which appear to have fallen under the pruning knife, but which are not unworthy of being gathered up here : —

"A plague on these haughty damsels, say I : — when they play their airs on their whining gallants, they ought to consider that we are the chief sufferers, — we have all their ill-humours at second-hand. Donna Louisa's cruelty to my master usually converts itself into blows, by the time it gets to me : — she can frown me black and blue at any time, and I shall carry the marks of the last box on the ear she gave him to my grave. Nay, if she smiles on any one else, I am the sufferer for it : — if she says a civil word to a rival, I am a rogue and a scoundrel ; and, if she sends him a letter, my back is sure to pay the postage."

In the scene between Ferdinand and Jerome (Act ii. scene 3.) the following lively speech of the latter was, I know not why, left out : —

" *Ferdin.* . . . . but he has never sullied his honour, which, with his title, has outlived his means.

" *Jerome.* Have they ? More shame for them ! — What business have honour or titles to survive, when property is extinct ? Nobility is but as a helpmate to a good fortune, and, like a Japanese wife, should perish on the funeral pile of the estate !"

In the first act, too, (scene 3.) where Jerome abuses the Duenna, there is an equally unaccountable omission of a sentence, in which he compares the old lady's face to " parchment, on which Time and Deformity have engrossed their titles."

Though some of the poetry of this opera is not much above that ordinary kind, to which music is so often doomed to be wedded — making up by her own sweetness for the dulness of her helpmate — by far the greater number of the songs are full of beauty, and some of them may rank among the best models of lyric writing. The verses "Had I a heart for falsehood framed," notwithstanding the stiffness of this word "framed," and one or two other slight blemishes, are not unworthy of living in recollection with the matchless air to which they are adapted.

There is another song, less known, from being connected with less popular music, which, for deep, impassioned feeling and natural eloquence, has not, perhaps, its rival, through the whole range of lyric poetry. As these verses, though contained in the common editions of The Duenna, are not to be found in the opera, as printed in The British Theatre, and still more strangely, are omitted in the late Collection of Mr. Sheridan's Works *, I should feel myself abundantly authorized in citing them here, even if their beauty were not a sufficient excuse for recalling them, under any circumstances, to the recollection of the reader : —

> " Ah, cruel maid, how hast thou chang'd
> The temper of my mind !
> My heart, by thee from love estrang'd,
> Becomes, like thee, unkind.

* For this Edition of his Works I am no further responsible than in having communicated to it a few prefatory pages, to account and apologize to the public for the delay of the Life.

" By fortune favour'd clear in fame,
    I once ambitious was;
And friends I had who fann'd the flame,
    And gave my youth applause.

" But now my weakness all accuse,
    Yet vain their taunts on me;
Friends, fortune, fame itself I'd lose,
    To gain one smile from thee.

" And only thou should'st not despise
    My weakness or my woe;
If I am mad in others' eyes,
    'Tis thou hast made me so.

" But days, like this, with doubting curst,
    I will not long endure —
Am I disdain'd — I know the worst,
    And likewise know my cure.

" If false, her vows she dare renounce,
    That instant ends my pain;
For, oh! the heart must break at once,
    That cannot hate again."

It is impossible to believe that such verses as
these had no deeper inspiration than the imaginary loves of an opera. They bear, burnt
into every line, the marks of personal feeling,
and must have been thrown off in one of those
passionate moods of the heart, with which the
poet's own youthful love had made him acquainted, and under the impression or vivid
recollection of which these lines were written.

In comparing this poem with the original words of the air to which it is adapted, (Parnell's pretty lines, "My days have been so wondrous free,") it will be felt, at once, how wide is the difference between the cold and graceful effusions of taste, and the fervid bursts of real genius — between the delicate product of the conservatory, and the rich child of the sunshine.

I am the more confirmed in the idea that this song was written previously to the opera, and from personal feeling, by finding among his earlier pieces the originals of two other songs — " I ne'er could any lustre see," and " What bard, oh Time, discover." The thought, upon which the latter turns, is taken from a poem already cited, addressed by him to Mrs. Sheridan in 1773 ; and the following is the passage that supplied the material : —

> " Alas, thou hast no wings, oh Time,
> It was some thoughtless lover's rhyme,
> Who, writing in his Chloe's view,
> Paid her the compliment through you.
> For, had he, if he truly lov'd,
> But once the pangs of absence prov'd,
> He'd cropt thy wings, and, in their stead,
> Have painted thee with heels of lead."

It will be seen presently that this poem was again despoiled of some of its lines, for an Epi-

logue which he began a few years after, upon a
very different subject. There is something, it
must be owned, not very sentimental in this con-
version of the poetry of affection to other and
less sacred uses — as if, like the ornaments of a
passing pageant, it might be broken up after the
show was over, and applied to more useful purposes. That the young poet should be guilty of
such sacrilege to Love, and thus steal back his
golden offerings from the altar, to melt them
down into utensils of worldly display, can only
be excused by that demand upon the riches of
his fancy, which the rapidity of his present career in the service of the Dramatic Muse occasioned.

There is not the same objection to the appro-
priation of the other song, which, it will be seen,
is a selection of the best parts of the following
Anacreontic verses : —

> " I ne'er could any lustre see *
> In eyes that would not look on me :
> When a glance aversion hints;
> I always think the lady squints.

* Another mode of beginning this song in the MS. : —

> " Go tell the maid who seeks to move
> My lyre to praise, my heart to love,
> No rose upon her cheek can live,
> Like those assenting blushes give."

CHAP.
IV.

1775.

I ne'er saw nectar on a lip,
But where my own did hope to sip.
No pearly teeth rejoice my view,
Unless a 'yes' displays their hue—
The prudish lip, that *noes* me back,
Convinces me the teeth are black.
To me the cheek displays no roses,
Like that th' assenting blush discloses;
But when with proud disdain 'tis spread,
To me 'tis but a scurvy red.
Would she have me praise her hair?
Let her place my garland there.
Is her hand so white and pure?
I must press it to be sure;
Nor can I be certain then,
Till it grateful press again.
Must I praise her melody?
Let her sing of love and me.
If she choose another theme,
I'd rather hear a peacock scream.
Must I, with attentive eye,
Watch her heaving bosom sigh?
I will do so, when I see
That heaving bosom sigh for me.
None but bigots will in vain
Adore a heav'n they cannot gain.
If I must religious prove
To the mighty God of Love,
Sure I am it is but fair
He, at least, should hear my prayer.
But, by each joy of his I've known,
And all I yet shall make my own,
Never will I, with humble speech,
Pray to a heav'n I cannot reach."

In the song, beginning "Friendship is the bond of reason," the third verse was originally thus : —

    " And, should I cheat the world and thee,
       One smile from her I love to win,
      Such breach of human faith would be
       A sacrifice and not a sin."

To the song " Give Isaac the nymph," there were at first two more verses, which, merely to show how judicious was the omission of them, I shall here transcribe. Next to the advantage of knowing what to put into our writings, is that of knowing what to leave out : —

" To one thus accomplish'd I durst speak my mind,
  And flattery doubtless would soon make her kind ;
  For the man that should praise her she needs must
    adore,
  Who ne'er in her life received praises before.

" But the frowns of a beauty in hopes to remove,
  Should I prate of her charms, and tell of my love ;
  No thanks wait the praise which she knows to be true,
  Nor smiles for the homage she takes as her due."

Among literary piracies or impostures, there are few more audacious than the Dublin edition of The Duenna, — in which, though the songs are given accurately, an entirely new dialogue is substituted for that of Sheridan, and his gold, as in the barter of Glaucus, exchanged for such copper as the following : —

"*Duen.* Well, sir, I don't want to stay in your house; but I must go and lock up my wardrobe.

"*Isaac.* Your wardrobe! when you came into my house you could carry your wardrobe in your comb-case, you could, you old dragon."

Another specimen : —

"*Isaac.* Her voice, too, you told me, was like a Virginian nightingale; why, it is like a cracked warming-pan : — and, as for dimples! — to be sure, she has the devil's own dimples. — Yes! and you told me she had a lovely down upon her chin, like the down of a peach; but, damn me if ever I saw such down upon any creature in my life, except once upon an old goat."

These jokes, I need not add, are all the gratuitous contributions of the editor.

Towards the close of the year 1775, it was understood that Garrick meant to part with his moiety of the patent of Drury Lane Theatre, and retire from the stage. He was then in the sixtieth year of his age, and might possibly have been influenced by the natural feeling, so beautifully expressed for a great actor of our own time by our greatest living writer : —

> ——" Higher duties crave
> Some space between the theatre and the grave;
> That, like the Roman in the Capitol,
> I may adjust my mantle, ere I fall." *

* Kemble's Farewell Address on taking leave of the Edinburgh stage, written by Sir Walter Scott.

The progress of the negotiation between him and Mr. Sheridan, which ended in making the latter patentee and manager, cannot better be traced than in Sheridan's own letters, addressed at the time to Mr. Linley, and most kindly placed at my disposal by Mr. Willam Linley.

" DEAR SIR,   Sunday, Dec. 31. 1775.

" I was always one of the slowest letter-writers in the world, though I have had more excuses than usual for my delay in this instance. The principal matter of business, on which I was to have written to you, related to our embryo negotiation with Garrick, of which I will now give you an account.

" Since you left town, Mrs. Ewart has been so ill, as to continue near three weeks at the point of death. This, of course, has prevented Mr. E. from seeing any body on business, or from accompanying me to Garrick's. However, about ten days ago, I talked the matter over with him by myself, and the result was, appointing Thursday evening last to meet him, and to bring Ewart, which I did accordingly. On the whole of our conversation that evening, I began (for the first time) to think him *really serious* in the business. He still, however, kept the reserve of giving the refusal to Colman, though at the same time he did not hesitate to assert his confidence that Colman would decline it. I was determined to push him on this point, (as it was really farcical for us to treat with him under such an evasion,) and at last he promised to put the question to Colman, and to give me a decisive answer by the ensuing Sunday (to-day). —Accordingly, within this hour, I have received a note from him, which (as I meant to show it my father) I here transcribe for you.

"' *Mr. Garrick presents his compliments to Mr. Sheridan, and as he is obliged to go into the country for three days, he should be glad to see him upon his return to town, either on Wednesday about 6 or 7 o'clock, or whenever he pleases. The party has no objection to the whole, but chooses no partner but Mr. G. — Not a word of this yet. Mr. G. sent a messenger on purpose* (i. e. *to Colman*). — *He would call upon Mr. S. but he is confined at home. Your name is upon our list.'*

" This *decisive answer* may be taken two ways. However, as Mr. G. informed Mr. Ewart and me, that he had no authority or pretensions to treat for *the whole*, it appears to me that Mr. Garrick's meaning in this note is, that Mr. Colman *declines* the purchase of *Mr. Garrick's share*, which is the point in debate, and the only part at present to be sold. I shall, therefore, wait on G. at the time mentioned, and, if I understand him right, we shall certainly without delay appoint two men of business and the law to meet on the matter, and come to a conclusion without further delay.

" *According* to his demand, the whole is valued at 70,000*l.* He appears very shy of letting his books be looked into, as the test of the profits on this sum, but says it must be, in its nature, a purchase on speculation. However, he has promised me a rough estimate, of *his own,* of the entire receipts for the last seven years. But, after all, it must certainly be a *purchase on speculation* without *money's worth* being *made out.* One point he solemnly avers, which is, that he will never part with it under the price above-mentioned.

" This is all I can say on the subject till Wednesday, though I can't help adding, that I think we might *safely* give five thousand pounds more on this purchase than richer people. The whole valued at 70,000*l.*, the annual interest is 3,500*l.* ; while this is *cleared,* the proprietors are *safe,* — but I think it must be *infernal* management indeed that does not double it.

" I suppose Mr. Stanley has written to you relative to your oratorio orchestra. The demand, I reckon, will be diminished one third, and the appearance remain very handsome, which, if the other affair takes place, you will find your account in ; and, if you discontinue your partnership with Stanley at Drury Lane, the orchestra

N 4

may revert to whichever wants it, on the other's paying his proportion for the use of it this year. This is Mr. Garrick's idea, and, as he says, might in that case be settled by arbitration.

" You have heard of our losing Miss Brown; however, we have missed her so little in The Duenna, that the managers have not tried to regain her, which I believe they might have done. I have had some books of the music these many days to send you down. I wanted to put Tom's name in the new music, and begged Mrs. L. to ask you, and let me have a line on her arrival, for which purpose I kept back the index of the songs. If you or he have no objection, pray, let me know. — I'll send the music to-morrow.

" I am finishing a two-act comedy for Covent-Garden, which will be in rehearsal in a week. We have given The Duenna a respite this Christmas, but nothing else at present brings money. We have every place in the house taken for the three next nights, and shall, at least, play it fifty nights, with only the Friday's intermission.

" My best love and the compliments of the season to all your fire-side.

" Your grandson is a very magnificent fellow.*

" Yours ever sincerely,

" R. B. Sheridan."

* Sheridan's first child, Thomas, born in the preceding year.

" Dear Sir,   January 4. 1776.

" I left Garrick last night too late to write
to you.   He has offered Colman the refusal, and
showed me his answer; which was (as in the
note) that he was willing to purchase the whole,
but would have no partner but Garrick.   On
this, Mr. Garrick appointed a meeting with his
partner, young Leasy, and, in presence of their
solicitor, treasurer, &c., declared to him that he
was absolutely on the point of settling, and, if
he was willing, he might have the same price
for his share; but that if he (Leasy) would not
sell, Mr. Garrick would, instantly, to another
party.   The result was, Leasy's declaring his
intention of not parting with his share.   Of this
Garrick again informed Colman, who immediately
gave up the whole matter.

" Garrick was extremely explicit, and, in short,
we came to a final resolution.   So that, if the
necessary matters are made out to all our satis-
factions, we may sign and seal a previous agreement within a fortnight.

" I meet him again to-morrow evening, when
we are to name a day for a conveyancer on
our side, to meet his solicitor, Wallace.   I have
pitched on a Mr. Phips, at the recommendation
and by the advice of Dr. Ford.   The three first
steps to be taken are these, — our lawyer is to
look into the titles, tenures, &c. of the house and

adjoining estate, the extent and limitations of
the patent, &c. We should then employ a builder
(I think, Mr. Collins,) to survey the state and
repair in which the whole premises are, to which
G. entirely assents. Mr. G. will then give us a
fair and attested estimate from his books of what
the profits have been, at an average, for these
last seven years.* This he has shown me in rough,
and valuing the property at 70,000*l.*, the interest
has exceeded ten per cent.

"We should, after this, certainly, make an
interest to get the King's promise, that, while
the theatre is well conducted, &c. he will grant
no patent for a third, — though G. seems confident that he never will. If there is any truth
in professions and appearances, G. seems likely
always to continue our friend, and to give every
assistance in his power.

"The method of our sharing the purchase, I
should think, may be thus, — Ewart to take
10,000*l.*, you, 10,000*l.*, and I, 10,000. — Dr.
Ford, agrees, with the greatest pleasure, to embark the other five ; and, if you do not choose
to venture so much, will, I dare say, share it with
you. Ewart is preparing his money, and I have

* These accounts were found among Mr. Sheridan's
papers. Garrick's income from the theatre for the year
1775-6 is thus stated : — Author, 400*l.*, salary, 800*l.*, manager, 500*l.*

a certainty of my part. We shall have a very useful ally in Doctor Ford ; and my father offers his services on our own terms. We cannot unite Garrick to our interests too firmly ; and I am convinced his influence will bring Leasy to our terms, if he should be ill-advised enough to desire to interfere in what he is totally unqualified for.

" I'll write to you to-morrow, relative to Leasy's mortgage (which Garrick has, and advises us to take,) and many other particulars. When matters are in a certain train (which I hope will be in a week), I suppose you will not hesitate to come to town for a day or two. Garrick proposes, when we are satisfied with the bargain, to sign a previous article, with a penalty of ten thousand pounds on the parties who break from fulfilling the purchase. When we are once satisfied and determined in the business (which, I own, is my case) the sooner that is done the better. I must urge it particularly, as my confidential connection with the other house is peculiarly distressing, till I can with prudence reveal my situation, and such a treaty (however prudently managed) cannot long be kept secret, especially as Leasy is now convinced of Garrick's resolution.

" I am exceedingly hurried at present, so excuse omissions, and do not flag, when we come to the point.   I'll answer for it, we shall see many golden campaigns.

" Yours ever,

" R. B. SHERIDAN.

" You have heard, I suppose, that Foote is likely never to show his face again."

" DEAR SIR,   January 31st, 1776.

" I am glad you have found a person who will let you have the money at 4 per cent.   The security will be very clear ; but, as there is some degree of risk, as in the case of fire, I think 4 per cent. uncommonly reasonable. — It will scarcely be any advantage to pay it off, for your houses and chapel, I suppose, bring in much more. Therefore, while you can raise money at 4 per cent. on the security of your theatrical share *only*, you will be right to alter, as little as you can, the present disposition of your property.

" As to your quitting Bath, I cannot see why you should doubt a moment about it.   Surely, the undertaking in which you embark such a sum as 10,000*l.* ought to be the chief object of your attention — and, supposing you did not chuse to give up all your time to the theatre, you may certainly employ yourself more profitably in London than in Bath.   But, if you are willing (as I suppose you will be) to make the

theatre the great object of your attention, rely
on it you may lay aside every doubt of not finding your account in it; for the fact is, we shall
have nothing but our own equity to consult in
making and obtaining any demand for exclusive
trouble. Leasy is utterly unequal to any department in the theatre. He has an opinion of
me, and is very willing to let the whole burthen
and ostensibility be taken off his shoulders. But
I certainly should not give up my time and labour (for his superior advantage, having so much
greater a share) without some exclusive advantage. Yet, I should by no means make the demand till I had shown myself equal to the task.
My father purposes to be with us but one year ;
and that only to give me what advantage he can
from his experience. He certainly must be paid
for his trouble, and so certainly must you. You
have experience and character equal to the line
you would undertake; and it never can enter
into any body's head that you were to give your
time or any part of your attention gratis, because
you had a share in the theatre. I have spoke
on this subject both to Garrick and Leasy, and
you will find no demur on any side to your gaining a *certain* income from the theatre — greater,
I think, than you could make out of it—and in
this the theatre will be acting only for its own
advantage. At the same time you may always

make leisure for a few select scholars, whose interest may also serve the greater cause of your patentee-ship.

" I have had a young man with me who wants to appear as a singer in plays or oratorios. I think you'll find him likely to be serviceable in either. He is not one-and-twenty, and has no conceit. He has a good tenor voice — very good ear, and a great deal of execution, of the right kind. He reads notes very quick, and can accompany himself. This is Betsey's verdict, who sat in judgment on him on Sunday last. I have given him no answer, but engaged him to wait till you come to town.

" You must not regard the reports in the paper about a third theatre — that's all nonsense.

" Betsey's and my love to all. Your grandson astonishes every body by his vivacity, his talents for music and poetry, and the most perfect integrity of mind.

" Yours most sincerely,

" R. B. Sheridan."

In the following June the contract with Garrick was perfected ; and, in a paper drawn up by Mr. Sheridan many years after, I find the shares of the respective purchasers thus stated : —

Mr. Sheridan, two fourteenths			
of the whole	-	-	10,000*l.*
Mr. Linley, ditto	-	-	10,000*l.*
Dr. Ford, 3 ditto	-	-	15,000*l.*

Mr. Ewart, it will be perceived, though ori-nally mentioned as one of the parties, had no concern in the final arrangement.

Though the letters, just cited, furnish a more detailed account than has yet been given to the public of this transaction by which Mr. Sheridan became possessed of his theatrical property, they still leave us in the dark with respect to the source, from which his own means of complet-ing the purchase were derived. Not even to Mr. Linley, while entering into all other details, does he hint at the fountain-head from which this supply is to come ; —

> ———" *gentes maluit ortus*
> *Mirari, quam nôsse, tuos.*"

There was, indeed, something mysterious and miraculous about all his acquisitions, whether in love, in learning, in wit, or in wealth. How or when his stock of knowledge was laid in, nobody knew ; it was as much a matter of marvel to those who never saw him read, as the mode of existence of the chamelion has been to those who fancied it never eat. His advances in the heart of his

mistress were, as we have seen, equally trackless
and inaudible;—and his triumph was the first that
even rivals knew of his love.   In like manner,
the productions of his wit took the world by surprize, — being perfected in secret, till ready for
display, and then seeming to break from under
the cloud of his indolence in full maturity of
splendour.   His financial resources had no less
an air of magic about them ; and the mode by
which he conjured up, at this time, the money
for his first purchase into the theatre, remains, as
far as I can learn, still a mystery.   It has been
said that Mr. Garrick supplied him with the
means — but a perusal of the above letters must
set that notion to rest.   There was evidently at
this time no such confidential understanding between them as an act of friendship of so signal
a nature would imply ; and it appears that Sheridan had the purchase money ready, even before the terms upon which Garrick would sell
were ascertained.   That Doctor Ford should
have advanced the money is not less improbable;
for the share of which, contrary to his first intention, he ultimately became proprietor, absorbed, there is every reason to think, the whole
of his disposable means.   He was afterwards a
sufferer by the concern to such an extent, as to
be obliged, in consequence of his embarrassments,
to absent himself for a considerable time from

England; and there are among the papers of
Mr. Sheridan, several letters of remonstrance
addressed to him by the son of Dr. Ford, in
which some allusion to such a friendly service,
had it ever occurred, would hardly have been
omitted.

About the end of this year some dissensions
arose between the new Patentees and Mr. Lacy,
in consequence of the expressed intention of the
latter to introduce two other partners into the
establishment, by the disposal of his share to
Captain Thomson and a Mr. Langford. By an
account of this transaction, which appears in a
Periodical Paper published at the time *, and
which from its correctness in other particulars I
rather think may be depended on, it would seem
that Sheridan, in his opposition to Lacy, had
proceeded to the extremity of seceding from his
own duties at the theatre, and inducing the principal actors to adopt the same line of conduct.

" Does not the rage (asks this writer) of the new managers, all directed against the innocent and justifiable
conduct of Mr. Lacy, look as if they meant to rule a
theatre, of which they have only a moiety among them,
and feared the additional weight and influence which
would be given to Mr. Lacy by the assistance of Captain
Thomson and Mr. Langford? If their intentions were
right, why should they fear to have their power balanced,

* The Selector.

VOL. I.   O

and their conduct examined? Is there a precedent in the annals of the theatre, where the acting manager deserted the general property, left the house, and seduced the actors from their duties — why? forsooth, because he was angry. Is not such conduct actionable? In any concern of common property, Lord Mansfield would make it so. And, what an insult to the public, from whose indulgence and favour this conceited young man, with his wife and family, are to receive their daily bread! Because Mr. Lacy, in his opinion, had used him ill — his patrons and benefactors might go to the devil! Mr. Lacy acted with great temper and moderation; and, in order that the public might not be wholly disappointed, he brought on old stock-plays — his brother-manager having robbed him of the means and instruments to do otherwise, by taking away the performers."

It is also intimated in the same publication that Mr. Garrick had on this occasion " given Mr. Sheridan credit on his banker for 20,000*l.* for law expenses, or for the purchase of Messrs. Langford and Thomson's shares."

The dispute, however, was adjusted amicably. Mr. Lacy was prevailed upon to write an apology to the public, and the design of disposing of his share in the theatre was for the present relinquished.

There is an allusion to this reconciliation in the following characteristic letter, addressed by Sheridan to Mr. Linley in the spring of the following year : —

" Dear Sir,

" You write to me, though you tell me you have nothing to say — now, I have reversed the case, and have not wrote to you, because I have had so much to say. However, I find I have delayed too long to attempt now to transmit you a long detail of our theatrical manœuvres ; but you must not attribute my not writing to idleness, but on the contrary to my *not* having been idle.

" You represent your situation of mind between *hopes* and *fears.* I am afraid I should argue in vain (as I have often on this point before) were I to tell you, that it is always better to encourage the former than the latter. It may be very prudent to mix a little *fear* by way of alloy with a good solid mass of *hope ;* but you, on the contrary, always deal in *apprehension* by the pound, and take *confidence* by the grain, and spread as thin as leaf gold. In fact, though a metaphor mayn't explain it, the truth is, that, in all undertakings which depend principally on ourselves, the surest way not to fail is to *determine to succeed.*

" It would be endless to say more at present about theatrical matters, only, that every thing is going on very well. Lacy promised me to write to you, which I suppose, however, he has not done. At our first meeting after you left

o 2

town, he cleared away all my doubts about his sincerity; and I dare swear we shall never have the least misunderstanding again, nor do I believe he will ever take any distinct council in future. Relative to your affair he has not the shade of an objection remaining, and is only anxious that you may not take amiss his boggling at first. We have, by and with the advice of the privy council, concluded to have Noverre over, and there is a species of pantomime to be shortly put on foot, which is to draw all the human kind to Drury.* This is become absolutely necessary on account of a marvellous preparation of the kind which is making at Covent-Garden.

" Touching the tragedies you mention, if you speak of them merely as certain tragedies that may be had, I should think it impossible we could find the least room, as you know Garrick saddles us with one which we *must* bring out. But, if you have any particular desire that one of them should be done, it is another affair, and I should be glad to see them. Otherwise, I would much rather you would save me the disagreeableness of giving my opinion to a fresh

---

* I find that the pantomime at Drury-Lane this year was a revival of " Harlequin's Invasion," and that at Covent-Garden, " Harlequin's Frolics."

tragic bard, being already in disgrace with about
nine of that irascible fraternity.

" Betsey has been alarmed about Tom, but
without reason. He is in my opinion better
than when you left him, at least to appearance,
and the cold he caught is gone. We sent to see
him at Battersea, and would have persuaded him
to remove to Orchard-Street; but he thinks the
air does him good, and he seems with people
where he is at home, and may divert himself,
which, perhaps, will do him more good than the
air, — but he is to be with us soon.

" Ormsby has sent me a silver branch on the
score of The Duenna. This will cost me, what
of all things I am least free of, a letter: and
it should have been a poetical one, too, if the
present had been any piece of plate, but a candlestick ! — I believe I must melt it into a bowl to
make verses on it, for there is no possibility of
bringing candle, candlestick, or snuffers, into
metre. However, as the gift was owing to the
muse, and the manner of it very friendly, I believe I shall try to jingle a little on the occasion;
at least, a few such stanzas as might gain a cup
of tea from the urn at Bath-Easton.

" Betsey is very well, and on the point of
giving Tom up to feed like a Christian and a
gentleman, or, in other words, of weaning, wain-
ing, or weening him. As for the young gentle-

man himself, his progress is so rapid, that one may plainly see the astonishment the sun is in of a morning, at the improvement of the night. Our loves to all.

" Yours ever, and truly,

" R. B. SHERIDAN."

The first contribution which the dramatic talent of the new manager furnished to the stock of the theatre, was an alteration of Vanbrugh's comedy, The Relapse, which was brought out on the 24th of February, 1777, under the title of " A Trip to Scarborough."

In reading the original play, we are struck with surprise, that Sheridan should ever have hoped to be able to *defecate* such dialogue, and, at the same time, leave any of the wit, whose whole spirit is in the lees, behind. The very life of such characters as Berinthia is their licentiousness, and it is with them, as with objects, that are luminous from putrescence, — to remove their taint is to extinguish their light. If Sheridan, indeed, had substituted some of his own wit for that which he took away, the inanition that followed the operation would have been much less sensibly felt. But to be so liberal of a treasure so precious, and for the enrichment of the work of another, could hardly have been expected from him. Besides, it may be doubted

whether the subject had not already yielded its
utmost to Vanbrugh, and whether, even in the
hands of Sheridan, it could have been brought
to bear a second crop of wit.   Here and there
through the dialogue, there are some touches
from his pen — more, however, in the style of his
farce than his comedy. For instance, that speech
of Lord Foppington, where, directing the hosier
not " to thicken the calves of his stockings so
much," he says, " You should always remember,
Mr. Hosier, that if you make a nobleman's spring
legs as robust as his autumnal calves, you commit a monstrous impropriety, and make no allowance for the fatigues of the winter."   Again, the
following dialogue : —

" *Jeweller*. I hope, my Lord, these buckles have had
the unspeakable satisfaction of being honoured with Your
Lordship's approbation?

" *Lord F.* Why, they are of a pretty fancy; but don't
you think them rather of the smallest?

" *Jeweller*. My Lord, they could not well be larger, to
keep on Your Lordship's shoe.

" *Lord F.* My good sir, you forget that these matters
are not as they used to be : formerly, indeed, the buckle
was a sort of machine, intended to keep on the shoe; but
the case is now quite reversed, and the shoe is of no
earthly use, but to keep on the buckle."

About this time Mrs. Sheridan went to pass a
few weeks with her father and mother at Bath,

while Sheridan himself remained in town, to superintend the concerns of the theatre. During this interval he addressed to her the following verses, which I quote, less from their own peculiar merit, than as a proof how little his heart had yet lost of those first feelings of love and gallantry, which too often expire in matrimony, as Faith and Hope do in heaven, and from the same causes —

" One lost in certainty, and one in joy." ·

" *To Laura.*

" Near Avon's ridgy bank there grows
 A willow of no vulgar size,
That tree first heard poor Silvio's woes,
 And heard how bright were Laura's eyes.

Its boughs were shade from heat or show'r,
 Its roots a moss-grown seat became ;
Its leaves would strew the maiden's bow'r,
 Its bark was shatter'd with her name !

Once on a blossom-crowned day
Of mirth-inspiring May,
Silvio, beneath this willow's sober shade
In sullen contemplation laid,

Did mock the meadow's flowery pride, —
 Rail'd at the dance and sportive ring ; —
The tabor's call he did deride,
 And said, *It was not Spring.*

He scorn'd the sky of azure blue,
   He scorn'd whate'er could mirth bespeak;
He chid the beam that drank the dew,
   And chid the gale that fann'd his glowing cheek.
Unpaid the season's wonted lay,
For still he sigh'd; and said it *was* not *May.*

' Ah, why should the glittering stream
   ' Reflect thus delusive the scene?
' Ah, why does a rosy-ting'd beam,
   ' Thus vainly enamel the green?
' To·me nor joy nor light they bring,
' I tell thee, Phœbus, *'tis not Spring.*

' Sweet tut'ress of music and love,
   ' Sweet bird, if 'tis thee that I hear,
' Why left you so early the grove,
   ' To lavish your melody here?
' Cease, then, mistaken thus to sing,
' Sweet nightingale! it *is* not *Spring.*

' The gale courts my locks but to tease,
   ' And, Zephyr, I call'd not on thee;
' Thy fragrance no longer can please,
   ' Then rob not the blossoms for me:
' But hence unload thy balmy wing,
' Believe me, Zephyr, 'tis *not Spring.*

' Yet the lily has drank of the show'r,
   ' And the rose 'gins to peep on the day;
' And yon bee seems to search for a flow'r,
   ' As busy as if it were May: —
' In vain, thou senseless flutt'ring thing,
' My heart informs me, *'tis not Spring.*'

May pois'd her roseate wings, for she had heard
 The mourner, as she pass'd the vales along;
And, silencing her own indignant bird,
 She thus reprov'd poor Silvio's song.

' How false is the sight of a lover;
' How ready his spleen to discover
 ' What reason would never allow !
' Why, — Silvio, my sunshine and showers,
' My blossoms, my birds, and my flow'rs,
 ' Were never more perfect than now.

' The water's reflection is true,
' The green is enamell'd to view,
 ' And Philomel sings on the spray;
' The gale is the breathing of Spring,
' 'Tis fragrance it bears on its wing,
 ' And the bee is assur'd it is *May.*'

' Pardon (said Silvio with a gushing tear),
' '*Tis* Spring, sweet nymph, *but Laura is not here.*' "

In sending these verses to Mrs. Sheridan, he
had also written her a description of some splendid party, at which he had lately been present,
where all the finest women of the world of
fashion were assembled. His praises of their
beauty, as well as his account of their flattering
attentions to himself, awakened a feeling of at
least poetical jealousy in Mrs. Sheridan, which
she expressed in the following answer to his
verses — taking occasion, at the same time, to
pay some generous compliments to the most

brilliant among his new fashionable friends.
Though her verses are of that kind which we
read more with interest than admiration, they
have quite enough of talent for the gentle themes
to which she aspired ; and there is, besides, a
charm about them, as coming from Mrs. Sheridan, to which far better poetry could not pre-
te nd.

" *To Silvio.*

" Soft flow'd the lay by Avon's sedgy side,
 While o'er its streams the drooping willow hung,
Beneath whose shadow Silvio fondly tried
 To check the opening roses as they sprung.

In vain he bade them cease to court the gale,
 That wanton'd balmy on the zephyr's wing;
In vain, when Philomel renew'd her tale,
 He chid her song, and said, ' *It was not Spring.'*

For still they bloom'd, tho' Silvio's heart was sad,
 Nor did sweet Philomel neglect to sing;
The zephyrs scorn'd them not, tho' Silvio had,
 For love and nature told them *it was Spring.* †

  * * * * *

To other scenes doth Silvio now repair,
 To nobler themes his daring Muse aspires ;
Around him throng the gay, the young, the fair,
 His lively wit the list'ning crowd admires.

 † As the poem altogether would be too long, I have here
omitted five or six stanzas.

And see, where radiant Beauty smiling stands,
    With gentle voice and soft beseeching eyes,
To gain the laurel from his willing hands,
    Her every art the fond enchantress tries.

What various charms the admiring youth surround,
    How shall he sing, or how attempt to praise?
So lovely all — where shall the bard be found,
    Who can to *one* alone attune his lays?

Behold with graceful step and smile serene,
    Majestic. Stella * moves to claim the prize;
' 'Tis thine,' he cries, ' for thou art Beauty's queen.'
    Mistaken youth! and see'st thou Myra's † eyes?

With beaming lustre see they dart at thee;
    Ah! dread their vengeance—yet withhold thy hand—
That deep'ning blush upbraids thy rash decree;
    Her's is the wreath — obey the just demand.

' Pardon, bright nymph,' (the wond'ring Silvio cries,)
    ' And oh, receive the wreath, thy beauty's due' —
His voice awards what still his hand denies,
    For beauteous Amoret ‡ now his eyes pursue.

With gentle step and hesitating grace,
    Unconscious of her power, the fair one came;
If, while he view'd the glories of that face,
    Poor Sylvia doubted, — who shall dare to blame?

---

    * According to the Key which has been given me, the name of Stella was meant to designate the Duchess of Rutland.
    † The Duchess of Devonshire.
    ‡ Mrs. (afterwards Lady) Crewe.

A rosy blush his ardent gaze reprov'd,
  The offer'd wreath she modestly declined; —
' If sprightly wit and dimpled smiles are lov'd,
  ' My brow, said Flavia*, ' shall that garland bind.'

With wanton gaiety the prize she seized —
  Sylvio in vain her snowy hand repell'd;
The fickle youth unwillingly was pleas'd,
  Reluctantly the wreath he yet withheld.

But Jessie's   all seducing form appears,
  Nor more the playful Flavia could delight:
Lovely in smiles, more lovely still in tears,
  Her every glance shone eloquently bright.

Those radiant eyes in safety none could view,
  Did not those fringed lids their brightness shade —
Mistaken youths! their beams, too late ye knew,
  Are by that soft defence more fatal made.

' O God of Love!' with transport Silvio cries,
  ' Assist me thou, this contest to decide;
' And since to *one* I cannot yield the prize,
  ' Permit thy slave the garland to divide.

' On Myra's breast the opening rose shall blow,
  ' Reflecting from her cheek a livelier bloom;
' For Stella shall the bright carnation glow —
  ' Beneath her eyes' bright radiance meet its doom.

' Smart pinks and daffodils shall Flavia grace,
  ' The modest eglantine and violet blue
' On gentle Amoret's placid brow I'll place —
  ' Of elegance and love an emblem true.'

* Lady Craven, afterwards Margravine of Anspach.
† The late Countess of Jersey.

CHAP.
IV.

1777.

In gardens oft a beauteous flow'r there grows,
    By vulgar eyes unnotic'd and unseen;
In sweet security it humbly blows,
    And rears its purple head to deck the green.

This flow'r, as nature's poet sweetly sings,
    Was once milk-white, and *heart's ease* was its name;
Till wanton Cupid pois'd his roseate wings,
    A vestal's sacred bosom to inflame.

With treacherous aim the god his arrow drew,
    Which she with icy coldness did repel;
Rebounding thence with feathery speed he flew,
    Till on this lonely flow'r at last it fell.

Heart's ease no more the wandering shepherds found,
    No more the nymphs its snowy form possess,
Its white now chang'd to purple by Love's wound,
    Heart's ease no more, 'tis ' Love in Idleness.'

' This flow'r, with sweet-brier join'd, shall thee adorn,
    ' Sweet Jessie, fairest 'mid ten thousand fair !
' But guard thy gentle bosom from the thorn,
    ' Which, tho' conceal'd, the sweet-brier still must
      bear.

' And place not Love, tho' *idle*, in thy breast,
    ' Tho' bright its hues, it boasts no other charm —
' So may thy future days be ever blest,
    ' And friendship's calmer joys thy bosom warm !'

But where does Laura pass her lonely hours ?
    Does she still haunt the grot and willow-tree?
Shall Silvio from his wreath of various flow'rs
    Neglect to cull one simple sweet for thee?

' Ah Laura, no,' the constant Silvio cries,
 ' For thee a never-fading wreath I'll twine,
' Though bright the rose, its bloom too swiftly flies,
 ' No emblem meet for love so true as mine.

' For thee, my love, the myrtle, ever-green,
 ' Shall every year its blossoms sweet disclose,
' Which when our spring of youth no more is seen,
 ' Shall still appear more lovely than the rose.'

' Forgive, dear youth,' the happy Laura said,
 ' Forgive each doubt, each fondly anxious fear,
' Which from my heart for ever now is fled —
 ' Thy love and truth, thus tried, are doubly dear.

' With pain I mark'd the various passions rise,
 ' When beauty so divine before thee mov'd;
' With trembling doubt beheld thy wandering eyes,
 ' For still I fear'd; — alas ! because I lov'd.

' Each anxious doubt shall Laura *now* forego,
 ' No more regret those joys so lately known,
' Conscious that tho' thy breast to *all* may glow,
 ' Thy faithful *heart* shall beat for *her* alone.

' Then, Silvio, seize again thy tuneful lyre,
 ' Nor yet sweet Beauty's pow'r forbear to praise;
' Again let charms divine thy strains inspire,
 ' And Laura's voice shall aid the poet's lays.' "

CHAP. V.

THE SCHOOL FOR SCANDAL.

Mr. Sheridan was now approaching the summit of his dramatic fame; — he had already produced the best opera in the language, and there now remained for him the glory of writing also the best comedy. As this species of composition seems, more, perhaps, than any other, to require that knowledge of human nature and the world which experience alone can give, it seems not a little extraordinary that nearly all our first-rate comedies should have been the productions of very young men. Those of Congreve were all written before he was five-and-twenty. Farquhar produced The Constant Couple in his two-and-twentieth year, and died at thirty. Vanbrugh was a young ensign when he sketched out The Relapse and The Provoked Wife, and Sheridan crowned his reputation with The School for Scandal at six-and-twenty.

It is, perhaps, still more remarkable to find, as in the instance before us, that works which, at this period of life, we might suppose to have been the rapid offspring of a careless, but vigorous fancy, — anticipating the results of experience by a sort of second-sight inspiration, — should, on the contrary, have been the slow result of many and doubtful experiments, gradually unfolding beauties unforeseen even by him who produced them, and arriving, at length, step by step, at perfection. That such was the tardy process by which The School for Scandal was produced, will appear from the first sketches of its plan and dialogue, which I am here enabled to lay before the reader, and which cannot fail to interest deeply all those who take delight in tracing the alchemy of genius, and in watching the first slow workings of the menstruum, out of which its finest transmutations arise.

"Genius," says Buffon, " is Patience;" or, (as another French writer has explained his thought,) — " La Patience cherche, et le Génie trouve;" and there is little doubt that to the co-operation of these two powers all the brighest inventions of this world are owing; — that Patience must first explore the depths where the pearl lies hid, before Genius boldly dives and brings it up full into light. There are, it is true, some striking exceptions to this rule; and our own times have witnessed more than one extraordinary intellect, whose depth has not prevented their treasures from lying ever ready within reach. But the records of Immortality furnish few such instances; and all we know of the works, that she has hitherto marked with her seal, sufficiently authorises the general position, — that nothing great and durable has ever been produced with ease, and that Labour is the parent of all the lasting wonders of this world, whether in verse or stone, whether poetry or pyramids.

The first Sketch of The School for Scandal that occurs was written, I am inclined to think, before The Rivals, or at least very soon after it; — and that it was his original intention to satirise some of the gossips of Bath appears from the title under which I find noted down, as follows, the very first hints, probably, that suggested themselves for the dialogue.

" THE SLANDERERS. — *A Pump-Room Scene.*

" Friendly caution to the newspapers.

" It is whispered ——

" She is a constant attendant at church, and very frequently takes Dr. M'Brawn home with her.

" Mr. Worthy is very good to the girl; — for my part, I dare swear he has no ill intention.

" What! Major Wesley's Miss Montague?

" Lud, ma'am; the match is certainly broke — no creature knows the cause; — some say a flaw in the lady's character, and others, in the gentleman's fortune.

" To be sure they do say ——

" I hate to repeat what I hear.

" She was inclined to be a little too plump before she went.

" The most intrepid blush ; — I've known her complexion stand fire for an hour together.

" ' She had twins,' — How ill-natured ! as I hope to be saved, ma'am, she had but one ! and that a little starved brat not worth mentioning."

The following is the opening scene of his first Sketch, from which it will be perceived that the original plot was wholly different from what it is at present, — Sir Peter and Lady Teazle being at that time not yet in existence.

" Lady Sneerwell *and* Spatter.

" *Lady S.* The paragraphs, you say, were all inserted.

" *Spat.* They were, madam.

" *Lady S.* Did you circulate the report of Lady Brittle's intrigue with Captain Boastall ?

" *Spat.* Madam, by this Lady Brittle is the talk of half the town ; and in a week will be treated as a demirep.

" *Lady S.* What have you done as to the innuendo of Miss Niceley's fondness for her own footman ?

" *Spat.* 'Tis in a fair train, ma'am. I told it to my hair-dresser, — he courts a milliner's girl in Pall-Mall, whose mistress has a first cousin who is waiting-woman to Lady Clackit. I think in about fourteen hours it must reach Lady Clackit, and then you know the business is done.

" *Lady S.* But is that sufficient, do you think ?

" *Spat.* O Lud, ma'am, I'll undertake to ruin the character of the primmest prude in London with half as much. Ha! ha! Did Your Ladyship never hear how poor Miss Shepherd lost her lover and her character last summer at Scarborough? this was the whole of it. One evening at Lady —————'s the conversation happened to turn on the difficulty of breeding Nova Scotia sheep in England. ' I have known instances,' says Miss ————, ' for last spring a friend of mine, Miss Shepherd of Ramsgate, had a Nova Scotia sheep that produced her twins.'— ' What!' cries the old deaf dowager Lady Bowlwell, ' has Miss Shepherd of Ramsgate been brought to-bed of twins?' This mistake, as you may suppose, set the company a laughing. However, the next day, Miss Verjuice Amarilla Lonely, who had been of the party, talking of Lady Bowlwell's deafness, began to tell what had happened; but, unluckily, forgetting to say a word of the sheep, it was understood by the company, and, in every circle, many believed, that Miss Shepherd of Ramsgate had actually been brought to-bed of a fine boy and girl; and, in less than a fortnight, there were people who could name the father, and the farm-house where the babes were put out to nurse.

" *Lady S.* Ha! ha! well, for a stroke of luck, it was a very good one. I suppose you find no difficulty in spreading the report on the censorious Miss ————.

" *Spat.* None in the world, — she has always been so prudent and reserved, that every body was sure there was some reason for it at the bottom.

" *Lady S.* Yes, a tale of scandal is as fatal to the credit of a prude as a fever to those of the strongest constitutions; but there is a sort of sickly reputation that outlives hundreds of the robuster character of a prude.

" *Spat.* True, ma'am, there are valetudinarians in re- putation as in constitutions; and both are cautious from their appreciation and consciousness of their weak side, and avoid the least breath of air. *

" *Lady S.* But, Spatter, I have something of greater confidence now to entrust you with. I think I have some claim to your gratitude.

" *Spat.* Have I ever shown myself one moment un- conscious of what I owe you?

" *Lady S.* I do not charge you with it, but this is an affair of importance. You are acquainted with my situ- ation, but not all my weaknesses. I was hurt, in the early part of my life, by the envenomed tongue of scan- dal, and ever since, I own, have no joy but in sullying the fame of others. In this I have found you an apt tool : you have often been the instrument of my revenge, but you must now assist me in a softer passion. A young widow with a little beauty and easy fortune is seldom driven to sue, — yet is that my case. Of the many you have seen here, have you ever observed me, secretly, to favour one?

" *Spat.* Egad! I never was more posed : I'm sure you cannot mean that ridiculous old knight, Sir Christopher Crab?

" *Lady S.* A wretch! his assiduities are my torment.

" *Spat.* Perhaps his nephew, the baronet, Sir Benjamin Backbite, is the happy man?

" *Lady S.* No, though he has ill-nature and a good

* This is one of the many instances where the improving effect of revision may be traced. The passage at present stands thus : — " There are valetudinarians in reputation as well as constitution ; who, being conscious of their weak part, avoid the least breath of air, and supply the want of stamina by care and circumspection."

person on his side, he is not to my taste. What think you of Clerimont ? †

" *Spat.* How ! the professed lover of your ward, Maria ; between whom, too, there is a mutual affection.

" *Lady S.* Yes, that insensible, that doater on an idiot, is the man.

" *Spat.* But how can you hope to succeed ?

" *Lady S.* By poisoning both with jealousy of the other, till the credulous fool, in a pique, shall be entangled in my snare.

" *Spat.* Have you taken any measure for it ?

" *Lady S.* I have. Maria has made me the confidante of Clerimont's love for her : in return, I pretended to entrust her with my affection for Sir Benjamin, who is her warm admirer. By strong representation of my passion, I prevailed on her not to refuse to see Sir Benjamin, which she once promised Clerimont to do. I entreated her to plead my cause, and even drew her in to answer Sir Benjamin's letters with the same intent. Of this I have made Clerimont suspicious ; but 'tis you must inflame him to the pitch I want.

" *Spat.* But will not Maria, on the least unkindness of Clerimont, instantly come to an explanation ?

" *Lady S.* This is what we must prevent by blinding
*   *   *   *"

The scene that follows, between Lady Sneerwell and Maria, gives some insight into the use that was to be made of this intricate groundwork ‡ ; and it was, no doubt, the difficulty of

† Afterwards called Florival.

‡ The following is his own arrangement of the Scenes of the Second Act : —

" Act II. Scene 1st. All. — 2d. Lady S. and Mrs. C. —

managing such an involvement of his personages dramatically, that drove him, luckily for the world, to the construction of a simpler, and, at the same time, more comprehensive plan. He might also, possibly, have been influenced by the consideration, that the chief movement of this plot must depend upon the jealousy of the lover, — a spring of interest which he had already brought sufficiently into play in The Rivals.

" *Lady Sneerwell.* Well, my love, have you seen Clerimont to-day?

" *Maria.* I have not, nor does he come as often as he used. Indeed, madam, I fear what I have done to serve you has by some means come to his knowledge, and injured me in his opinion. I promised him faithfully never to see Sir Benjamin. What confidence can he ever have in me, if he once finds I have broken my word to him?

" *Lady S.* Nay, you are too grave. If he should suspect any thing, it will always be in my power to undeceive him.

" *Mar.* Well, you have involved me in deceit, and I must trust to you to extricate me.

" *Lady S.* Have you answered Sir Benjamin's last letter in the manner I wished?

3d. Lady S. and * * Em. and Mrs. C. listening. — 4th. L. S. and Flor. shows him into the room, — bids him return the other way. — L. S. and Emma. — Emma and Florival; — fits, — maid. — Emma fainting and sobbing: — ' Death, don't expose me!' — enter maid, — will call out — all come on with cards and smelling-bottles."

"*Mar.* I have written exactly as you desired me; but I wish you would give me leave to tell the whole truth to Clerimont at once. There is a coldness in his manner of late, which I can no ways account for.

Lady S. (*aside.*) I'm glad to find I have worked on him so far;—fie, Maria, have you so little regard for me? would you put me to the shame of being known to love a man who disregards me? Had you entrusted me with such a secret, not a husband's power should have forced it from me. But, do as you please. Go, forget the affection I have shown you : forget that I have been as a mother to you, whom I found an orphan. Go, break through all ties of gratitude, and expose me to the world's derision, to avoid one sullen hour from a moody lover.

" *Mar.* Indeed, madam, you wrong me ; and you who know the apprehension of love should make allowance for its weakness. My love for Clerimont is so great —

" *Lady S.* Peace ; it cannot exceed mine.

" *Mar.* For Sir Benjamin, perhaps not, ma'am —— and, I am sure, Clerimont has as sincere an affection for me.

" *Lady S.* Would to heaven I could say the same !

" *Mar.* Of Sir Benjamin : — I wish so too, ma'am. But I am sure you would be extremely hurt, if, in gaining your wishes, you were to injure me in the opinion of Clerimont.

" *Lady S.* Undoubtedly ; I would not for the world — Simple fool ! (*aside.*) But my wishes, my happiness depend on you — for, I doat so on the insensible, that it kills me to see him so attached to you. Give me but Clerimont, and —

" *Mar.* Clerimont !

" *Lady S.* Sir Benjamin, you know, I mean. Is he not attached to you ? am I not slighted for you ? Yet, do I bear any enmity to you, as my rival? I only request your friendly intercession, and you are so ungrateful, you would deny me that.

Mar. Nay, madam, have I not done every thing you wished? For you, I have departed from truth, and contaminated my mind with falsehood — what could I do more to serve you?

" *Lady S.* Well, forgive me, I was too warm; I know you would not betray me. I expect Sir Benjamin and his uncle this morning — why, Maria, do you always leave our little parties?

" *Mar.* I own, madam, I have no pleasure in their conversation. I have myself no gratification in uttering detraction, and therefore none in hearing it.

" *Lady S.* Oh fie, you are serious — 'tis only a little harmless raillery.

" *Mar.* I never can think that harmless which hurts the peace of youth, draws tears from beauty, and gives many a pang to the innocent.

" *Lady S.* Nay, you must allow that many people of sense and wit have this foible — Sir Benjamin Backbite, for instance.

" *Mar.* He may, but I confess I never can perceive wit where I see malice.

" *Lady S.* Fie, Maria, you have the most unpolished way of thinking! It is absolutely impossible to be witty without being a little ill-natured. The malice of a good thing is the barb that makes it stick. I protest now when I say an ill-natured thing, I have not the least malice against the person; and, indeed, it may be of one whom I never saw in my life; for I hate to abuse a friend — but I take it for granted, they all speak as ill-naturedly of me.

" *Mar.* Then you are, very probably, conscious you

deserve it—for my part, I shall only suppose myself ill-spoken of, when I am conscious I deserve it.

" *Enter Servant.*

" *Ser.* Mrs. Candour.

" *Mar.* Well, I'll leave you.

" *Lady S.* No, no, you have no reason to avoid her, she is good nature itself.

" *Mar.* Yes, with an artful affectation of candour, she does more injury than the worst backbiter of them all.

" *Enter* MRS. CANDOUR.

" *Mrs. Cand.* So, Lady Sneerwell, how d'ye do? Maria, child, how dost? Well, who is't you are to marry at last? Sir Benjamin or Clerimont. The town talks of nothing else."

Through the remainder of this scene the only difference in the speeches of Mrs. Candour is, that they abound more than at present in ludicrous names and anecdotes, and occasionally straggle into that loose wordiness, which, knowing how much it weakens the sap of wit, the good taste of Sheridan was always sure to lop away. The same may be said of the greater part of that scene of scandal, which at present occurs in the second Act, and in which all that is now spoken by Lady Teazle, was originally put into the mouths of Sir Christopher Crab and others — the caustic remarks of Sir Peter

Teazle being, as well as himself, an after creation.

It is chiefly, however, in Clerimont, the embryo of Charles Surface, that we perceive how imperfect may be the first lineaments that Time and Taste contrive to mould gradually into beauty. The following is the scene that introduces him to the audience, and no one ought to be disheartened by the failure of a first attempt after reading it. The spiritless language — the awkward introduction of the sister into the plot — the antiquated expedient * of dropping the letter — all, in short, is of the most undramatic and most unpromising description, and as little like what it afterwards turned to as the block is to the statue, or the grub to the butterfly.

" *Sir C.* This Clerimont is, to be sure, the drollest mortal ! he is one of your moral fellows, who does unto others as he would they should do unto him.

" *Lady Sneer.* Yet he is sometimes entertaining.

" *Sir C.* Oh hang him ! no — he has too much good nature to say a witty thing himself, and is too ill-natured to praise wit in others.

" *Enter* CLERIMONT.

" *Sir B.* So, Clerimont — we were just wishing for you to enliven us with your wit and agreeable vein.

* This objection seems to have occurred to himself; for one of his memorandums is — " Not to drop the letter, but take it from the maid."

" *Cler.* No, Sir Benjamin, I cannot join you.

" *Sir B.* Why, man, you look as grave as a young lover the first time he is jilted.

" *Cler.* I have some cause to be grave, Sir Benjamin. A word with you all. I have just received a letter from the country, in which I understand that my sister has suddenly left my uncle's house, and has not since been heard of.

" *Lady S.* Indeed ! and on what provocation ?

" *Cler.* It seems they were urging her a little too hastily to marry some country squire that was not to her taste.

" *Sir B.* Positively I love her for her spirit.

" *Lady S.* And so do I, and would protect her, if I knew where she was.

" *Cler.* Sir Benjamin, a word with you — (*takes him apart*). I think, sir, we have lived for some years on what the world calls the footing of friends.

" *Sir B.* To my great honour, sir. — Well, my dear friend ?

" *Cler.* You know that you once paid your addresses to my sister. My uncle disliked you ; but I have reason to think you were not indifferent to her.

" *Sir B.* I believe you are pretty right there ; but what follows ?

" *Cler.* Then I think I have a right to expect an implicit answer from you, whether you are in any respect privy to her elopement ?

" *Sir B.* Why, you certainly have a right to ask the question, and I will answer you as sincerely — which is, that though I make no doubt but that she would have gone with me to the world's end, I am at present entirely ignorant of the whole affair. This I declare to you upon my honour — and, what is more,

I assure you my devotions are at present paid to another lady — one of your acquaintance, too.

" *Cler.* (*aside.*) Now, who can this other be whom he alludes to? — I have sometimes thought I perceived a kind of mystery between him and Maria — but I rely on her promise, though, of late, her conduct to me has been strangely reserved.

" *Lady S.* Why, Clerimont, you seem quite thoughtful. Come with us ; we are going to kill an hour at ombre — your mistress will join us?

" *Cler.* Madam, I attend you.

" *Lady S.* (*taking Sir B. aside.*) Sir Benjamin, I see Maria is now coming to join us — do you detain her awhile, and I will contrive that Clerimont should see you, and then drop this letter.   [*Exeunt all but Sir B.*

" *Enter* MARIA.

" *Mar.* I thought the company were here, and Clerimont — —

" *Sir B.* One, more your slave than Clerimont, is here.

" *Mar.* Dear Sir Benjamin, I thought you promised me to drop this subject. If I have really any power over you, you will oblige me — —

" *Sir B.* Power over me! What is there you could not command me in? Have you not wrought on me to proffer my love to Lady Sneerwell? Yet though you gain this from me, you will not give me the smallest token of gratitude.

" *Enter* CLERIMONT *behind.*

" *Mar.* How can I believe your love sincere, when you continue still to importune me.

" *Sir B.* I ask but for your friendship, your esteem.

" *Mar.* That you shall ever be entitled to — then I may depend upon your honour?

" *Sir B.* Eternally — dispose of my heart as you please.

" *Mar.* Depend upon it I shall study nothing but its happiness. I need not repeat my caution as to Clerimont?

" *Sir B.* No, no, he suspects nothing as yet.

" *Mar.* For, within these few days, I almost believed that he suspects me.

" *Sir B.* Never fear, he does not love well enough to be quick-sighted; for just now he taxed me with eloping with his sister.

" *Mar.* Well, we had now best join the company.
[*Exeunt.*

" *Cler.* So, now — who can ever have faith in woman? D—d deceitful wanton! why did she not fairly tell me that she was weary of my addresses? that woman, like her mind, was changed, and another fool succeeded.

" *Enter* LADY SNEERWELL.

" *Lady S.* Clerimont, why do you leave us? Think of my losing this hand. (*Cler.* She has no heart.) —Five mate — (*Cler.* Deceitful wanton!) spadille.

" *Cler.* Oh yes, ma'am — 'twas very hard.

" *Lady S.* But you seem disturbed; and where are Maria and Sir Benjamin? I vow I shall be jealous of Sir Benjamin.

" *Cler.* I dare swear they are together very happy,— but, Lady Sneerwell — you may perhaps often have perceived that I am discontented with Maria. I ask you to tell me sincerely — have you ever perceived it?

" *Lady S.* I wish you would excuse me.

" *Cler.* Nay, you have perceived it — I know you hate deceit.   *   *   *   *   *

*   *   *   * "

I have said that the other Sketch, in which Sir Peter and Lady Teazle are made the leading personages, was written subsequently to that of which I have just given specimens. Of this, however, I cannot produce any positive proof. There is no date on the manuscripts, nor any other certain clue, to assist in deciding the precedency of time between them. In addition to this, the two plans are entirely distinct, — Lady Sneerwell and her associates being as wholly excluded from the one, as Sir Peter and Lady Teazle are from the other; so that it is difficult to say, with certainty, which existed first, or at what time the happy thought occurred of blending all that was best in each into one.

The following are the Dramatis Personæ of the second plan : —

> Sir Rowland Harpur.   ,
> —— Plausible.
> Capt. Harry Plausible.
> Freeman.
> Old Teazle. †   (*Left off trade.*)
>
> Mrs. Teazle.
> Maria.

† The first intention was, as appears from his introductory speech, to give Old Teazle the Christian name of So-

From this list of the personages we may conclude that the quarrels of Old Teazle and his
wife, the attachment between Maria and one of
the Plausibles, and the intrigue of Mrs. Teazle
with the other, formed the sole materials of the
piece, as then constructed.* There is reason, too,
to believe, from the following memorandum,
which occurs in various shapes through these
manuscripts, that the device of the screen was
not yet thought of, and that the discovery was
to be effected in a very different manner: —

" Making love to aunt and niece — meeting wrong in
the dark — some one coming — locks up the aunt, thinking it to be the niece."

I shall now give a scene or two from the
Second Sketch — which shows, perhaps, even

---

lomon. Sheridan was, indeed, most fastidiously changeful
in his names. The present Charles Surface was at first
Clerimont, then Florival, then Captain Harry Plausible, then
Harry Pliant or Pliable, then Young Harrier, and then
Frank — while his elder brother was successively Plausible,
Pliable, Young Pliant, Tom, and, lastly, Joseph Surface.
Trip was originally called Spunge ; the name of Snake was,
in the earlier sketch, Spatter, and, even after the union of
the two plots into one, all the business of the opening scene
with Lady Sneerwell, at present transacted by Snake, was
given to a character, afterwards wholly omitted, Miss Verjuice.

* This was most probably the " Two-act Comedy," which
he announced to Mr. Linley as preparing for representation
in 1775.

more strikingly than the other, the volatilising and condensing process which his wit must have gone through, before it attained its present proof and flavour.

" ACT I. — Scene I.

" Old Teazle, *alone.*

" In the year 44, I married my first wife; the wedding was at the end of the year — ay, 'twas in December; yet, before Ann. Dom. 45, I repented. A month before, we swore we preferred each other to the whole world — perhaps we spoke truth; but, when we came to promise to love each other till death, there I am sure we lied. Well, Fortune owed me a good turn; in 48 she died. Ah, silly Solomon, in 52 I find thee married again! Here, too, is a catalogue of ills — Thomas, born February 12.; Jane, born Jan. 6.; so they go on to the number of five. However, by death I stand credited but by one. Well, Margery, rest her soul! was a queer creature; when she was gone, I felt awkward at first, and being sensible that wishes availed nothing, I often wished for her return. For ten years more I kept my senses and lived single. Oh, blockhead, dolt Solomon! Within this twelvemonth thou art married again — married to a woman thirty years younger than thyself; a fashionable woman. Yet I took her with caution; she had been educated in the country; but now she has more extravagance than the daughter of an Earl, more levity than a Countess. What a defect it is in our laws, that a man who has once been branded in the forehead should be hanged for the second offence.

"*Enter* JARVIS.

" *Teaz.* Who's there? Well, Jarvis?

" *Jarv.* Sir, there are a number of my mistress's tradesmen without, clamorous for their money.

" *Teaz.* Are those their bills in your hand?

" *Jarv.* Something about a twentieth part, sir.

" *Teaz.* What! have you expended the hundred pounds I gave you for her use.

" *Jarv.* Long ago, sir, as you may judge by some of the items: — ' Paid the coachmaker for lowering the front seat of the coach.'

" *Teaz.* What the deuce was the matter with the seat?

" *Jarv.* Oh Lord, the carriage was too low for her by a foot when she was dressed — so that it must have been so, or have had a tub at top like a hat-case on a travelling trunk. Well, sir, (*reads,*) ' Paid her two footmen half a year's wages, 50*l.*'

" *Teaz.* 'Sdeath and fury! does she give her footmen a hundred a year?

" *Jarv.* Yes, sir, and I think, indeed, she has rather made a good bargain, for they find their own bags and bouquets.

" *Teaz.* Bags and bouquets for footmen! — halters and bastinadoes! *

" *Jarv.* ' Paid for my lady's own nosegays, 50*l.*'

" *Teaz.* Fifty pounds for flowers! enough to turn the Pantheon into a green-house, and give a Fête Champêtre at Christmas.

" † *Lady Teaz.* Lord, Sir Peter, I wonder you should

* Transferred afterwards to Trip and Sir Oliver.
† We observe here a change in his plan, with respect both to the titles of Old Teazle and his wife, and the pre-

grudge me the most innocent articles in dress — and then, for the expense — flowers cannot be cheaper in winter — you should find fault with the climate, and not with me. I am sure I wish with all my heart, that it was Spring all the year round, and roses grew under one's feet.

" *Sir P.* Nay, but, madam, then you would not wear them; but try snow-balls, and icicles. But tell me, madam, how can you feel any satisfaction in wearing these, when you might reflect that one of the rose-buds would have furnished a poor family with a dinner?

" *Lady T.* Upon my word, Sir Peter, begging your pardon, that is a very absurd way of arguing. By that rule, why do you indulge in the least superfluity? I dare swear a beggar might dine tolerably on your great-coat, or sup off your laced waistcoat — nay, I dare say, he wouldn't eat your gold-headed cane in a week. Indeed, if you would reserve nothing but necessaries, you

---

sence of the latter during this scene, which was evidently not at first intended.

From the following skeleton of the scenes of this piece, it would appear that (inconsistently, in some degree, with my notion of its being the two-act Comedy announced in 1775,) he had an idea of extending the plot through five acts.

" Act 1st, Scene 1st, Sir Peter and Steward — 2d, Sir P. and Lady — then Young Pliable.

" Act 2d, Sir P. and Lady — Young Harrier — Sir P. and Sir Rowland, and Old Jeremy — Sir R. and Daughter — Y. P. and Y. H.

" Act 3d, Sir R., Sir P., and O. J. — 2d, Y. P. and Company Y. R. O. R. — 3d, Y. H. and Maria — Y. O. R. H., and Young Harrier, to borrow.

" Act 4th, Y. P. and Maria, to borrow his money; gets away what he had received from his uncle — Y. P., Old Jer., and tradesmen — P. and Lady T.," &c. &c.

should give the first poor man you meet your wig, and walk the streets in your night-cap, which, you know, becomes you very much.

" *Sir P.* Well, go on to the articles.

" *Jarv.* (*reading.*) ' Fruit for my lady's monkey, 5*l.* per week.'

" *Sir P.* Five pounds for the monkey ! — why 'tis a dessert for an alderman !

" *Lady T.* Why, Sir Peter, would you starve the poor animal? I dare swear he lives as reasonably as other monkeys do.

" *Sir P.* Well, well, go on.

" *Jarv.* ' China for ditto' —

" *Sir P.* What, does he eat out of china ?

" *Lady T.* Repairing china that he breaks — and I am sure no monkey breaks less.

" *Jarv.* ' Paid Mr. Warren for perfumes—milk of roses, .30*l.*'

" *Lady T.* Very reasonable.

" *Sir P.* 'Sdeath, madam, if you had been born to these expenses I should not have been so much amazed ; but I took you, madam, an honest country squire's daughter —

" *Lady T.* Oh, filthy; don't name it. Well, heaven forgive my mother, but I do believe my father must have been a man of quality.

" *Sir P.* Yes, madam, when first I saw you, you were drest in a pretty figured linen gown, with a bunch of keys by your side ; your occupations, madam, to superintend the poultry ; your accomplishments, a complete knowledge of the family receipt-book — then you sat in a room hung round with fruit in worsted of your own working ; your amusements were to play country-dances on an old spinet to your father while he went asleep after a fox-chase — to read Tillotson's Sermons to your aunt Deborah. These, madam, were your re-creations, and these the accomplishments that captivated me. Now, forsooth, you must have two footmen to your chair, and a pair of white dogs in a phaeton; you forget when you used to ride double behind the butler on a docked bay coach-horse. . . . . . . Now you must have a French hair-dresser; do you think you did not look as well when you had your hair combed smooth over a roller? . . . . . Then you could be content to sit with me, or walk by the side of the Ha! Ha!

" *Lady T.* True, I did; and, when you asked me if I could love an old fellow, who would deny me nothing, I simpered and said, ' 'Till death.'

" *Sir P.* Why did you say so?

" *Lady T.* Shall I tell you the truth?

" *Sir P.* If it is not too great a favour.

" *Lady T.* Why, then, the truth is I was heartily tired of all these agreeable recreations you have so well remembered, and having a spirit to spend and enjoy fortune, I was determined to marry the first fool I should meet with . . . . . . you made me a wife, for which I am much obliged to you, and if you have a wish to make me more grateful still, make me a widow." †

* * * * * *

" *Sir P.* Then, you never had a desire to please me, or add to my happiness?

" *Lady T.* Sincerely, I never thought about you; did you imagine that age was catching? I think you have been overpaid for all you could bestow on me. Here am I surrounded by half a hundred lovers, not

† The speeches which I have omitted consist merely of repetitions of the same thoughts, with but very little vari-ation of the language.

one of whom but would buy a single smile by a thousand such baubles as you grudge me.

" *Sir P.* Then you wish me dead ?

" *Lady T.* You know I do not, for you have made no settlement on me.

    *   *   *   *   *

" *Sir P.* I am but middle-aged.

" *Lady T.* There's the misfortune; put yourself on, or back, twenty years, and either way I should like you the better.

    *   *   *   *   *

Yes, sir, and then your behaviour too was different ; you would dress, and smile, and bow; fly to fetch me any thing I wanted; praise every thing I did or said; fatigue your stiff face with an eternal grin ; nay, you even committed poetry, and muffled your harsh tones into a lover's whisper to sing it yourself, so that even my mother said you were the smartest old bachelor she ever saw — a billet-doux engrossed on buckram ! ! ! ! ! ! †

    *   *   *   *

Let girls take my advice and never marry an old bachelor. He must be so either because he could find nothing to love in women, or because women could find nothing to love in him."

The greater part of this dialogue is evidently *experimental*, and the play of repartee protracted with no other view, than to take the chance of a trump of wit or humour turning up.

In comparing the two characters in this sketch with what they are at present, it is impossible

† These notes of admiration are in the original, and seem meant to express the surprise of the author at the extravagance of his own joke.

not to be struck by the signal change that they have undergone. The transformation of Sir Peter into a gentleman has refined, without weakening the ridicule of his situation; and there is an interest created by the respectability and amiableness of his sentiments, which, contrary to the effect produced in general by elderly gentlemen so circumstanced, makes us rejoice, at the end, that he has his young wife all to himself. The improvement in the character of Lady Teazle is still more marked and successful. Instead of an ill-bred young shrew, whose readiness to do wrong leaves the mind in but little uncertainty as to her fate, we have a lively and innocent, though imprudent country girl, transplanted into the midst of all that can bewilder and endanger her, but with still enough of the purity of rural life about her heart, to keep the blight of the world from settling upon it permanently.

There is, indeed, in the original draught a degree of glare and coarseness, which proves the eye of the artist to have been fresh from the study of Wycherley and Vanbrugh; and this want of delicacy is particularly observable in the subsequent scene between Lady Teazle and Surface — the chastening down of which to its present tone is not the least of those triumphs of taste and skill, which every step in the elaboration of this fine Comedy exhibits.

" *Scene* * — YOUNG PLIANT's *Room.*

" *Young P.* I wonder Her Ladyship is not here : she promised me to call this morning. I have a hard game to play here, to pursue my designs on Maria. I have brought myself into a scrape with the mother-in-law. However, I think we have taken care to ruin my brother's character with my uncle, should he come to-morrow. Frank has not an ill quality in his nature ; yet, a neglect of forms, and of the opinion of the world, has hurt him in the estimation of all his graver friends. I have profited by his errors, and contrived to gain a character, which now serves me as a mask to lie under.

" *Enter* LADY TEAZLE.

" *Lady T.* What, musing, or thinking of me ?

" *Young P.* I was thinking unkindly of you ; do you know now that you must repay me for this delay, or I must be coaxed into good humour ?

" *Lady T.* Nay, in faith you should pity me — this old curmudgeon of late is grown so jealous, that I dare scarce go out, till I know he is secure for some time.

" *Young P.* I am afraid the insinuations we have had spread about Frank have operated too strongly on him — we meant only to direct his suspicions to a wrong object.

" *Lady T.* Oh, hang him ! I have told him plainly that

---

* The Third of the Fourth Act in the present form of the Comedy. This scene underwent many changes afterwards, and was oftener put back into the crucible than any other part of the play.

if he continues to be so suspicious, I'll leave him entirely, and make him allow me a separate maintenance.

" *Young P.* But, my charmer, if ever that should be the case, you see before you the man who will ever be attached to you. But you must not let matters come to extremities ; you can never be revenged so well by leaving him, as by living with him, and let my sincere affection make amends for his brutality.

" *Lady T.* But how shall I be sure now that you are sincere ? I have sometimes suspected, that you loved my niece. *

" *Young P.* Oh, hang her ! a puling idiot, without sense or spirit.

" *Lady T.* But what proofs have I of your love to me, for I have still so much of my country prejudices left, that if I were to do a foolish thing (and I think I can't promise) it shall be for a man who would risk every thing for me alone. How shall I be sure you love me?

" *Young P.* I have dreamed of you every night this week past.

" *Lady T.* That's a sign you have slept every night for this week past ; for my part, I would not give a pin for a lover who could not wake for a month in absence.

" *Young P.* I have written verses on you out of number.

" *Lady T.* I never saw any.

" *Young P.* No — they did not please me, and so I tore them.

" *Lady T.* Then it seems you wrote them only to divert yourself.

" *Young P.* Am I doomed for ever to suspense ?

" *Lady T.* I don't know — if I was convinced ——

* He had not yet decided whether to make Maria the daughter-in-law or niece of Lady Teazle.

" *Young P.* Then let me on my knees ——

" *Lady T.* Nay, nay, I will have no raptures either. This much I can tell you, that if I am to be seduced to do wrong, I am not to be taken by storm, but by deliberate capitulation, and that only where my reason or my heart is convinced.

" *Young P.* Then, to say it at once — the world gives itself liberties ——

" *Lady T.* Nay, I am sure without cause; for I am as yet unconscious of any ill, though I know not what I may be forced to.

" *Young P.* The fact is, my dear Lady Teazle, that your extreme innocence is the very cause of your danger; it is the integrity of your heart that makes you run into a thousand imprudences which a full consciousness of error would make you guard against. Now, in that case, you can't conceive how much more circumspect you would be.

" *Lady T.* Do you think so?

" *Young P.* Most certainly. Your character is like a person in a plethora, absolutely dying of too much health.

" *Lady T.* So then you would have me sin in my own defence, and part with my virtue to preserve my reputation. †

" *Young P.* Exactly so, upon my credit, ma'am."

* * * * * *

It will be observed, from all I have cited, that much of the original material is still preserved

† This sentence seems to have haunted him — I find it written in every direction, and without any material change in its form, over the pages of his different memorandum-books.

throughout; but that, like the ivory melting in the hands of Pygmalion, it has lost all its first rigidity and roughness, and, assuming at every touch some variety of aspect, seems to have gained new grace by every change.

> " *Mollescit ebur, positoque rigore*
> *Subsidit digitis, ceditque ut Hymettia sole*
> *Cera remollescit, tractataque pollice multas*
> *Flectitur in facies, ipsoque fit utilis usu.*"

Where'er his fingers move, his eye can trace
The once rude ivory softening into grace—
Pliant as wax that, on Hymettus' hill,
Melts in the sunbeam, it obeys his skill;
At every touch some different aspect shows,
And still, the oftener touch'd, the lovelier grows.

I need not, I think, apologise for the length of the extracts I have given, as they cannot be otherwise than interesting to all lovers of literary history. To trace even the mechanism of an author's style through the erasures and alterations of his rough copy, is, in itself, no ordinary gratification of curiosity; and the *brouillon* of Rousseau's Heloise, in the library of the Chamber of Deputies at Paris, affords a study in which more than the mere "auceps syllabarum" might delight. But it is still more interesting to follow thus the course of a writer's thoughts—to watch the kindling of new fancies as he goes — to accompany him in the change of plans, and see the various vistas that open upon him at every step. It is, indeed, like being admitted by some magical power, to witness the mysterious processes of the natural world — to see the crystal forming by degrees round its primitive nucleus, or observe the slow ripening of

> " the imperfect ore,
> " And know it will be gold another day !"

In respect of mere style, too, the workmanship of so pure a writer of English as Sheridan is well worth the attention of all who would learn the difficult art of combining ease with polish, and being, at the same time, idiomatic and elegant. There is not a page of these manuscripts that does not bear testimony to the fastidious care with which he selected, arranged, and moulded his language, so as to form it into that transparent channel of his thoughts, which it is at present.

His chief objects in correcting were to condense and simplify — to get rid of all unnecessary phrases and epithets, and, in short, to strip away from the thyrsus of his wit every leaf that could render it less light and portable. One instance out of many will show the improving

effect of these operations. * The following is the
original form of a speech of Sir Peter's : —

“ People who utter a tale of scandal, knowing it to be
forged, deserve the pillory more than for a forged bank-
note.   They can't pass the lie without putting their
names on the back of it.   You say no person has a right
to come on you because you didn't invent it ; but you
should know that, if the drawer of the lie is out of the
way, the injured party has a right to come on any of the
indorsers.”

When this is compared with the form in which
the same thought is put at present, it will be
perceived how much the wit has gained in lightness and effect by the change : —

“ *Mrs. Candour.* But sure you would not be quite so
severe on those who only report what they hear ?
“ *Sir P.* Yes, madam, I would have Law-merchant for

---

* In one or two sentences he has left a degree of stiffness
in the style, not so much from inadvertence as from the
sacrifice of ease to point.   Thus, in the following example,
he has been tempted by an antithesis into an inversion of
phrase by no means idiomatic.   “ The plain state of the
matter is this—I am an extravagant young fellow *who want
money to borrow;* you, I take to be a prudent old fellow who
have got money to lend.”
In the Collection of his Works this phrase is given differ-
ently —but without authority from any of the manuscript
copies.

them too, and in all cases of slander currency *, whenever the drawer of the lie was not to be found, the injured party should have a right to come on any of the indorsers."

Another great source of the felicities of his style, and to which he attended most anxiously in revision, was the choice of epithets; in which he has the happy art of making these accessary words not only minister to the clearness of his meaning, but bring out new effects in his wit by the collateral lights which they strike upon it — and even where the principal idea has but little significance, he contrives to enliven it into point by the quaintness or contrast of his epithets.

Among the many rejected scraps of dialogue that lie about, like the chippings of a Phidias, in this workshop of wit, there are some precious enough to be preserved, at least, as relics. For instance, — " she is one of those, who convey a libel in a frown, and wink a reputation down." The following touch of costume, too, in Sir Peter's description of the rustic dress of Lady Teazle before he married her : — " You forget when a little wire and gauze, with a few beads,

* There is another simile among his memorandums of the same mercantile kind : — " A sort of broker in scandal, who transfers lies without fees."

made you a fly-cap not much bigger than a blue-bottle."

The specimen which Sir Benjamin Backbite gives of his poetical talents was taken, it will be seen, from the following verses, which I find in Mr. Sheridan's hand-writing — one of those trifles, perhaps, with which he and his friend Tickell were in the constant habit of amusing themselves, and written apparently with the intention of ridiculing some women of fashion : —

" Then, behind, all my hair is done up in a plat,
And so, like a cornet's, tuck'd under my hat.
Then I mount on my palfrey as gay as a lark,
And, follow'd by John, take the dust * in High Park.
In the way I am met by some smart macaroni,
Who rides by my side on a little bay pony —
No sturdy Hibernian, with shoulders so wide,
But as taper and slim as the ponies they ride ;
Their legs are as slim, and their shoulders no wider,
Dear sweet little creatures, both pony and rider !

But sometimes, when hotter, I order my chaise,
And manage, myself, my two little greys.
Sure never were seen two such sweet little ponies,
Other horses are clowns, and these macaronies,
And to give them this title, I'm sure isn't wrong,
Their legs are so slim, and their tails are so long.
In Kensington Gardens to stroll up and down,
You know was the fashion before you left town, —

* This phrase is made use of in the dialogue : — " As Lady Betty Curricle was taking the dust in Hyde Park."

The thing's well enough, when allowance is made
For the size of the trees and the depth of the shade,
But the spread of their leaves such a shelter affords
To those noisy, impertinent creatures call'd birds,
Whose ridiculous chirruping ruins the scene,
Brings the country before me, and gives me the spleen.

Yet, tho' 'tis too rural — to come near the mark,
We all herd in *one* walk, and that, nearest the Park,
There with ease we may see, as we pass by the wicket,
The chimneys of Knightsbridge and — footmen at cricket.
I must tho', in justice, declare that the grass,
Which, worn by our feet, is diminish'd apace,
In a little time more will be brown and as flat
As the sand at Vauxhall or as Ranelagh mat.
Improving thus fast, perhaps, by degrees,
We may see rolls and butter spread under the trees,
With a small pretty band in each seat of the walk,
To play little tunes and enliven our talk."

Though Mr. Sheridan appears to have made more easy progress after he had incorporated his two first plots into one, yet, even in the details of the new plan, considerable alterations were subsequently made — whole scenes suppressed or transposed, and the dialogue of some entirely re-written. In the third Act, for instance, as it originally stood, there was a long scene, in which Rowley, by a minute examination of Snake, drew from him, in the presence of Sir Oliver and Sir Peter, a full confession of his designs against the reputation of Lady Teazle.

Nothing could be more ill-placed and heavy; it was accordingly cancelled, and the confession of Snake postponed to its natural situation, the conclusion. The scene, too, where Sir Oliver, as Old Stanley, comes to ask pecuniary aid of Joseph, was at first wholly different from what it is at present; and in some parts approached much nearer to the confines of caricature than the watchful taste of Mr. Sheridan would permit. For example, Joseph is represented in it as giving the old suitor only half-a-guinea, which the latter indignantly returns, and leaves him; upon which Joseph, looking at the half-guinea, exclaims, " Well, let him starve — this will do for the opera."

It was the fate of Mr. Sheridan, through life, —and, in a great degree, his policy, — to gain credit for excessive indolence and carelessness, while few persons, with so much natural brilliancy of talents, ever employed more art and circumspection in their display. This was the case, remarkably, in the instance before us. Notwithstanding the labour which he bestowed upon this comedy, (or we should rather, perhaps, say in consequence of that labour) the first representation of the piece was announced before the whole of the copy was in the hands of the actors. The manuscript, indeed, of the five last scenes bears evident marks of this haste in finishing,——there being but one rough draught of them, scribbled upon detached pieces of paper; while, of all the preceding acts, there are numerous transcripts, scattered promiscuously through six or seven books, with new interlineations and memorandums to each. On the last leaf of all, which exists just as we may suppose it to have been despatched by him to the copyist, there is the following curious specimen of doxology, written hastily, in the hand-writing of the respective parties, at the bottom:——

" Finished at last, Thank God!

" R. B. SHERIDAN."

" Amen!

" W. HOPKINS." *

The cast of the play, on the first night of representation (May 8, 1777), was as follows:——

Sir Peter Teazle .	.	*Mr. King.*
Sir Oliver Surface .	.	*Mr. Yates.*
Joseph Surface .	.	*Mr. Palmer.*
Charles . .	.	*Mr. Smith.*
Crabtree . .	.	*Mr. Parsons.*
Sir Benjamin Backbite	.	*Mr. Dodd.*
Rowley . .	.	*Mr. Aickin.*
Moses . .	.	*Mr. Baddeley.*
Trip . .	.	*Mr. Lamash.*
Snake . .	.	*Mr. Packer.*
Careless . .	.	*Mr. Farren.*
Sir Harry Bumper	.	*Mr. Gawdry.*

* The Prompter.

Lady Teazle	.	.	*Mrs. Abington.*
Maria	.	.	*Miss P. Hopkins.*
Lady Sneerwell	.	.	*Miss Sherry.*
Mrs. Candour	.	.	*Miss Pope.*

The success of such a play, so acted, could not be doubtful. Long after its first uninterrupted run, it continued to be played regularly two or three times a week ; and a comparison of the receipts of the first twelve nights, with those of a later period, will show how little the attraction of the piece had abated by repetition : —

May 8th, 1777.			£	s.	d.	
School for Scandal	.	.	225	9	0	
Ditto	.	. .	195	6	0	
Ditto A. B. (Author's night)			73	10	0	(Expenses;
Ditto	.	. .	257	4	6	
Ditto	.	. .	243	0	0	
Ditto A. B.	.	. .	73	10	0	
Committee	.	.	65	6	6	
School for Scandal	.	.	262	19	6	
Ditto	.	. .	263	13	6	
Ditto A. B.	.	.	73	10	0	
Ditto K. (the King)	.	.	272	9	6	
Ditto	.	. .	247	15	0	
Ditto	.	. .	255	14	0	

The following extracts are taken at hazard from an account of the weekly receipts of the Theatre, for the year 1778, kept with exemplary neatness and care by Mrs. Sheridan herself : * —

* It appears from a letter of Holcroft to Mrs. Sheridan, (given in his Memoirs, vol. i. p. 275.) that she was also in

1778.			£	s.	d.
Jan. 3. Twelfth Night	. Queen Mab	.	139	14	6
5. Macbeth .	. Queen Mab	.	212	19	0
6. Tempest .	. Queen Mab	.	107	15	6
7. School for Scandal	. Comus	.	292	16	0
8. School for Fathers	. Queen Mab	.	181	10	6
9. School for Scandal	. Padlock	.	281	6	0
Mar. 14. School for Scandal	. Deserter	.	263	18	6
16. Venice Preserved	. Balphegor (New)		195	3	6
17. Hamlet .	. Balphegor	.	160	19	0
19. School for Scandal	. Balphegor	.	261	10	0

Such, indeed, was the predominant attraction
of this comedy during the two years subsequent
to its first appearance, that, in the official account of receipts for 1779, we find the following
remark subjoined by the Treasurer:— " School
for Scandal damped the new pieces." I have
traced it by the same unequivocal marks of success through the years 1780 and 1781, and find
the nights of its representation always rivalling
those on which the King went to the theatre, in
the magnitude of their receipts.

The following note from Garrick * to the

---

the habit of reading for Sheridan the new pieces sent in by
dramatic candidates : — " Mrs. Crewe (he says) has spoken
to Mr. Sheridan concerning it (the Shepherdess of the Alps)
as he informed me last night, desiring me at the same time
to send it to you, who, he said, would not only read it yourself, but remind him of it."

* Murphy tells us, that Mr. Garrick attended the re-
hearsals, and " was never known on any former occasion to
be more anxious for a favourite piece. He was proud of

author, dated May 12. (four days after the first
appearance of the comedy), will be read with
interest by all those for whom the great names
of the drama have any charm : —

" MR. GARRICK's best wishes and compliments
to Mr. Sheridan.

" How is the Saint to-day ?   A gentleman
who is as mad as myself about y⁰ School remark'd, that the characters upon the stage at y⁵
falling of the screen stand too long before they
speak ; — I thought so too y⁰ first night : — he
said it was the same on y⁰ 2ⁿᵈ, and was remark'd
by others ; — tho' they should be astonish'd, and
a little petrify'd, yet it may be carry'd to too
great a length. — All praise at Lord Lucan's
last night."

The beauties of this Comedy are so universally known and felt, that criticism may be
spared the trouble of dwelling upon them very
minutely.   With but little interest in the plot,
with no very profound or ingenious developement of character, and with a group of personages, not one of whom has any legitimate claims

---

the new manager ; and in a triumphant manner boasted of
the genius to whom he had consigned the conduct of the
theatre." — *Life of Garrick.*

upon either our affection or esteem, it yet, by the admirable skill with which its materials are managed, — the happy contrivance of the situations, at once both natural and striking, — the fine feeling of the ridiculous that smiles throughout, and that perpetual play of wit which never tires, but seems, like running water, to be kept fresh by its own flow, — by all this general animation and effect, combined with a finish of the details almost faultless, it unites the suffrages, at once, of the refined and the simple, and is not less successful in ministering to the natural enjoyment of the latter, than in satisfying and delighting the most fastidious tastes among the former. And this is the true triumph of genius in all the arts ; — whether in painting, sculpture, music, or literature, those works which have pleased the greatest number of people of all classes, for the longest space of time, may, without hesitation be pronounced the best ; and, however mediocrity may enshrine itself in the admiration of the select few, the palm of excellence can only be awarded by the many.

The defects of The School for Scandal, if they can be allowed to amount to defects, are, in a great measure, traceable to that amalgamation of two distinct plots, out of which, as I have already shown, the piece was formed. From this cause, — like an accumulation of wealth

from the union of two rich families, — has de-
volved that excessive opulence of wit, with which,
as some critics think, the dialogue is overloaded;
and which, Mr. Sheridan himself used often to
mention, as a fault of which he was conscious in
his work.   That he had no such scruple, however, in writing it, appears evident from the
pains which he took to string upon his new plot
every bright thought and fancy which he had
brought together for the two others; and it is
not a little curious, in turning over his manuscript, to see how the out-standing jokes are
kept in recollection upon the margin, till he can
find some opportunity of funding them to advantage in the text.   The consequence of all this
is, that the dialogue, from beginning to end, is
a continued sparkling of polish and point: and
the whole of the Dramatis Personæ might be
comprised under one common designation of
Wits.   Even Trip, the servant, is as pointed and
shining as the rest, and has his master's wit, as
he has his birth-day clothes, " with the gloss
on." *   The only personage among them that
shows any " temperance in jesting," is Old Row-

---

* This is one of the phrases that seem to have perplexed
the taste of Sheridan, — and upon so minute a point, as,
whether it should be " with the gloss on," or, " with the
gloss on them."   After various trials of it in both ways, he
decided, as might be expected from his love of idiom, for
the former.

ley ; and he, too, in the original, had his share
in the general largess of *bon-mots*, — one of the
liveliest in the piece * being at first given to him,
though afterwards transferred, with somewhat
more fitness, to Sir Oliver.   In short, the entire
Comedy is a sort of El-Dorado of wit, where the
precious metal is thrown about by all classes, as
carelessly as if they had not the least idea of its
value.

Another blemish that hypercriticism has noticed, and which may likewise be traced to the
original conformation of the play, is the useless-
ness of some of the characters to the action or
business of it — almost the whole of the " Scandalous College " being but, as it were, excrescences, through which none of the life-blood of
the plot circulates.   The cause of this is evident : — Sir Benjamin Backbite, in the first plot
to which he belonged, was a principal personage ; but, being transplanted from thence into
one with which he has no connection, not only
he, but his uncle Crabtree, and Mrs. Candour,
though contributing abundantly to the animation
of the dialogue, have hardly any thing to do
with the advancement of the story ; and, like
the accessories in a Greek drama, are but as a

---

* The answer to the remark, that " charity begins at
home," — " and his, I presume, is of that domestic sort
which never stirs abroad at all."

sort of Chorus of Scandal throughout. That this defect, or rather peculiarity, should have been observed at first, when criticism was freshly on the watch for food, is easily conceivable; and I have been told by a friend, who was in the pit on the first night of performance, that a person who sat near him, said impatiently, during the famous scene at Lady Sneerwell's, in the Second Act,—" I wish these people would have done talking, and let the play begin."

It has often been remarked as singular, that the lovers, Charles and Maria, should never be brought in presence of each other till the last scene; and Mr. Sheridan used to say, that he was aware, in writing the Comedy, of the apparent want of dramatic management which such an omission would betray; but that neither of the actors, for whom he had destined those characters, was such as he could safely trust with a love scene. There might, perhaps, too, have been, in addition to this motive, a little consciousness, on his own part, of not being exactly in his element in that tender style of writing, which such a scene, to make it worthy of the rest, would have required; and of which the specimens left us in the serious parts of The Rivals are certainly not among his most felicitous efforts.

By some critics the incident of the screen has

been censured, as a contrivance unworthy of the dignity of comedy. * But in real life, of which comedy must condescend to be the copy, events of far greater importance are brought about by accidents as trivial; and in a world like ours, where the falling of an apple has led to the discovery of the laws of gravitation, it is surely too fastidious to deny to the dramatist the discovery of an intrigue by the falling of a screen. There is another objection as to the manner of employing this machine, which, though less grave, is perhaps less easily answered. Joseph, at the commencement of the scene, desires his servant to draw the screen before the window, because " his opposite neighbour is a maiden lady of so anxious a temper; " yet, afterwards, by placing Lady Teazle between the screen and the window, he enables this inquisitive lady to indulge her curiosity at leisure. It might be said, indeed, that Joseph, with the alternative of exposure to either the husband or neighbour, chooses the lesser evil; — but the oversight hardly requires a defence.

* " In the old comedy, the catastrophe is occasioned, in general, by a change in the mind of some principal character, artfully prepared and cautiously conducted; — in the modern, the unfolding of the plot is effected by the overturning of a screen, the opening of a door, or some other equally dignified machine." — GIFFORD, *Essay on the Writings of Massinger.*

From the trifling nature of these objections to the dramatic merits of The School for Scandal, it will be seen that, like the criticism of Momus on the creaking of Venus's shoes, they only show how perfect must be the work in which no greater faults can be found. But a more serious charge has been brought against it on the score of morality ; and the gay charm thrown around the irregularities of Charles is pronounced to be dangerous to the interests of honesty and virtue. There is no doubt that, in this character, only the fairer side of libertinism is presented, — that the merits of being in debt are rather too fondly insisted upon, and with a grace and spirit that might seduce even creditors into admiration. It was, indeed, playfully said, that no tradesman who applauded Charles could possibly have the face to dun the author afterwards. In looking, however, to the race of rakes that had previously held possession of the stage, we cannot help considering our release from the contagion of so much coarseness and selfishness to be worth even the increased risk of seduction that may have succeeded to it; and the remark of Burke, however questionable in strict ethics, is, at least, true on the stage, — that " vice loses half its evil by losing all its grossness."

It should be recollected, too, that, in other

respects, the author applies the lash of moral satire very successfully. The group of slanderers who, like the Chorus of the Eumenides, go searching about for their prey with " eyes that drop poison," represent a class of persons in society who richly deserve such ridicule, and who — like their prototypes in Æschylus trembling before the shafts of Apollo — are here made to feell the full force of the archery of wit. It is a proof of the effect and use of such satire, that the name of " Mrs. Candour" has become one of those formidable by-words, which have more power in putting folly and ill-nature out of countenance, than whole volumes of the wisest remonstrance and reasoning.

The poetical justice exercised upon the Tartuffe of sentiment, Joseph, is another service to the cause of morals, which should more than atone for any dangerous embellishment of wrong, that the portraiture of the younger brother may exhibit. Indeed, though both these characters are such as the moralist must visit with his censure, there can be little doubt to which we should, in real life, give the preference ; — the levities and errors of the one, arising from warmth of heart and of youth, may be merely like those mists that exhale from summer streams, obscuring them awhile to the eye, without affecting the native purity of their waters ; while the hypocrisy of the other is like the *mirage* of the desert, shining with promise on the surface, but all false and barren beneath.

In a late work, professing to be the Memoirs of Mr. Sheridan, there are some wise doubts expressed as to his being really the author of The School for Scandal, to which, except for the purpose of exposing absurdity, I should not have thought it worth while to allude. It is an old trick of Detraction, — and one, of which it never tires, — to father the works of eminent writers upon others ; or, at least, while it kindly leaves an author the credit of his worst performances, to find some one in the back-ground to ease him of the fame of his best. When this sort of charge is brought against a cotemporary, the motive is intelligible ; but, such an abstract pleasure have some persons in merely unsettling the crowns of Fame, that a worthy German has written an elaborate book to prove, that The Iliad was written, not by that particular Homer the world supposes, but by some *other* Homer! In truth, if mankind were to be influenced by those *Qui tam* critics, who have, from time to time, in the course of the history of literature, exhibited informations of plagiarism against great authors, the property of fame would pass from its present holders into the hands of persons with whom the world is but little acquainted. Aristotle must refund to one Ocellus Lucanus — Virgil must make a *cessio bonorum* in favour of Pisander — the Metamorphoses of Ovid must be credited to the account of Parthenius of Nicæa, and (to come to a modern instance) Mr. Sheridan must, according to his biographer, Dr. Watkins, surrender the glory of having written The School for Scandal to a certain anonymous young lady, who died of a consumption in Thames Street !

To pass, however, to less hardy assailants of the originality of this comedy, — it is said that the characters of Joseph and Charles were suggested by those of Bliful and Tom Jones ; that the incident of the arrival of Sir Oliver from India is copied from that of the return of Warner in Sidney Biddulph ; and that the hint of the famous scandal scene at Lady Sneerwell's is borrowed from a comedy of Moliere.

Mr. Sheridan, it is true, like all men of genius, had, in addition to the resources of his own wit, a quick apprehension of what suited his purpose in the wit of others, and a power of enriching whatever he adopted from them with such new grace, as gave him a sort of claim of paternity over it, and made it all his own. " C'est mon bien," said Moliere, when accused of borrowing, " et je le reprens partout où je le trouve ; " and next to creation, the re-production, in a new and

more perfect form, of materials already existing,
or the full developement of thoughts that had
but half blown in the hands of others, are the
noblest miracles for which we look to the hand
of genius. It is not my intention, therefore, to
defend Mr. Sheridan from this kind of plagiarism,
of which he was guilty in common with the rest
of his fellow-descendants from Prometheus, who
all steal the spark wherever they can find it.
But the instances, just alleged, of his obligations
to others, are too questionable and trivial to be
taken into any serious account. Contrasts of
character, such as Charles and Joseph exhibit,
are as common as the lights and shadows of a
landscape, and belong neither to Fielding or
Sheridan, but to nature. It is in the manner of
transferring them to the canvass that the whole
difference between the master and the copyist
lies; and Charles and Joseph would, no doubt,
have been what they are, if Tom Jones had never
existed. With respect to the hint supposed to
be taken from the novel of his mother, he at
least had a right to consider any aid from that
quarter as " son bien "— talent being the only
patrimony to which he had succeeded. But the
use made of the return of a relation in the play
is wholly different from that to which the same
incident is applied in the novel. Besides, in
those golden times of Indian delinquency, the

arrival of a wealthy relative from the East was no very unobvious ingredient in a story.

The imitation of Moliere, (if, as I take for granted, The Misanthrope be the play, in which the origin of the famous scandal scene is said to be found) is equally faint and remote, and, except in the common point of scandal, untraceable. Nothing, indeed, can be more unlike than the manner in which the two scenes are managed. Célimene, in Moliere, bears the whole *frais* of the conversation; and this female in La Bruyere's tedious and solitary dissections of character would be as little borne on the English stage, as the quick and dazzling movement of so many lancets of wit as operate in The School for Scandal would be tolerated on that of the French.

It is frequently said that Mr. Sheridan was a good deal indebted to Wycherley; and he himself gave in some degree, a colour to the charge, by the suspicious impatience which he betrayed whenever any allusion was made to it. He went so far, it is said, as to deny ever having read a line of Wycherley (though of Vanbrugh's dialogue he always spoke with the warmest admiration);—and this assertion, as well as some others equally remarkable, such as, that he never saw Garrick on the stage, that he never had seen a play throughout in his life, however strange and startling they may appear, are, at

least, too curious and characteristic not to be
put upon record. His acquaintance with Wycherley was possibly but at second-hand, and
confined, perhaps, to Garrick's alteration of The
Country Wife, in which the incident, already
mentioned as having been borrowed for The
Duenna, is preserved. There is, however, a
scene in The Plain Dealer (Act II.), where
Nevil and Olivia attack the characters of the
persons with whom Nevil had dined, of which
it is difficult to believe that Mr. Sheridan was
ignorant; as it seems to contain much of that
Hyle, or First Matter, out of which his own
more perfect creations were formed.

In Congreve's Double Dealer, too, (Act III.
Scene 10.) there is much which may, at least,
have mixed itself with the recollections of Sheridan, and influenced the course of his fancy; —
it being often found that the images with which
the memory is furnished, like those pictures
hung up before the eyes of pregnant women at
Sparta, produce insensibly a likeness to themselves in the offspring which the imagination
brings forth. The admirable drollery in Congreve about Lady Froth's verses on her coach-
man —

" For as the sun shines every day,
    So of our Coachman I may say " —

is by no means unlikely to have suggested the doggerel of Sir Benjamin Backbite; and the scandalous conversation in this scene, though far inferior in delicacy and ingenuity to that of Sheridan, has somewhat, as the reader will see, of a parental resemblance to it : —

" *Lord Froth.* Hee, hee, my dear; have you done? Won't you join with us? We were laughing at my Lady Whifler and Mr. Sneer.

" *Lady F.* Ay, my dear, were you? Oh filthy Mr. Sneer ! he is a nauseous figure, a most fulsamick fop. He spent two days together in going about Covent Garden to suit the lining of his coach with his complexion.

" *Ld. F.* Oh, silly ! yet his aunt is as fond of him, as if she had brought the ape into the world herself.

" *Brisk.* Who? my Lady Toothless? Oh, she is a mortifying spectacle; she's always chewing the cud like an old ewe.

" *Ld. F.* Then she's always ready to laugh, when Sneer offers to speak; and sits in expectation of his no jest, with her gums bare, and her mouth open —

" *Brisk.* Like an oyster at low ebb, egad — ha, ha, ha !

" *Cynthia.* (*aside.*) Well, I find there are no fools so inconsiderable themselves, but they can render other people contemptible by exposing their infirmities.

" *Lady F.* Then that t'other great strapping Lady — I can't hit off her name; the old fat fool, that paints so exorbitantly.

" *Brisk.* I know whom you mean — but, deuce take her, I can't hit off her name either — paints, d'ye say? Why she lays it on with a trowel. Then she has a great beard that bristles through it, and makes her look as if she was plastered with lime and hair, let me perish."

It would be a task not uninteresting, to enter into a detailed comparison of the characteristics and merits of Mr. Sheridan, as a dramatic writer, with those of the other great masters of the art ; and to consider how far they differed or agreed with each other, in the structure of their plots and management of their dialogue — in the mode of laying the train of their repartee, or pointing the artillery of their wit. But I have already devoted to this part of my subject a much ampler space than to some of my readers will appear either necessary or agreeable; — though by others, more interested in such topics, my diffuseness will, I trust, be readily pardoned. In tracking Mr. Sheridan through his two distinct careers of literature and of politics, it is on the highest point of his elevation in each that the eye naturally rests; and The School for Scandal in one, and the Begum speeches in the other, are the two grand heights — the " *summa biverticis umbra Parnassi*" — from which he will stand out to after times, and round which, therefore, his biographer may be excused for lingering with most fondness and delay.

It appears singular that, during the life of Mr. Sheridan, no authorised or correct edition of this play should have been published in England.

He had, at one time, disposed of the copyright to Mr. Ridgway of Piccadilly, but, after repeated applications from the latter for the manuscript, he was told by Mr. Sheridan, as an excuse for keeping it back, that he had been nineteen years endeavouring to satisfy himself with the style of The School for Scandal, but had not yet succeeded. Mr. Ridgway, upon this, ceased to give him any further trouble on the subject.

The edition printed in Dublin is, with the exception of a few unimportant omissions and verbal differences, perfectly correct. It appears that, after the success of the comedy in London, he presented a copy of it to his eldest sister, Mrs. Lefanu, to be disposed of, for her own advantage, to the manager of the Dublin Theatre. The sum of a hundred guineas, and free admissions for her family, were the terms upon which Ryder, the manager at that period, purchased from this lady the right of acting the play; and it was from the copy thus procured that the edition afterwards published in Dublin was printed. I have collated this edition with the copy given by Mr. Sheridan to Lady Crewe, (the last, I believe, ever revised by himself*,) and find it, with the few exceptions already mentioned, correct throughout.

* Among the corrections in this copy, (which are in his own hand-writing, and but few in number,) there is one which shows not only the retentiveness of his memory, but

The School for Scandal has been translated into most of the languages of Europe, and, among the French particularly, has undergone a variety of metamorphoses. A translation, undertaken, it appears, with the permission of Sheridan himself, was published in London, in the year 1789, by a Monsr. Bunell Delille, who, in a Dedication to "Milord Macdonald," gives the following account of the origin of his task: "Vous savez, Milord, de quelle manière mystérieuse cette pièce, qui n'a jamais été imprimé que furtivement, se trouva l'été dernier sur ma table, en manuscrit, in-folio; et si vous daignez vous le rappeler, après vous avoir fait part de l'aventure, je courus chez Monsieur Sheridan pour lui demander la permission," &c. &c.

The scenes of the Auction and the Screen were introduced, for the first time, I believe, on the French stage, in a little piece called "*Les*

---

the minute attention which he paid to the structure of his sentences. Lady Teazle, in her scene with Sir Peter in the Second Act, says, " That's very true, indeed, Sir Peter; and, after having married you, I should never pretend to taste again, I allow." It was thus that the passage stood at first in Lady Crewe's copy, — as it does still, too, in the Dublin edition, and in that given in the Collection of his Works : — but in his final revision of this copy, the original reading of the sentence, such as I find it in all his earlier manuscripts of the play, is restored : — " That's very true, indeed, Sir Peter; and, after having married you, I am sure I should never pretend to taste again."

Deux Neveux," acted in the year 1788, by the young comedians of the Comte de Beaujolais. Since then, the story has been reproduced under various shapes and names : — " Les Portraits de Famille, " " Valsain et Florville, " and, at the Théâtre Français, under the title of the " Tartuffe de Mœurs." Lately, too, the taste for the subject has revived. The Vaudeville has founded upon it a successful piece, called " Les Deux Cousins ; " and there is even a melodrame at the Porte St. Martin, entitled " L'Ecole du Scandale."

CHAP. VI.

FURTHER PURCHASE OF THEATRICAL PROPERTY. — MO-
NODY TO THE MEMORY OF GARRICK. — ESSAY ON METRE.
— THE CRITIC. — ESSAY ON ABSENTEES. — POLITICAL
CONNECTIONS. — THE " ENGLISHMAN." — ELECTED FOR
STAFFORD.

THE document in Mr. Sheridan's hand-writing, already mentioned, from which I have stated the sums paid in 1776 by him, Dr. Ford, and Mr. Linley, for Garrick's moiety of the Drury Lane Theatre, thus mentions the new purchase; by which he extended his interest in this property in the year 1778: — " Mr. Sheridan afterwards was obliged to buy Mr. Lacy's moiety at a price exceeding 45,000*l.*: this was in the year 1778." He then adds, — what it may be as well to cite, while I have the paper before me, though relating to subsequent changes in the property: — " In order to enable Mr. S. to complete this purpose, he afterwards consented to divide his original share between Dr. Ford and Mr. Linley, so as to make up each of theirs a quarter. But the price at which they purchased from Mr.

s 4

Sheridan was not at the rate which he bought from Lacy, though at an advance on the price paid to Garrick. Mr. S. has since purchased Dr. Ford's quarter for the sum of 17,000*l.*, subject to the increased incumbrance of the additional renters."

By what spell all these thousands were conjured up, it would be difficult accurately to ascertain. That happy art — in which the people of this country are such adepts — of putting the future in pawn for the supply of the present, must have been the chief resource of Mr. Sheridan in all these later purchases.

Among the visible signs of his increased influence in the affairs of the theatre, was the appointment this year of his father to be manager; — a reconciliation having taken place between them, which was facilitated, no doubt, by the brightening prospects of the son, and by the generous confidence which his prosperity gave him in making the first advances towards such a re-union.

One of the novelties of the year was a musical entertainment called The Camp, which was falsely attributed to Mr. Sheridan at the time, and has since been inconsiderately admitted into the Collection of his Works. This unworthy trifle (as appears from a rough copy of it in my possession) was the production of Tickell, and the patience with which his friend submitted to the imputation of having written it was a sort of " martyrdom of fame" which few but himself could afford.

At the beginning of the year 1779 Garrick died, and Sheridan, as chief mourner, followed him to the grave. He also wrote a Monody to his memory, which was delivered by Mrs. Yates, after the play of The West Indian, in the month of March following. During the interment of Garrick in Poets' Corner, Mr. Burke had remarked that the statue of Shakspeare seemed to point to the grave where the great actor of his works was laid. This hint did not fall idly on the ear of Sheridan, as the following *fixation* of the thought, in the verses which he afterwards wrote, proved : —

" The throng that mourn'd as their dead favourite pass'd,
   The grac'd respect that claim'd him to the last ;
   While Shakspeare's image, from its hallow'd base,
   Seem'd to prescribe the grave and point the place."

This Monody, which was the longest flight ever sustained by its author in verse, is more remarkable, perhaps, for refinement and elegance, than for either novelty of thought or depth of sentiment. There is, however, a fine burst of poetical eloquence in the lines beginning

" Superior hopes the poet's bosom fire;" and
this passage, accordingly, as being the best in
the poem, was, by the gossiping critics of the
day, attributed to Tickell, — from the same
laudable motives that had induced them to attribute Tickell's bad farce to Sheridan. There
is no end to the variety of these small missiles
of malice with which the Gullivers of the world
of literature are assailed by the Lilliputians
around them.

The chief thought which pervades this poem,
— namely, the fleeting nature of the actor's art
and fame, — had already been more simply expressed by Garrick himself in his Prologue to
The Clandestine Marriage : —

" The painter's dead, yet still he charms the eye,
While England lives, his fame can never die;
But he, who struts his hour upon the stage,
Can scarce protract his fame through half an age;
Nor pen nor pencil can the actor save ;
The art and artist have one common grave."

Colley Cibber, too, in his portrait (if I remember right) of Betterton, breaks off into the
same reflection, in the following graceful passage, which is one of those instances where
prose could not be exchanged for poetry without
loss : — " Pity it is that the momentary beauties,
flowing from an harmonious elocution, can-

not, like those of poetry, be their own record;
that the animated graces of the player can live
no longer than the instant breath and motion
that presents them, or, at best, can but faintly
glimmer through the memory of a few surviving
spectators."

With respect to the style and versification of
the Monody, the heroic couplet in which it is
written has long been a sort of Ulysses' bow, at
which Poetry tries her suitors, and at which
they almost all fail. Redundancy of epithet and
monotony of cadence are the inseparable com-
panions of this metre in ordinary hands; nor
could all the taste and skill of Sheridan keep it
wholly free from these defects in his own. To
the subject of metre, he had, nevertheless, paid
great attention. There are among his papers
some fragments of an Essay * which he had

---

* Or rather memorandums collected, as was his custom,
with a view to the composition of such an Essay. He had
been reading the writings of Dr. Foster, Webb, &c. on this
subject, with the intention, apparently, of publishing an
answer to them. The following (which is one of the few
consecutive passages I can find in these notes) will show
how little reverence he entertained for that antient prosody,
upon which, in the system of English education, so large
and precious a portion of human life is wasted: — " I never
desire a stronger proof that an author is on a wrong scent
on these subjects, than to see Quintilian, Aristotle, &c.,
quoted on a point where they have not the least business.
All poetry is made by the ear, which must be the sole judge

commenced on the nature of poetical accent and emphasis ; and the adaptation of his verses to

———

— it is a sort of musical rhythmus. If, then, we want to reduce our practical harmony to rules, every man, with a knowledge of his own language and a good ear, is at once competent to the undertaking. Let him trace it to music — if he has no knowledge, let him enquire.

" We have lost all notion of the antient accent ; — we have lost their pronunciation ; — all puzzling about it is ridiculous, and trying to find out the melody of our own verse by theirs is still worse. We should have had all our own metres, if we never had heard a word of their language,—this I affirm. Every nation finds out for itself a national melody ; and we may say of it, as of religion, no place has been discovered without music. A people, likewise, as their language improves, will introduce a music into their poetry, which is simply (that is to say, the numerical part of poetry, which must be distinguished from the imaginary,) the transferring the time of melody into speaking. What then have the Greeks or Romans to do with our music? It is plain that our admiration of their verse is mere pedantry, because we could not adopt it. Sir Philip Sidney failed. If it had been melody, we should have had it ; our language is just as well calculated for it.

" It is astonishing that the excessive ridiculousness of a Gradus or Prosodial Dictionary has never struck our scholars. The idea of looking into a book to see whether the *sound* of a syllable be short or long is absolutely as much a bull of Bœotian pedantry as ever disgraced Ireland." He then adds, with reference to some mistakes which Dr. Foster had appeared to him to have committed in his accentuation of English words : — " What strange effects has this system brought about ! It has so corrupted the ear, that absolutely our scholars cannot tell an English long syllable from a short one. If a boy were to make the *a* in " cano " or the airs in The Duenna — even allowing for the aid which he received from Mrs. Sheridan — shows a degree of musical feeling, from which a much greater variety of cadence might be expected, than we find throughout the versification of this poem. The taste of the time, however, was not prepared for any great variations in the music of the couplet. The regular foot-fall, established so long, had yet been but little disturbed ; and the only licence of this kind hazarded through the poem — " All perishable " — was objected to by some of the author's critical friends, who suggested, that it would be better thus : " All doomed to perish."

Whatever, in more important points, may be the inferiority of the present school of poetry to that which preceded it, in the music of versification there can be but little doubt of its improvement ; nor has criticism, perhaps, ever

---

" amo " long, Dr. F. would no doubt feel his ear hurt, and yet * * * "

Of the style in which some of his observations are committed to paper, the following is a curious specimen :—
" Dr. Foster says that short syllables, when inflated with that emphasis which the sense demands, swell in height, length, and breadth beyond their natural size. — The devil they do! Here is a most omnipotent power in emphasis. Quantity and accent may in vain toil to produce a little effect, but emphasis comes at once and monopolizes the power of them both."

rendered a greater service to the art, than in helping to unseal the ears of its worshippers to that true spheric harmony of the elders of song, which, during a long period of our literature, was as unheard as if it never existed.

The Monody does not seem to have kept the stage more than five or six nights : — nor is this surprising. The recitation of a long, serious address must always be, to a certain degree, ineffective on the stage; and though this subject contained within it many strong sources of interest, as well personal as dramatic, they were not, perhaps, turned to account by the poet with sufficient warmth and earnestness on his own part, to excite a very ready response of sympathy in others. Feeling never wanders into generalities ; — it is only by concentrating his rays upon one point that even Genius can kindle strong emotion ; and, in order to produce any such effect in the present instance upon the audience, Garrick himself ought to have been kept prominently and individually before their eyes in almost every line. Instead of this, however, the man is soon forgotten in his Art, which is then deliberately compared with other Arts, and the attention, through the greater part of the poem, is diffused over the transitoriness of actors in general, instead of being brought strongly to a focus upon the particular loss just sustained.

Even in those parts, which apply most directly
to Garrick, the feeling is a good deal diluted by
this tendency to the abstract ; and, sometimes,
by a false taste of personification, like that in the
very first line, —

    " If dying *excellence* deserves a tear,"

where the substitution of a quality of the man
for the man himself * puts the mind, as it were,
one remove further from the substantial object
of its interest, and disturbs that sense of reality,
on which the operations even of Fancy itself
ought to be founded.

But it is very easy to play the critic — so
easy as to be a task of but little glory. For one
person who could produce such a poem as this,
how many thousands exist and have existed,
who could shine in the exposition of its faults !
Though insufficient, perhaps, in itself, to create
a reputation for an author, yet, as a " *stella Co-
ronæ*," — one of the stars in that various crown,
which marks the place of Sheridan in the firma-

---

* Another instance of this fault occurs in his song " When
sable Night : " —

    " As some fond mother, o'er her babe deploring,
      Wakes *its beauty* with a tear ; "

where the clearness and reality of the picture are spoiled by
the affectation of representing the *beauty* of the child as
waked, instead of the child itself.

ment of Fame, — it not only well sustains its own part in the lustre, but draws new light from the host of brilliancy around it.

It was in the course of this same year that he produced the entertainment of The Critic — his last legitimate offering on the shrine of the Dramatic Muse. In this admirable farce we have a striking instance of that privilege which, as I have already said, Genius assumes, of taking up subjects that had passed through other hands, and giving them a new value and currency by his stamp. The plan of a Rehearsal was first adopted, for the purpose of ridiculing Dryden, by the Duke of Buckingham ; but, though there is much laughable humour in some of the dialogue between Bayes and his friends, the salt of the satire altogether was not of a very conservative nature, and the piece continued to be served up to the public long after it had lost its relish. Fielding tried the same plan in a variety of pieces — in his Pasquin, his Historical Register, his Author's Farce, his Eurydice, &c., — but without much success, except in the comedy of Pasquin, which had, I believe, at first a prosperous career, though it has since, except with the few that still read it for its fine tone of pleasantry, fallen into oblivion. It was reserved for Sheridan to give vitality to this form of dramatic humour, and to invest even his satirical portraits

— as in the instance of Sir Fretful Plagiary, which, it is well known, was designed for Cumberland —with a generic character, which, without weakening the particular resemblance, makes them representatives for ever of the whole class to which the original belonged. Bayes, on the contrary, is a caricature——made up of little more than personal peculiarities, which may amuse as long as reference can be had to the prototype, but like those supplemental features furnished from the living subject by Taliacotius, fall lifeless the moment the individual that supplied them is defunct.

It is evident, however, that Bayes was not forgotten in the composition of The Critic. His speech, where the two Kings of Brentford are singing in the clouds, may be considered as the exemplar which Sheridan had before him in writing some of the rehearsal-scenes of Puff : —

" *Smith.* Well, but methinks the sense of this song is not very plain.

" *Bayes.* Plain ! why did you ever hear any people in the clouds sing plain ? They must be all for flight of fancy at its fullest range, without the least check or controul upon it. When once you tie up spirits and people in clouds to speak plain, you spoil all."

There are particular instances of imitation still more direct. Thus, in The Critic : —

" *Enter* Sir Walter Raleigh *and* Sir Christopher
Hatton.

" *Sir Christ. H.* True, gallant Raleigh.—
" *Dangle.* What, they had been talking before ?
" *Puff.* Oh yes, all the way as they came along."

In the same manner in The Rehearsal, where
the Physician and Usher of the two Kings
enter : —

" *Phys.* Sir, to conclude —
" *Smith.* What, before he begins ?
" *Bayes.* No, sir, you must know they had been talk-
ing of this a pretty while without.
" *Smith.* Where? in the tyring room ?
" *Bayes.* Why, ay, sir.   He's so dull."

Bayes, at the opening of the Fifth Act, says,
" Now, gentlemen, I will be bold to say, I'll
show you the greatest scene that England ever
saw ; I mean not for words, for those I don't
value, but for state, show, and magnificence."
Puff announces his grand scene in much the
same manner : — " Now then for my magnificence! my battle! my noise! and my procession!"

In Fielding, too, we find numerous hints or
germs, that have come to their full growth of
wit in The Critic.   For instance, in Trapwit (a
character in " Pasquin ") there are the rudiments
of Sir Fretful as well as of Puff : —

" *Sneerwell.* Yes, faith, I think I would cut that last speech.

" *Trapwit.* Sir, I'll sooner cut off an ear or two; sir, that's the very best thing in the whole play   *   *

*   *   *   *   *   *   *

" *Trapwit.* Now, Mr. Sneerwell, we shall begin my third and last act; and I believe I may defy all the poets who have ever writ, or ever will write, to produce its equal; it is, sir, so cramm'd with drums and trumpets, thunder and lightning, battles and ghosts, that I believe the audience will want no entertainment after it."

The manager, Marplay, in " The Author's Farce," like him of Drury Lane in The Critic, " does the town the honour of writing himself;" and the following incident in " The Historical Register" suggested, possibly, the humorous scene of Lord Burleigh : —

" *Enter Four Patriots from different Doors, who meet in the centre and shake Hands.*

" *Sour-wit.* These patriots seem to equal your greatest politicians in their silence.

" *Medley.* Sir, what they think now cannot well be spoke, but you may conjecture a good deal from their shaking their heads.

Such coincidences, whether accidental or de-signed, are at least curious, and the following is another of somewhat a different kind :—" Steal! (says Sir Fretful) to be sure they may; and egad, serve your best thoughts as gipsies do stolen children, disfigure them, to make 'em pass for their own." * Churchill has the same idea in nearly the same language : —

> " Still pilfers wretched plans and makes them worse,
> Like gipsies, lest the stolen brat be known,
> Defacing first, then claiming for their own."

The character of Puff, as I have already shown, was our author's first dramatic attempt ; and, having left it unfinished in the porch as he entered the Temple of Comedy, he now, we see, made it worthy of being his farewell oblation in quitting it.   Like Eve's flowers, it was his

> " Early visitation, and his last."

We must not, however, forget a lively Epilogue which he wrote this year, for Miss Hannah More's tragedy of Fatal Falsehood, in which there is a description of a blue-stocking lady, executed with all his happiest point.   Of this dense, epigrammatic style, in which every line is a cartridge of wit in itself, Sheridan was, both in prose and verse, a consummate master; and if any one could hope to succeed after Pope, in a

* This simile was again made use of by him in a speech upon Mr. Pitt's India Bill, which he declared to be " nothing more than a bad plagiarism on Mr. Fox's; disfigured, indeed, as gipsies do stolen children, in order to make them pass for their own."

Mock Epic, founded upon fashionable life, it
would have been, we should think, the writer of
this epilogue.   There are some verses, written on
the " *Immortelle Emilie*" of Voltaire, in which
her employments, as a *savante* and a woman of
the world, are thus contrasted : —

> " *Tout lui plait, tout convient à son vaste génie,*
> *Les livres, les bijoux, les compas, les pompons,*
> *Les vers, les diamans, les beribis, l'optique,*
> *L'algèbre, les soupers, le Latin, les jupons,*
> *L'opéra, les procès, le bal, et la physique.*"

How powerfully has Sheridan, in bringing
out the same contrasts, shown the difference
between the raw material of a thought, and the
fine fabric as it comes from the hands of a work-
man ; —

> " What motley cares Corilla's mind perplex,
> Whom maids and metaphors conspire to vex !
> In studious deshabille behold her sit,
> A letter'd gossip and a housewife wit:
> At once invoking, though for different views,
> Her gods, her cook, her milliner, and muse.
> Round her strew'd room a frippery chaos lies,
> A chequer'd wreck of notable and wise.
> Bills, books, caps, couplets, combs, a varied mass,
> Oppress the toilet and obscure the glass ;
> Unfinish'd here an epigram is laid,
> And there a mantua-maker's bill unpaid.
> There new-born plays foretaste the town's applause,
> There dormant patterns pine for future gauze.

A moral essay now is all her care,
A satire next, and then a bill of fare.
A scene she now projects, and now a dish,
Here Act the First, and here ' Remove with Fish.'
Now, while this eye in a fine frenzy rolls,
That soberly casts up a bill for coals ;
Black pins and daggers in one leaf she sticks,
And tears, and threads, and bowls, and thimbles mix."

We must now prepare to follow the subject of
this Memoir into a field of display, altogether
different, where he was in turn to become an
actor before the public himself, and where, instead of indicting lively speeches for others, he
was to deliver the dictates of his eloquence and
wit from his own lips. However the lovers of
the drama may lament this diversion of his
talents, and doubt whether even the chance of
another School for Scandal were not worth more
than all his subsequent career, yet to the individual himself, full of ambition and conscious
of versatility of powers, such an opening into a
new course of action and fame, must have been
like one of those sudden turnings of the road in
a beautiful country, which dazzle the eyes of the
traveller with new glories, and invite him on to
untried paths of fertility and sunshine.

It has been before remarked how early, in a
majority of instances, the dramatic talent has
come to its fullest maturity. Mr. Sheridan would

possibly never have exceeded what he had already
done, and his celebrity had now reached that
point of elevation, where, by a sort of optical
deception in the atmosphere of fame, to remain
stationary is to seem, in the eyes of the spectators, to fall.   He had, indeed, enjoyed only the
triumphs of talent, and without even descending
to those ovations, or minor triumphs, which in
general are little more than celebrations of escape
from defeat, and to which they, who surpass all
but themselves, are often capriciously reduced.
It is questionable, too, whether, in any other
walk of literature, he would have sustained the
high reputation which he acquired by the drama.
Very rarely have dramatic writers, even of the
first rank, exhibited powers of equal rate, when
out of the precincts of their own art; while, on
the other hand, poets of a more general range,
whether epic, lyric, or satiric, have as rarely
succeeded on the stage.   There is, indeed, hardly
one of our celebrated dramatic authors (and the
remark might be extended to other countries)
who has left works worthy of his reputation in
any other line; and Mr. Sheridan, perhaps, might
only have been saved from adding to the list of
failures, by such a degree of prudence or of
indolence as would have prevented him from
making the attempt.   He may, therefore, be
said to have closed his account with literature,

when not only the glory of his past successes, but the hopes of all that he might yet have achieved, were set down fully, and without any risk of forfeiture, to his credit ; and, instead of being left, like Alexander, to sigh for new worlds to vanquish, no sooner were his triumphs in one sphere of action complete than another opened to invite him to new conquests.

We have already seen that Politics, from the very commencement of his career, had held divided empire with Literature in the tastes and studies of Sheridan ; and, even in his fullest enjoyment of the smiles of the Comic Muse, while he stood without a rival in *her* affections, the " *Musa severior*" of politics was estranging the constancy of *his* —

" *Te tenet, absentes alios suspirat amores.*"

" Ev'n while perfection lies within his arms,
    He strays in thought and sighs for other charms."

Among his manuscripts there are some sheets of an Essay on Absentees, which, from the allusions it contains to the measures then in contemplation for Ireland, must have been written, I rather think, about the year 1778—when The School for Scandal was in its first career of success, and The Critic preparing, at no very long interval, to partake its triumph. It is obvious, from some expressions used in this pamphlet,

that his intention was, if not to publish it in Ireland, at least to give it the appearance of having
been written there; — and, except the pure unmixed motive of rendering a service to his country, by the discussion of a subject so closely
connected with her interests, it is difficult to
conceive what inducement he could have had to
select at that moment such a topic for his pen.
The plain, unpretending style of the greater part
of the composition sufficiently proves that literary display was not the object of it; while the
absence of all criminatory matter against the
government precludes the idea of its having
originated in party zeal.

As it is curious to observe how soberly his
genius could yoke itself to grave matter of fact,
after the winged excursions in which it had been
indulging, I shall here lay some paragraphs of
this pamphlet before the reader.

In describing the effects of the prevailing
system of pasturage — one of the evils attributed
by him to Absentees, — he thus, with occasional
irradiations of eloquence and ingenuity, expresses
himself : —

" Now it must ever be the interest of the Absentee to
place his estates in the hands of as few tenants as possible, by which means there will be less difficulty or
hazard in collecting his rents, and less intrusted to an

agent, if his estate require one. The easiest method of effecting this is by laying the land out for pasturage, and letting it in gross to those who deal only in ' a fatal living crop'—whose produce we are not allowed a market for when manufactured, while we want art, honesty, and encouragement to fit it for home consumption. Thus the indolent extravagance of the lord becomes subservient to the interest of a few mercenary graziers — shepherds of most unpastoral principles — while the veteran husbandman may lean on the shattered, unused plough, and view himself surrounded with flocks that furnish raiment without food. Or, if his honesty be not proof against the hard assaults of penury, he may be led to revenge himself on these dumb innovators of his little field—then learn too late that some portion of the soil is reserved for a crop more fatal even than that which tempted and destroyed him.

" Without dwelling on the particular ill effects of non-residence in this case, I shall conclude with representing that principal and supreme prerogative which the Absentee foregoes—the prerogative of mercy, of charity. The estated resident is invested with a kind of relieving providence — a power to heal the wounds of undeserved misfortune — to break the blows of adverse fortune, and leave chance no power to undo the hopes of honest, persevering industry. There cannot surely be a more happy station than that wherein prosperity and worldly interest are to be best forwarded by an exertion of the most endearing offices of humanity. This is his situation who lives on the soil which furnishes him with means to live. It is his interest to watch the devastation of the storm, the ravage of the flood—to mark the pernicious extremes of the elements, and, by a judicious indulgence and assistance, to convert the sorrows and repinings of

the sufferer into blessings on his humanity. By such a
conduct he saves his people from the sin of unrighteous
murmurs, and makes Heaven his debtor for their resignation.

"It will be said that the residing in another kingdom
will never erase from humane minds the duty and attention which they owe to those whom they have left to
cultivate their demesnes. I will not say that absence
lessens their humanity, or that the superior dissipation
which they enjoy in it contracts their feelings to coarser
enjoyments — without this, we know that agents and
stewards are seldom intrusted with full powers of aiding
and remitting. In some, compassion would be injustice.
They are, in general, content with the virtue of justice
and punctuality towards their employer; part of which
they conceive to be a rigorous exaction of his rents, and,
where difficulty occurs, their process is simply to distrain
and to eject — a rigour that must ever be prejudicial to
an estate, and which, practised frequently, betrays either
an original negligence, or want of judgment in choosing
tenants, or an extreme inhumanity towards their inci-
dental miscarriages.

"But, granting an undiminished benevolence to exist
on the part both of the landlord and the agent, yet can
we expect any great exertion of pathetic eloquence to
proceed from the latter to palliate any deficiency of the
tenants? — or, if there were, do we not know how much
lighter an impression is made by distresses related to us
than by those which are 'oculis subjecta fidelibus?' The
heart, the seat of charity and compassion, is more accessible to the senses than the understanding. Many, who
would be unmoved by any address to the latter, would
melt into charity at the eloquent persuasion of silent
sorrow. When he sees the widow's tear, and hears the

orphan's sigh, every one will act with a sudden uniform rectitude because he acts from the divine impulse of ' free love dealt equally to all.' "

The blind selfishness of those commercial laws, which England so long imposed upon Ireland, — like ligatures to check the circulation of the empire's life-blood, — is thus adverted to :

" Though I have mentioned the decay of trade in Ireland as insufficient to occasion the great increase of emigration, yet is it to be considered as an important ill effect, arising from the same cause. It may be said that trade is now in higher repute in Ireland, and that the exports and imports (which are always supposed the test of it) are daily increasing. This may be admitted to be true, yet cannot it be said that the trade of the kingdom flourishes. The trade of a kingdom should increase in exact proportion to its luxuries, and those of the nations connected with it. Therefore it is no argument to say, that, on examining the accounts of customs fifty years back, they appear to be trebled now ; for England, by some sudden stroke, might lose such a proportion of its trade, as would ruin it as a commercial nation, yet the amount of what remained might be tenfold of what it enjoyed in the reign of Queen Elizabeth. Trade, properly speaking, is the commutations of the product of each country — this extends itself to the exchange of commodities in which art has fixed a price. Where a nation hath free power to export the works of its industry, the balance in such articles will certainly be in its favour. Thus had we in Ireland power to export our manufactured silks, stuffs, and woollens, we should be assured that it would be our interest to import and cultivate their materials. But, as this is not the case, the gain of individuals is no proof that the nation is benefited by such commerce. For instance, the exportation of unwrought wool may be very advantageous to the dealer, and, through his hands, bring money, or a beneficial return of commodities into the kingdom ; — but trace the ill effects of depopulating such tracts of land as are necessary for the support of flocks to supply this branch, and number those who are deprived of support and employment by it, and so become a dead weight on the community — we shall find that the nation, in fact, will be the poorer for this apparent advantage. This would be remedied were we allowed to export it manufactured; because the husbandman might get his bread as a manufacturer.

" Another principal cause that the trade may increase, without proportionally benefiting the nation, is that a great part of the stock which carries on the foreign trade of Ireland belongs to those who reside out of the country — thus the ultimate and material profits on it are withdrawn to another kingdom. It is likewise to be observed, that, though the exportations may appear to exceed the importations, yet may this in part arise from the accounts of the former being of a more certain nature, and those of the latter very conjectural, and always falling short of the fact."

Though Mr. Sheridan afterwards opposed a Union with Ireland, the train of reasoning which he pursued in this pamphlet naturally led him to look forward to such an arrangement between the two countries, as, perhaps, the only chance

of solving the long-existing problem of their re-
lationship to each other.

" It is the state, (he continues,) the luxury, and
fashions of the wealthy, that give life to the artificers of
elegance and taste; — it is their numerous train that
sends the rapid shuttle through the loom; and, when
they leave their country, they not only beggar these de-
pendents but the tribes that live by clothing them.

" An extravagant passion for luxuries hath been in
all nations a symptom of an approaching dissolution.
However, in commercial states, while it predominates
only among the higher ranks, it brings with it the con-
ciliating advantage of being greatly beneficial to trade
and manufactures. But, how singularly unfortunate is
that kingdom, where the luxurious passions of the great
beggar those who should be supported by them, — a
kingdom, whose wealthy members keep equal pace with
their numbers in the dissipated and fantastical pursuits
of life, without suffering the lower class to glean even
the dregs of their vices. While this is the case with
Ireland the prosperity of her trade must be all forced
and unnatural; and if, in the absence of its wealthy and
estated members the state already feels all the disadvantages of a Union, it cannot do better than endeavour
at a free trade by effecting it in reality."

Having demonstrated, at some length, the
general evil of Absenteeism, he thus proceeds to
enquire into the most eligible remedy for it: —

" The evil complained of is simply the absence of the
proprietors of a certain portion of the landed property.
This is an evil unprovided against by the legislature;—

therefore, we are not to consider whether it might not with propriety have been guarded against, but whether a remedy or alleviation of it can now be attempted consistently with the spirit of the constitution. On examining all the most obvious methods of attempting this, I believe there will appear but two practicable. The First will be by enacting a law for the frequent summoning the proprietors of landed property to appear *de facto* at stated times. The Second will be the voting a supply to be raised from the estates of such as do never reside in the kingdom.

" The First, it is obvious, would be an obligation of no use, without a penalty was affixed to the breach of it, amounting to the actual forfeiture of the estate of the recusant. This, we are informed, was once the case in Ireland. But at present, whatever advantage the kingdom might reap by it, it could not possibly be reconciled to the genius of the Constitution : and, if the fine were trifling, it would prove the same as the second method, with the disadvantage of appearing to treat as an act of delinquency what in no way infringes the municipal laws of the kingdom.

" In the Second method the legislature is, in no respect, to be supposed to regard the *person* of the Absentee. It prescribes no place of residence to him, nor attempts to summon or detain him. The light it takes up the point in is this — that the welfare of the whole is injured by the produce of a certain portion of the soil being sent out of the kingdom. * * * It will be said that the produce of the soil is not exported by being carried to our own markets : but if the value received in exchange for it, whatever it be, whether money or commodities, be exported, it is exactly the same in its ultimate effects as if the grain, flocks, &c. were literally sent to England. In this light, then, if the state is found to suffer by such an exportation, its deducting a small part from the produce is simply a reimbursing the public, and putting the loss of the public (to whose welfare the interest of individuals is always to be subservient) upon those very members who occasion that loss.

" This is only to be effected by a tax."

Though to a political economist of the present day much of what is so loosely expressed in these extracts will appear but the crudities of a tyro in the science, yet, at the time when they were written, — when both Mr. Fox and Mr. Burke could expatiate on the state of Ireland, without a single attempt to develope or enforce those simple, but wise principles of commercial policy, every one of which had been violated in the restrictions on her industry, — it was no small merit in Mr. Sheridan to have advanced even thus far in a branch of knowledge so rare and so important.

In addition to his own early taste for politics, the intimacies which he had now formed with some of the most eminent public men of the day must have considerably tended to turn his ambition in that direction. At what time he first became acquainted with Mr. Fox I have no means of ascertaining exactly. Among the letters addressed to him by that statesman, there is one which, from the formality of its style, must have been written at the very commencement of their

acquaintance — but, unluckily it is not dated.
Lord John Townshend, who first had the happiness
of bringing two such men together, has given the
following interesting account of their meeting,
and of the impressions which they left upon the
minds of each other. His Lordship, however, has
not specified the period of this introduction : —

"I made the first dinner-party at which they
met, having told Fox that all the notions he
might have conceived of Sheridan's talents and
genius from the comedy of The Rivals, &c. would
fall infinitely short of the admiration of his astonishing powers, which I was sure he would entertain at the first interview. The first interview
between them (there were very few present, only
Tickell and myself, and one or two more,) I shall
never forget. Fox told me, after breaking up
from dinner, that he had always thought Hare,
after my uncle, Charles Townshend, the wittiest
man he ever met with, but that Sheridan surpassed them both infinitely ; and Sheridan told
me next day that he was quite lost in admiration
of Fox, and that it was a puzzle to him to say
what he admired most, his commanding superiority of talents and universal knowledge, or his
playful fancy, artless manners, and benevolence
of heart, which showed itself in every word he
uttered."

With Burke Mr. Sheridan became acquainted

at the celebrated Turk's Head Club, — and, if
any incentive was wanting to his new passion for
political distinction, the station to which he saw
his eloquent fellow-countryman exalted, with no
greater claims from birth or connection than his
own, could not have failed to furnish it. His
intimacy with Mr. Windham began, as we have
seen, very early at Bath, and the following letter,
addressed to him by that gentleman from Norfolk,
in the year 1778, is a curious record not only of the
first political movements of a person so celebrated
as Mr. Windham, but of the interest with which
Sheridan then entered into the public measures
of the day : —

                                    " Jan. 5. 1778.

" I fear my letter will greatly disappoint your
hopes.* I have no account to send you of my
answering Lord Townshend — of hard-fought
contests — spirited resolves — ballads, mobs,
cockades, and Lord North burnt in effigy. We
have had a bloodless campaign, but not from

---

* Mr. Windham had gone down to Norfolk, in consequence of a proposed meeting in that county, under the
auspices of Lord Townshend, for the purpose of raising a
subscription in aid of government, to be applied towards
carrying on the war with the American colonies. In about
three weeks after the date of this letter, the meeting was
held, and Mr. Windham, in a spirited answer to Lord Townshend, made the first essay of his eloquence in public.

backwardness in our troops, but for the most creditable reason that can be — want of resolution in the enemy to encounter us. When I got down here early this morning, expecting to find a room prepared, a chair set for the president, and nothing wanting but that the orators should begin, I was surprised to learn that no advertisement had appeared on the other part; but that Lord T. having dined at a meeting, where the proposal was received very coldly, had taken fright, and for the time at least had dropped the proposal. It had appeared, therefore, to those whom I applied to (and I think very rightly) that till an advertisement was inserted by them, or was known for certain to be intended, it would not be proper for any thing to be done by us. In this state, therefore, it rests. The advertisement which we agreed upon is left at the printer's, ready to be inserted upon the appearance of one from them. We lie upon our arms, and shall begin to act upon any motion of the enemy. I am very sorry that things have taken this turn, as I came down in full confidence of being able to accomplish something distinguished. I had drawn up, as I came along, a tolerably good paper, to be distributed to-morrow in the streets, and settled pretty well in my head the terms of a protest — besides some pretty smart pieces of oratory, delivered upon Newmarket Heath. I never felt so much disposition to exert myself before — I hope from my never having before so fair a prospect of doing it with success. When the coach comes in, I hope I shall receive a packet from you, which shall not be lost, though it may not be used immediately.

" I must leave off writing, for I have got some other letters to send by to-night's post. Writing in this ink is like speaking with respect to the utter annihilation of what is past ; — by the time it gets to you, perhaps, it may have become legible, but I have no chance of reading over my letter myself.

" I shall not suffer this occasion to pass over entirely without benefit.

" Believe me yours most truly,

" W. WINDHAM.

" Tell Mrs. Sheridan that I hope she will have a closet ready, where I may remain till the heat of the pursuit is over. My friends in France have promised to have a vessel ready upon the coast.

" *Richard Brinsley Sheridan, Esq.,*
   Queen Street, Lincoln's Inn Fields."

The first political service rendered by Mr. Sheridan to the party with whom he now closely connected himself, was the active share which he took in a periodical paper called The Englishman, set up by the Whigs for the purpose of seconding, out of parliament, the crimination and invective of which they kept up such a brisk fire within. The intention, as announced by Sheridan in the first Number *, was, like Swift in the Drapier's Letters, to accommodate the style of the publication to the comprehension of persons in " that class of the community, who are commonly called the *honest* and *industrious.*" But this plan, — which not even Swift, independent as was his humour of the artifices of style, could adhere to, — was soon abandoned, and there is in most of Sheridan's own papers a finesse and ingenuity of allusion, which only the most cultivated part of his readers could fully enjoy. For instance, in exposing the inconsistency of Lord North, who had lately consented in a Committee of the whole House, to a motion which he had violently opposed in the House itself, — thus " making (says Sheridan) that respectable assembly disobey its own orders, and the members reject with contempt, under the form of a Chairman, the resolutions they had imposed on themselves under the authority of a Speaker," — he proceeds in a strain of refined raillery, as little suited to the " honest and industrious " class of the community, as Swift's references to Locke, Molyneux,

* Published 13th of March, 1779.

and Sydney, were to the readers for whom he also professed to write : —

" The burlesque of any plan, I know, is rather a recommendation of it to Your Lordship; and the ridicule you might throw on this assembly, by continuing to support this Athanasian distinction of powers in the unity of an apparently corporate body, might in the end compensate to you for the discredit you have incurred in the attempt.

" A deliberative body of so *uncommon a form,* would probably be deemed a kind of STATE MONSTER by the ignorant and the vulgar. This might at first increase their *awe* for it, and so far counteract Your Lordship's intentions. They would probably approach it with as much reverence as Stephano does the monster in The Tempest : — ' What, one body and two voices — a most delicate monster !' However, they would soon grow familiarized to it, and probably hold it in as little respect as they were wished to do. They would find it on many occasions ' a very shallow monster,' and particularly ' a most poor *credulous* monster,' — while Your Lordship, as keeper, would enjoy every advantage and profit that could be made of it. You would have the benefit of the *two voices,* which would be the MONSTER's great excellencies, and would be peculiarly serviceable to Your Lordship. With the ' forward voice ' you would aptly promulgate those vigorous schemes and productive resources, in which Your Lordship's fancy is so pregnant; while ' the backward voice ' might be kept solely for *recantation.* The MONSTER, to maintain its character, must appear no novice in the science of flattery, or in the talents of servility, — and while it could never scruple to bear any burdens Your Lordship should please to lay on it, you would always, on the *approach of a storm,* find a shelter under its gabardine."

The most celebrated of these papers was the attack upon Lord George Germaine, written also by Mr. Sheridan, — a composition which, for unaffected strength of style and earnestness of feeling, may claim a high rank among the models of political vituperation. To every generation its own contemporary press seems always more licentious than any that had preceded it; but it may be questioned, whether the boldness of modern libel has ever gone beyond the direct and undisguised personality, with which one cabinet minister was called a liar and another a coward, in this and other writings of the popular party at that period. The following is the concluding paragraph of this paper against Lord George Germaine, which is in the form of a Letter to the Freeholders of England : —

" It would be presuming too much on your attention, at present, to enter into an investigation of the measures and system of war which this minister has pursued, — these shall certainly be the subject of a future paper. At present I shall only observe that, however mortifying it may be to reflect on the ignominy and disasters which this inauspicious character has brought on his country, yet there are consoling circumstances to be drawn even from his ill success. The calamities which may be laid to his account are certainly great; but, had the case been otherwise, it may fairly be questioned whether the example of a degraded and reprobated officer (preposterously elevated to one of the first stations of honour and confidence in the state) directing the military enterprizes of this country with unlooked-for prosperity, might not ultimately be the cause of more extensive evils than even those, great as they are, which we at present experience: whether from so fatal a precedent we might not be led to introduce characters under similar disqualifications into every department: — to appoint Atheists to the mitre, *Jews* to the exchequer, — to select a treasury-bench from the *Justitia*, to place *Brown Dignam* on the woolsack, and Sir Hugh Palliser at the head of the admiralty."

The Englishman, as might be expected from the pursuits and habits of those concerned in it, was not very punctually conducted, and, after many apologies from the publisher for its not appearing at the stated times (Wednesdays and Saturdays), ceased altogether on the 2d of June. From an imperfect sketch of a new Number, found among Mr. Sheridan's manuscripts, it appears that there was an intention of reviving it a short time after — probably towards the autumn of the same year, from the following allusion to Mr. Gibbon, whose acceptance of a seat at the Board of Trade took place, if I recollect right, in the summer of 1779 : —

" This policy is very evident among the majority in both houses, who, though they make no scruple in private to acknowledge the total incapacity of ministers, yet, in

public, speak and vote as if they believed them to have
every virtue under heaven; and, on this principle, some
gentlemen, — as Mr. Gibbon, for instance, — while, in
private, they indulge their opinion pretty freely, will yet,
in their zeal for the public good, even condescend to
accept a place, in order to give a colour to their confidence in the wisdom of the government."

It is needless to say that Mr. Sheridan had
been for some time among the most welcome
guests at Devonshire-House, — that rendezvous
of all the wits and beauties of fashionable life,
where Politics was taught to wear its most attractive form, and sat enthroned, like Virtue,
among the Epicureans, with all the Graces and
Pleasures for handmaids.

Without any disparagement of the many and
useful talents, which are at present no where
more conspicuous than in the upper ranks of
society, it may be owned that for wit, social
powers, and literary accomplishments, the political men of the period under consideration
formed such an assemblage as it would be flattery to say that our own times can parallel. The
natural tendency of the French Revolution was
to produce in the higher classes of England an
increased reserve of manner, and, of course, a
proportionate restraint on all within their circle,
which have been fatal to conviviality and humour, and not very propitious to wit — subduing

both manners and conversation to a sort of polished level, to rise above which is often thought almost as vulgar as to sink below it. Of the greater ease of manners that existed some forty or fifty years ago, one trifling, but not the less significant indication, was the habit, then prevalent among men of high station, of calling each other by such familiar names as Dick, Jack, Tom, &c.* — a mode of address, that brings with it, in its very sound, the notion of conviviality and playfulness, and, however, unrefined, implies at least, that ease and *sea-room*, in which wit spreads its canvass most fearlessly.

With respect to literary accomplishments, too, — in one branch of which, poetry, almost all the leading politicians of that day distinguished themselves — the change that has taken place in the times, independently of any want of such talent, will fully account for the difference that we witness, in this respect, at present. As the public mind becomes more intelligent and watchful, statesmen can the less afford to trifle with their talents, or to bring suspicion upon their fitness for their own vocation, by the failures which they risk in deviating into others. Besides, in poetry, the temptation of distinction no longer exists, — the commonness of that

* Dick Sheridan, Ned Burke, Jack Townshend, Tom Grenville, &c. &c.

talent in the market, at present, being such
as to reduce the value of an elegant copy of
verses, very far below the price it was at when
Mr. Hayley enjoyed an almost exclusive monopoly of the article.

In the clever Epistle, by Tickell, " from the
Hon. Charles Fox, partridge-shooting, to the
Hon. John Townshend, cruising," some of .the
most shining persons in that assemblage of wits
and statesmen, who gave a lustre to Brooks's
Club-House at the period of which we are
speaking, are thus agreeably grouped : —

" Soon as to Brooks's * thence thy footsteps bend,
  What gratulations thy approach attend !
  See Gibbon rap his box — auspicious sign
  That classic compliment and wit combine ;
  See Beauclerc's cheek a tinge of red surprize,
  And friendship give what cruel health denies ; —
      *   *   *   *
      *   *   *   *

  On that auspicious night, supremely grac'd
  With chosen guests, the pride of liberal taste,

* The well-known lines on Brooks himself are perhaps
the perfection of this drawing-room style of humour : —

" And know, I've bought the best champagne from Brooks ;
  From liberal Brooks, whose speculative skill
  Is hasty credit, and a distant bill ;
  Who nurs'd in clubs, disdains a vulgar trade,
  Exults to trust, and blushes to be paid."

Not in contentious heat, nor madd'ning strife,
Not with the busy ills, nor cares of life,
We'll waste the fleeting hours — far happier themes
Shall claim each thought and chase ambition's dreams.
Each *beauty* that *sublimity* can boast
He best shall tell, who still unites them most.
Of wit, of taste, of fancy we'll debate,
If Sheridan, for once, be not too late:
But scarce a thought on politics we'll spare,
Unless on Polish politics, with Hare.
Good-natured Devon! oft shall then appear
The cool complacence of thy friendly sneer:
Oft shall Fitzpatrick's wit and Stanhope's ease
And Burgoyne's manly sense unite to please.
And while each guest attends our various feats
Of scattered covies and retreating fleets,
Me shall they wish some better sport to gain,
And Thee more glory, from the next campaign."

In the society of such men the destiny of
Mr. Sheridan could not be long in fixing. On
the one side, his own keen thirst for distinction,
and, on the other, a quick and sanguine appreciation of the service that such talents might
render in the warfare of party, could not fail to
hasten the result that both desired.

His first appearance before the public as a
political character was in conjunction with
Mr. Fox, at the beginning of the year 1780,
when the famous Resolutions on the State of the
Representation, signed by Mr. Fox as chairman
of the Westminster Committee, together with a

Report on the same subject from the Sub-Committee, signed by Sheridan, were laid before the public. Annual parliaments and Universal Suffrage were the professed objects of this meeting ; and the first of the Resolutions, subscribed by Mr. Fox, stated that " Annual Parliaments are the undoubted right of the people of England."

Notwithstanding this strong declaration, it may be doubted whether Sheridan was, any more than Mr. Fox, a very sincere friend to the principle of Reform ; and the manner in which he masked his disinclination or indifference to it was strongly characteristic both of his humour and his tact. Aware that the wild scheme of Cartwright and others, which these Resolutions recommended, was wholly impracticable, he always took refuge in it when pressed upon the subject, and would laughingly advise his political friends to do the same : —— " Whenever any one," he would say, " proposes to you a specific plan of Reform, always answer that you are for nothing short of Annual Parliaments and Universal Suffrage — there you are safe." He also had evident delight, when talking on this question, in referring to a jest of Burke, who said that there had arisen a new party of Reformers, still more orthodox than the rest, who thought Annual Parliaments far from being sufficiently frequent, and who, founding themselves on the latter words of the statute of Edward III., that " a parliament shall be holden every year once, and *more often if need be*," were known by the denomination of the *Oftener-if-need-bes*. " For my part," he would add, in relating this, " I am an Oftener-if-need-be." Even when most serious on the subject (for, to the last, he professed himself a warm friend to Reform) his arguments had the air of being ironical and insidious. To Annual Parliaments and Universal Suffrage, he would say, the principles of representation naturally and necessarily led, — any less extensive proposition was a base compromise and a dereliction of right ; and the first encroachment on the people was the act of Henry VI., which limited the power of election to forty-shilling freeholders within the county, whereas the real right was in the " outrageous and excessive " number of people, by whom the preamble recites * that the choice had been made of late. — Such were the arguments by which he affected to support his cause, and it is not difficult to detect the eyes of the snake glistening from under them.

* " Elections of knights of shires have now of late been made by very great outrageous and excessive number of people, dwelling within the same counties, of the which most part was people of small substance and of no value." 8 H. 6. c. 7.

The Dissolution of Parliament that took place in the autumn of this year (1780) afforded at length the opportunity to which his ambition had so eagerly looked forward. It has been said, I know not with what accuracy, that he first tried his chance of election at Honiton — but Stafford was the place destined to have the honour of first choosing him for its representative ; and it must have been no small gratification to his independent spirit, that, unfurnished as he was with claims from past political services, he appeared in parliament, not as the nominee of any aristocratic patron, but as member for a borough, which, whatever might be its purity in other respects, at least enjoyed the freedom of choice. Elected conjointly with Mr. Monckton, to whose interest and exertions he chiefly owed his success, he took his seat in the new parliament which met in the month of October ; — and, from that moment giving himself up to the pursuit of politics, bid adieu to the worship of the Dramatic Muse for ever : —

> " *Comœdia luget ;*
> *Scena est deserta : hinc ludus risusque jocusque*
> *Et numeri innumeri simul omnes collacrumarunt.*"

Comedy mourns — the Stage neglected sleeps —
Ev'n Mirth in tears his languid laughter steeps,
And Song, through all her various empire, weeps.

CHAP. VII.

UNFINISHED PLAYS AND POEMS.

BEFORE I enter upon the sketch of Mr. Sheridan's political life, I shall take this opportunity of laying before the reader such information with respect to his unfinished literary designs, both dramatic and poetic, as the papers in my possession enable me to communicate.

Some of his youthful attempts in literature have already been mentioned, and there is a dramatic sketch of his, founded on The Vicar of Wakefield, which, from a date on the manuscript (1768), appears to have been produced at a still earlier age, and when he was only in his seventeenth year. A scene of this piece will be sufficient to show how very soon his talent for lively dialogue displayed itself: —

" SCENE II.

" THORNHILL *and* ARNOLD.

" *Thornhill.* Nay, prithee, Jack, no more of that if you love me. What, shall I stop short with the game in full view? Faith, I believe the fellow's turned puritan. What think you of turning methodist, Jack? You have a tolerable good canting countenance, and, if escaped being taken up for a Jesuit, you might make a fortune in Moorfields.

" *Arnold.* I was serious, Tom.

" *Thorn.* Splenetic you mean. Come, fill your glass, and a truce to your preaching. Here's a pretty fellow has let his conscience sleep for these five years, and has now plucked morality from the leaves of his grandmother's bible, beginning to declaim against what he has practised half his life-time. Why, I tell you once more, my schemes are all come to perfection. I am now convinced Olivia loves me — at our last conversation, she said she would rely wholly on my honour.

" *Arn.* And therefore you would deceive her.

" *Thorn.* Why no — deceive her? — why — indeed — as to that — but — but, for God's sake, let me hear no more on this subject, for 'faith, you make me sad, Jack. If you continue your admonitions, I shall begin to think you have yourself an eye on the girl. You have promised me your assistance, and, when you came down into the country, were as hot on the scheme as myself : but, since you have been two or three times with me at Primrose's, you have fallen off strangely. No encroachments, Jack, on my little rosebud — if you have a mind to beat up game in this quarter, there's her sister — but no poaching.

" *Arn.* I am not insensible to her sister's merit, but have no such views as you have. However, you have promised me that if you find in this lady that real virtue which you so firmly deny to exist in the sex, you will give up the pursuit, and, foregoing the low consider-ations of fortune, make atonement by marriage.

" *Thorn.* Such is my serious resolution.

" *Arn.* I wish you'd forego the experiment. But, you have been so much in raptures with your success, that I have, as yet, had no clear account how you came acquainted in the family.

" *Thorn.* Oh, I'll tell you immediately. You know Lady Patchet?

" *Arn.* What, is she here?

" *Thorn.* It was by her I was first introduced. It seems that, last year, her ladyship's reputation began to suffer a little; so that she thought it prudent to retire for a while, till people learned better manners or got worse memories. She soon became acquainted with this little family, and, as the wife is a prodigious admirer of quality, grew in a short time to be very intimate, and, imagining that she may one day make her market of the girls, has much ingratiated herself with them. She introduced me — I drank, and abused this degenerate age with the father — promised wonders to the mother for all her brats — praised her gooseberry wine, and ogled the daughters, by which means in three days I made the progress I related to you.

" *Arn.* You have been expeditious indeed. I fear where that devil Lady Patchet is concerned there can be no good — but is there not a son?

" *Thorn.* Oh! the most ridiculous creature in na-ture. He has been bred in the country a bumpkin all his life, till within these six years, when he was sent to the University, but the misfortunes that have reduced his father falling out, he is returned, the most ridiculous animal you ever saw, a conceited, disputing blockhead. So there is no great matter to fear from *his* penetration.

But come, let us begone, and see this moral family, we shall meet them coming from the field, and you will see a man who was once in affluence, maintaining by hard labour a numerous family.

"*Arn.* Oh! Thornhill, can you wish to add infamy to their poverty? [*Exeunt.*"

There also remain among his papers three Acts of a Drama, without a name, — written evidently in haste, and with scarcely any correction, — the subject of which is so wild and unmanageable, that I should not have hesitated in referring it to the same early date, had not the introduction into one of the scenes of "Dry be that tear, be hush'd that sigh," proved it to have been produced after that pretty song was written.

The chief personages upon whom the story turns are a band of outlaws, who, under the name and disguise of *Devils*, have taken up their residence in a gloomy wood, adjoining a village, the inhabitants of which they keep in perpetual alarm by their incursions and apparitions. In the same wood resides a hermit, secretly connected with this band, who keeps secluded within his cave the beautiful Reginilla, hid alike from the light of the sun and the eyes of men. She has, however, been indulged in her prison with a glimpse of a handsome young huntsman, whom she believes to be a phantom, and is encouraged in her belief by the hermit, by whose contrivance this huntsman (a prince in disguise) has been thus presented to her. The following is — as well as I can make it out from a manuscript not easily decipherable — the scene that takes place between the fair recluse and her visitant. The style, where style is attempted, shows, as the reader will perceive, a taste yet immature and unchastened : —

" *Scene draws, and discovers* REGINILLA *asleep in the Cave.*

" *Enter* PEVIDOR *and other Devils, with the* HUNTSMAN *— unbind him, and exeunt.*

" *Hunts.* Ha ! Where am I now ? Is it indeed the dread abode of guilt, or refuge of a band of thieves ? it cannot be a dream. (*sees* REGINILLA.) Ha ! if this be so, and I *do* dream, may I never wake — it is — my beating heart acknowledges my dear, gentle Reginilla. I'll not wake her, lest, if it be a phantom, it should vanish. Oh, balmy breath ! but for thy soft sighs that come to tell me it is no image, I should believe . . . . . (*bends down towards her.*) a sigh from her heart ! — thus let me arrest thee on thy way. (*kisses her.*) A deeper blush has flushed her cheek — sweet modesty ! that even in sleep is conscious and resentful. — She will not wake, and yet some fancy calls up those frequent sighs — how her heart beats in its ivory cage, like an imprisoned bird — or as if to reprove the hand that dares approach its sanctuary ! Oh, would she but wake, and bless this gloom with her bright eyes ! — Soft, here's a lute — perhaps her soul will hear the call of harmony.

* " Oh yield, fair lids, the treasures of my heart,
   Release those beams, that make this mansion bright;
From her sweet sense, Slumber! tho' sweet thou art,
   Begone, and give the air she breathes in light.

" Or while, oh Sleep, thou dost those glances hide,
   Let rosy slumbers still around her play,
Sweet as the cherub Innocence enjoy'd,
   When in thy lap, new-born, in smiles he lay.

" And thou, oh Dream, that com'st her sleep to cheer,
   Oh take my shape, and play a lover's part;
Kiss her from me, and whisper in her ear,
   Till her eyes shine, 'tis night within my heart.

" *Reg.* (*waking.*) The phantom, father! (*seizes his hand.*) ah, do not, do not wake me then. (*rises.*)
" *Hunts.* (*kneeling to her.*) Thou beauteous sun of this dark world, that mak'st a place, so like the cave of death, a heaven to me, instruct me how I may approach thee — how address thee and not offend.
" *Reg.* Oh how my soul would hang upon those lips! speak on — and yet, methinks, he should not kneel so — why are you afraid, sir? indeed, I cannot hurt you.
" *Hunts.* Sweet innocence, I'm sure thou would'st not.

* I have taken the liberty here of supplying a few rhymes and words that are wanting in the original copy of the song. The last line of all runs thus in the manuscript : —

   " Till her eye shines I live in darkest night."

which, not rhyming as it ought, I have ventured to alter as above.

"*Reg.* Art thou not he to whom I told my name, and didst thou not say thine was —

"*Hunts.* Oh blessed be the name that then thou told'st — it has been ever since my charm, and kept me from distraction. But, may I ask how such sweet excellence as thine could be hid in such a place?

"*Reg.* Alas, I know not — for such as thou I never saw before, nor any like myself.

"*Hunts.* Nor like thee ever shall — but would'st thou leave this place, and live with such as I am?

"*Reg.* Why may not you live here with such as I?

"*Hunts.* Yes — but I would carry thee where all above an azure canopy extends, at night bedropt with gems, and one more glorious lamp, that yields such bashful light as love enjoys — while underneath, a carpet shall be spread of flowers to court the pressure of thy step, with such sweet whispered invitations from the leaves of shady groves or murmuring of silver streams, that thou shalt think thou are in Paradise.

"*Reg.* Indeed!

"*Hunts.* Ay, and I'll watch and wait on thee all day, and cull the choicest flowers, which while thou bind'st in the mysterious knot of love, I'll tune for thee no vulgar lays, or tell thee tales shall make thee weep yet please thee — while thus I press thy hand, and warm it thus with kisses.

"*Reg.* I doubt thee not — but then my Governor has told me many a tale of faithless men who court a lady but to steal her peace and fame, and then to leave her.

"*Hunts.* Oh never such as thou art — witness all . . .

"*Reg.* Then wherefore could'st thou not live here? For I do feel, though tenfold darkness did surround this spot, I could be blest, would you but stay here; and, if it made you sad to be imprison'd thus, I'd sing and play for thee, and dress thee sweetest fruits, and, though you chid me, would kiss thy tear away and hide my blushing face upon thy bosom — indeed, I would. Then what avails the gaudy day, and all the evil things I'm told inhabit there, to those who have within themselves all that delight and love, and heaven can give?

" *Hunts.* My angel, thou hast indeed the soul of love.

" *Reg.* It is no ill thing, is it?

" *Hunts.* Oh most divine — it is the immediate gift of heaven, which steals into our breast   *   *

    *   *   *   *   *

'tis that which makes me sigh thus, look thus — fear and tremble for thee.

" *Reg.* Sure I should learn it too, if you would teach me.

              " (*Sound of horn without — Huntsman starts.*

" *Reg.*   You must not go — this is but a dance preparing for my amusement — oh we have, indeed, some pleasures here — come, I will sing for you the while.

               " *Song.*

" Wilt thou then leave me? canst thou go from me,
    To woo the fair that love the gaudy day?
Yet, ev'n among those joys, thou'lt find that she,
    Who dwells in darkness, loves thee more than they.
For these poor hands, and these unpractised eyes
And this poor heart is thine without disguise.

" But, if thou'lt stay with me, my only care
    Shall be to please and make thee love to stay
    With music, song, and dance   *   *
  *   *   *   *   *

  But, if you go, nor music, song, nor dance,
  *   *   *   *   *

" If thou art studious, I will read
Thee tales of pleasing woe —
If thou art sad, I'll kiss away
The tears . . . . . . that flow.

" If thou would'st play, I'll kiss thee till I blush,
Then hide that blush upon thy breast,
If thou would'st sleep . . . . . .
Shall rock thy aching head to rest.

" *Hunts.* My soul's wonder, I will never leave thee.

" (*The Dance. — Allemande by two Bears.*)

" *Enter* PEVIDOR.

" *Pev.* So fond, so soon ! I cannot bear to see it.
What ho, within, (*Devils enter.*) secure him.
" (*Seize and bind the Huntsman.*"

The Duke or sovereign of the country, where these events are supposed to take place, arrives at the head of a military force, for the purpose of investing the haunted wood, and putting down, as he says, those " lawless renegades, who, in infernal masquerade, make a hell around him." He is also desirous of consulting the holy hermit of the wood, and availing himself of his pious consolations and prayers — being haunted with remorse for having criminally gained possession of the crown by contriving the shipwreck of the rightful heir, and then banishing from the court his most virtuous counsellors. In addition to these causes of dis-

quietude, he has lately lost, in a mysterious manner, his only son, who, he supposes, has fallen a
victim to these Satanic outlaws, but who, on the
contrary, it appears, has voluntarily become an
associate of their band, and is amusing himself,
heedless of his noble father's sorrow, by making
love, in the disguise of a dancing bear, to a
young village coquette of the name of Mopsa.
A short specimen of the manner, in which this
last farcical incident is managed, will show how
wide even Sheridan was, at first, of that true
vein of comedy, which, on searching deeper into
the mine, he so soon afterwards found : —

" SCENE.— *The Inside of the Cottage.* — MOPSA, LUBIN
(*her father*), *and* COLIN (*her lover*), *discovered.*

" *Enter* PEVIDOR, *leading the Bear, and singing.*

" And he dances, dances, dances,
    And goes upright like a Christian swain,
And he shows you pretty fancies,
    Nor ever tries to shake off his chain.

" *Lubin.* Servant, master. Now, Mopsa, you are
happy — it is, indeed, a handsome creature. What
country does your bear come from ?
" *Pev.* Dis bear, please your worship, is of de race of
dat bear of St. Antony, who was de first convert he made
in de woods. St. Antony bade him never more meddle
with man, and de bear observed de command to his
dying day.
" *Lub.* Wonderful !

" *Pev.* Dis generation be all de same — all born widout toots.

" *Colin.* What, can't he bite? (*puts his finger to the Bear's mouth, who bites him.*) Oh Lord, no toots! why you ——

" *Pev.* Oh dat be only his gum.   (*Mopsa laughs.*

" *Col.* For shame, Mopsa — now, I say, Maister Lubin, mustn't she give me a kiss to make it well?

" *Lub.* Ay, kiss her, kiss her, Colin.

" *Col.* Come, Miss.

"   " (*Mopsa runs to the Bear, who kisses her.*"

The following scene of the Devils, drinking in their subterraneous dwelling, though cleverly imagined, is such as, perhaps, no cookery of style could render palateable to an English audience.

" SCENE. — *The Devils' Cave.*

" 1*st Dev.* Come, Urial, here's to our resurrection:

" 2*d Dev.* It is a toast I'd scarcely pledge — by my life, I think we're happier here.

" 3*d Dev.* Why, so think I — by Jove, I would despise the man, who could but wish to rise again to earth, unless we were to lord there.   What! sneaking pitiful in bondage, among vile money-scrapers, treacherous friends, fawning flatterers — or, still worse, deceitful mistresses. Shall we, who reign lords here, again lend ourselves to swell the train of tyranny and usurpation? By my old father's memory, I'd rather be the blindest mole that ever skulked in darkness, the lord of one poor hole where he might say ' I'm master here.'

" 2*d Dev.* You are too hot — where shall concord be

found, if even the devils disagree. — Come, fill the glass, and add thy harmony — while we have wine to enlighten us, the sun be hanged ! I never thought he gave so fine a light, for my part — and then, there are such vile inconveniences — high winds and storms, rains, &c.—oh hang it ! living on the outside of the earth is like sleeping on deck, when one might, like us, have a snug birth in the cabin.

" 1*st Dev.* True, true, — Helial, where is thy catch ?

" In the earth's center let me live,
   There, like a rabbit will I thrive,
Nor care if fools should call my life infernal ;
   While men on earth crawl lazily about,
   Like snails upon the surface of the nut,
We are, like maggots, feasting in the kernel.

" 1*st Dev.* Bravo, by this glass, Meli, what say you?
" 3*d Dev.* Come, here's to my Mina — I used to toast her in the upper regions.
" 1*st Dev.* Ay, we miss them here.

" *Glee.*

" What's a woman good for ?
   Rat me, sir, if I know.
   *   *   *   *   *

   She's a savour to the glass,
   An excuse to make it pass.
   *   *   *   *   *

" 1*st Dev.* I fear we are like the wits above, who abuse women only because they can't get them, — and, after all, it must be owned they are a pretty kind of creatures.
" *All.* Yes, yes.

" *Catch.*

" 'Tis woman after all
        Is the blessing of this ball,
    'Tis she keeps the balance of it even.
        We are devils, it is true,
        But had we women too,
    Our Tartarus would turn to a Heaven !"

A scene in the Third Act, where these devils bring the prisoners whom they have captured to trial, is an overcharged imitation of the satire of Fielding, and must have been written, I think, after a perusal of that author's Satirical Romance, " A Journey from this World to the Next," — the first half of which contains as much genuine humour and fancy as are to be found in any other production of the kind. The interrogatories of Minos in that work suggested, I suspect, the following scene : —

" *Enter a number of Devils.— Others bring in* LUDOVICO.

" 1*st Dev.* Just taken, in the wood, sir, with two more.

" *Chorus of Devils.*

" Welcome, welcome   *   *
    *   *   *   *   *   *

" *Pev.* What art thou ?
" *Ludov.* I went for a man in the other world.
" *Pev.* What sort of man ?
" *Ludov.* A soldier at your service.

" *Pev.* Wast thou in the battle of —— ?

" *Ludov.* Truly I was.

" *Pev.* What was the quarrel ?

" *Ludov.* I never had time to ask. The children of peace, who make our quarrels, must be Your Worship's informants there.

" *Pev.* And art thou not ashamed to draw the sword for thou know'st not what—and to be the victim and food of others' folly ?

· " *Ludov.* Vastly.

" *Pev. (to the Devils.)* Well, take him for to-day, and only score his skin and pepper it with powder—then chain him to a cannon, and let the Devils practise at his head — his be the reward who hits it with a single ball.

" *Ludov.* Oh mercy, mercy !

" *Pev.* Bring Savodi.

" *(A Devil brings in* Savodi.*)*

" *Chorus as before.*

" Welcome, welcome, &c.

" *Pev.* Who art thou ?

" *Sav.* A courtier at Your Grace's service.

" *Pev.* Your name ?

" *Sav.* Savodi, an' please Your Highnesses.

" *Pev.* Your use ?

" *Sav.* A foolish utensil of state — a clock kept in the waiting-chamber, to count the hours.

" *Pev.* Are you not one of those who fawn and lie, and cringe like spaniels to those a little higher, and take revenge by tyranny on all beneath ?

" *Sav.* Most true, Your Highnesses.

" *Pev.* Is't not thy trade to promise what thou canst not do, — to gull the credulous of money, to shut the royal door on unassuming merit — to catch the scandal for thy master's ear, and stop the people's voice ....

" *Sav.* Exactly, an' please Your Highnesses' Worships.

" *Pev.* Thou dost not now deny it?

" *Sav.* Oh no, no, no.

" *Pev.* Here — baths of flaming sulphur ! — quick — stir up the cauldron of boiling lead — this crime deserves it.

" 1*st Dev.* Great Judge of this infernal place, allow him but the mercy of the court.

" *Sav.* Oh kind Devil ! — yes, Great Judge, allow.

" 1*st Dev.* The punishment is undergone already — truth from him is something.

" *Sav.* Oh, most unusual — sweet Devil !

" 1*st Dev.* Then, he is tender, and might not be able to endure —

" *Sav.* Endure ! I shall be annihilated by the thoughts of it — dear Devil.

" 1*st Dev.* Then let him, I beseech you, in scalding brimstone be first soaked a little, to inure and prepare him for the other.

" *Sav.* Oh hear me, hear me.

" *Pev.* Well, be it so.

" (*Devils take him out and bring in* PAMPHILES.)

" *Pev.* This is he we rescued from the ladies — a dainty one, I warrant.

" *Pamphil.* (*affectedly.*) This is Hell certainly by the smell.

" *Pev.* What, art thou a soldier too?

" *Pamphil.* No, on my life — a Colonel, but no soldier — innocent even of a review, as I exist.

" *Pev.* How rose you then? come, come — the truth.

" *Pamphil.* Nay, be not angry, sir — if I was preferred it was not my fault — upon my soul, I never did any thing to incur preferment.

" *Pev.* Indeed! what was thy employment then, friend?

" *Pamphil.* Hunting —

" *Pev.* 'Tis false.

" *Pamphil.* Hunting women's reputations.

" *Pev.* What, thou wert amorous?

" *Pamphil.* No, on my honour, sir, but vain, confounded vain — the character of bringing down my game was all I wished, and, like a true sportsman, I would have given my birds to my pointers.

" *Pev.* This crime is new — what shall we do with him?" &c. &c.

This singular Drama does not appear to have been ever finished. With respect to the winding up of the story, the hermit, we may conclude, would have turned out to be the banished counsellor, and the devils, his followers; while the young huntsman would most probably have proved to be the rightful heir of the dukedom.

In a more crude and unfinished state are the fragments that remain of his projected opera, " The Foresters." To this piece, (which appears to have been undertaken at a later period than the preceding one,) Mr. Sheridan often alluded in conversation — particularly when any regret was expressed at his having ceased to assist Old Drury with his pen, — " wait, he would say smiling) till I bring out my Foresters." The plot, as far as can be judged from the few meagre scenes that exist, was intended to be an improvement upon that of the Drama just described — the Devils being transformed into Foresters, and the action commencing, not with the loss of a son but the recovery of a daughter, who had fallen by accident into the hands of these freebooters. At the opening of the piece the young lady has just been restored to her father by the heroic Captain of the Foresters, with no other loss than that of her heart, which she is suspected of having left with her preserver. The list of the Dramatis Personæ (to which however he did not afterwards adhere) is as follows : —

> Old Oscar.
> Young Oscar.
> Colona.
> Morven.
> Harold.
> Nico.
> Miza.
> Malvina.
> Allanda.
> Dorcas.
> Emma.

To this strange medley of nomenclature is appended a memorandum—" *Vide* Petrarch for names."

The first scene represents the numerous lovers

of Malvina rejoicing at her return, and celebrat-
ing it by a chorus; after which, Oscar, her father,
holds the following dialogue with one of them: —

"*Osc.* I thought, son, you would have been among
the first and most eager to see Malvina upon her return.

"*Colin.* Oh father, I would give half my flock to think
that my presence would be welcome to her.

"*Osc.* I am sure you have never seen her prefer any
one else.

. "*Col.* There's the torment of it — were I but once
sure that she loved another better, I think I should be
content — at least she should not know but that I was
so. My love is not of that jealous sort that I should
pine to see her happy with another — nay, I could even
regard the man that would make her so.

"*Osc.* Haven't you spoke with her since her return?

"*Col.* Yes, and I think she is colder to me than ever.
My professions of love used formerly to make her laugh,
but now they make her weep — formerly she seemed
wholly insensible; now, alas! she seems to feel — but as
if addressed by the wrong person," &c. &c.

In a following scene are introduced two brothers, both equally enamoured of the fair Malvina, yet preserving their affection unaltered
towards each other. With the recollection of
Sheridan's own story fresh in our minds, we
might suppose that he meant some reference to
it in this incident, were it not for the exceeding
niaiserie that he has thrown into the dialogue.
For instance: —

" *Osc.* But we are interrupted — here are two more of her lovers — brothers, and rivals, but friends.

" *Enter* Nico *and* Lubin.

" So, Nico — how comes it you are so late in your enquiries after your mistress?

" *Nic.* I should have been sooner; but Lubin would stay to make himself fine — though he knows he has no chance of appearing so to Malvina.

" *Lubin.* No, in truth — Nico says right — I have no more chance than himself.

" *Osc.* However, I am glad to see you reconciled, and that you live together, as brothers should do.

" *Nico.* Yes, ever since we found your daughter cared for neither of us, we grew to care for one another. There is a fellowship in adversity that is consoling; and it is something to think that Lubin is as unfortunate as myself.

" *Lub.* Yes, we are well matched — I think Malvina dislikes him, if possible more than me, and that's a great comfort.

" *Nico.* We often sit together, and play such woeful tunes on our pipes, that the very sheep are moved at it.

" *Osc.* But why don't you rouse yourselves, and since you can meet with no requital of your passion, return the proud maid scorn for scorn.

" *Nico.* Oh mercy, no — we find a great comfort in our sorrow — don't we, Lubin?

" *Lubin.* Yes, if I meet no crosses, I shall be undone in another twelvemonth — I let all go to wreck and ruin.

" *Osc.* But suppose Malvina should be brought to give you encouragement.

" *Nico.* Heaven forbid! that would spoil all.

"*Lubin.* Truly I was almost assured within this fortnight that she was going to relax.

"*Nico.* Ay, I shall never forget how alarmed we were at the appearance of a smile one day," &c. &c.

Of the poetical part of this opera, the only specimens he has left are a skeleton of a chorus, beginning "Bold Foresters we are," and the following song, which, for grace and tenderness, is not unworthy of the hand that produced The Duenna : —

> " We two, each other's only pride,
> Each other's bliss, each other's guide,
> Far from the world's unhallow'd noise,
> Its coarse delights and tainted joys,
> Through wilds will roam and deserts rude —
> For, Love, thy home is solitude.

> " There shall no vain pretender be,
> To court thy smile and torture me,
> No proud superior there be seen, ,
> But nature's voice shall hail thee, queen.

> " With fond respect and tender awe,
> I will receive thy gentle law,
> Obey thy looks, and serve thee still,
> Prevent thy wish, foresee thy will,
> And, added to a lover's care,
> Be all that friends and parents are."

But, of all Mr. Sheridan's unfinished designs, the Comedy which he meditated on the subject of Affectation is that of which the abandonment is most to be regretted. To a satirist, who would not confine his ridicule to the mere outward demonstrations of this folly, but would follow and detect it through all its windings and disguises, there could hardly perhaps be a more fertile theme. Affectation, merely of *manner*, being itself a sort of acting, does not easily admit of any additional colouring on the stage, without degenerating into farce ; and, accordingly, fops and fine ladies — with very few exceptions — are about as silly and tiresome in representation as in reality. But the aim of the dramatist, in this comedy, would have been far more important and extensive ; — and how anxious he was to keep before his mind's eye the whole wide horizon of folly which his subject opened upon him, will appear from the following list of the various species of Affectation, which I have found written by him, exactly as I give it, on the inside cover of the memorandum-book, that contains the only remaining vestiges of this play : —

" An Affectation of Business.
    of Accomplishments.
    of Love of Letters and Wit.
       Music.
    of Intrigue.
    of Sensibility.
    of Vivacity.
    of Silence and Importance.
    of Modesty.
    of Profligacy.
    of Moroseness."

In this projected comedy he does not seem to have advanced as far as even the invention of the plot, or the composition of a single scene. The memorandum-book alluded to—on the first leaf of which he had written in his neatest hand (as if to encourage himself to begin) " Affectation" — contains, besides the names of three of the intended personages, Sir Babble Bore, Sir Peregrine Paradox, and Feignwit, nothing but unembodied sketches of character, and scattered particles of wit, which seem waiting, like the imperfect forms and seeds in chaos, for the brooding of genius to nurse them into system and beauty.

The reader will not, I think, be displeased at seeing some of these curious materials here. They will show that in this work, as well as in The School for Scandal, he was desirous of making the vintage of his wit as rich as possible, by distilling into it every drop that the collected fruits of his thought and fancy could supply. Some of the jests are far-fetched, and others, perhaps, abortive—but it is pleasant to track him in his pursuit of a point, even when he misses. The very failures of a man of real wit are often more delightful than the best successes of others— the quicksilver, even in escaping from his grasp, shines; " it still eludes him, but it glitters still."

I shall give the memorandums as I find them,

with no other difference, than that of classing together those that have relation to the same thought or subject.

" *Character.* — Mr. Bustle.

" A man who delights in hurry and interruption — will take any one's business for them — leaves word where all his plagues may follow him — governor of all hospitals, &c. — share in Ranelagh — speaker every where, from the Vestry to the House of Commons — ' I am not at home — gad, now he has heard me and I must be at home.' — ' Here am I so plagued, and there is nothing I love so much as retirement and quiet.' — ' You never sent after me.' — Let servants call in to him such a message as ' 'Tis nothing but the window-tax,' he hiding in a room that communicates. — A young man tells him some important business in the middle of fifty trivial interruptions, and the calling in of idlers; such as fiddlers, wild-beast men, foreigners with recommendatory letters, &c. — answers notes on his knee, ' and so your uncle died ? — for your obliging enquiries — and left you an orphan — to cards in the evening.'

" Can't bear to be doing nothing. — ' Can I do anything for any body any where ? ' — ' Have been to the Secretary — written to the Treasury.' — ' Must proceed to meet the Commissioners, and write Mr. Price's little boy's exercise.' — The most active idler and laborious trifler.

" He does not in reality love business — only the appearance of it, ' Ha ! ha ! did my Lord say that I was always very busy ? — What, plagued to death ? '

" Keeps all his letters and copies — ' Mem. To meet the Hackney-coach Commissioners — to arbitrate between, &c. &c.'

" Contrast with the man of indolence, his brother.—
' So, brother, just up ! and I have been, &c. &c.'— one
will give his money from indolent generosity, the other
his time from restlessness — ' 'Twill be shorter to pay
the bill than look for the receipt.'— Files letters, answered and unanswered — ' Why, here are more un-
opened than answered !'

" He regulates every action by a love for fashion —
will grant annuities though he doesn't want money —
appear to intrigue, though constant ; to drink, though
sober — has some fashionable vices — affects to be distressed in his circumstances, and, when his new vis-à-vis
comes out, procures a judgment to be entered against
him — wants to lose, but by ill-luck wins five thousand
pounds.

" One who changes sides in all arguments the moment any one agrees with him.
" An irresolute arguer, to whom it is a great misfortune that there are not three sides to a question — a
libertine in argument ; conviction, like enjoyment, palls
him, and his rakish understanding is soon satiated with
truth — more capable of being faithful to a paradox —
' I love truth as I do my wife ; but sophistry and pa-
radoxes are my mistresses — I have a strong domestic
respect for her, but for the other the passion due to a
mistress.'
" One, who agrees with every one, for the pleasure
of speaking their sentiments for them — so fond of talking that he does not contradict only because he can't
wait to hear people out.
" A tripping casuist, who veers by others' breath, and

gets on to information by tacking between the two sides — like a hoy, not made to go straight before the wind.

" The more he talks, the farther he is off the argument, like a bowl on a wrong bias.

" What are the affectations you chiefly dislike?

" There are many in this company, so I'll mention others. — To see two people affecting intrigue, having their assignations in public places only; he, affecting a warm pursuit, and the lady, acting the hesitation of retreating virtue —' Pray, ma'am, don't you think, &c.' — while neither party have words between 'em to conduct the preliminaries of gallantry, nor passion to pursue the object of it.

" A plan of public flirtation — not to get beyond a profile.

" Then I hate to see one, to whom heaven has given real beauty, settling her features at the glass of fashion, while she speaks — not thinking so much of what she says as how she looks, and more careful of the action of her lips than of what shall come from them.

" A pretty woman studying looks and endeavouring to recollect an ogle, like Lady ——, who has learned to play her eyelids like Venetian blinds.*

" An old woman endeavouring to put herself back to a girl.

" A true trained wit lays his plan like a general — foresees the circumstances of the conversation — sur-

---

* This simile is repeated in various shapes through his manuscripts — " She moves her eyes up and down like Venetian blinds." — " Her eyelids play like a Venetian blind," &c. &c.

veys the ground and contingencies — detaches a question to draw you into the palpable ambuscade of his ready-made joke.

" A man intriguing, only for the reputation of it — to his confidential servant: ' Who am I in love with now?' — ' The newspapers give you so and so — you are laying close siege to Lady L. in The Morning Post, and have succeeded with Lady G. in The Herald — Sir F. is very jealous of you in The Gazetteer.' — ' Remember to-morrow, the first thing you do, to put me in love with Mrs. C.'

" ' I forgot to forget the billet-doux at Brooks's. — ' By the bye, an't I in love with you?' — ' Lady L. has promised to meet me in her carriage to-morrow — where is the most public place?'

" ' You were rude to her!' — ' Oh no, upon my soul, I made love to her directly.'

" An old man, who affects intrigue, and writes his own reproaches in The Morning Post, trying to scandalise himself into the reputation of being young, as if he could obscure his age by blotting his character — though never so little candid as when he's abusing himself.

" ' Shall you be at Lady ——'s ? — I'm told the Bramin is to be there, and the new French philosopher.' — ' No — it will be pleasanter at Lady ——'s conversazione — the cow with two heads will be there.'

" ' I shall order my valet to shoot me the very first thing he does in the morning.'

" ' You are yourself affected and don't know it — you would pass for morose.'

" He merely wanted to be singular, and happened to find the character of moroseness unoccupied in the society he lived with.

" He certainly has a great deal of fancy and a very good memory; but with a perverse ingenuity he employs these qualities as no other person does — for he employs his fancy in his narratives, and keeps his recollections for his wit — when he makes his jokes you applaud the accuracy of his memory, and 'tis only when he states his facts, that you admire the flights of his imagination.*

" A fat woman trundling into a room on castors — in sitting can only lean against her chair — rings on her fingers, and her fat arms strangled with bracelets, which belt them like corded brawn — rolling and heaving when she laughs with the rattles in her throat, and a most apoplectic ogle — you wish to draw her out, as you would an opera-glass.

" A long lean man, with all his limbs rambling — no way to reduce him to compass, unless you could double him like a pocket rule — with his arms spread, he'd lie on the bed of Ware like a cross on a Good Friday bun — standing still, he is a pilaster without a base — he appears rolled out or run up against a wall — so thin, that his front face is but the moiety of a profile — if he stands cross-legged, he looks like a caduceus, and put him in a fencing attitude, you would take him for a piece of chevaux-de-frise — to make any use of him, it

* The reader will find how much this thought was improved upon afterwards.

must be as a spontoon or a fishing-rod—when his wife's by, he follows like a note of admiration — see them together, one's a mast, and the other all hulk — she's a dome and he's built like a glass-house—when they part, you wonder to see the steeple separate from the chancel, and were they to embrace, he must hang round her neck like a skein of thread on a lace-maker's bolster — to sing her praise you should choose a rondeau, and to celebrate him you must write all Alexandrines.

" I wouldn't give a pin to make fine men in love with me — every coquette can do that, and the pain you give these creatures is very trifling. I love out-of-the-way conquests ; and as I think my attractions are singular, I would draw singular objects.

" The loadstone of true beauty draws the heaviest substances — not like the fat dowager, who frets herself into warmth to get the notice of a few *papier mâché* fops as you rub Dutch sealing-wax to draw paper.

" If I were inclined to flatter I would say that, as you are unlike other women, you ought not to be won as they are. Every woman can be gained by time, therefore you ought to be by a sudden impulse. Sighs, devotion, attention weigh with others; but they are so much your due that no one should claim merit from them, ...

" You should not be swayed by common motives — how heroic to form a marriage for which no human being can guess the inducement — what a glorious unaccountableness ! all the world will wonder what the devil you could see in me; and, if you should doubt your singularity, I pledge myself to you that I never yet was endured by woman; so that I should owe every thing

to the effect of your bounty, and not by my own superfluous deserts make it a debt, and so lessen both the obligation and my gratitude. In short, every other woman
follows her inclination, but you, above all things, should
take me, if you do not like me. You will, besides, have
the satisfaction of knowing that we are decidedly the
worst match in the kingdom — a match, too, that must
be all your own work, in which fate could have no hand,
and which no foresight could foresee.

" A lady who affects poetry. — ' I made regular approaches to her by sonnets and rebusses — a rondeau of
circumvallation — her pride sapped by an elegy, and her
reserve surprised by an impromptu—proceeding to storm
with Pindarics, she, at last, saved the further effusion of
ink by a capitulation.'

" Her prudish frowns and resentful looks are as ridiculous as 'twould be to see a board with notice of spring-
guns set in a highway, or of steel-traps in a common —
because they imply an insinuation that there is something
worth plundering where one would not, in the least, suspect it.

" The expression of her face is at once a denial of all
love-suit, and a confession that she never was asked —
the sourness of it arises not so much from her aversion
to the passion, as from her never having had an opportunity to show it. — Her features are so unfortunately
formed that she could never dissemble or put on sweetness enough to induce any one to give her occasion to
show her bitterness. — I never saw a woman to whom
you would more readily give credit for perfect chastity.

" *Lady Clio.* ' What am I reading ? — have I drawn nothing lately ? — is the work-bag finished ? — how accomplished I am ! — has the man been to untune the harpsichord ? — does it look as if I had been playing on it ?

" ' Shall I be ill to-day ? — shall I be nervous ? ' — ' Your La'ship was nervous yesterday.' — ' Was I ? — then I'll have a cold — I haven't had a cold this fortnight — a cold is becoming — no — I'll not have a cough ; that's fatiguing — I'll be quite well.' — ' You become sickness — your La'ship always looks vastly well when you're ill.'

" ' Leave the book half read and the rose half finished — you know I love to be caught in the fact.'

" One who knows that no credit is ever given to his assertions has the more right to contradict his words.

" He goes the western circuit, to pick up small fees and impudence.

" A new wooden leg for Sir Charles Easy.

" An ornament which proud peers wear all the year round — chimney-sweepers only on the first of May.

" In marriage if you possess any thing very good, it makes you eager to get every thing else good of the same sort.

" The critic when he gets out of his carriage should always recollect, that his footman behind is gone up to judge as well as himself.

" She might have escaped in her own clothes, but I suppose she thought it more romantic to put on her brother's regimentals."

The rough sketches and fragments of poems, which Mr. Sheridan left behind him, are numerous; but those among them that are sufficiently finished to be cited, bear the marks of having been written when he was very young, and would not much interest the reader—while of the rest it is difficult to find four consecutive lines, that have undergone enough of the *toilette* of composition to be presentable in print. It was his usual practice, when he undertook any subject in verse, to write down his thoughts first in a sort of poetical prose,—with, here and there, a rhyme or a metrical line, as they might occur—and then, afterwards to reduce, with much labour, this anomalous compound to regular poetry. The birth of his prose being, as we have already seen, so difficult, it may be imagined how painful was the travail of his verse. Indeed, the number of tasks which he left unfinished are all so many proofs of that despair of perfection, which those best qualified to attain it are always the most likely to feel.

There are some fragments of an Epilogue, apparently intended to be spoken in the character of a woman of fashion, which give a lively notion of what the poem would have been when

complete.   The high carriages, that had just then
come into fashion, are thus adverted to : —

" My carriage stared at ! — none so high or fine —
  Palmer's mail-coach shall be a sledge to mine.
  *   * .   *   *   *   *
  No longer now the youths beside us stand,
  And talking lean, and leaning press the hand;
  But, ogling upward, as aloft we sit,
  Straining, poor things, their ancles and their wit,
  And, much too short the inside to explore,
  Hang like supporters half way up the door."

The approach of a " veteran husband," to
disturb these flirtations and chase away the
lovers, is then hinted at : —

" To persecuted virtue yield assistance,
  And for one hour teach younger men their distance,
  Make them, in very spite, appear discreet,
  And mar the public mysteries of the street."

The affectation of appearing to make love,
while talking on indifferent matters, is illustrated
by the following simile : —

" So when dramatic statesmen talk apart,
  With practis'd gesture and heroic start,
  The plot's their theme, the gaping galleries guess,
  While Hull and Fearon think of nothing less."

The following lines seem to belong to the same
Epilogue : —

" The Campus Martius of St. James's Street,
　Where the beau's cavalry pace to and fro,
　Before they take the field in Rotten Row ;
　Where Brooks's Blues and Weltze's Light Dragoons
　Dismount in files, and ogle in platoons."

He had also begun another Epilogue, directed against female gamesters, of which he himself repeated a couplet or two to Mr. Rogers a short time before his death, and of which there remain some few scattered traces among his papers : —

" A night of fretful passion may consume,
　All that thou hast of beauty's gentle bloom,
　And one distemper'd hour of sordid fear
　Print on thy brow the wrinkles of a year. †
　　*　　　　*　　　　*~　　　　*　　　　*

　Great figure loses, little figure wins.
　　*　　　　*　　　　*　　　　*　　　 *　*

　Ungrateful blushes and disorder'd sighs,
　Which love disclaims nor even shame supplies.
　　*　　　　*　　　　*　　　　*　　　　*

　Gay smiles, which once belong'd to mirth alone,
　And starting tears, which pity dares not own."

The following stray couplet would seem to have been intended for his description of Corilla : —

† These four lines, as I have already remarked, are taken — with little change of the words, but a total alteration of the sentiment — from the verses which he addressed to Mrs. Sheridan in the year 1773.　See page 120.

> " A crayon Cupid, redd'ning into shape,
>   Betrays her talents to design and scrape."

The Epilogue, which I am about to give, though apparently finished, has not, as far as I can learn, yet appeared in print, nor am I at all aware for what occasion it was intended: —

> " In this gay month when, through the sultry hour,
>   The vernal sun denies the wonted shower,
>   When youthful Spring usurps maturer sway,
>   And pallid April steals the blush of May,
>   How joys the rustic tribe, to view display'd
>   The liberal blossom and the early shade !
>   But ah ! far other air our soil delights;
>   *Here* ' charming weather ' is the worst of blights.
>   No genial beams rejoice our rustic train,
>   Their harvest's still the better for the rain.
>   To summer suns our groves no tribute owe,
>   They thrive in frost, and flourish best in snow.
>   When other woods resound the feather'd throng,
>   Our groves, our woods, are destitute of song.
>   The thrush, the lark, all leave our mimic vale,
>   No more we boast our Christmas nightingale;
>   Poor Rossignol — the wonder of his day,
>   Sung through the winter — but is mute in May.
>   Then bashful Spring that gilds fair nature's scene,
>   O'ercasts our lawns, and deadens every green;
>   Obscures our sky, embrowns the wooden shade,
>   And dries the channel of each tin cascade !
>   " Oh hapless we, whom such ill fate betides,
>   Hurt by the beam which cheers the world besides !
>   Who love the ling'ring frost, nice, chilling showers,
>   While Nature's *Benefit* — is death to ours;

Who, witch-like, best in noxious mists perform,
Thrive in the tempest, and enjoy the storm.
Oh hapless we — unless your generous care
Bids us no more lament that Spring is fair,
But plenteous glean from the dramatic soil,
The vernal harvest of our winter's toil.
For April suns to us no pleasure bring —
Your presence here is all we feel of Spring;
May's riper beauties here no bloom display,
Your fostering smile alone proclaims it May."

A poem upon Windsor Castle, half ludicrous
and half solemn, appears, from the many experiments which he made upon it, to have cost him
considerable trouble.   The Castle he says,

" Its base a mountain, and itself a rock,
    In proud defiance of the tempests' rage,
    Like an old grey-hair'd veteran stands each shock —
    The sturdy witness of a nobler age."

He then alludes to the " cockney " improve-
ments that had lately taken place, among which
the venerable castle appears, like

" A helmet on a macaroni's head —
    Or like old Talbot turn'd into a fop,
    With coat embroider'd and scratch wig at top."

Some verses, of the same mixed character, on
the short duration of life and the changes that
death produces, thus begin : —

" Of that same tree which gave the box,
 Now rattling in the hand of FOX,
 Perhaps his coffin shall be made. —"

He then rambles into prose, as was his custom, on a sort of knight-errantry after thoughts and images : — " The lawn thou hast chosen for thy bridal shift—thy shroud may be of the same piece. That flower thou hast bought to feed thy vanity — from the same tree thy corpse may be decked. Reynolds shall, like his colours, fly ; and Brown, when mingled with the dust, manure the grounds he once laid out. Death is life's second childhood ; we return to the breast from whence we came, are weaned,   *   *   * "
There are a few detached lines and couplets of a poem, intended to ridicule some fair invalid, who was much given to falling in love with her physicians : —

" Who felt her pulse, obtain'd her heart."

The following couplet, in which he character-ises an amiable friend of his, Dr. Bain, with whom he did not become acquainted till the year 1792, proves these fragments to have been writ-ten after that period : —

" Not savage   *   *   *   nor gentle BAIN —
She was in love with Warwick Lane."

An " Address to the Prince," on the exposed style of women's dress, consists of little more than single lines, not yet wedded into couplets ; such as—" The more you show, the less we wish to see."—" And bare their bodies, as they mask their minds," &c. This poem, however, must have been undertaken many years after his entrance into Parliament, as the following curious political memorandum will prove : — " I like it no better for being from France — whence all ills come — altar of liberty, begrimed at once with blood and mire."

There are also some Anacreontics — lively, but boyish and extravagant. For instance, in expressing his love of bumpers : —

> " Were mine a goblet that had room
> For a whole vintage in its womb,
> I still would have the liquor swim
> An inch or two above the brim."

The following specimen is from one of those poems, whose length and completeness prove them to have been written at a time of life when he was more easily pleased, and had not yet arrived at that state of glory and torment for the poet, when

> " Toujours mécontent de ce qu'il vient de faire,
> Il plait à tout le monde et ne sçaurait se plaire :" —

" The Muses call'd, the other morning,
On Phœbus, with a friendly warning
That invocations came so fast,
They must give up their trade at last,
And if he meant to' assist them all,
The aid of Nine would be too small.
Me then, as clerk, the Council chose,
To tell this truth in humble prose.—
But Phœbus, possibly intending
To show what all their hopes must end in,
To give the scribbling youths a sample,
And frighten them by my example,
Bade me ascend the poet's throne,
And give them verse — much like their own.

" Who has not heard each poet sing
The powers of Heliconian spring ?
Its noble virtues we are told
By all the rhyming crew of old.
Drink but a little of its well,
And straight you could both write and spell,
While such rhyme-giving pow'rs run through it,
A quart would make an epic poet." &c. &c.

A poem on the miseries of a literary drudge
begins thus promisingly : —

" Think ye how dear the sickly meal is bought,
By him who works at verse and trades in thought ?"

The rest is hardly legible; but there can be
little doubt that he would have done this subject
justice ; — for he had himself tasted of the bitter-

ness with which the heart of a man of genius overflows, when forced by indigence to barter away (as it is here expressed) " the reversion of his thoughts," and

" Forestall the blighted harvest of his brain."

It will be easily believed that, in looking over the remains, both dramatic and poetical, from which the foregoing specimens are taken, I have been frequently tempted to indulge in much ampler extracts. It appeared to me, however, more prudent, to rest satisfied with the selections here given; for, while less would have disappointed the curiosity of the reader, more might have done injustice to the memory of the author.

CHAP. VIII.

THE period at which Mr. Sheridan entered upon
his political career was, in every respect, remarkable.   A persevering and vindictive war against
America, with the folly and guilt of which the
obstinacy of the Court and the acquiescence of
the people are equally chargeable, was fast approaching that crisis, which every unbiassed spec-
tator of the contest had long foreseen, — and
at which, however humiliating to the haughty
pretensions of England, every friend to the liberties of the human race rejoiced.   It was, perhaps, as difficult for this country to have been
long and virulently opposed to such principles as
the Americans asserted in this contest, without
being herself corrupted by the cause which she
maintained, as it was for the French to have
fought, in the same conflict, by the side of the
oppressed, without catching a portion of that

enthusiasm for liberty, which such an alliance was calculated to inspire. Accordingly, while the voice of Philosophy was heard along the neighbouring shores, speaking aloud those oracular warnings, which preceded the death of the Great Pan of Despotism, the courtiers and lawyers of England were, with an emulous spirit of servility, advising and sanctioning such strides of power, as would not have been unworthy of the most dark and slavish times.

When we review, indeed, the history of the late reign, and consider how invariably the arms and councils of Great Britain, in her Eastern wars, her conflict with America, and her efforts against revolutionary France, were directed to the establishment and perpetuation of despotic principles, it seems little less than a miracle that her own liberty should have escaped with life from the contagion. Never, indeed, can she be sufficiently grateful to the few patriot spirits of that period, to whose courage and eloquence she owes the high station of freedom yet left to her; — never can her sons pay a homage too warm to the memory of such men as a Chatham, a Fox, and a Sheridan; who, however much they may have sometimes sacrificed to false views of expediency, and, by compromise with friends and coalition with foes, too often weakened their hold upon public confidence; however the at-

traction of the Court may have sometimes made
them librate in their orbit, were yet the saving
lights of Liberty in those times, and alone preserved the ark of the Constitution from founder-
ing in the foul and troubled waters that encom-
passed it.

Not only were the public events, in which Mr.
Sheridan was now called to take a part, of a
nature more extraordinary and awful than had
often been exhibited on the theatre of politics,
but the leading actors in the scene were of that
loftier order of intellect, which Nature seems to
keep in reserve for the ennoblement of such
great occasions. Two of these, Mr. Burke and
Mr. Fox, were already in the full maturity of
their fame and talent, — while the third, Mr.
Pitt, was just upon the point of entering, with
the most auspicious promise, into the same
splendid career : —

" Nunc cuspide Patris
Inclytus, Herculeas olim moture sagittas."

Though the administration of that day, like
many other ministries of the same reign, was
chosen more for the pliancy than the strength
of its materials, yet Lord North himself was no
ordinary man, and, in times of less difficulty and
under less obstinate dictation, might have ranked
as a useful and most popular minister. It is

true, as the defenders of his measures state, that some of the worst aggressions upon the rights of the Colonies had been committed before he succeeded to power. But his readiness to follow in these rash footsteps, and to deepen every fatal impression which they had made;—his insulting reservation of the Tea Duty, by which he contrived to embitter the only measure of concession that was wrung from him;—the obsequiousness, with which he made himself the channel of the vindictive feelings of the Court, in that memorable declaration (rendered so truly mock-heroic by the event) that "a total repeal of the Port Duties could not be thought of, till America was prostrate at the feet of England;"—all deeply involve him in the shame of that disastrous period, and identify his name with measures as arbitrary and headstrong, as have ever disgraced the annals of the English monarchy.

The playful wit and unvarying good-humour of this nobleman formed a striking contrast to the harsh and precipitate policy, which it was his lot, during twelve stormy years, to enforce:—and, if his career was as headlong as the torrent near its fall, it may also be said to have been as shining and as smooth. These attractive qualities secured to him a considerable share of personal popularity; and, had fortune ultimately smiled on his councils, success would, as usual, have reconciled the people of England to any means, however arbitrary, by which it had been attained. But the calamities, and, at last, the hopelessness of the conflict inclined them to moralise upon its causes and character. The hour of Lord North's ascendant was now passing rapidly away, and Mr. Sheridan could not have joined the Opposition, at a conjuncture more favourable to the excitement of his powers, or more bright in the views which it opened upon his ambition.

He made his first speech in Parliament on the 20th of November, 1780, when a petition was presented to the House, complaining of the undue election of the sitting members (himself and Mr. Monckton) for Stafford. It was rather lucky for him that the occasion was one in which he felt personally interested, as it took away much of that appearance of anxiety for display, which might have attended his first exhibition upon any general subject. The fame, however, which he had already acquired by his literary talents, was sufficient, even on this question, to awaken all the curiosity and expectation of his audience ; and accordingly we are told in the report of his speech, that " he was heard with particular attention, the House being uncommonly still while he was speaking." The indignation, which he expressed on this occasion at the charges brought by the petition against the electors of Stafford, was coolly turned into ridicule by Mr. Rigby, Paymaster of the Forces. But Mr. Fox, whose eloquence was always ready at the call of good nature, and, like the shield of Ajax, had " ample room and verge enough," to protect not only himself but his friends, came promptly to the aid of the young orator; and, in reply to Mr. Rigby, observed, that " though those ministerial members, who chiefly robbed and plundered their constituents, might afterwards affect to despise them, yet gentlemen, who felt properly the nature of the trust allotted to them, would always treat them and speak of them with respect."

It was on this night, as Woodfall used to relate, that Mr. Sheridan, after he had spoken, came up to him in the gallery, and asked, with much anxiety, what he thought of his first attempt. The answer of Woodfall, as he had the courage afterwards to own, was " I am sorry to say I do not think that this is your line — you had much better have stuck to your former pursuits." On hearing which, Sheridan rested his head upon his hand for a few minutes, and then vehemently exclaimed, " It is in me, however, and, by G——, it shall come out."

It appears, indeed, that upon many persons besides Mr. Woodfall the impression produced by this first essay of his oratory was far from answerable to the expectations that had been formed. The chief defect remarked in him was a thick and indistinct mode of delivery, which, though he afterwards greatly corrected it, was never entirely removed.

It is not a little amusing to find him in one of his early speeches, gravely rebuking Mr. Rigby and Mr. Courtenay* for the levity and raillery with which they treated the subject before the House, — thus condemning the use of that weapon in other hands, which soon after became so formidable in his own. The remarks by which Mr. Courtenay (a gentleman whose lively wit found afterwards a more congenial air on the benches of Opposition) provoked the reprimand of the new senator for Stafford, are too humorous to be passed over without, at least, a specimen of their spirit. In ridiculing the conduct of the Opposition, he observed : —

" Oh liberty ! Oh virtue ! Oh my country ! had been the pathetic, though fallacious cry of former Oppositions; but the present he was sure acted on purer motives. They wept over their bleeding country, he had no doubt. Yet the patriot ' eye in a fine frenzy rolling ' sometimes deigned to cast a wishful squint on the riches and

* Feb. 26. — On the second reading of the Bill for the better regulation of His Majesty's Civil List Revenue.

honours enjoyed by the minister and his venal supporters.
If he were not apprehensive of hazarding a ludicrous
allusion, (which he knew was always improper on a
serious subject) he would compare their conduct to that
of the sentimental alderman in one of Hogarth's prints,
who, when his daughter is expiring, wears indeed a
parental face of grief and solicitude, but it is to secure
her diamond ring which he is drawing gently from her
finger."

" Mr. Sheridan (says the report) rose and reprehended
Mr. Courtenay for turning every thing that passed into
ridicule; for having introduced into the House a style
of reasoning, in his opinion, every way unsuitable to the
gravity and importance of the subjects that came under
their discussion. If they would not act with dignity, he
thought they might, at least, debate with decency. He
would not attempt to answer Mr. Courtenay's arguments,
for it was impossible seriously to reply to what, in every
part, had an infusion of ridicule in it. Two of the
honourable gentleman's similes, however, he must take
notice of. The one was his having insinuated that Opposition was envious of those who basked in court sunshine; and desirous merely to get into their places. He
begged leave to remind the honourable gentleman that,
though the sun afforded a genial warmth, it also occasioned an intemperate heat, that tainted and infected
every thing it reflected on. That this excessive heat
tended to corrupt as well as to cherish; to putrefy as
well as to animate; to dry and soak up the wholesome
juices of the body politic, and turn the whole of it into
one mass of corruption. If those, therefore, who sat
near him did not enjoy so genial a warmth as the honourable gentleman, and those who like him kept close
to the Noble Lord in the blue ribbon, he was certain

they breathed a purer air, an air less infected and less corrupt."

This florid style, in which Mr. Sheridan was not very happy, he but rarely used in his speeches afterwards.

The first important subject that drew forth any thing like a display of his oratory was a motion which he made on the 5th of March, 1781, " For the better regulation of the Police of Westminster." The chief object of the motion was to expose the unconstitutional exercise of the prerogative that had been assumed, in employing the military to suppress the late riots, without waiting for the authority of the civil power. These disgraceful riots, which proved to what Christianly consequences the cry of " No Popery " may lead, had the effect, which follows all tumultuary movements of the people, of arming the Government with new powers, and giving birth to doctrines and precedents permanently dangerous to liberty. It is a little remarkable that the policy of blending the army with the people and considering soldiers as citizens, which both Montesquieu and Blackstone recommend as favourable to freedom, should, as applied by Lord Mansfield on this occasion, be pronounced, and perhaps with more justice, hostile to it; — the tendency of such a practice

being, it was said, to weaken that salutary jealousy, with which the citizens of a free state
should ever regard a soldier, and thus familiarise
the use of this dangerous machine, in every possible service to which capricious power may apply it. The Opposition did not deny that the
measure of ordering out the military, and em-
powering their officers to act at discretion without any reference to the civil magistrate, was,
however unconstitutional, not only justifiable
but wise, in a moment of such danger. But the
refusal of the minister to acknowledge the ille-
gality of the proceeding by applying to the
House for an Act of Indemnity, and the trans-
mission of the same discretionary orders to the
soldiery throughout the country, where no such
imminent necessity called for it, were the points
upon which the conduct of the Government was
strongly, and not unjustly, censured.

Indeed, the manifest design of the ministry,
at this crisis, to avail themselves of the impression produced by the riots, as a means of extending the frontier of their power, and fortify-
ing the doctrines by which they defended it,
spread an alarm among the friends of constitutional principles, which the language of some of
the advocates of the Court was by no means
calculated to allay. Among others, a Noble Earl,
— one of those awkward worshippers of power,

who bring ridicule alike upon their idol and themselves, — had the foolish effrontery, in the House of Lords, to eulogise the moderation which His Majesty had displayed, in not following the recent example of the King of Sweden, and employing the sword, with which the hour of difficulty had armed him, for the subversion of the Constitution and the establishment of despotic power. Though this was the mere ebullition of an absurd individual, yet the bubble on the surface often proves the strength of the spirit underneath, and the public were justified by a combination of circumstances, in attributing designs of the most arbitrary nature to such a Court and such an Administration. Meetings were accordingly held in some of the principal counties, and resolutions passed, condemning the late unconstitutional employment of the military. Mr. Fox had adverted to it strongly at the opening of the session, and it is a proof of the estimation in which Mr. Sheridan already stood with his party, that he was the person selected to bring forward a motion, upon a subject in which the feelings of the public were so much interested. In the course of his speech he said:—

" If this doctrine was to be laid down, that the Crown could give orders to the military to interfere, when, where, and for what length of time it pleases, then we might bid farewell to freedom. If this was the law, we should then be reduced to a military government of the very worst species, in which we should have all the evils of a despotic state, without the discipline or the security. But we were given to understand, that we had the best protection against this evil, in the virtue, the moderation, and the constitutional principles of the sovereign. No man upon earth thought with more reverence than himself of the virtues and moderation of the sovereign; but this was a species of liberty which he trusted would never disgrace an English soil. The liberty that rested on the virtuous inclinations of any one man, was but suspended despotism; the sword was not. indeed upon their necks, but it hung by the small and brittle thread of human will."

The following passage of this speech affords an example of that sort of antithesis of epithet, which, as has been already remarked, was one of the most favourite contrivances of his style:—

" Was not the conduct of that man or men criminal, who had permitted those Justices to continue in the commission? Men of *tried inability* and *convicted deficiency!* Had no attempt been made to establish some more effectual system of police, in order that we might still depend upon the remedy of the bayonet, and that the military power might be called in to the aid of *contrived weakness* and *deliberate inattention?*"

One of the few instances in which he ever differed with his friend, Mr. Fox, occurred during this session, upon the subject of a Bill which the latter introduced for the repeal of the Marriage

Act, and which he prefaced by a speech as characteristic of the ardour, the simplicity, the benevolence and fearlessness of his disposition, as any
ever pronounced by him in public. Some parts,
indeed, of this remarkable speech are in a strain
of feeling so youthful and romantic, that they
seem more fit to be addressed to one of those
Parliaments of Love, which were held during
the times of Chivalry, than to a grave assembly
employed about the sober realities of life, and
legislating with a view to the infirmities of human
nature.

The hostility of Mr. Fox to the Marriage Act
was hereditary, as it had been opposed with equal
vehemence by his father, on its first introduction
in 1753, when a debate not less memorable took
place, and when Sir Dudley Ryder, the Attorney-
general of the day, did not hesitate to advance,
as one of his arguments in favour of the Bill, that
it would tend to keep the aristocracy of the country pure, and prevent their mixture by intermar-
riage with the mass of the people. However this
anxiety for the " streams select" of noble blood,
or views, equally questionable, for the accumulation of property in great families, may have
influenced many of those with whom the Bill
originated,—however cruel, too, and mischievous,
some of its enactments may be deemed, yet the
general effect which the measure was intended to

produce, of diminishing as much as possible the number of imprudent marriages, by allowing the pilotage of parental authority to continue till the first quicksands of youth are passed, is, by the majority of the civilised world, acknowledged to be desirable and beneficial. Mr. Fox, however, thought otherwise, and though — " bowing," as he said, " to the prejudices of mankind," — he consented to fix the age at which young people should be marriageable without the consent of parents, at sixteen years for the woman and eighteen for the man, his own opinion was decidedly for removing all restriction whatever, and for leaving the " heart of youth" which, in these cases, was " wiser than the head of age," without limit or controul, to the choice which its own desires dictated.

He was opposed in his arguments, not only by Mr. Sheridan, but by Mr. Burke, whose speech on this occasion was found among his manuscripts after his death, and is enriched, though short, by some of those golden sentences, which he " scattered from his urn " upon every subject that came before him.* Mr. Sheridan, for whose

* In alluding to Mr. Fox's too favourable estimate of the capability of very young persons to choose for themselves, he pays the following tribute to his powers : — " He is led into it by a natural and to him inevitable and real mistake, that the ordinary race of mankind advance as fast towards maturity of judgment and understanding as he has done."

---

opinions upon this subject the well-known history of his own marriage must have secured no ordinary degree of attention, remarked that —

> " His honourable friend, who brought in the Bill, appeared not to be aware that, if he carried the clause enabling girls to marry at sixteen, he would do an injury to that liberty of which he had always shown himself the friend, and promote domestic tyranny, which he could consider only as little less intolerable than public tyranny. If girls were allowed to marry at sixteen, they would, he conceived, be abridged of that happy freedom of intercourse, which modern custom had introduced between the youth of both sexes; and which was, in his opinion, the best nursery of happy marriages. Guardians would, in that case, look on their wards with a jealous eye, from a fear that footmen and those about them might take advantage of their tender years and immature judgment, and persuade them into marriage, as soon as they attained the age of sixteen."

It seems somewhat extraordinary that, during the very busy interval which passed between Mr. Sheridan's first appearance in Parliament and his appointment under Lord Rockingham's administration in 1782, he should so rarely have taken a part in the debates that occurred — interesting

His concluding words are : — " Have mercy on the youth of both sexes; protect them from their ignorance and inexperience; protect one part of life by the wisdom of another; protect them by the wisdom of laws and the care of nature."

as they were, not only from the importance of
the topics discussed, but from the more than
usual animation now infused into the warfare of
parties, by the last desperate struggles of the
Ministry and the anticipated triumph of the
Opposition. Among the subjects, upon which
he appears to have been rather unaccountably
silent, was the renewal of Mr. Burke's Bill for
the regulation of the Civil List, — an occasion
memorable as having brought forth the maiden
speech of Mr. Pitt, and witnessed the first accents
of that eloquence, which was destined, ere long,
to sound, like the shell of Misenus, through
Europe, and call kings and nations to battle by
its note. The debate upon the legality of petitions from delegated bodies, in which Mr. Dun-
ning sustained his high and rare character of a
patriot lawyer ; — the bold proposal of Mr.
Thomas Pitt, that the Commons should withhold
the supplies, till pledges of amendment in the
administration of public affairs should be given ;
— the Bill for the exclusion of Excise Officers
and Contractors from Parliament, which it was
reserved for a Whig Administration to pass ; —
these and other great constitutional questions,
through which Mr. Burke and Mr. Fox fought,
side by side, lavishing at every step the inex-
haustible ammunition of their intellect, seem to
have passed away without once calling into action

the powers of their new and brilliant auxiliary, Sheridan.

The affairs of Ireland, too, had assumed, at this period, under the auspices of Mr. Grattan and the example of America, a character of grandeur, as passing as it was bright, — but which will be long remembered with melancholy pride by her sons, and as long recall the memory of that admirable man, to whose patriotism she owed her brief day of freedom, and upon whose name that momentary sunshine of her sad history rests. An opportunity of adverting to the events, which had lately taken place in Ireland, was afforded by Mr. Fox in a motion for the recommitment of the Mutiny Bill; and on this subject, perhaps, the silence of Mr. Sheridan may be accounted for, from his reluctance to share the unpopularity attached by his countrymen to those high notions of the supremacy of England, which, on the great question of the independence of the Irish Parliament, both Mr. Fox and Mr. Burke were known to entertain.*

* As the few beautiful sentences spoken by Burke on this occasion, in support of his friend's motion, have been somewhat strangely omitted in the professed Collection of all his Speeches, I shall give them here as they are reported in the Parliamentary History : — " Mr. Burke said, so many and such great revolutions had happened of late, that he was not much surprised to hear the Right Hon. Gentleman (Mr. Jenkinson) treat the loss of the supremacy of this country

A A 4

Even on the subject of the American war,
which was now the important point that called
forth all the resources of attack and defence on
both sides, the co-operation of Mr. Sheridan appears to have been but rare and casual.   The only
occasions, indeed, connected with this topic, upon
which I can trace him as having spoken at any
length, were the charges brought forward by Mr.
Fox against the Admiralty for their mismanage-
ment of the naval affairs of 1781, and the Resolution of censure on His Majesty's Ministers
moved by Lord John Cavendish.   His remarks
in the latter debate upon the two different sets
of opinions, by which (as by the double soul,
imagined in Xenophon,) the speaking and the
voting of Mr. Rigby were actuated, are very
happy : —

" The Right Hon. Gentleman, however, had acted in
this day's debate with perfect consistency.   He had assured the House that he thought the Noble Lord ought
to resign his office ; and yet he would give his vote for
his remaining in it.   In the same manner he had long

over Ireland as a matter of very little consequence.   Thus,
one star, and that the brightest ornament of our orrery,
having been suffered to be lost, those who were accustomed
to inspect and watch our political heaven ought not to
wonder that it should be followed by the loss of another. —

So star would follow star, and light light,
Till all was darkness and eternal night."

declared, that he thought the American war ought to be abandoned; yet had uniformly given his vote for its continuance. He did not mean, however, to insinuate any motives for such conduct;—he believed the Right Hon. Gentleman to have been sincere; he believed that, as a member of Parliament, as a Privy Counsellor, as a private gentleman, he had always detested the American war as much as any man; but that he had never been able to persuade the Paymaster that it was a bad war; and unfortunately, in whatever character he spoke, it was the Paymaster who always voted in that House."

The infrequency of Mr. Sheridan's exertions upon the American question combines with other circumstances to throw doubt upon an anecdote, which has been, however, communicated to me as coming from an authority worthy in every respect of the most implicit belief. He is said to have received, towards the close of this war, a letter from one of the leading persons of the American Government, expressing high admiration of his talents and political principles, and informing him that the sum of twenty thousand pounds had been deposited for him in the hands of a certain banker, as a mark of the value which the American people attached to his services in the cause of liberty. To this Mr. S. returned an answer (which, as well as the letter, was seen, it is said, by the person with whom the anecdote originated,) full of the most respectful gratitude for the opinion entertained of his services, but

begging leave to decline a gift under such circumstances. That this would have been the
nature of his answer, had any such proposal occurred, the generally high tone of his political
conduct forbids us to feel any doubt, —but, with
respect to the credibility of the transaction altogether, it is far less easy to believe that the
Americans had so much money to give, than that
Mr. Sheridan should have been sufficiently high-
minded to refuse it.

Not only were the occasions very few and
select, on which he offered himself to the attention of the House at this period, but, whenever
he did speak, it was concisely and unpretend-
ingly, with the manner of a person who came to
learn a new road to fame, — not of one who laid
claim to notice upon the credit of the glory he
brought with him. Mr. Fox used to say that he
considered his conduct in this respect as a most
striking proof of his sagacity and good taste ; —
such rare and unassuming displays of his talents
being the only effectual mode he could have
adopted, to win on the attention of his audience
and gradually establish himself in their favour.
He had, indeed, many difficulties and disadvantages to encounter, of which his own previous
reputation was not the least. Not only did he
risk a perilous comparison between his powers as
a speaker and his fame as a writer, but he had

also to contend with that feeling of monopoly, which pervades the more worldly classes of talent, and which would lead politicians to regard as an intruder upon their craft, a man of genius thus aspiring to a station among them, without the usual qualifications of either birth or apprenticeship to entitle him to it.* In an assembly, too, whose deference for rank and property is such as to render it lucky that these instruments of influence are so often united with honesty and talent, the son of an actor and proprietor of a theatre had, it must be owned, most fearful odds against him, in entering into competition with the sons of Lord Holland and Lord Chatham.

With the same discretion that led him to obtrude himself but seldom on the House, he never

* There is an anecdote strongly illustrative of this observation, quoted by Lord John Russel in his able and lively work " On the Affairs of Europe from the Peace of Utrecht." — " Mr. Steele (in alluding to Sir Thomas Hanmer's opposition to the Commercial Treaty in 1714) said, ' I rise to do him honour'— on which many members who had before tried to interrupt him, called out ' Tatler, Tatler ;' and, as he went down the House, several said ' It is not so easy a thing to speak in the House ;' ' He fancies, because he can scribble, &c. &c.' — Slight circumstances, indeed, (adds Lord John,) but which show at once the indisposition of the House to the Whig party, and the natural envy of mankind, long ago remarked by Cicero, towards all who attempt to gain more than one kind of pre-eminence."

spoke at this period but after careful and even verbal preparation. Like most of our great orators at the commencement of their careers, he was in the habit of writing out his speeches before he delivered them; and, though subsequently he scribbled these preparatory sketches upon detached sheets, I find that he began by using for this purpose the same sort of copybooks, which he had employed in the first rough draughts of his plays.

However ill the affairs of the country were managed by Lord North, in the management of Parliament few ministers have been more smoothly dexterous; and through the whole course of those infatuated measures, which are now delivered over, without appeal, to the condemnation of History, he was cheered along by as full and triumphant majorities, as ever followed in the wake of ministerial power. At length, however, the spirit of the people, that last and only resource against the venality of parliaments and the obstinacy of kings, was roused from its long and dangerous sleep by the unparalleled exertions of the Opposition leaders, and spoke out with a voice, always awfully intelligible, against the men and the measures that had brought England to the brink of ruin. The effect of this popular feeling soon showed itself in the upper regions. The country gentlemen, those birds of political omen, whose migrations are so portentous of a change of weather, began to flock in numbers to the brightening quarter of Opposition; and at last, Lord North, after one or two signal defeats, (in spite even of which the Court for some time clung to him, as the only hope of its baffled, but persevering revenge,) resigned the seals of office in the month of March, 1782, and an entirely new Administration was formed under the promising auspices of the Marquis of Rockingham.

Mr. Sheridan, as might be expected, shared in the triumph of his party, by being appointed one of the Under Secretaries of State; and, no doubt, looked forward to a long and improving tenure of that footing in office which his talents had thus early procured for him. But, however prosperous on the surface the complexion of the ministry might be, its intestine state was such as did not promise a very long existence. Whiggism is a sort of political Protestantism, and pays a similar tax for the freedom of its creed, in the multiplicity of opinions which that very freedom engenders — while true Toryism, like Popery, holding her children together by the one common doctrine of the infallibility of the Throne, takes care to repress any schism inconvenient to their general interest, and keeps them, at least for all intents and purposes of place-holding, unanimous.

Between the two branches of Opposition that composed the present Administration, there were some very important, if not essential, differences of opinion. Lord Shelburne, the pupil and friend of Lord Chatham, held the same high but unwise opinions, with respect to the recognition of American independence, which " the swan-like end" of that great man has consecrated in our imaginations, however much our reason may condemn them. " Whenever," said Lord Shel-burne, " the Parliament of Great Britain shall acknowledge the independence of America, from that moment the sun of England is set for ever." With regard to the affairs of India, too, and the punishment of those who were accused of mis-managing them, the views of the Noble Lord wholly differed from those of Mr. Fox and his followers — as appeared from the decided part in favour of Mr. Hastings, which he took in the subsequent measure of the Impeachment. In addition to these fertile seeds of disunion, the retention in the cabinet of a person like Lord Thurlow, whose views of the Constitution were all through the wrong end of the telescope, and who did not even affect to conceal his hostility to the principles of his colleagues, seemed such

a provision, at starting, for the embarrassment
of the Ministry, as gave but very little hope of
its union or stability.

The only Speech, of which any record remains as having been delivered by Mr. Sheridan during his short official career, was upon a motion made by Mr. Eden, the late Secretary for Ireland, " to repeal so much of the Act of George I. as asserted a right in the King and Parliament of Great Britain, to make laws to bind the Kingdom of Ireland." This motion was intended to perplex the new ministers, who, it was evident from the speech of Mr. Fox on the subject, had not yet made up their minds to that surrender of the Legislative Supremacy of Great Britain, which Ireland now, with arms in her hands, demanded.* Mr. Sheridan concurred with the Honourable Secretary in deprecating such a hasty and insidious agitation of the question, but at the same time expressed, in a much more unhesitating manner, his opinion of that

---

* Mr. Fox, in his speech upon the Commercial Propositions of 1785, acknowledged the reluctance that was felt at this period, in surrendering the power of external or commercial legislation over Ireland :— " a power," he said, " which, in their struggles for independence, the Irish had imprudently insisted on having abolished, and which he had himself given up in compliance with the strong prejudices of that nation, though with a reluctance that nothing but irresistible necessity could have overcome."

law of Subjection from which Ireland now rose
to release herself : —

" If he declared himself (he said) so decided an
enemy to the principle of the Declaratory Law in question, which he had always regarded as a tyrannous
usurpation in this country, he yet could not but repro-
bate the motives which influenced the present mover for
its repeal — but, if the House divided on it, he should
vote with him."

The general sense of the House being against
the motion, it was withdrawn. But the spirit of
the Irish nation had advanced too far on its
march, to be called back even by the most
friendly voice. All that now remained for the
ministers was to yield, with a confiding frankness, what the rash measures of their predecessors and the weakness of England had put it
out of their power with safety to refuse. This
policy, so congenial to the disposition of Mr.
Fox, was adopted. His momentary hesitation
was succeeded by such a prompt and generous
acquiescence in the full demands of the Irish
Parliament, as gave all the grace of a favour to
what necessity would, at all events, have extorted ; — and, in the spirited assertion of the
rights of freemen on one side, and the cordial
and entire recognition of them on the other, the
names of Grattan and Fox, in that memorable

moment, reflected a lustre on each other which associates them in its glory for ever.

Another occasion upon which Mr. Sheridan spoke while in office, — though no report of his Speech has been preserved — was a motion for a Committee to examine into the State of the Representation, brought forward by the youthful reformer, Mr. William Pitt, whose zeal in the cause of freedom was at that time, perhaps, sincere, and who little dreamed of the war he was destined to wage with it afterwards. Mr. Fox and Mr. Sheridan spoke strongly in favour of the motion ; while, in compliance with the request of the former, Mr. Burke absented himself from the discussion, — giving the cause of Reform, for once, a respite from the thunders of his eloquence, like the sleep of Jove in Homer, which leaves the Greeks for the moment masters of the field.

Σφιν κυδος οπαζε, μινυνθα περ, οφρ' ετι ευδει
Ζευς.*

Notwithstanding all this, however, the question was lost by a majority of 161 to 141.

Immediately on his accession to office Mr. Sheridan received the following letter from his brother Charles Francis, who had been called to

* " And, while the moment lasts of Jove's repose,
    Make victory theirs."   Cowper.

the Irish bar in 1778 or 9, but was at this time practising as a Special Pleader : —

    " DEAR DICK,   Dublin, March 27. 1782.

    " I am much obliged to you for your early intelligence concerning the fate of the Ministry, and give you joy on the occasion, notwithstanding your sorrow for the departure of the good Opposition. I understand very well what you mean by this sorrow — but as you may be now in a situation in which you may obtain some substantial advantage for yourself, for God's sake improve the opportunity to the utmost, and don't let dreams of empty fame (of which you have had enough in conscience) carry you away from your solid interests.

    " I return you many thanks for Fox's letter. I mean for your intention to make him write one —for as your good intentions always satisfy your conscience, and that you seem to think the carrying them into execution to be a mere trifling ceremony, as well omitted as not, your friends must always take the *will* for the *deed*. I will forgive you, however, on condition that you will for once in your life consider that though the *will* alone may perfectly satisfy yourself, your friends would be a little more gratified if they were sometimes to see it accompanied by the deed — and let me be the first upon whom you

try the experiment. If the people here are not
to share the fate of their patrons, but are suffered to continue in the government of this
country, I believe you will have it in your
power, as I am certain it will be in your inclination, to fortify my claims upon them by recom-
mendations from your side of the water, in such
a manner as to insure to me what I have a right
to expect from them, but of which I can have
no certainty without that assistance. I wish the
present people may continue here, because I
certainly have claims upon them, and considering the footing that Lord C—— and Charles
Fox are on, a recommendation from the latter
would now have every weight, — it would be
drawing a bill upon Government here, payable
at sight, which they dare not protest. So, dear
Dick, I shall rely upon you that will *really* be
done ; and, to confess the truth, unless it be
done and that speedily, I shall be completely
ruined, for this damned annuity, payable to my
uncle, plays the devil with me. If there is any
intention of recalling the people here, I beg you
will let me know it as soon as possible that I
may take my measures accordingly, — and I
think I may rely upon you also that whoever
comes over here as Lord L——t, I shall not be
forgot among the number of those who shall be
recommended to them.

" As to our politics here, I send you a newspaper, — read the resolutions of the volunteers, and you will be enabled to form some idea of the spirit which at present pervades this country. A declaration of the independency of our Parliament upon yours will *certainly* pass our House of Commons immediately after the recess ; government here dare not, cannot oppose it ; you will see the volunteers have pledged their lives and fortunes in support of the measure. The grand juries of every county have followed their example, and some of the staunchest friends of government have been, much against their inclinations, compelled to sign the most spirited Resolutions.

" A call of the House is ordered for the first Tuesday after the recess, and circular letters from the Speaker worded in this remarkable manner, " that the members do attend on that day as *they tender the rights of Ireland.*" In short, nothing will satisfy the people but the most unequivocal assertion of the total independence of the Irish legislature. This flame has been raised within this six weeks, and is entirely owing either to the insidious design or unpardonable inattention of the late administration, in including, or suffering to be included, the name of Ireland in no less than five British statutes passed last sessions. People here were ignorant of this till Grattan produced the five Acts to the House of Commons, one of which Eden had been so imprudent as to publish in the Dublin Gazette. Previous to this the general sense of the country was, that the mere question of right should be suffered to sleep, provided the *exercise* of the power claimed under it should never again be resorted to in a single instance.

" The sooner you repeal the 6th of G. 1. the better ; for, believe me, nothing short of that can now preserve union and cordiality between the two countries.

" I hope my father and you are very good friends by this. I shall not be able to send you the remaining 50*l.* till October, as I have been disappointed as to the time of payment of the money I expected to receive this month. — Let me entreat you to write to me shortly a few words. I beg my love to Mrs. S. and Tom.

" I am, dear Dick,

" Your very affectionate brother,

" C. F. SHERIDAN."

The expectations of the writer of this letter were not disappointed. The influence of Mr. Sheridan, added to his own claims, procured for him the office of Secretary of War in Ireland, — a situation, which the greater pliancy of his political principles contrived to render a more permanent benefit to him than any that his Whig brother was ever able to secure for himself.

The death of the Marquis of Rockingham broke up this short-lived Ministry, which, during the four months of its existence, did more perhaps for the principles of the Constitution, than any one administration that England had seen since the Revolution. They were betrayed, it is true, into a few awkward overflowings of loyalty, which the rare access of Whigs to the throne may at once account for and excuse ; — and Burke, in particular, has left us a specimen of his taste for extremes, in that burst of optimism with which he described the King's message, as " the best of messages to the best of people from the best of kings." But these first effects of the atmosphere of a court, upon heads unaccustomed to it, are natural and harmless, — while the measures that passed during that brief interval, directed against the sources of Parliamentary corruption, and confirmatory of the best principles of the Constitution, must ever be remembered to the honour of the party from which they emanated. The exclusion of contractors from the House of Commons — the disqualification of revenue-officers from voting at elections — the disfranchisement of corrupt voters at Cricklade, by which a second precedent * was

* The first was that of the borough of Shoreham in 1771.

furnished towards that plan of gradual Reform, which has, in our own time, been so forcibly recommended by Lord John Russell — the diminution of the patronage of the Crown, by Mr. Burke's celebrated Bill * — the return to the old constitutional practice † of making the revenues of the Crown pay off their own incumbrances, which salutary principle was again lost in the hands of Mr. Pitt — the atonement at last made to the violated rights of electors, by the rescinding of the Resolutions relative to Wilkes — the frank and cordial understanding entered into with Ireland, which identifies the memory of Mr. Fox and this ministry with the only *oäsis* in the whole desert of Irish history — so many and such important recognitions of the best principles of Whiggism, followed up, as they were, by the Resolutions of Lord John Cavendish at the close of the Session, pledging the ministers to a perseverance in the same task of purification and retrenchment, give an aspect to

---

* This Bill, though its circle of retrenchment was, as might be expected, considerably narrowed, when the Treasury Bench became the centre from which he described it, was yet eminently useful, as an acknowledgment from ministerial authority of the necessity of such occasional curtailments of the Royal influence.

† First departed from in 1769. See Burke's powerful exposure of the mischiefs of this innovation, in his " Thoughts on the Causes of the present Discontents."

this short period of the annals of the late reign, to which the eye turns for relief from the arbitrary complexion of the rest; and furnish us with, at least, *one* consoling instance, where the principles professed by statesmen, when in opposition, were retained and sincerely acted upon by them in power.

On the death of the Marquis of Rockingham, Lord Shelburne, without, as it appears, consulting any of the persons attached to that nobleman, accepted the office of first Lord of the Treasury; in consequence of which Mr. Fox, and the greater number of his friends — among whom were Mr. Burke and Mr. Sheridan — sent in their resignations; while General Conway, the Duke of Richmond, and one or two other old allies of the party, remained in office.

To a disposition so social as that of Mr. Fox, the frequent interruption and even loss of friendships, which he had to sustain in the course of his political career, must have been a sad alloy to its pleasure and its pride. The fable of the sheep that leaves its fleece on the bramble bush is but too apt an illustration of the fate of him, who thus sees himself stripped of the comforts of friendship by the tenacious and thorny hold of politics. On the present occasion, however, the desertion of his standard by a few who had followed him cordially in his ascent to power, but did not show the same alacrity in accompanying his voluntary fall, was amply made up to him by the ready devotion with which the rest of the party shared his fortunes. The disinterestedness of Sheridan was the more meritorious, if, as there is every reason to believe, he considered the step of resignation at such a moment to be, at least, hasty, if not wholly wrong. In this light it was, indeed, viewed by many judicious persons at the time, and the assurances given by the Duke of Richmond and General Conway, of the continued adherence of the cabinet to the same principles and measures, to which they were pledged at the first formation of the ministry, would seem to confirm the justice of the opinion. So much temper, however, had, during the few months of their union, been fermenting between the two great masses of which the Administration was composed, that it would have been difficult, if not impossible, for the Rockingham party to rally, with any cordiality, round Lord Shelburne, as a leader — however they might still have been contented to co-operate with him, had he remained in the humble station which he himself had originally selected. That noble Lord, too, who felt that the sacrifice which he had considerately made, in giving up the supremacy of station to Lord Rockingham, had, so far from being duly

appreciated by his colleagues, been repaid only
with increased alienation and distrust, could
hardly be expected to make a second surrender
of his advantages, in favour of persons who had,
he thought, so ungraciously requited him for
the first.   In the mean time the Court, to which
the Rockingham party was odious, had, with its
usual policy, hollowed the ground beneath them,
so as to render their footing neither agreeable
nor safe.   The favourite object in that quarter
being to compose a ministry of those convenient
ingredients, called " King's friends," Lord Shelburne was but made use of as a temporary instrument, to clear away, in the first place, the
chief obstacles to such an arrangement, and
then, in his turn, be sacrificed himself, as soon as
a more subservient system could be organised.
It was, indeed, only upon a strong representation from his Lordship of the impossibility of
carrying on his government against such an
Opposition, without the infusion of fresh and
popular talent, that the royal consent was obtained to the appointment of Mr. Pitt — the
memory of whose uncompromising father, as
well as the first achievements on his own youthful shield, rendered him no very promising
accession to such a scheme of government, as
was evidently then contemplated by the Court.

In this state of affairs, the resignation of

Mr. Fox and his friends was but a prompt and
spirited anticipation of what must inevitably
have taken place, under circumstances much
less redounding to the credit of their independence and disinterestedness. There is little
doubt, indeed, that with the great majority of
the nation, Mr. Fox by this step considerably
added to his popularity, — and, if we were desired to point out the meridian moment of his
fame, we should fix it perhaps at this splendid
epoch before the ill-fated Coalition had damped
the confidence of his friends, or the ascendancy
of his great rival had multiplied the number of
his enemies.

There is an anecdote of Mr. Burke, connected
with this period, the credibility of which must
be left to the reader's own judgment. It is
said that, immediately upon the retirement of
Mr. Fox, while Lord John Cavendish (whose
resignation was for a short time delayed by the
despatch of some official business,) was still a
minister, Mr. Burke, with a retrospect to the
sweets of office which showed that he had not
wholly left hope behind, endeavoured to open a
negotiation through the medium of Lord John,
for the purpose of procuring, by some arrangement, either for himself or his son, a Tellership
then in the possession of a relative of Lord Orford. It is but fair to add that this curious

anecdote rests chiefly upon the authority of the latter nobleman. * The degree of faith it receives will, therefore, depend upon the balance that may be struck in our comparative estimate between the disinterestedness of Burke and the veracity of Lord Orford.

At the commencement of the following session that extraordinary Coalition was declared, which had the ill-luck attributed to the conjunction of certain planets, and has shed an unfavourable influence over the political world ever since. Little is, I believe, known of the private negociations that led to this ill-assorted union of parties; but, from whichever side the first advances may have come, the affair seems to have been dispatched with the rapidity of a Siamese courtship; and while to Mr. Eden (afterwards Lord Auckland) is attributed the credit of having gained Lord North's consent to the union, Mr. Burke is generally supposed to have been the person, who sung the " Hymen, oh Hymenæe" in the ears of Mr. Fox.

With that sagacity, which in general directed his political views, Mr. Sheridan foresaw all the consequences of such a defiance of public opinion, and exerted, it is said, the whole power of his persuasion and reasoning, to turn aside his sanguine and uncalculating friend from a mea-

* Unpublished Papers.

sure so likely to embarrass his future career. Unfortunately, however, the advice was not taken, — and a person, who witnessed the close of a conversation, in which Sheridan had been making a last effort to convince Mr. Fox of the imprudence of the step he was about to. take, heard the latter, at parting, express his final resolution in the following decisive words : — " It is as fixed as the Hanover succession."

To the general principle of Coalitions, and the expediency and even duty of forming them, in conjunctures that require and justify such a sacrifice of the distinctions of party, no objection, it appears to me, can rationally be made by those who are satisfied with the manner in which the Constitution has worked, since the new modification of its machinery introduced at the Revolution. The Revolution itself was, indeed, brought about by a Coalition, in which Tories, surrendering their doctrines of submission, arrayed themselves by the side of Whigs, in defence of their common liberties. Another Coalition, less important in its object and effects, but still attended with results most glorious to the country, was that which took place in the year 1757, when, by a union of parties from whose dissension much mischief had flowed, the interests of both king and people were reconciled, and the good genius of England triumphed at home and abroad.

On occasions like these, when the public liberty or safety is in peril, it is the duty of every honest statesman to say, with the Roman, " *Non me impedient privatæ offensiones, quo minus pro reipublicæ salute etiam cum inimicissimo consentiam.*" Such cases, however, but rarely occur ; and they have been in this respect, among others, distinguished from the ordinary occasions, on which the ambition or selfishness of politicians resorts to such unions, that the voice of the people has called aloud for them in the name of the public weal ; and that the cause round which they have rallied has been sufficiently general, to merge all party titles in the one undistinguishing name of Englishman. By neither of these tests can the junction between Lord North and Mr. Fox be justified. The people at large, so far from calling for this ill-omened alliance, would on the contrary — to use the language of Mr. Pitt — have " forbid the banns ;" and, though it is unfair to suppose that the interests of the public did not enter into the calculations of the united leaders, yet, if the real watchword of their union were to be demanded of them in " the Palace of Truth," there can be little doubt that the answer of each would be, distinctly and unhesitatingly, "Ambition."

One of the most specious allegations in defence of the measure is, that the extraordinary favour which Lord Shelburne enjoyed at court, and the arbitrary tendencies known to prevail in that quarter, portended just then such an overflow of Royal influence, as it was necessary to counteract by this double embankment of party. In the first place, however, it is by no means so certain that the noble minister at this period did actually enjoy such favour. On the contrary, there is every reason to believe that his possession of the Royal confidence did not long survive that important service, to which he was made instrumental, of clearing the cabinet of the Whigs; and that, like the bees of Virgil, he had left the soul of his own power in the wound which he had been the means of inflicting upon that of others. In the second place, whatever might have been the designs of the Court, — and of its encroaching spirit no doubt can be entertained, — Lord Shelburne had assuredly given no grounds for apprehending, that he would ever, like one of the chiefs of this combination against him, be brought to lend himself precipitately or mischievously to its views. Though differing from Mr. Fox on some important points of policy, and following the example of his friend, Lord Chatham, in keeping himself independent of Whig confederacies, he was not the less attached to the true principles of that party, and, throughout his whole political career, invariably maintained them. This argument, therefore, — the only plausible one in defence of the Coalition, — fails in the two chief assumptions on which it is founded.

It has been truly said of Coalitions, considered abstractedly, that such a union of parties, when the public good requires it, is to be justified on the same grounds on which Party itself is vindicated. But the more we feel inclined to acknowledge the utility of party, the more we must dread and deprecate any unnecessary compromise, by which a suspicion of unsoundness may be brought upon the agency of so useful a principle — the more we should discourage, as a matter of policy, any facility in surrendering those badges of opinion, on which the eyes of followers are fondly fixed, and by which their confidence and spirit are chiefly kept alive — the more, too, we must lament that a great popular leader, like Mr. Fox, should ever have lightly concurred in such a confusion of the boundaries of opinion, and, like that mighty river, the Mississippi, whose waters lose their own colour in mixing with those of the Missouri, have sacrificed the distinctive hue of his own political creed to this confluence of interests with a party so totally opposed to it.

"Court and Country," says Hume[*], "which are the genuine offspring of the British government, are a kind of mixed parties, and are influenced both by principle and by interest. The heads of the factions are commonly most governed by the latter motive; the inferior members of them by the former." Whether this be altogether true or not, it will, at least, without much difficulty be conceded, that the lower we descend in the atmosphere of Party, the more quick and inflammable we find the feeling that circulates through it. Accordingly, actions and professions, which, in that region of indifference, high life, may be forgotten as soon as done or uttered, become recorded as pledges and standards of conduct, among the lower and more earnest adherents of the cause; and many a question, that has ceased to furnish even a jest in the drawing-rooms of the great, may be still agitated, as of vital importance, among the humbler and less initiated disputants of the party. Such being the tenacious nature of partisanship, and such the watch kept upon every movement of the higher political bodies, we can well imagine what a portent it must appear to distant and unprepared observers, when the stars

[*] Essay "On the Parties of Great Britain."

to which they trusted for guidance are seen to "shoot madly from their spheres," and not only lose themselves for the time in another system, but unsettle all calculations with respect to their movements for the future.

The steps by which, in general, the principals in such transactions are gradually reconciled to their own inconsistency — the negotiations that precede and soften down the most salient difficulties — the value of the advantages gained, in return for opinions sacrificed — the new points of contact brought out by a change of circumstances, and the abatement or extinction of former differences, by the remission or removal of the causes that provoked them, — all these conciliatory gradations and balancing adjustments, which to those who are in the secret may account for, and more or less justify, the alliance of statesmen who differ in their general views of politics, are with difficulty, if at all, to be explained to the remote multitude of the party, whose habit it is to judge and feel in the gross, and who, as in the case of Lord North and Mr. Fox, can see only the broad and but too intelligible fact, that the leaders for whom both parties had sacrificed so much — those on one side their interest, and those on the other, perhaps, their consciences — had deserted them to patch up a suspicious alliance with each other, the only open

and visible motive to which was the spoil that it
enabled them to partition between them.

If, indeed, in that barter of opinions and interests, which must necessarily take place in Coalitions between the partisans of the People and of the Throne, the former had any thing like an equality of chance, the mere probability of gaining thus any concessions in favour of freedom might justify to sanguine minds the occasional risk of the compromise. But it is evident that the result of such bargains must generally be to the advantage of the Crown — the alluvions of power all naturally tend towards that shore. Besides, where there are places as well as principles to be surrendered on one side, there must in return be so much more of principles given up on the other, as will constitute an equivalent to this double sacrifice. The centre of gravity will be sure to lie in that body, which contains within it the source of emoluments and honours, and the other will be forced to revolve implicitly round it.

The only occasion at this period on which Mr. Sheridan seems to have alluded to the Coalition, was during a speech of some length on the consideration of the Preliminary Articles of Peace. Finding himself obliged to advert to the subject, he chose rather to recriminate on the opposite party for the anomaly of their own alliances, than to vindicate that which his distinguished friend had just formed, and which, in his heart, as has been already stated, he wholly disapproved. The inconsistency of the Tory Lord Advocate (Dundas) in connecting himself with the patron of Equal Representation, Mr. Pitt, and his support of that full recognition of American independence, against which, under the banners of Lord North, he had so obstinately combated, afforded to Sheridan's powers of raillery an opportunity of display, of which, there is no doubt, he with his accustomed felicity availed himself. The reporter of the speech, however, has, as usual, contrived, with an art near akin to that of reducing diamonds to charcoal, to turn all the brilliancy of his wit into dull and opake verbage.

It was during this same debate, that he produced that happy retort upon Mr. Pitt, which, for good-humoured point and seasonableness, has seldom, if ever, been equalled.

" Mr. Pitt (say the Parliamentary Reports) was pointedly severe on the gentlemen who had spoken against the Address, and particularly on Mr. Sheridan. ' No man admired more than he did the abilities of that Right Honourable Gentleman, the elegant sallies of his thought, the gay effusions of his fancy, his dramatic turns and his epigrammatic point; and if they were reserved for the proper stage, they would, no doubt, receive what the Honourable Gentleman's abilities always did receive, the plaudits of the audience; and it would be his fortune ' *sui plausu gaudere theatri.*' But this was not the proper scene for the exhibition of those elegancies.' Mr. Sheridan, in rising to explain, said that ' On the particular sort of personality which the Right Honourable Gentleman had thought proper to make use of, he need not make any comment. The propriety, the taste, the gentlemanly point of it, must have been obvious to the House. But, said Mr. Sheridan, let me assure the Right Honourable Gentleman, that I do now, and will at any time he chooses to repeat this sort of allusion, meet it with the most sincere good-humour. Nay, I will say more — flattered and encouraged by the Right Honourable Gentleman's panegyric on my talents, if ever I again engage in the compositions he alludes to, I may be tempted to an act of presumption — to attempt an improvement on one of Ben Jonson's best characters, the character of the Angry Boy in the Alchemist.' "

Mr. Sheridan's connection with the stage, though one of the most permanent sources of his glory, was also a point, upon which, at the commencement of his political career, his pride was most easily awakened and alarmed. He, himself, used to tell of the frequent mortifications which he had suffered, when at school, from taunting allusions to his father's profession — being called by some of his school-fellows " the player-boy," &c. Mr. Pitt had therefore selected the most sensitive spot for his sarcasm ;

and the good temper as well as keenness, with which the thrust was returned, must have been felt even through all that pride of youth and talent, in which the new Chancellor of the Exchequer was then enveloped. There could hardly, indeed, have been a much greater service rendered to a person in the situation of Mr. Sheridan, than thus affording him an opportunity of silencing, once for all, a battery to which this weak point of his pride was exposed, and by which he might otherwise have been kept in continual alarm. This gentleman-like retort, combined with the recollection of his duel, tended to place him for the future in perfect security against any indiscreet tamperings with his personal history.*

* The following *jeu d'esprit*, written by Sheridan himself upon this occurrence, has been found among his manuscripts : —

" ADVERTISEMENT EXTRAORDINARY.

" We hear that, in consequence of a hint, lately given in the House of Commons, the Play of the Alchemist is certainly to be performed by a set of Gentlemen for our diversion, in a private apartment of Buckingham-House.

" The Characters, thus described in the old editions of Ben Jonson, are to be represented in the following manner —the old practice of men's playing the female parts being adopted : —

" SUBTLE (*the Alchemist*) - Lord Sh—lb—e.
FACE (*the House-keeper*) - The Lord·Ch—ll—r.
DOLL COMMON (*their Colleague*) The L—d Adv—c—te.

In the Administration, that was now forced upon the court by the Coalition, Mr. Sheridan held the office of Secretary of the Treasury — the other Secretary being Mr. Richard Burke, the brother of the orator. His exertions in the House, while he held this office, were chiefly confined to financial subjects, for which he, perhaps, at this time, acquired the taste, that tempted him afterwards, upon most occasions, to bring his arithmetic into the field against Mr. Pitt. His defence of the Receipt Tax,— which like all other long-lived taxes, was borne with difficulty,— appears, as far as we can judge of it from the Report, to have been highly amusing. Some country-gentleman having recommended a tax upon grave-stones as a substitute for it, Sheridan replied that

" Such a tax, indeed, was not easily evaded, and could not be deemed oppressive, as it would only be once paid; but so great was the spirit of clamour against any tax on receipts, that he should not wonder if it ex-

DRUGGER (*a Tobacco-man*) -	Lord Eff—ng—m.	
EPICURE MAMMON - -	Mr. R—gby.	
TRIBULATION - - -	Dr. J—nk—s—n.	
ANANIAS (*a little Pastor*) -	Mr. H—ll.	
KASTRIL (*the Angry Boy*) -	Mr. W. P—tt.	
DAME PLIANT - - -	Gen. C—nw—y.	
	and	
SURLY - - - -	His ————."	

tended to them; and that it should be asserted, that persons having paid the last debt,—the debt of nature, —government had resolved they should pay a receipt-tax, and have it stamped over their grave. Nay, with so extraordinary a degree of inveteracy were some Committees in the city, and elsewhere, actuated, that if a receipt-tax of the nature in question was enacted, he should not be greatly surprised if it were soon after published, that such Committees had unanimously resolved that they would never be buried, in order to avoid paying the tax; but had determined to lie above ground, or have their ashes consigned to family-urns, in the manner of the ancients."

He also took an active share in the discussions relative to the restoration of Powell and Bembridge to their offices by Mr. Burke:—a transaction which, without fixing any direct stigma upon that eminent man, subjected him, at least, to the unlucky suspicion of being less scrupulous in his notions of official purity, than became the party which he espoused or the principles of Reform that he inculcated.

Little as the Court was disposed, during the late reign, to retain Whigs in its service any longer than was absolutely necessary, it must be owned that neither did the latter, in general, take very courtier-like modes of continuing their connection with Royalty; but rather chose to meet the hostility of the Crown half-way, by some overt act of imprudence or courage, which at once brought the matter to an issue between them. Of this hardihood the India Bill of Mr. Fox was a remarkable example — and he was himself fully aware of the risk which he ran in proposing it. " He knew," he said, in his speech upon first bringing forward the question, " that the task he had that day set himself was extremely arduous and difficult; he knew that he had considerable risk in it; but when he took upon himself an office of responsibility, he had made up his mind to the situation and the danger of it."

Without agreeing with those who impute to Mr. Fox the extravagant design of investing himself, by means of this Bill, with a sort of perpetual Whig Dictatorship, independent of the will of the Crown, it must nevertheless be allowed that, together with the interests of India, which were the main object of this decisive measure, the future interests and influence of his own party were in no small degree provided for; and that a foundation was laid by it for their attainment of a more steady footing in power than, from the indisposition of the Court towards them, they had yet been able to accomplish. Regarding — as he well might, after so long an experience of Tory misrule — a government upon Whig principles as essential to the true interests of England, and hopeless of seeing the experiment at all fairly tried, as long as the political existence of the servants of the Crown was left dependent upon the caprice or treachery of their master, he would naturally welcome such an accession to the influence of the party, as might strengthen their claims to power when out of office, and render their possession of it, when in, more secure and useful. These objects the Bill in question would have, no doubt, effected. By turning the Pactolus of Indian patronage into the territories of Whiggism, it would have attracted new swarms of settlers to that region,— the Court would have found itself outbid in the market,— and, however the principles of the party might eventually have fared, the party itself would have been so far triumphant. It was indeed, probably, the despair of ever obtaining admission for Whiggism, in its unalloyed state, into the councils of the Sovereign, that reconciled Mr. Fox to the rash step of debasing it down to the Court standard by the Coalition — and, having once gained possession of power by these means, he saw, in the splendid provisions of the India Bill, a chance of being able to transmit it as an heir-loom to his party, which, though conscious of the hazard, he was determined to try. If his intention, therefore, was, as his enemies say, to establish a Dictatorship in his own person, it

was, at the worst, such a Dictatorship as the
Romans sometimes created, for the purpose of
averting the plague, and would have been directed merely against that pestilence of Toryism,
under which the prosperity of England had, he
thought, languished so long.

It was hardly, however, to be expected of
Royalty, — even after the double humiliation
which it had suffered, in being vanquished by
rebels under one branch of the Coalition, and
brow-beaten into acknowledging their independence by the other— that it would tamely submit
to such an undisguised invasion of its sanctuary;
particularly when the intruders had contrived
their operations so ill, as to array the people in
hostility against them, as well as the Throne.
Never was there an outcry against a ministry so
general and decisive. Dismissed insultingly by
the King on one side, they had to encounter the
indignation of the people on the other; and,
though the House of Commons, with a fidelity
to fallen ministers sufficiently rare, stood by
them for a time in a desperate struggle with
their successors, the voice of the Royal Prerogative, like the horn of Astolpho, soon scattered
the whole body in consternation among their
constituents, " *di quà, di là, di su, di giù,*" and
the result was a complete and long-enjoyed triumph to the Throne and Mr. Pitt.

Though the name of Mr. Fox is indissolubly
connected with this Bill, and though he bore it
aloft, as fondly as Cæsar did his own Commentaries, through all this troubled sea of opposition,
it is to Mr. Burke that the first daring outline of
the plan, as well as the chief materials for filling
it up, are to be attributed, — whilst to Sir Ar-
thur Pigot's able hand was entrusted the legal
task of drawing the Bill. The intense interest
which Burke took in the affairs of India had led
him to lay in such stores of information on the
subject, as naturally gave him the lead in all
deliberations connected with it. His labours for
the Select Committee, the Ninth Report of
which is pregnant with his mighty mind, may be
considered as the source and foundation of this
Bill; — while of the under-plot, which had in
view the strengthening of the Whig interest, we
find the germ in his "Thoughts on the present
Discontents," where, in pointing out the advantage to England of being ruled by such a
confederacy, he says, "In one of the most fortunate periods of our history, this country was
governed by a connection; I mean the great
connection of Whigs in the reign of Queen
Anne."

Burke was, indeed, at this time the actuating
spirit of the party — as he must have been of
any party to which he attached himself. Keep-

ing, as he did, the double engines of his genius and his industry incessantly in play over the minds of his more indolent colleagues, with an intentness of purpose that nothing could divert, and an impetuosity of temper that nothing could resist, it is not wonderful that he should have gained such an entire mastery over their wills, or that the party who obeyed him should so long have exhibited the mark of his rash spirit imprinted upon their measures. The yielding temper of Mr. Fox, together with his unbounded admiration of Burke, led him easily, in the first instance, to acquiesce in the views of his friend; and then the ardour of his own nature, and the self-kindling power of his eloquence, threw an earnestness and fire into his public enforcement of those views, which made even himself forget that they were but adopted from another, and impressed upon his hearers the conviction that they were all, and from the first, his own.

We read his speeches in defence of the India Bill with a sort of breathless anxiety, which no other political discourses, except those, perhaps, of Demosthenes, could produce. The importance of the stake which he risks — the boldness of his plan — the gallantry with which he flings himself into the struggle, and the frankness of personal feeling that breathes throughout—all throw around him an interest, like that which encircles a hero of romance ; nor could the most candid autobiography that ever was written exhibit the whole character of the man more transparently through it.

The death of this ill-fated Ministry was worthy of its birth. Originating in a Coalition of Whigs and Tories, which compromised the *principles* of freedom, it was destroyed by a Coalition of King and People, which is even, perhaps, more dangerous to its *practice.** The conduct, indeed, of all estates and parties, during this short interval, was any thing but laudable. The leaven of the unlucky alliance with Lord North was but too visible in many of the measures of the Ministry — in the jobbing terms of the Loan, the resistance to Mr. Pitt's plan of retrenchment, and the diminished numbers on the side of Parlia-

---

* " This assumption (says Burke) of the Tribunitian power by the Sovereign was truly alarming. When Augustus Cæsar modestly consented to become the Tribune of the people, Rome gave up into the hands of that prince the only remaining shield she had to protect her liberty. The Tribunitian power in this country, as in ancient Rome, was wisely kept distinct and separate from the executive power : in this government it was constitutionally lodged where it was naturally to be lodged, in the House of Commons ; and to that House the people ought first to carry their complaints, even when they were directed against the measures of the House itself. But now the people were taught to pass by the door of the House of Commons and supplicate the Throne for the protection of their liberties." — *Speech on moving his Representation to the King, in June,* 1784.

mentary Reform. * On the other hand, Mr. Pitt
and his party, in their eagerness for place, did
not hesitate to avail themselves of the ambidex-
terous and unworthy trick of representing the
India Bill to the people, as a Tory plan for the
increase of Royal influence, and to the King, as
a Whig conspiracy for the curtailment of it.
The King, himself, in his arbitrary interference
with the deliberations of the Lords, and the
Lords, in the prompt servility with which so
many of them obeyed his bidding, gave specimens of their respective branches of the Constitution, by no means creditable — while finally
the people, by the unanimous outcry with which
they rose, in defence of the monopoly of Leadenhall Street and the sovereign will of the Court,
proved how little of the " *vox Dei* " there may
sometimes be in such clamour.

Mr. Sheridan seems to have spoken but once
during the discussions on the India Bill, and
that was on the third reading, when it was carried

---

* The consequences of this alloy were still more visible
in Ireland. " The Coalition Ministry," says Mr. Hardy,
" displayed itself in various employments — but there was
no harmony. The old courtiers hated the new, and being
more dexterous, were more successful." In stating that
Lord Charlemont was but coldly received by the Lord Lieutenant, Lord Northington, Mr. Hardy adds, " It is to be
presumed that some of the old Court, who, in consequence
of the Coalition, had crept once more into favour, influenced
his conduct in this particular."

so triumphantly through the House of Commons. The report of his speech is introduced with the usual tantalising epithets, " witty," " entertaining," &c. &c. ; but, as usual, entails disappointment in the perusal — " *at cum intraveris, Dii Deæque, quam nihil in medio invenies!*" * There is only one of the announced pleasantries forthcoming, in any shape, through the speech. Mr. Scott (the present Lord Eldon) had, in the course of the debate, indulged in a licence of Scriptural parody, which he would himself, no doubt, be among the first to stigmatise as blasphemy in others, and had affected to discover the rudiments of the India Bill in a Chapter of the Book of Revelations, — Babylon being the East India Company, Mr. Fox and his seven Commissioners the Beast with the seven heads, and the marks on the hand and forehead, imprinted by the Beast upon those around him, meaning, evidently, he said, the peerages, pensions, and places distributed by the minister. In answering this strange sally of forensic wit, Mr. Sheridan quoted other passages from the same Sacred Book, which (as the Reporter gravely assures us) " told strongly for the Bill," and which proved that Lord Fitzwilliam and his fellow Commissioners, instead of being the seven heads of the Beast, were seven Angels " clothed in pure and white linen !"

* Pliny.

CHAP. IX.

The Whigs, who had now every reason to be convinced of the aversion with which they were regarded at court, had lately been, in some degree, compensated for this misfortune by the accession to their party of the Heir Apparent, who had, since the year 1783, been in the enjoyment of a separate establishment, and taken his seat in the House of Peers as Duke of Cornwall. That a young prince, fond of pleasure and impatient of restraint, should have thrown himself into the arms of those who were most likely to be indulgent to his errors, is nothing surprising, either in politics or ethics. But that mature and enlightened statesmen, with the lessons of all history before their eyes, should have been equally ready to embrace such a rash alliance, or should count upon it as any more than a temporary instrument of faction, is, to say the least of it, one of those self-delusions of the wise, which show how vainly the voice of the Past may speak amid the loud appeals and temptations of the Present. The last Prince of Wales, it is true, by whom the popular cause was espoused, had left the lesson imperfect, by dying before he came to the throne. But this deficiency has since been amply made up; and future Whigs, who may be placed in similar circumstances, will have, at least, one historical warning before their eyes, which ought to be enough to satisfy the most unreflecting and credulous.

In some points, the breach that now took place between the Prince and the King bore a close resemblance to that which had disturbed the preceding reign. In both cases the Royal parents were harsh and obstinate — in both cases money was the chief source of dissension — and in both cases the genius, wit, and accomplishments of those with whom the Heir Apparent connected himself, threw a splendour round the political bond between them, which prevented even themselves from perceiving its looseness and fragility.

In the late question of Mr. Fox's India Bill, the Prince of Wales had voted with his political friends in the first division. But, upon finding afterwards that the King was hostile to the measure, His Royal Highness took the prudent step

(and with Mr. Fox's full concurrence) of absent-
ing himself entirely from the second discussion,
when the Bill, as it is known, was finally defeated. This circumstance, occurring thus early
in their intercourse, might have proved to each
of the parties in this ill-sorted alliance, how difficult it was for them to remain long and credit-
ably united. * On the one side, there was a

* The following sensible remarks upon this first interruption of the political connection between the Heir Apparent
and the Opposition, are from an unfinished Life of Mr.
Sheridan now in my possession — written by one whose
boyhood was passed in the society of the great men whom
he undertook to commemorate, and whose station and
talents would have given to such a work an authenticity and
value, that would have rendered the humble memorial, which
I have attempted, unnecessary : —

" His Royal Highness acted upon this occasion by Mr.
Fox's advice and with perfect propriety. At the same time
the necessity under which he found himself of so acting
may serve as a general warning to Princes of the Blood in
this country, to abstain from connecting themselves with
party, and engaging either as active supporters or opponents
of the administration of the day. The ties of family, the
obligations of their situation, the feelings of the public assuredly will condemn them, at some time or other, as in the
present instance, to desert their own public acts, to fail in
their private professions, and to leave their friends at the
very moment, in which service and support are the most
imperiously required.

" Princes are always suspected proselytes to the popular
side. Conscious of this suspicion, they strive to do it away
by exaggerated professions, and by bringing to the party

character to be maintained with the people, which a too complacent toleration of the errors of Royalty might, —and, as it happened, —*did* compromise ; while, on the other side, there were the obligations of filial duty, which, as in this instance of the India Bill, made desertion decorous, at a time when co-operation would have been most friendly and desirable. There was also the perpetual consciousness of being destined to a higher station, in which, while duty would perhaps demand an independence of all party whatever, convenience would certainly dictate a release from the restraints of Whiggism.

It was most fortunate for Mr. Sheridan, on the rout of his party that ensued, to find himself safe in his seat for Stafford once more, and the following document, connected with his election, is sufficiently curious, in more respects than one, to be laid before the reader : —

_____

which they espouse more violent opinions and more un-measured language than any which they find. These mighty promises they soon find it unreasonable, impossible, inconvenient to fulfil. Their dereliction of their principles becomes manifest and indefensible, in proportion to the vehemence with which they have pledged themselves always to maintain them ; and the contempt and indignation which accompanies their retreat is equivalent to the expectations excited by the boldness and determination of their advance.'"

*R. B. Sheridan, Esq.   Expenses at the Borough
of Stafford for Election, Anno 1784.*

248 Burgesses, paid £ 5   5   0 each......... £ 1,302   0   0

Yearly Expenses since.

	£.	s.	d.			
House-rent and taxes.........	23	6	6			
Servant at 6s. per week, } board wages............... }	15	12	0			
Ditto, yearly wages............	8	8	0			
Coals, &c.......................	10	0	0			
				57	6	6
Ale tickets.....................	40	0	0			
Half the members' plate........	25	0	0			
Swearing young burgesses...	10	0	0			
Subscription to the infirmary	5	5	0			
Ditto clergymen's widows....	2	2	0			
Ringers	4	4	0			
				86	11	0
One year..................	143	17	6			
Multiplied by years......		6				
				863	5	0

Total expense of six years' parliament, exclusive
of expense incurred during the time of election,
and your own annual expenses.................£2,165   5   0

The followers of the Coalition had been defeated in almost all directions, and it was com-
puted that no less than 160 of them had been
left upon the field, — with no other consolation
than what their own wit afforded them, in the
title which they bestowed upon themselves of
" Fox's Martyrs."

This reduction in the ranks of his enemies, at the very commencement of his career, left an open space for the youthful minister, which was most favourable to the free display of his energies. He had, indeed, been indebted, throughout the whole struggle, full as much to a lucky concurrence of circumstances as to his talents and name for the supremacy to which he so rapidly rose. All the other eminent persons of the day had either deeply entangled themselves in party ties, or taken the gloss off their reputations by some unsuccessful or unpopular measures; and as he was the only man independent enough of the House of Commons to be employed by the King as a weapon against it, so was he the only one sufficiently untried in public life, to be able to draw unlimitedly on the confidence of the people, and array them, as he did, in all the enthusiasm of ignorance, on his side. Without these two advantages, which he owed to his youth and inexperience, even loftier talents than his would have fallen far short of his triumph.

The financial affairs of the country, which the war had considerably deranged, and which none of the ministries that ensued felt sure enough of themselves to attend to, were, of course, among the first and most anxious objects of his administration; and the wisdom of the measures which he brought forward for their amelioration was

not only candidly acknowledged by his opponents at the time, but forms at present the least
disputable ground, upon which his claim to reputation as a finance-minister rests.   Having
found, on his accession to power, an annual deficiency of several millions in the revenue, he,
in the course of two years, raised the income of
the country so high as to afford a surplus for the
establishment of his Sinking Fund. Nor did his
merit lie only in the mere increase of income,
but in the generally sound principles of the taxation by which he accomplished it, in the im-
provements introduced into the collection of the
revenue, and the reform effected in the offices
connected with it, by the simplification of the
mode of keeping public accounts.

Though Mr. Sheridan delivered his opinion
upon many of the taxes proposed, his objections
were rather to the details than the general object
of the measures ; and it may be reckoned, indeed,
a part of the good fortune of the minister, that
the financial department of Opposition at this
time was not assumed by any more adventurous
calculator, who might have perplexed him, at
least, by ingenious cavils, however he might
have failed to defeat him by argument.   As it
was, he had the field almost entirely to himself ;
for Sheridan, though acute, was not industrious
enough to be formidable, and Mr. Fox, from a

struggle, perhaps, between candour and party-feeling, absented himself almost entirely from the discussion of the new taxes. *

The only question, in which the angry spirit of the late conflict still survived, were the Westminster Scrutiny and Mr. Pitt's East India Bill. The conduct of the minister in the former transaction showed that his victory had not brought with it those generous feelings towards the vanquished, which, in the higher order of minds, follows as naturally as the calm after a tempest. There must, indeed, have been something peculiarly harsh and unjust in the proceedings against his great rival on this occasion, which could induce so many of the friends of the minister — then in the fulness of his popularity and power— to leave him in a minority and vote against the continuance of the Scrutiny. To this persecution, however, we are indebted for a speech of Mr. Fox, which is (as he, himself, in his opening, pronounced it *would* be) one of his best and noblest; and which is reported, too, with such evident fidelity, as well as spirit, that we seem to

* " He had absented himself," he said, " upon principle; that, though he might not be able to approve of the measures which had been adopted, he did not at the same time think himself authorised to condemn them, or to give them opposition, unless he had been ready to suggest others less distressing to the subject." — *Speech on Navy Bills, &c. &c.*

hear, while we read, the " *Demosthenem ipsum* " uttering it.

Sheridan had, it appears, written a letter, about this time, to his brother Charles, in which, after expressing the feelings of himself and his brother Whigs, at the late unconstitutional victory over their party, he added, " But you are all so void of principle, in Ireland, that you cannot enter into our situation." Charles Sheridan, who, in the late changes, had not thought it necessary to pay his principles the compliment of sacrificing his place to them, considered himself, of course, as included in this stigma ; and the defence of time-serving politics which he has set up in his answer, if not so eloquent as that of the great Roman master of this art in his letter to Lentulus, is, at least, as self-conscious and laboured, and betrays altogether a feeling but too worthy of the political meridian from which it issued.

" Dublin Castle, 10th March, 1784.

" MY DEAR DICK,

" I am much obliged to you for the letter you sent me by Orde ; I began to think you had forgot I was in existence, but I forgive your past silence on account of your recent kind attention. The new Irish administration have come with the olive branch in their hand, and very wisely,

I think ; the system, the circumstances, and the manners of the two countries are so totally different, that I can assure you nothing could be so absurd as any attempt to extend the party-distinctions which prevail on your side of the water, to this. Nothing, I will venture to assert, can possibly preserve the connection between England and Ireland, but a permanent government here, acting upon fixed principles, and pursuing systematic measures. For this reason a change of Chief Governor, ought to be nothing more than a simple transfer of government, and by no means to make any change in that political system respecting this country, which England must adopt, let who will be the minister and whichever party may acquire the ascendancy, if she means to preserve Ireland as a part of the British empire.

" You will say that this is a very good plan for people in place, as it tends to secure them against all contingencies ; but this, I give you my word, is not my reason for thinking as I do. I must, in the first place, acquaint you that there never can be hereafter in this country any such thing as party connections founded upon political principles ; we have obtained all the great objects for which Ireland had contended for many years, and there does not now remain one national object of sufficient importance to unite

men in the same pursuit. Nothing but such
objects ever did unite men in this kingdom, and
that not from principle, but because the spirit of
the people was so far roused with respect to
points in which the pride, the interest, the commerce, and the prosperity of the nation at large
was so materially concerned, that the House of
Commons, if they had not the virtue to forward,
at least wanted the courage to oppose, the general and determined wish of the whole kingdom ; they therefore made a virtue of necessity,
joined the standard of a very small popular
party ; both *Ins* and *Outs* voted equally against
government, the latter of course, and the former
because each individual thought himself safe in
the number who followed his example.

" This is the only instance, I believe, in the
history of Irish politics, where a party ever appeared to act upon public principle ; and as the
cause of this singular instance has been removed
by the attainment of the only objects which
could have united men in one pursuit, it is not
probable that we shall in future furnish any other
example that will do honour to our public spirit.
If you reflect an instant, you will perceive that
our subordinate situation necessarily prevents
the formation of any party among us, like those
you have in England, composed of persons acting upon certain principles, and pledged to sup-

port each other. I am willing to allow you that your exertions are directed by public spirit; but if those exertions did not lead to *power*, you must acknowledge that it is probable they would not be made, or if made, that they would not be of much use. The object of a party in England is either to obtain power for themselves, or to take it from those who are in possession of it — they may do this from the purest motives, and with the truest regard for the public good, but still you must allow that power is a very tempting object, the hopes of obtaining it no small incentive to their exertions, and the consequences of success to the individuals of which the party is composed, no small strengthening to the bands which unite them together. Now, if you were to expect similar parties to be formed in Ireland, you would exact of us more virtue than is necessary for yourselves. From the peculiar situation of this country it is impossible that the exertions of any party here can ever lead to *power*. Here then is one very tempting object placed out of our reach, and, with it, all those looked-for consequences to individuals, which, with you, induce them to pledge themselves to each other; so that nothing but poor public spirit would be left to keep our Irish party together, and consequently a greater degree of disinterestedness would be necessary in them, than is requisite in one of your English parties.

" That no party exertion here can ever lead to power is obvious when you reflect, that we have in fact no *Irish government;* all power here being lodged in a branch of the *English* government, we have no cabinet, no administration of our own, no great offices of state, every office we have is merely ministerial, it confers no power but that of giving advice, which may or may not be followed by the Chief Governor. As all power, therefore, is lodged solely in the English government, of which the Irish is only a branch, it necessarily follows that no exertion of any party here could ever lead to power, unless they overturned the English government in this country, or unless the efforts of such a party in the Irish House of Commons could overturn the British administration in England, and the leaders of it get into their places ; — the first, you will allow, would not be a very wise object, and the latter you must acknowledge to be impossible.

" Upon the same principle, it would be found very difficult to form a party in this country which should co-operate with any particular party in England, and consent to stand or fall with them. The great leading interests in this kingdom are, of course, strongly averse to forming any such connections on your side of the water, as it would tend to create a fluctuation in the affairs of this country, that would destroy all their consequence ; and, as to the personal friends which a party in England may possibly have in this country, they must in the nature of things be few in number, and consequently could only injure themselves by following the fortunes of a party in England, without being able to render that party the smallest service. And, at all events, to such persons this could be nothing but a losing game. It would be, to refuse to avail themselves of their connections or talents in order to obtain office or honours, and to rest all their pretensions upon the success of a party in another kingdom, to which success they could not in the smallest degree contribute. You will admit that to a party in England, no friends on this side of the water would be worth having who did not possess connections or talents ; and if they did possess these, they must, of course, force themselves into station, let the government of this country be in whose hands it may, and that upon a much more permanent footing than if they were connected with a party in England. What therefore could they gain by such a connection ? nothing but the virtue of self-denial, in continuing out of office as long as their friends were so, the chance of coming in, when their

friends attained power, and only the chance, for
there are interests in this country which must
not be offended ; and the certainty of going out
whenever their friends in England should be
dismissed. So that they would exchange the
certainty of station upon a permanent footing
acquired by their own efforts, connections, or
talents, for the chance of station upon a most
precarious footing, in which they would be
placed in the insignificant predicament of doing
nothing for themselves, and resting their hopes
and ambition upon the labours of others.

" In addition to what I have said respecting
the consequences of the subordinate situation of
this country, you are to take into consideration
how peculiarly its inhabitants are circumstanced.
Two out of three millions are Roman Catholics
— I believe the proportion is still larger — and
two-thirds of the remainder are violent rank
Presbyterians, who have always been, but most
particularly of late, strongly averse to all government placed in the hands of the members
of the church of England ; nine-tenths of the
property, the landed property of the country I
mean, is in the possession of the latter. You
will readily conceive how much these circumstances must give persons of property in this
kingdom a leaning towards government ; how
necessarily they must make them apprehensive

for themselves, placed between such potent enemies; and how naturally it must make them look up to English government, in whatever hands it may be, for that strength and support, which the smallness of their numbers prevents their finding among themselves; and, consequently, you will equally perceive that those political or party principles, which create such serious differences among you in England, are matters of small importance to the persons of landed property in this country, when compared with the necessity of their having the constant support of an English government. — Here, my dear Dick, is a very long answer to a very few lines in your postscript. But I could not avoid *boring* you on the subject, when you say ' that we are all so void of principle that we cannot enter into your situation.'

" I have received with the greatest pleasure the accounts of the very considerable figure you have made this sessions in the House of Commons. As I have no doubt but that your Parliament will be dissolved, God send you success a second time at Stafford, and the same to your friend at Westminster. I will not forgive you if you do not give me the first intelligence of both those events. I shall say nothing to you on the subject of your English politics, only that I feel myself much more partial to one side of the question than, in my present situation, it would be of any use to me to avow. — I am the happiest domestic man in the world, and am in daily expectation of an addition to that happiness; and own that a home, which I never leave without regret, nor return to without delight, has somewhat abated my passion for politics, and that warmth I once felt about public questions. But it has not abated the warmth of my private friendships; it has not abated my regard for Fitzpatrick, my anxiety for you, and the warmth of my wishes for the success of your friends, considering them as such. — I beg my love to Mrs. Sheridan and Tom, and am, dear Dick,

" Most affectionately yours,

" C. F. SHERIDAN."

With respect to the Bill for the better government of India, which Mr. Pitt substituted for that of his defeated rival, its provisions are now, from long experience, so familiarly known, that it would be superfluous to dwell upon either their merits or defects. * The two important points in which it differed from the measure of

* Three of the principal provisions were copied from the Propositions of Lord North in 1781 — in allusion to which Mr. Powys said of the measure, that " it was the voice of Jacob, but the hand of Esau."

Mr. Fox were, in leaving the management of their commercial concerns still in the hands of the Company, and in making the Crown the virtual depositary of Indian patronage *, instead of suffering it to be diverted into the channels of the Whig interest, — never, perhaps, to find its way back again. In which of these directions such an accession of power might, with least mischief to the Constitution, be bestowed, having the experience only of the use made of it on one side, we cannot, with any certainty, pretend to determine. One obvious result of this transfer of India to the Crown has been that smoothness

* " Mr. Pitt's Bill continues the form of the Company's government, and professes to leave the patronage under certain conditions, and the commerce without condition, in the hands of the Company ; but places all matters relating to the *civil* and *military* government and *revenues* in the hands of six Commissioners, to be nominated and appointed by His Majesty, under the title of ' Commissioners of the Affairs of India,' which Board of Commissioners is vested with the ' superintendence and controul over all the British territorial possessions in the East Indies, and over the affairs of the United Company of Merchants trading thereto.' " — *Comparative Statement of the Two Bills,* read from his place by Mr. Sheridan, on the Discussion of the Declaratory Acts in 1788, and afterwards published.

In another part of this Statement he says, " The present Board of Controul have, under Mr. Pitt's Bill, usurped those very imperial prerogatives from the Crown, which were falsely said to have been given to the new Board of Directors under Mr. Fox's Bill.

so remarkable in the movements of the system
ever since, — that easy and noiseless play of its
machinery, which the lubricating contact of influence alone could give, and which was wholly
unknown in Indian policy, till brought thus by
Mr. Pitt under ministerial controul. When we
consider the stormy course of Eastern politics
before that period — the enquiries, the exposures,
the arraignments that took place — the constant
hunt after Indian delinquency, in which Ministers joined no less keenly than the Opposition —
and then compare all this with the tranquillity
that has reigned, since the halcyon incubation of
the Board of Controul over the waters, — though
we may allow the full share that actual reform
and a better system of government may claim in
this change, there is still but too much of it to
be attributed to causes of a less elevated nature,
— to the natural abatement of the watchfulness
of the minister, over affairs no longer in the
hands of others, and to that power of 'Influence,
which, both at home and abroad, is the great
and ensuring bond of tranquillity, and, like the
Chain of Silence mentioned in old Irish poetry,
binds all that come within its reach in the same
hushing spell of compromise and repose.

It was about this time that, in the course of
an altercation with Mr. Rolle, the member for
Devonshire, Mr. Sheridan took the opportunity

CHAP.
IX.

of disavowing any share in the political satires then circulating, under the titles of " The Rolliad" and the " Probationary Odes." " He was aware," he said, " that the Honourable Gentleman had suspected that he was either the author of those compositions, or some way or other concerned in them ; but he assured him, upon his honour, he was not — nor had he ever seen a line of them till they were in print in the newspaper."

Mr. Rolle, the hero of The Rolliad, was one of those unlucky persons, whose destiny it is to be immortalised by ridicule, and to whom the world owes the same sort of gratitude for the wit of which they were the butts, as the merchants did, in Sinbad's story, to those pieces of meat to which diamonds adhered. The chief offence, besides his political obnoxiousness, by which he provoked this satirical warfare, (whose plan of attack was all arranged at a club held at Becket's,) was the lead which he took in a sort of conspiracy, formed on the ministerial benches, to interrupt, by coughing, hawking, and other unseemly noises, the speeches of Mr. Burke. The chief writers of these lively productions were Tickell, General Fitzpatrick *, Lord John

* To General Fitzpatrick some of the happiest pleasantries are to be attributed ; among others, the verse on Brooke Watson, those on the Marquis of Graham, and " The Liars."

Townshend *, Richardson, George Ellis, and Dr.
Lawrence. †   There were also a few minor contributions from the pens of Bate Dudley, Mr.
O'Beirne (afterwards Bishop of Meath), and
Sheridan's friend, Read.   In two of the writers,
Mr. Ellis and Dr. Lawrence, we have a proof
of the changeful nature of those atoms whose
concourse for the time constitutes Party, and of
the volatility with which, like the motes in the
sunbeam, described by Lucretius, they can

" *Commutare viam, retroque repulsa reverti*
Nunc huc, nunc illuc, in cunctas denique partes."

Change their light course, as fickle chance may guide,
Now here, now there, and shoot from side to side.

Doctor Lawrence was afterwards a violent
supporter of Mr. Pitt, and Mr. Ellis‡ showed the

* Lord John Townshend, the only survivor, at present, of
this confederacy of wits was the author, in conjunction
with Tickell, of the admirable Satire, entitled " Jekyll," —
Tickell having contributed only the lines parodied from Pope.
To the exquisite humour of Lord John we owe also the
Probationary Ode for Major Scott, and the playful parody
on " *Donec gratis eram tibi.*"

† By Doctor Lawrence the somewhat ponderous irony of
the prosaic department was chiefly managed.   In allusion
to the personal appearance of this eminent civilian, one of
the wits of the day thus parodied a passage of Virgil : —
" *Quo tetrior alter*
Non fuit, excepto Laurentis *corpore Turni.*"

‡ It is related that, on one occasion, when Mr. Ellis was
dining with Mr. Pitt, and embarrassed naturally by the re-

CHAP.
IX.

versatility of his wit, as well as of his politics, by becoming one of the most brilliant contributors to The Antijacobin.

The Rolliad and The Antijacobin may, on their respective sides of the question, be considered as models of that style of political satire *,

---

collection of what he had been guilty of towards his host in The Rolliad, some of his brother wits, to amuse themselves at his expense, endeavoured to lead the conversation to the subject of this work, by asking him various questions as to its authors, &c., — which Mr. Pitt overhearing, from the upper end of the table, leaned kindly towards Ellis and said,

" *Immo age, et a prima, dic, hospes, origine nobis.*"

The word " *hospes*," applied to the new convert, was happy, and the " *erroresque tuos*," that follows, was, perhaps, left to be implied.

* The following just observations upon The Rolliad and Probationary Odes occur in the manuscript Life of Sheridan which I have already cited: — " They are, in most instances, specimens of the powers of men, who, giving themselves up to ease and pleasure, neither improved their minds with great industry, nor exerted them with much activity; and have therefore left no very considerable nor durable memorials of the happy and vigorous abilities, with which nature had certainly endowed them. The effusions themselves are full of fortunate allusions, ludicrous terms, artful panegyric, and well-aimed satire. The verses are at times far superior to the occasion, and the whole is distinguished by a taste, both in language and matter, perfectly pure and classical; but they are mere occasional productions. They will sleep with the papers of The Craftsman, so vaunted in their own time, but which are never now raked up, except by the curiosity of the historian and the man of literature.

whose lightness and vivacity give it the appearance of proceeding rather from the wantonness of wit than of ill-nature, and whose very malice, from the fancy with which it is mixed up, like certain kinds of fireworks, explodes in sparkles. They, however, who are most inclined to forgive, in consideration of its polish and playfulness, the personality in which the writers of both these works indulged, will also readily admit that by no less shining powers can a licence so questionable be either assumed or palliated, and that nothing but the lively effervescence of the draught can make us forget the bitterness infused into it. At no time was this truth ever more strikingly exemplified than at present, when a separation seems to have taken place between satire and wit, which leaves the former like the toad, *without* the " jewel in its head ;"

" Wit, being generally founded upon the manners and characters of its own day, is crowned in that day, beyond all other exertions of the mind, with splendid and immediate success. But there is always something that equalises. In return, more than any other production, it suffers suddenly and irretrievably from the hand of Time. It receives a character the most opposite to its own. From being the most generally understood and perceived, it becomes of all writing the most difficult and the most obscure. Satires, whose meaning was open to the multitude, defy the erudition of the scholar, and comedies, of which every line was felt as soon as it was spoken, require the labour of an antiquary to explain them."

and when the hands, into which the weapon of personality has chiefly fallen, have brought upon it a stain and disrepute, that will long keep such writers as those of The Rolliad and Antijacobin from touching it again.

Among other important questions, that occupied the attention of Mr. Sheridan at this period, was the measure brought forward under the title of " Irish Commercial Propositions " for the purpose of regulating and finally adjusting the commercial intercourse between England and Ireland. The line taken by him and Mr. Fox in their opposition to this plan was such as to accord, at once, with the prejudices of the English manufacturers and the feelings of the Irish patriots, —the former regarding the measure as fatal to their interests, and the latter rejecting with indignation the boon which it offered, as coupled with a condition for the surrender of the legislative independence of their country.

In correct views of political economy, the advantage throughout this discussion was wholly on the side of the minister; and, in a speech of Mr. Jenkinson, we find (advanced, indeed, but incidentally, and treated by Mr. Fox as no more than amusing theories,) some of those liberal principles of trade which have since been more fully developed, and by which the views of all practical statesmen are, at the present day, directed. The little interest attached by Mr. Fox to the science of Political Economy—so remarkably proved by the fact of his never having read the work of Adam Smith on the subject—is, in some degree, accounted for by the scepticism of the following passage, which occurs in one of his animated speeches on this very question. Mr. Pitt having asserted, in answer to those who feared the competition of Ireland in the market from her low prices of labour, that " great capital would in all cases overbalance cheapness of labour," Mr. Fox questions the abstract truth of this position, and adds,— " General positions of all kinds ought to be very cautiously admitted; indeed, on subjects so infinitely complex and mutable as politics and commerce, a wise man hesitates at giving too implicit a credit to any general maxim of any denomination."

If the surrender of any part of her legislative power could have been expected from Ireland in that proud moment, when her new-born Independence was but just beginning to smile in her lap, the acceptance of the terms then proffered by the Minister, might have averted much of the evils, of which she was afterwards the victim. The proposed plan being in itself (as Mr. Grattan called it,) " an incipient and creeping Union," would have prepared the way less violently for the completion of that fated measure, and spared at least the corruption and the blood which were the preliminaries of its perpetration at last. But the pride, so natural and honourable to the Irish — had fate but placed them in a situation to assert it with any permanent effect — repelled the idea of being bound even by the commercial regulations of England. The wonderful eloquence of Grattan, which, like an eagle guarding her young, rose grandly in defence of the freedom to which itself had given birth, would alone have been sufficient to determine a whole nation to his will. Accordingly, such demonstrations of resistance were made both by people and parliament, that the Commercial Propositions were given up by the minister, and this apparition of a Union withdrawn from the eyes of Ireland — merely to come again, in another shape, with many a " mortal murder on its crown, and push her from her stool."

As Mr. Sheridan took a strong interest in this question, and spoke at some length on every occasion when it was brought before the House, I will, in order to enable the reader to judge of his manner of treating of it, give a few passages from his speech on the discussion of that Resolution, which stipulated for England a controul over the external legislation of Ireland : —

" Upon this view, it would be an imposition on common sense to pretend, that Ireland could in future have the exercise of free will or discretion upon any of those subjects of legislation, on which she now stipulated to follow the edicts of Great Britain; and it was a miserable sophistry to contend, that her being permitted the ceremony of placing those laws upon her own Statute-book, as a form of promulgating them, was an argument, that it was not the British but the Irish Statutes that bound the people of Ireland. For his part, if he were a member of the Irish Parliament, he should prefer the measure of enacting by one decisive vote, that all British laws, to the purposes stipulated, should have immediate operation in Ireland as in Great Britain; choosing rather to avoid the mockery of enacting without deliberation, and deciding where they had no power to dissent. — Where fetters were to be worn, it was a wretched ambition to contend for the distinction of fastening our own shackles."

* * * *

" All had been delusion, trick, and fallacy; a new scheme of commercial arrangement is proposed to the Irish as a boon ; and the surrender of their Constitution is tacked to it as a mercantile regulation. Ireland newly escaped from harsh trammels and severe discipline, is treated like a high-mettled horse, hard to catch ; and the Irish Secretary is to return to the field, soothing and coaxing him, with a sieve of provender in one hand, but with a bridle in the other, ready to slip over his head while he is snuffling at the food. But this political jockeyship, he was convinced, would not succeed."

In defending the policy, as well as generosity of the concessions made to Ireland by Mr. Fox in 1782, he says, —

" Fortunately for the peace and future union of the two kingdoms, no such miserable and narrow policy entered into the mind of his Right Honourable friend ; he disdained the injustice of bargaining with Ireland on such a subject ; nor would Ireland have listened to him if he had attempted it. She had not applied to purchase a Constitution ; and if a tribute or contribution had been demanded in return for what was then granted, those patriotic spirits who were at that time leading the oppressed people of that insulted country to the attainment of their just rights, would have pointed to other modes of acquiring them ; — would have called to them in the words of Camillus, *arma aptare atque ferro non auro patriam et libertatem recuperare.*"

The following passage is a curious proof of the short-sighted views which prevailed at that period, even among the shrewdest men, on the subject of trade : —

" There was one point, however, in which he most completely agreed with the manufacturers of this country ; namely, in their assertion, that if the Irish trader should be enabled to meet the British merchant and manufacturer in the British market, the gain of Ireland must be the loss of England.* This was a fact not to be controverted on any principle of common sense or reasonable argument. The pomp of general declamation and waste of fine words, which had on so many occasions been employed to disguise and perplex this plain simple truth, or, still more fallaciously to endea-

* Mr. Fox also said, " Ireland cannot make a single acquisition but to the proportionate loss of England."

vour to prove, that Great Britain would find her balance in the Irish market, had only tended to show the weakness and inconsistency of the doctrine they were meant to support. The truth of the argument was with the manufacturers; and this formed, in Mr. Sheridan's mind, a ground of one of the most vehement objections he had to the present plan."

It was upon the clamour, raised at this time by the English manufacturers, at the prospect of the privileges about to be granted to the trade of Ireland, that Tickell, whose wit was always on the watch for such opportunities, wrote the following fragment, found among the papers of Mr. Sheridan : —

" A Vision.

" After supping on a few Colchester oysters and a small Welsh rabbit, I went to bed last Tuesday night at a quarter before eleven o'clock. I slept quietly for near two hours, at the expiration of which period, my slumber was indeed greatly disturbed by the oddest train of images I ever experienced. I thought that every individual article of my usual dress and furniture was suddenly gifted with the powers of speech, and all at once united to assail me with clamorous reproaches, for my unpardonable neglect of their common interests, in the great question of surrendering our British commerce to Ireland. My hat, my coat, and every button on it, my Manchester waistcoat, my silk breeches, my Birmingham buckles, my shirt-buttons, my shoes, my stockings, my garters, and, what was more troublesome, my night-cap, all joined in a dissonant volley of petitions and remon-strances — which, as I found it impossible to wholly suppress, I thought it most prudent to moderate, by soliciting them to communicate their ideas individually. It was with some difficulty they consented to even this proposal, which they considered as a device to extin-guish their general ardour, and to break the force of their united efforts ; nor would they by any means ac-cede to it, till I had repeatedly assured them, that, as soon as I heard them separately, I would appoint an *early hour* for receiving them in a joint body. Accord-ingly, having fixed these preliminaries, my Night-cap thought proper to slip up immediately over my ears, and, disengaging itself from my temples, called upon my Waistcoat, who was rather carelessly reclining on a chair, to attend him immediately at the foot of the bed. My Sheets and Pillow-cases, being all of Irish extrac-tion, stuck close to me, however, — which was uncom-monly fortunate, for, not only my Curtains had drawn off to the foot of the bed, but my Blankets also had the audacity to associate themselves with others of the woollen fraternity, at the first outset of this household meeting. Both my Towels attended as evidence at the bar, — but my Pocket-bandkerchief, notwithstanding his uncommon forwardness to hold forth the banner of sedition, was thought to be a character of so mixed a complexion, as rendered it more decent for him to re-serve his interference till my Snuff-box could be heard — which was settled accordingly.

" At length, to my inconceivable astonishment, my Night-cap, attended as I have mentioned, addressed me in the following terms : —"

*　　　*　　　*　　　*　　　*

Early as was the age at which Sheridan had
been transplanted from Ireland — never to set
foot upon his native land again — the feeling of
nationality remained with him warmly through
life, and he was, to the last, both fond and proud
of his country. The zeal with which he entered,
at this period, into Irish politics, may be judged
of from some letters, addressed to him by
Mr. Isaac Corry, who was at that time a member of the Irish Opposition, and combated the
Commercial Propositions as vigorously as he
afterwards, when Chancellor of the Exchequer,
defended their " consummate flower," the Union.
A few extracts from these letters will give some
idea of the interest attached to this question by
the popular party in both countries.

The following, dated August 5. 1785, was
written during the adjournment of ten days, that
preceded Mr. Orde's introduction of the Propositions : —

" Your most welcome letter, after hunting
me some days through the country, has at length
reached me. I wish you had sent some notes
of your most excellent speech ; but such as we
have must be given to the public — admirable
commentary upon Mr. Pitt's *apology to the People of Ireland*, which must also be published in
the manner fitting it. The addresses were sent

round to all the towns in the kingdom, in order to give currency to the *humbug*. Being upon the spot, I have my troops in perfect order, and am ready at a moment's warning, for any manœuvre which may, when we meet in Dublin previous to the next sitting, be thought necessary to follow the petitions for postponing.

" We hear astonishing accounts of *your* greatness in particular. Paddy will, I suppose, some *beau jour* be voting you another 50,000*, if you go on as you have done.

" I send to-day down to my friend, O'Neil, who waits for a signal only, and we shall go up together. Brownlow is just beside me, and I shall ride over this morning to get him up to consultation · in town . . . . . . we must get our Whig friends in England to engraft a few slips of Whiggism here—till that is done, there will be neither Constitution for the people nor stability for the government.

" Charlemont and I were of opinion that we should not make the volunteers speak upon the present business; so I left it out in the Resolutions at our late review. They are as tractable as we could desire, and we can manage them completely. We inculcate all moderation — were we to slacken in that, they would instantly step forward."

* Alluding to the recent vote of that sum to Mr. Grattan.

The date of the following letter is August 10th — two days before Mr. Orde brought forward the Propositions : —

" We have got the Bill entire, sent about by Orde. The more it is read, the less it is liked. I made notable use of the clause you sent me before the whole arrived. We had a select meeting to day of the D. of Leinster, Charlemont, Conolly, Grattan, Forbes, and myself. We think of moving an address to postpone to-morrow till the 15th of January, and have also some Resolutions ready *pro re natá*, as we don't yet know what shape they will put the business into ; — Conolly to move. To-morrow morning we settle the Address and Resolutions, and after that, to-morrow, meet more at large at Leinster House. All our troops muster pretty well — Mountmorris is here, and to be with us to-morrow morning. We reckon on something like a hundred, and some are sanguine enough to add near a score above it — that is too much. The report of to-night is that Orde is not yet ready for us, and will beg a respite of a few days — Beresford is not yet arrived, and that is said to be the cause. Mornington and Poole are come — their muster is as strict as ours. If we divide any thing like a hundred, they will not dare to take a victory over us. Adieu, yours most truly,   " I. C."

The motion for bringing in the bill was carried only by a majority of nineteen, which is thus announced to Mr. Sheridan by his correspondent :—

." I congratulate with you on 108 minority — against 127. The business never can go on. They were astonished, and looked the sorriest devils you can imagine. Orde's exhibition was pitiful indeed — the support of his party weak and open to attack — the debate on their part really poor. On ours, Conolly, O'Neill, and the other country gentlemen, strong and of great weight — Grattan able and eloquent in an uncommon degree—every body in high spirits, and altogether a force that was irresistible. We divided at nine this morning, on leave to bring in a Bill for the settlement. The ground fought upon was the Fourth Resolution, and the principle of that in the others. The commercial detail did not belong accurately to the debate, though some went over it in a cursory way. Grattan, two hours and a half — Flood as much — the former brilliant, well attended to, and much admired — the latter tedious from detail ; of course, not so well heard, and answered by Foster in detail, to refutation.

" The Attorney General defended the constitutional safety under the Fourth-Resolution
principle. Orde mentioned the Opposition in
England twice in his opening speech, with im-
putations, or insinuations at least, not very
favourable. You were not left undefended.
Forbes exerted his warm attachment to you
with great effect — Burgh, the flag-ship of the
Leinster squadron, gave a well-supported fire
pointed against Pitt, and covering you. Hardy
(the Bishop of Down's friend) in a very elegant
speech gave you due honour ; and I had the
satisfaction of a slight skirmish which called up
the Attorney General, &c. . . . ."

On the 15th of August Mr. Orde withdrew
his Bill, and Mr. Corry writes — " I wish you
joy a thousand times of our complete victory.
Orde has offered the Bill — moved its being
printed for his own justification to the country,
and no more of it this session. We have the
effects of a complete victory."

Another question of much less importance, but
more calculated to call forth Sheridan's various
powers, was the Plan of the Duke of Richmond
for the fortification of dock-yards, which Mr. Pitt
brought forward (it was said, with much reluctance,) in the session of 1786, and which Sheridan
must have felt the greater pleasure in attacking,

from the renegade conduct of its noble author in politics. In speaking of the Report of a Board of General Officers, which had been appointed to examine into the merits of this plan, and of which the Duke himself was President, he thus ingeniously plays with the terms of the art in question, and fires off his wit, as it were, *en ricochet*, making it bound lightly from sentence to sentence : —

" Yet the Noble Duke deserved the warmest panegyrics for the striking proofs he had given of his genius as an engineer ; which appeared even in the planning and construction of the paper in his hand ! The professiona ability of the Master-General shone as conspicuously there, as it could upon our coasts. He had made it an argument of posts ; and conducted his reasoning upon principles of trigonometry, as well as logic. There were certain detached data, like advanced works, to keep the enemy at a distance from the main object in debate. Strong provisions covered the flanks of his assertions. His very queries were in casements. No impression, therefore, was to be made on this fortress of sophistry by desultory observations ; and it was necessary to sit down before it, and assail it by regular approaches. It was fortunate, however, to observe, that notwithstanding all the skill employed by the noble and literary engineer, his mode of defence on paper was open to the same objection which had been urged against his other fortifications ; that if his adversary got possession of one of his posts, it became strength against him, and the means of subduing the whole line of his argument."

He also spoke at considerable length, upon the Plan brought forward by Mr. Pitt for the Redemption of the National Debt, — that grand object of the calculator and the financier, and equally likely, it should seem, to be attained by the dreams of the one as by the experiments of the other. Mr. Pitt himself seemed to dread the suspicion of such a partnership, by the care with which he avoided any acknowledgment to Dr. Price, whom he had nevertheless personally consulted on the subject, and upon whose visions of compound interest this fabric of finance was founded.

In opening the Plan of his new Sinking Fund to the House, Mr. Pitt, it is well known, pronounced it to be " a firm column, upon which he was proud to flatter himself his name might be inscribed." Tycho Brahe would have said the same of his Astronomy, and Des Cartes of his Physics ; — but these baseless columns have long passed away, and the Plan of paying debt with borrowed money well deserves to follow them. The delusion, indeed, of which this Fund was made the instrument, during the war with France, is now pretty generally acknowledged ; and the only question is, whether Mr. Pitt was so much the dupe of his own juggle, as to persuade himself that thus playing with a debt, from one hand to the other, was paying it, — or whe-

ther, aware of the inefficacy of his Plan for any
other purpose than that of keeping up a blind
confidence in the money-market, he yet gravely
went on, as a sort of High Priest of Finance,
profiting by a miracle in which he did not himself
believe, and, in addition to the responsibility of
the uses to which he applied the money, incur-
ring that of the fiscal imposture by which he
raised it.

Though, from the prosperous state of the revenue at the time of the institution of this Fund,
the absurdity was not yet committed of borrowing money to maintain it, we may perceive by the
following acute pleasantry of Mr. Sheridan, (who
denied the existence of the alleged surplus of
income,) that he already had a keen insight into
the fallacy of that Plan of Redemption afterwards
followed : — " At present," he said, " it was
clear there was no surplus ; and the only means
which suggested themselves to him were, a loan
of a million for the especial purpose — for the
Right Hon. Gentleman might say, with the person
in the comedy, ' *If you won't lend me the money,
how can I pay you ?*' "

CHAP. X.

THE calm security into which Mr. Pitt's Administration had settled, after the victory which the Tory alliance of King and people had gained for him, left but little to excite the activity of party-spirit, or to call forth those grand explosions of eloquence, which a more electric state of the political world produces. The orators of Opposition might soon have been reduced, like Philoctetes wasting his arrows upon geese at Lemnos *, to expend the armoury of their wit upon the Grahams and Rolles of the Treasury-bench. But a subject now presented itself—the impeachment of Warren Hastings — which, by embodying the cause of a whole country in one individual, and thus combining the extent and grandeur of a national question with the direct aim and singleness of a personal attack, opened as wide a field for display as the most versatile

* " *Pinnigero, non armigero in corpore tela exerceantur.*"
— *Accius, ap. Ciceron.* lib. vii. ep. 33.

talents could require, and to Mr. Sheridan, in particular, afforded one of those precious opportunities, of which, if Fortune but rarely offers them to genius, it is genius alone that can fully and triumphantly avail itself.

The history of the rise and progress of British power in India — of that strange and rapid vicissitude, by which the ancient Empire of the Moguls was transferred into the hands of a Company of Merchants in Leadenhall Street — furnishes matter, perhaps, more than any other that could be mentioned, for those strong contrasts and startling associations, to which eloquence and wit often owe their most striking effects. The descendants of a Throne, once the loftiest in the world, reduced to stipulate with the servants of traders for subsistence — the dethronement of Princes converted into a commercial transaction, and a ledger-account kept of the profits of Revolutions — the sanctity of Zenanas violated by search-warrants, and the chicaneries of English Law transplanted, in their most mischievous luxuriance, into the holy and peaceful shades of the Bramins, — such events as these, in which the poetry and the prose of life, its pompous allusions and mean realities, are mingled up so sadly and fantastically together, were of a nature, particularly when recent, to lay hold of the imagination as well as the feelings, and to furnish

eloquence with those strong lights and shadows, CI
of which her most animated pictures are composed.

It is not wonderful, therefore, that the warm
fancy of Mr. Burke should have been early and
strongly excited by the scenes of which India
was the theatre, or that they should have (to use
his own words) " constantly preyed upon his
peace, and by night and day dwelt on his imagination." His imagination, indeed, — as will naturally happen, where this faculty is restrained
by a sense of truth — was always most livelily
called into play by events of which he had not
himself been a witness ; and, accordingly, the
sufferings of India and the horrors of revolutionary France were the two subjects upon which
it has most unrestrainedly indulged itself. In
the year 1780 he had been a member of the
Select Committee, which was appointed by the
House of Commons, to take the affairs of India
into consideration, and through some of whose
luminous Reports we trace that powerful intellect, which " stamped an image of itself" on
every subject that it embraced. Though the
reign of Clive had been sufficiently fertile in
enormities, and the treachery practised towards
Omichund seemed hardly to admit of any parallel, yet the loftier and more prominent iniquities of Mr. Hastings's government were supposed

to have thrown even these into shadow. Against him, therefore, — now rendered a still nobler object of attack by the haughty spirit with which he defied his accusers, — the whole studies and energies of Mr. Burke's mind were directed.

It has already been remarked that to the impetuous zeal, with which Burke at this period rushed into Indian politics, and to that ascendancy over his party by which he so often compelled them to " swell with their tributary urns his flood," the ill-fated East India Bill of Mr. Fox in a considerable degree owed its origin. In truth, the disposition and talents of this extraordinary man made him at least as dangerous as useful to any party with which he connected himself. Liable as he was to be hurried into unsafe extremes, impatient of contradiction, and with a sort of *feudal* turn of mind, which exacted the unconditional service of his followers, it required, even at that time, but little penetration to foresee the violent schism that ensued some years after, or to pronounce that, whenever he should be unable to command his party, he would desert it.

The materials which he had been collecting on the subject of India, and the indignation with which these details of delinquency had filled him, at length burst forth (like that mighty cloud, described by himself as " pouring its whole contents over the plains of the Carnatic") in his wonderful speech on the Nabob of Arcot's debts * — a speech, whose only rivals, perhaps, in all the records of oratory, are to be found among three or four others of his own, which, like those poems of Petrarch called *Sorelle* from their kindred excellence, may be regarded as sisters in beauty, and equalled only by each other.

Though the charges against Mr. Hastings had long been threatened, it was not till the present year that Mr. Burke brought them formally forward. He had been, indeed, defied to this issue by the friends of the Governor-General, whose reliance, however, upon the sympathy and support of the ministry (accorded, as a matter of course, to most State-delinquents,) was, in this instance, contrary to all calculation, disappointed. Mr. Pitt, at the commencement of the proceedings, had shown strong indications of an intention to take the cause of the Governor-General under his protection. Mr. Dundas, too, had

* Isocrates, in his Encomium upon Helen, dwells much on the advantage to an orator of speaking upon subjects from which but little eloquence is expected — περι των φαυλων και ταπεινων. There is little doubt, indeed, that *surprise* must have considerable share in the pleasure, which we derive from eloquence on such unpromising topics as have inspired three of the most masterly speeches that can be selected from modern oratory — that of Burke on the Nabob of Arcot's Debts — of Grattan on Tithes, and of Mr. Fox on the Westminster Scrutiny.

exhibited one of those convenient changes of opinion, by which such statesmen can accommodate themselves to the passing hue of the Treasury-bench, as naturally as the Eastern insect does to the colour of the leaf on which it feeds. Though one of the earliest and most active denouncers of Indian misgovernment, and even the mover of those strong Resolutions in 1782 * on which some of the chief charges of the present prosecution were founded, he now, throughout the whole of the opening scenes of the Impeachment, did not scruple to stand forth as the warm eulogist of Mr. Hastings, and to endeavour by a display of the successes of his administration to dazzle away attention from its violence and injustice.

This tone, however, did not long continue :— in the midst of the anticipated triumph of Mr. Hastings, the Minister suddenly " changed his hand, and checked his pride." On the occasion of the Benares Charge, brought forward in the House of Commons by Mr. Fox, a majority was, for the first time, thrown into the scale of the accusation ; and the abuse that was in conse-

* In introducing the Resolutions he said, that " he was urged to take this step by an account, which had lately arrived from India, of an act of the most flagrant violence and oppression and of the grossest breach of faith, committed by Mr. Hastings against Cheyt Sing, the Raja of Benares."

quence showered upon Mr. Pitt and Mr. Dundas, through every channel of the press, by the friends of Mr. Hastings, showed how wholly unexpected, as well as mortifying, was the desertion.

As but little credit was allowed to conviction in this change, — it being difficult to believe that a Minister should come to the discussion of such a question, so lightly ballasted with opinions of his own as to be thrown from his equilibrium by the first wave of argument he encountered, — various statements and conjectures were, at the time, brought forward to account for it. Jealousy of the great and increasing influence of Mr. Hastings at court was, in general, the motive assigned for the conduct of the Minister. It was even believed that a wish expressed by the King, to have his new favourite appointed President of the Board of Control, was what decided Mr. Pitt to extinguish, by co-operating with the Opposition, every chance of a rivalry, which might prove troublesome, if not dangerous, to his power. There is no doubt that the arraigned ruler of India was honoured at this period with the distinguished notice of the Court — partly, perhaps, from admiration of his proficiency in that mode of governing, to which all Courts are, more or less, instinctively inclined; and partly from a strong distaste to those who were his accusers, which would have been sufficient to recommend any person or measure to which they were opposed.

But whether Mr. Pitt, in the part which he now took, was actuated merely by personal motives, or (as his eulogists represent) by a strong sense of impartiality and justice, he must at all events have considered the whole proceeding, at this moment, as a most seasonable diversion of the attacks of the Opposition, from his own person and government to an object so little connected with either. The many restless and powerful spirits now opposed to him would soon have found, or made, some vent for their energies, more likely to endanger the stability of his power ; — and, as an expedient for drawing off some of that perilous lightning, which flashed around him from the lips of a Burke, a Fox, and a Sheridan, the prosecution of a great criminal like Mr. Hastings furnished as efficient a conductor as could be desired.

Still, however, notwithstanding the accession of the Minister, and the impulse given by the majorities which he commanded, the projected Impeachment was but tardy and feeble in its movements, and neither the House nor the public went cordially along with it. Great talents, united to great power — even when, as in the instance of Mr. Hastings, abused — is a com-

bination before which men are inclined to bow
implicitly. The iniquities, too, of Indian rulers
were of that gigantic kind, which seemed to
outgrow censure, and even, in some degree,
challenge admiration. In addition to all this,
Mr. Hastings had been successful ; and success
but too often throws a charm round injustice,
like the dazzle of the necromancer's shield in
Ariosto, before which every one falls : —

" Con gli occhi abbacinati, e senza mente."

The feelings, therefore, of the public were, at
the outset of the prosecution, rather for than
against the supposed delinquent. Nor was this
tendency counteracted by any very partial leaning towards his accusers. Mr. Fox had hardly
yet recovered his defeat on the India Bill, or —
what had been still more fatal to him — his victory in the Coalition. Mr. Burke, in spite of
his great talents and zeal, was by no means popular. There was a tone of dictatorship in his
public demeanor against which men naturally
rebelled ; and the impetuosity and passion, with
which he flung himself into every favourite subject, showed a want of self-government but little
calculated to inspire respect. Even his eloquence,
various and splendid as it was, failed in general
to win or command the attention of his hearers,

and, in this great essential of public speaking, must be considered inferior to that ordinary, but practical kind of oratory *, which reaps its harvest at the moment of delivery, and is afterwards remembered less for itself than its effects. There was a something — which those who have but read him can with difficulty conceive — that marred the impression of his most sublime and glowing displays. In vain did his genius put forth its superb plumage, glittering all over with the hundred eyes of fancy, — the gait of the bird was heavy and awkward, and its voice seemed rather to scare than attract. Accordingly, many of those masterly discourses, which, in their present form, may proudly challenge comparison with all the written eloquence upon record, were, at the time when they were pronounced, either coldly listened to, or only welcomed as a signal and excuse for not listening at all. To such a length was this indifference carried, that, on the evening when he delivered his great Speech on the Nabob of Arcot's debts, so faint was the impression it produced upon the House, that Mr. Pitt and Lord Grenville, as I have heard, not only consulted with each other

* " Whoever, upon comparison, is deemed by a common audience the greatest orator, ought most certainly to be pronounced such by men of science and erudition."—*Hume*, Essay 13.

as to whether it was necessary they should take the trouble of answering it, but decided in the negative. Yet doubtless, at the present moment, if Lord Grenville — master as he is of all the knowledge that belongs to a statesman and a scholar—were asked to point out from the stores of his reading the few models of oratorical composition, to the perusal of which he could most frequently, and with unwearied admiration, return, this slighted and unanswered speech would be among the number.

From all these combining circumstances it arose that the prosecution of Mr. Hastings, even after the accession of the Minister, excited but a slight and wavering interest ; and, without some extraordinary appeal to the sympathies of the House and the country — some startling touch to the chord of public feeling — it was questionable whether the enquiry would not end as abortively as all the other Indian inquests * that had preceded it.

In this state of the proceeding, Mr. Sheridan brought forward, on the 7th of February, in the House of Commons, the charge relative to the Begum Princesses of Oude, and delivered that

* Namely, the fruitless prosecution of Lord Clive by General Burgoyne, the trifling verdict upon the persons who had imprisoned Lord Pigot, and the Bill of Pains and Penalties against Sir Thomas Rumbold, finally withdrawn.

G G

celebrated Speech, whose effect upon its hearers has no parallel in the annals of ancient or modern eloquence.* When we recollect the men by whom the House of Commons was at that day adorned, and the conflict of high passions and interests in which they had been so lately engaged; — when we see them all, of all par-

---

* Mr. Burke declared it to be "the most astonishing effort of eloquence, argument, and wit united, of which there was any record or tradition." Mr. Fox said, " All that he had ever heard, all that he had ever read, when compared with it, dwindled into nothing, and vanished like vapour before the sun ;" — and Mr. Pitt acknowledged " that it surpassed all the eloquence of ancient and modern times, and possessed every thing that genius or art could furnish, to agitate and controul the human mind."

There were several other tributes, of a less distinguished kind, of which I find the following account in the Annual Register : —

" Sir William Dolben immediately moved an adjournment of the debate, confessing, that, in the state of mind in which Mr. Sheridan's speech had left him, it was impossible for him to give a determinate opinion. Mr. Stanhope seconded the motion. When he had entered the House, he was not ashamed to acknowledged, that his opinion inclined to the side of Mr. Hastings. But such had been the wonderful efficacy of Mr. Sheridan's convincing detail of facts, and irresistible eloquence, that he could not but say that his sentiments were materially changed. Nothing, indeed, but information almost equal to a miracle, could determine him not to vote for the Charge ; but he had just felt the influence of such a miracle, and he could not but ardently desire to avoid an immediate decision. Mr. Matthew Montagu confessed, that he had felt a similar revolution of sentiment."

ties, brought (as Mr. Pitt expressed it) " under the wand of the enchanter," and only vying with each other in their description of the fascination by which they were bound ; — when we call to mind, too, that he, whom the first statesmen of the age thus lauded, had but lately descended among them from a more aërial region of intellect, bringing trophies falsely supposed to be incompatible with political prowess ; — it is impossible to imagine a moment of more entire and intoxicating triumph. The only alloy that could mingle with such complete success must be the fear that it was too perfect ever to come again ; — that his fame had then reached the meridian point, and from that consummate moment must date its decline.

Of this remarkable Speech there exists no Report ; — for it would be absurd to dignify with that appellation the meagre and lifeless sketch, the

> " Tenuem sine viribus umbram
> In faciem Æneæ,"

which is given in the Annual Registers and Parliamentary Debates. Its fame, therefore, remains like an empty shrine — a cenotaph still crowned and honoured, though the inmate is wanting. Mr. Sheridan was frequently urged to furnish a Report himself, and from his habit of preparing and writing out his speeches, there is little doubt that he could have accomplished such a task without much difficulty. But, whether from indolence or design, he contented himself with leaving to imagination, which, in most cases, he knew, transcends reality, the task of justifying his eulogists, and perpetuating the tradition of their praise. Nor, in doing thus, did he act perhaps unwisely for his fame. We may now indulge in dreams of the eloquence that could produce such effects *, as we do of the music of the ancients and the miraculous powers attributed to it, with as little risk of having our fancies chilled by the perusal of the one, as there is of our faith being disenchanted by hearing a single strain of the other.

After saying thus much, it may seem a sort of wilful profanation, to turn to the spiritless

---

* The following anecdote is given as a proof of the irresistible power of this speech in a note upon Mr. Bisset's History of the Reign of George III. : —

" The late Mr. Logan, well known for his literary efforts, and author of a most masterly defence of Mr. Hastings, went that day to the House of Commons, prepossessed for the accused and against the accuser. At the expiration of the first hour he said to a friend, ' All this is declamatory assertion without proof :' — when the second was finished, ' This is a most wonderful oration :' — at the close of the third, ' Mr. Hastings has acted very unjustifiably :' — the fourth, ' Mr. Hastings is a most atrocious criminal ;' — and, at last, ' Of all monsters of iniquity the most enormous is Warren Hastings !' "

abstract of this speech, which is to be found in
all the professed reports of Parliamentary oratory,
and which stands, like one of those half-clothed
mummies in the Sicilian vaults, with, here and
there, a fragment of rhetorical drapery, to give
an appearance of life to its marrowless frame.
There is, however, one passage so strongly
marked with the characteristics of Mr. Sheridan's
talent, that it may be looked upon as a pretty
faithful representation of what he spoke, and
claim a place among the authentic specimens of
his oratory. Adverting to some of those admirers of Mr. Hastings, who were not so implicit in their partiality as to give unqualified
applause to his crimes, but found an excuse for
their atrocity in the greatness of his mind, he
thus proceeds : —

" To estimate the solidity of such a defence, it would
be sufficient merely to consider in what consisted this
prepossessing distinction, this captivating characteristic
of greatness of mind. Is it not solely to be traced in
great actions directed to great ends ? In them, and them
alone, we are to search for true estimable magnanimity.
To them only can we justly affix the splendid title and
honours of real greatness. There was indeed another
species of greatness, which displayed itself in boldly
conceiving a bad measure, and undauntedly pursuing it
to its accomplishment. But had Mr. Hastings the merit
of exhibiting either of these descriptions of greatness, —
even of the latter ? He saw nothing great — nothing

magnanimous — nothing open — nothing direct in his measures, or in his mind. On the contrary, he had too often pursued the worst objects by the worst means. His course was an eternal deviation from rectitude. He either tyrannised or deceived; and was by turns a Dionysius and a Scapin. * As well might the writhing obliquity of the serpent be compared to the swift directness of the arrow, as the duplicity of Mr. Hastings's ambition to the simple steadiness of genuine magnanimity. In his mind all was shuffling, ambiguous, dark, insidious, and little: nothing simple, nothing unmixed: all affected plainness, and actual dissimulation; — a heterogeneous mass of contradictory qualities; with nothing great but his crimes; and even those contrasted by the littleness of his motives, which at once denoted both his baseness and his meanness, and marked him for a traitor and a trickster. Nay, in his style and writing there was the same mixture of vicious contrarieties; — the most grovelling ideas were conveyed in the most inflated language, giving mock consequence to low cavils, and uttering quibbles in heroics; so that his compositions disgusted the mind's taste, as much as his actions excited the soul's abhorrence. Indeed this mixture of character seemed by some unaccountable, but inherent quality, to be appropriated, though in inferior degrees, to every thing that concerned his employers. He remembered to have heard an honourable and learned gentleman (Mr. Dundas) remark, that there was something in the first frame and constitution of the Company, which extended the sordid principles of their origin over all their successive operations; connecting with their civil policy,

* The spirit of this observation has been well condensed in the compound name given by the Abbé de Pradt to Napoleon — ' Jupiter' Scapin."

and even with their boldest achievements, the meanness of a pedlar and the profligacy of pirates. Alike in the political and the military line could be observed *auction-eering ambassadors* and *trading generals;* — and thus we saw a revolution brought about by *affidavits;* an army employed in *executing an arrest;* a town besieged on *a note of hand;* a prince dethroned for the *balance of an account.* Thus it was they exhibited a government, which united the mock majesty of a bloody sceptre, and the little *traffic of a merchant's counting-house,* wielding a truncheon with one hand, and *picking a pocket with the other."*

The effect of this Speech, added to the line taken by the Minister, turned the balance against Hastings, and decided the Impeachment.

Congratulations on his success poured in upon Mr. Sheridan, as may be supposed, from all quarters ; and the letters that he received from his own family on the occasion were preserved by him carefully and fondly through life. The following extract from one written by Charles Sheridan is highly honourable to both brothers : —

" Dublin Castle, 13th February, 1787.

" MY DEAR DICK,

" Could I for a moment forget you were my brother, I should merely as an Irishman, think myself bound to thank you, for the high credit you have done your country. You may be assured, therefore, that the sense of national pride, which I in common with all your countrymen on this side of the water must feel on this splendid occasion, acquires no small increase of personal satisfaction, when I reflect to whom Ireland is indebted, for a display of ability so unequalled, that the honour derived from it seems too extensive to be concentered in an individual, but ought to give, and I am persuaded will give, a new respect for the name of Irishman. I have heard and read the accounts of your speech, and of the astonishing impression it made, with tears of exultation — but what will flatter you more — I can solemnly declare it to be a fact, that I have, since the news reached us, seen good honest *Irish* pride, national pride I mean, bring tears into the eyes of many persons, on this occasion, who never saw you. I need not, after what I have stated, assure you, that it is with the most heartfelt satisfaction that I offer you my warmest congratulations.   *   *   * ”

The following is from his eldest sister, Mrs. Joseph Lefanu : —

“ 16th February, 1787.

“ MY DEAR BROTHER,

“ The day before yesterday I received the account of your glorious speech. Mr. Crauford was so good as to write a more particular and

satisfactory one to Mr. Lefanu than we could
have received from the papers. I have watched
the first interval of ease from a cruel and almost
incessant head-ache to give vent to my feelings,
and tell you how much I rejoice in your success.
May it be entire ! May the God who fashioned
you, and gave you powers to sway the hearts of
men and controul their wayward wills, be equally
favourable to you in all your undertakings, and
make your reward here and hereafter ! Amen,
from the bottom of my soul ! My affection for
you has been ever ' passing the love of women.'
Adverse circumstances have deprived me of the
pleasure of your society, but have had no effect
in weakening my regard for you. I know your
heart too well to suppose that regard is indifferent to you, and soothingly sweet to me is the
idea that in some pause of thought from the important matters that occupy your mind, your
earliest friend is sometimes recollected by you.

" I know you are much above the little vanity
that seeks its gratification in the praises of the
million, but you must be pleased with the applause of the discerning, — with the tribute I
may say of affection paid to the goodness of
your heart. People love your character as much
as they admire your talents. My father is, in a
degree that I did not expect, gratified with the
general attention you have excited here : he

seems truly pleased that men should say, 'There goes the father of Gaul.' If your fame has shed a ray of brightness over all so distinguished as to be connected with you, I am sure I may say it has infused a ray of gladness into my heart, deprest as it has been with ill health and long confinement.   *   *   * ''

There is also another letter from this lady, of the same date, to Mrs. Sheridan, which begins thus enthusiastically :—

"MY DEAR SHERI.
" Nothing but death could keep me silent on such an occasion as this. I wish you joy — I am sure you feel it : ' oh moments worth whole ages past, and all that are to come.' You may laugh at my enthusiasm if you please — I glory in it.   *   *   * ''

In the month of April following, Mr. Sheridan opened the Seventh Charge, which accused Hastings of corruption, in receiving bribes and presents. The orator was here again lucky in having a branch of the case allotted to him, which, though by no means so susceptible of the ornaments of eloquence as the former, had the advantage of being equally borne out by testimony, and formed one of the most decided features of the cause. The avidity, indeed, with

which Hastings exacted presents, and then concealed them as long as there was a chance of his
being able to appropriate them to himself, gave
a mean and ordinary air to iniquities, whose
magnitude would otherwise have rendered them
imposing, if not grand.

The circumstances, under which the present
from Cheyte Sing was extorted, shall be related
when I come to speak of the great Speech in
Westminster Hall. The other strong cases of
corruption, on which Mr. Sheridan now dwelt,
were the sums given by the Munny Begum (in
return for her appointment to a trust for which,
it appears, she was unfit,) both to Hastings himself and his useful agent, Middleton. This
charge, as far as regards the latter, was never
denied ; — and the suspicious lengths to which
the Governor-general went, in not only refusing
all enquiry into his own share of the transaction,
but having his accuser, Nuncomar, silenced by
an unjust sentence of death, render his acquittal
on this charge such a stretch of charity, as nothing but a total ignorance of the evidence and
all its bearings can justify.

The following passage, with which Sheridan
wound up his Speech on this occasion, is as
strong an example as can be adduced of that
worst sort of florid style, which prolongs metaphor into allegory, and, instead of giving in a

single sentence the essence of many flowers, spreads the flowers themselves, in crude heaps, over a whole paragraph : —

" In conclusion, (he observed,) that, although within this rank, but infinitely too fruitful wilderness of iniquities—within this dismal and unhallowed labyrinth — it was most natural to cast an eye of indignation and concern over the wide and towering forest of enormities — all rising in the dusky magnificence of guilt ; and to fix the dreadfully-excited attention upon the huge trunks of revenge, rapine, tyranny, and oppression ; — yet it became not less necessary to trace out the poisonous weeds, the baleful brushwood, and all the little, creeping, deadly plants, which were, in quantity and extent, if possible, more noxious. The whole range of this far-spreading calamity was sown in the hot-bed of corruption ; and had risen, by rapid and mature growth, into every species of illegal and atrocious violence."

At the commencement of the proceedings against Hastings, an occurrence, immediately connected with them, had brought Sheridan and his early friend Halhed together, under circumstances as different as well can be imagined from those under which they had parted, as boys. The distance, indeed, that had separated them in the interval was hardly greater than the divergence that had taken place in their pursuits ; for, while Sheridan had been converted into a senator and statesman, the lively Halhed had become an East Indian Judge, and a learned commentator on the Gentoo Laws. Upon the subject, too, on which they now met, their views and interests were wholly opposite, — Sheridan being the accuser of Hastings, and Halhed his friend. The following are the public circumstances that led to their interview.

In one of the earliest debates on the Charges against the Governor-General, Major Scott having asserted that, when Mr. Fox was preparing his India Bill, overtures of accommodation had been made, by his authority, to Mr. Hastings, added that he (Major Scott) " entertained no doubt that, had Mr. Hastings then come home, he would have heard nothing of all this calumny, and all these serious accusations." Mr. Fox, whom this charge evidently took by surprise, replied that he was totally ignorant of any such overtures, and that " whoever made, or even hinted, at such an offer, as coming from him, did it without the smallest shadow of authority." By an explanation, a few days after, from Mr. Sheridan, it appeared that he was the person who had taken the step alluded to by Major Scott. His interference, however, he said, was solely founded upon an opinion which he had himself formed with respect to the India Bill, — namely, that it would be wiser, on grounds of expediency, not to make it retrospective in any of its clauses. In consequence of this opinion,

he had certainly commissioned a friend to enquire of Major Scott, whether, if Mr. Hastings
were recalled, he would come home; — but
" that there had been the most distant idea of
bartering with Mr. Hastings for his support of
the Indian Bill, he utterly denied." In conclusion, he referred, for the truth of what he had
now stated, to Major Scott, who, instantly rising,
acknowledged that, from enquiries which he had
since made of the gentleman deputed to him by
Mr. Sheridan on the occasion, he was ready to
bear testimony to the fairness of the statement
just submitted to the House, and to admit his
own mistake in the interpretation which he had
put on the transaction.

It was in relation to this misunderstanding
that the interview took place in the year 1786
between Sheridan and Halhed — the other persons present being Major Scott and Doctor Parr,
from whom I heard the circumstance. The
feelings of this venerable scholar towards " iste
Scotus" (as he calls Major Scott in his Preface
to Bellendenus) were not, it is well known, of
the most favourable kind; and he took the opportunity of this interview to tell that gentleman
fully what he thought of him : — " for ten
minutes," said the Doctor, in describing his aggression, " I poured out upon him hot, scalding
abuse — 'twas lava, sir ! ''

Among the other questions that occupied the attention of Mr. Sheridan during this session, the most important were the Commercial Treaty with France, and the Debts of the Prince of Wales.

The same erroneous views, by which the opposition to the Irish Commercial Propositions was directed, still continued to actuate Mr. Fox and his friends in their pertinacious resistance to the Treaty with France; —a measure which reflects high honour upon the memory of Mr. Pitt, as one of the first efforts of a sound and liberal policy to break through that system of restriction and interference, which had so long embarrassed the flow of international commerce.

The wisdom of leaving trade to find its own way into those channels, which the reciprocity of wants established among mankind opens to it, is one of those obvious truths that have lain long on the highways of knowledge, before practical statesmen would condescend to pick them up. It has been shown, that the sound principles of commerce, which have at last forced their way from the pages of thinking men into the councils of legislators, were more than a hundred years since promulgated by Sir Dudley North * ;— and in the Querist of Bishop Berkeley may be

* M'Culloch's Discourse on the Science of Political Economy.

found the outlines of all that the best friends not only of free trade but of free religion would recommend to the rulers of Ireland at the present day. Thus frequently does Truth, before the drowsy world is prepared for her, like

> " The nice Morn on the Indian steep,
> From her cabin'd loophole peep."

Though Mr. Sheridan spoke frequently in the course of the discussions, he does not appear to have, at any time, encountered the main body of the question, but to have confined himself chiefly to a consideration of the effects, which the Treaty would have upon the interests of Ireland; — a point which he urged with so much earnestness, as to draw down upon him from one of the speakers the taunting designation of " Self-appointed Representative of Ireland."

Mr. Fox was the most active antagonist of the Treaty; and his speeches on the subject may be counted among those feats of prowess, with which the chivalry of Genius sometimes adorns the cause of Error. In founding, as he did, his chief argument against commercial intercourse upon the " natural enmity " between the two countries, he might have referred, it is true, to high Whig authority: — " The late Lord Oxford told me," says Lord Bolingbroke, "that my Lord Somers being pressed, I know not on what occasión or by whom, on the unnecessary and ruinous continuation of the war, instead of giving reasons to show the necessity of it, contented himself to reply that he had been bred up in a hatred to France." — But no authority, however high, can promote a prejudice into a reason, or conciliate any respect for this sort of vague, traditional hostility, which is often obliged to seek its own justification in the very mischiefs which itself produces. If Mr. Fox ever happened to peruse the praises, which his *Antigallican* sentiments on this occasion procured for him, from the tedious biographer of his rival, Mr. Gifford, he would have suspected, like Phocion, that he must have spoken something unworthy of himself, to have drawn down upon his head a panegyric from such a quarter.

Another of Mr. Fox's arguments against entering into commercial relations with France, was the danger lest English merchants, by investing their capital in foreign speculations, should become so entangled with the interests of another country as to render them less jealous than they ought to be of the honour of their own, and less ready to rise in its defence, when wronged or insulted. But, assuredly, a want of pugnacity is not the evil to be dreaded among nations, — still less between two, whom the orator had just represented as inspired by a

" natural enmity " against each other. He ought rather, upon this assumption, to have welcomed the prospect of a connection, which, by transfusing and blending their commercial interests, and giving each a stake in the prosperity of the other, would not only soften away the animal antipathy attributed to them, but, by enlisting selfishness on the side of peace and amity, afford the best guarantee against wanton warfare, that the wisdom of statesmen or philosophers has yet devised.

Mr. Burke, in affecting to consider the question in an enlarged point of view, fell equally short of its real dimensions ; and even descended to the weakness of ridiculing such commercial arrangements, as unworthy altogether of the contemplation of the higher order of statesmen. " The Right Honourable Gentleman," he said, " had talked of the treaty as if it were the affair of two little counting-houses, and not of two great countries. He seemed to consider it as a contention between the sign of the Fleur-de-lis, and the sign of the Red Lion, which house should obtain the best custom. Such paltry considerations were below his notice."

In such terms could Burke, from temper or waywardness of judgment, attempt to depreciate a speech which may be said to have contained the first luminous statement of the principles of commerce, with the most judicious views of their application to details, that had ever, at that period, been presented to the House.

The wise and enlightened opinions of Mr. Pitt, both with respect to Trade, and another very different subject of legislation, Religion, would have been far more worthy of the imitation of some of his self-styled followers, than those errors which they are so glad to shelter under the sanction of his name. For encroachments upon the property and liberty of the subject, for financial waste and unconstitutional severity, they have the precedent of their great master ever ready on their lips. But, in all that would require wisdom and liberality in his copyists — in the repugnance he felt to restrictions and exclusions, affecting either the worldly commerce of man with man, or the spiritual intercourse of man with his God — in all this, like the Indian that quarrels with his idol, these pretended followers not only dissent from their prototype themselves, but violently denounce, as mischievous, his opinions when adopted by others.

In attributing to party feelings the wrong views entertained by the Opposition on this question, we should but defend their sagacity at the expence of their candour; and the cordiality with which they came forward this year to

H H 2

praise the spirited part taken by the Minister in the affairs of Holland — even allowing that it would be difficult for Whigs not to concur in a measure so national — sufficiently acquits them of any such perverse spirit of party, as would, for the mere sake of opposition, go wrong because the Minister was right. To the sincerity of one of their objections to the Treaty — namely, that it was a design, on the part of France, to detach England, by the temptation of a mercantile advantage, from her ancient alliance with Holland and her other continental connections — Mr. Burke bore testimony, as far as himself was concerned, by repeating the same opinions, after an interval of ten years, in his testamentary work, the " Letters on a Regicide Peace."

The other important question which I have mentioned as engaging, during the session of 1787, the attention of Mr. Sheridan, was the application to Parliament for the payment of the Prince of Wales's debts. The embarrassments of the Heir-Apparent were but a natural consequence of his situation ; and a little more graciousness and promptitude on the part of the King, in interposing to relieve His Royal Highness from the difficulties under which he laboured, would have afforded a chance of detaching him from his new political associates, of

which, however the affection of the Royal parent
may have slumbered, it is strange that his sagacity did not hasten to avail itself. A contrary
system, however, was adopted. The haughty
indifference both of the monarch and his minister threw the Prince entirely on the sympathy
of the Opposition. Mr. Pitt identified himself
with the obstinacy of the father, while Mr. Fóx
and the Opposition committed themselves with
the irregularities of the son ; and the proceedings of both parties were such as might have
been expected from their respective connections ; — the Royal mark was but too visible
upon each.

One evil consequence, that was on the point
of resulting from the embarrassed situation in
which the Prince now found himself, was his
acceptance of a loan which the Duke of Orleans
had proffered him, and which would have had
the perilous tendency of placing the future Sovereign of England in a state of dependence, as
creditor, on a Prince of France. That the negotiations in this extraordinary transaction had
proceeded farther than is generally supposed,
will appear from the following letters of the
Duke of Portland to Sheridan : —

H H 3

" Dear Sheridan, Sunday noon, 13. Dec.
" Since I saw you I have received a confirmation of the intelligence which was the subject of our conversation. The particulars varied in no respect from those I related to you — except in the addition of a pension, which is to take place immediately on the event which entitles the creditors to payment, and is to be granted for life to a nominee of the D. of O———s. The loan was mentioned in a mixed company by two of the Frenchwomen and a Frenchman (none of whose names I know) in *Calonne*'s presence, who interrupted them, by asking, how they came to know any thing of the matter, then set them right in two or three particulars which they had misstated, and afterwards begged them, for God's sake, not to talk of it, because it might be their complete ruin.

" I am going to Bulstrode — but will return at a moment's notice, if I can be of the least use in getting rid of this odious engagement, or preventing its being entered into, if it should not be yet completed.

" Yours ever,
" P."

" Dear Sheridan,
" I think myself much obliged to you for what you have done. I hope I am not too san-

guine in looking to a good conclusion of this bad
business. I will certainly be in town by two
o'clock.

" Yours, ever,

" Bulstrode, Monday, 14. Dec.   P.
" 9 A. M."

Mr. Sheridan, who was now high in the confidence of the Prince, had twice, in the course of
the year 1786, taken occasion to allude publicly
to the embarrassments of His Royal Highness.
Indeed, the decisive measure which this Illustrious Person himself had adopted, in reducing
his establishment and devoting a part of his
income to the discharge of his debts, sufficiently
proclaimed the true state of affairs to the public.
Still, however, the strange policy was persevered
in, of adding the discontent of the Heir-Apparent
to the other weapons in the hands of the Opposition ; — and, as might be expected, they were
not tardy in turning it to account. In the spring
of 1787, the embarrassed state of His Royal
Highness's affairs was brought formally under the
notice of parliament by Alderman Newenham.

During one of the discussions to which the
subject gave rise, Mr. Rolle, the member for
Devonshire, a strong adherent of the ministry,
in deprecating the question about to be agitated,
affirmed that " it went immediately to affect our

Constitution in Church and State." In these solemn words it was well understood, that he alluded
to a report at that time generally believed, and
acted upon by many in the etiquette of private life,
that a marriage had been solemnized between the
Prince of Wales and Mrs. Fitzherbert, a lady of the
Roman Catholic persuasion, who, with more danger
to her own peace than to that of either Church
or State, had for some time been the distinguished
object of His Royal Highness's affection.

Even had an alliance of this description taken
place, the provisions of the Royal Marriage Act
would have nullified it into a mere ceremony,
inefficient, as it was supposed, for any other purpose than that of satisfying the scruples of one of
the parties. But that dread of Popery, which in
England starts at its own shadow, took alarm at
the consequences of an intercourse so heterodox ;
and it became necessary, in the opinion of the
Prince and his friends, to put an end to the apprehensions that were abroad on the subject.

Nor can it be denied that, in the minds of those
who believed that the marriage had been actually
solemnized *, there were, in one point of view,
very sufficient grounds of alarm. By the Statute

* Horne Tooke, in his insidious pamphlet on the subject,
presumed so far on this belief as to call Mrs. Fitzherbert
" Her Royal Highness."

of William and Mary, commonly called the Bill of Rights, it is enacted, among other causes of exclusion from the throne, that " every person who shall marry a Papist shall be excluded and for ever be incapable to inherit the crown of this realm." — In such cases (adds this truly revolutionary Act) " the people of these realms shall be and are hereby absolved of their allegiance." Under this Act, which was confirmed by the Act of Settlement, it is evident that the Heir-Apparent would, by such a marriage as was now attributed to him, have forfeited his right of succession to the throne. From so serious a penalty, however, it was generally supposed, he would have been exempted by the operation of the Royal Marriage Act (12 George III.), which rendered null and void any marriage contracted by any descendant of George II. without the previous consent of the King, or a twelve months' notice given to the Privy Council.

That this Act would have nullified the alleged marriage of the Prince of Wales there is, of course, no doubt ; — but that it would have also exempted him from the forfeiture incurred by marriage with a Papist, is a point which, in the minds of many, still remains a question. There are, it is well known, analogous cases in Law, where the nullity of an illegal transaction does not do away the penalty attached to it.* . To persons, therefore, who believed that the actual solemnization of the marriage could be proved by witnesses present at the ceremony, this view of the case, which seemed to promise an interruption of the Succession, could not fail to suggest some disquieting apprehensions and speculations, which nothing short, it was thought, of a public and authentic disavowal of the marriage altogether would be able effectually to allay.

If in politics Princes are unsafe allies, in connections of a tenderer nature they are still more perilous partners; and a triumph over a Royal lover is dearly bought by the various risks and humiliations which accompany it. Not only is a lower standard of constancy applied to persons of that rank, but when once love-affairs are converted into matters of state, there is an end to

---

* Thus, a man by contracting a second marriage, pending the first marriage, commits a felony; and the crime, according to its legal description, consists in marrying, or contracting a marriage — though what he does is no more a marriage than that of the Heir-Apparent would be under the circumstances in question.

The same principle runs through the whole Law of Entails both in England and Scotland, and a variety of cases might be cited, in which, though the act done is void, yet the doing of it creates a forfeiture.

all the delicacy and mystery that ought to encircle them. The disavowal of a Royal marriage in the Gazette would have been no novelty in English history * ; and the disclaimer, on the present occasion, though intrusted to a less official medium, was equally public, strong, and unceremonious.

Mr. Fox, who had not been present in the House of Commons when the member for Devonshire alluded to the circumstance, took occasion, on the next discussion of the question, and, as he declared, with the immediate authority of the Prince, to contradict the report of the marriage in the fullest and most unqualified terms : — it was, he said, " a miserable calumny, a low malicious falsehood, which had been propagated without doors, and made the wanton sport of the vulgar ; — a tale, fit only to impose upon the lowest orders, a monstrous invention, a report of a fact which had not the smallest degree of foundation, actually impossible to have happened." To an observation from Mr. Rolle that " they all knew there was an Act of Parliament which forbade such a marriage ; but,

---

* See in Ellis's Letters of History, vol. iii., the declarations of Charles II. with respect to his marriage with " one Mrs. Walters," signed by himself, and published in The London Gazette.

that, though it could not be done under the formal sanction of the law, there were ways in which it might have taken place, and in which that law, in the minds of some persons, might have been satisfactorily evaded," — Mr. Fox replied, that " he did not deny the calumny in question merely with regard to certain existing laws, but that he denied it *in toto*, in point of fact as well as of law : — it not only never could have happened legally, but it never did happen in any way whatsoever, and had from the beginning been a base and malicious falsehood."

Though Mr. Rolle, from either obstinacy or real distrust, refused, in spite of the repeated calls of Mr. Sheridan and Mr. Grey, to declare himself satisfied with this declaration, it was felt by the minister to be at least sufficiently explicit and decisive, to leave him no further pretext, in the eyes of the public, for refusing the relief which the situation of the Prince required. Accordingly, a message from the Crown on the subject of His Royal Highness's debts was followed by an addition to his income of 10,000*l.* yearly out of the Civil List ; an issue of 161,000*l.* from the same source, for the discharge of his debts, and 20,000*l.* on account of the works at Carlton-House.

In the same proportion that this authorised declaration was successful in satisfying the public mind, it must naturally have been painful and humiliating to the person whose honour was involved in it. The immediate consequence of this feeling was a breach between that person and Mr. Fox, which, notwithstanding the continuance, for so many years after, of the attachment of both to the same illustrious object, remained, it is understood, unreconciled to the last.

If, in the first movement of sympathy with the pain excited in that quarter, a retractation of this public disavowal was thought of, the impossibility of finding any creditable medium, through which to convey it must soon have suggested itself to check the intention. Some middle course, however, it was thought might be adopted, which, without going the full length of retracting, might tend at least to unsettle the impression left upon the public, and, in some degree, retrieve that loss of station, which a disclaimer, coming in such an authentic shape, had entailed. To ask Mr. Fox to discredit his own statement was impossible. An application was, therefore, made to a young member of the party, who was then fast rising into the eminence which he has since so nobly sustained, and whose answer to the proposal is said to have betrayed some of that unaccommodating highmindedness, which, in more than one collision with Royalty, has proved him but an unfit adjunct to a Court. The reply to his refusal was, " Then, I must get Sheridan to say something ;" — and hence, it seems, was the origin of those few dexterously unmeaning compliments, with which the latter, when the motion of Alderman Newenham was withdrawn, endeavoured, without in the least degree weakening the declaration of Mr. Fox, to restore that equilibrium of temper and self-esteem, which such a sacrifice of gallantry to expediency had naturally disturbed. In alluding to the offer of the Prince, through Mr. Fox, to answer any questions upon the subject of his reported marriage, which it might be thought proper to put to him in the House, Mr. Sheridan said,—" That no such idea had been pursued, and no such enquiry had been adopted, was a point which did credit to the decorum, the feelings, and the dignity of Parliament. But whilst His Royal Highness's feelings had no doubt been considered on this occasion, he must take the liberty of saying, however some might think it a subordinate consideration, that there was another person entitled, in every delicate and honourable mind, to the same attention ; one,

whom he would not otherwise venture to describe or allude to, but by saying it was a
name, which malice or ignorance alone could
attempt to injure, and whose character and
conduct claimed and were entitled to the truest
respect."

CHAP. XI.

IMPEACHMENT OF MR. HASTINGS.

THE motion of Mr. Burke on the 10th of May, 1787, " That Warren Hastings, Esq., be impeached," having been carried without a division, Mr. Sheridan was appointed one of the Managers, " to make good the Articles " of the Impeachment, and, on the 3d of June in the following year, brought forward the same Charge in Westminster Hall which he had already enforced with such wonderful talent in the House of Commons.

To be called upon for a second great effort of eloquence, on a subject of which all the facts and the bearings remained the same, was, it must be acknowledged, no ordinary trial to even the most fertile genius ; and Mr. Fox, it is said, hopeless of any second flight ever rising to the grand elevation of the first, advised that the former Speech should be, with very little change, repeated. But such a plan, however welcome it might be to the indolence of his friend, would have looked too like an acknowledgment of exhaustion on the subject, to be submitted to by one so justly confident in the resources both of his reason and fancy. Accordingly, he had the glory of again opening, in the very same field, a new and abundant spring of eloquence, which, during four days, diffused its enchantment among an assembly of the most illustrious persons of the land, and of which Mr. Burke pronounced at its conclusion, that " of all the various species of oratory, of every kind of eloquence that had been heard, either in ancient or modern times; whatever the acuteness of the bar, the dignity of the senate, or the morality of the pulpit, could furnish, had not been equal to what that House had that day heard in Westminster Hall. No holy religionist, no man of any description as a literary character, could have come up, in the one instance, to the pure sentiments of morality, or in the other, to the variety of knowledge, force of imagination, propriety and vivacity of allusion, beauty and elegance of diction, and strength of expression, to which they had that day listened. From poetry up to eloquence there was not a species of composition of which a complete and perfect specimen might not have been culled, from one part or the other of the speech to which he alluded, and which, he was persuaded, had left too strong an impression on the minds of that House to be easily obliterated."

As some atonement to the world for the loss of the Speech in the House of Commons, this second master-piece of eloquence on the same subject has been preserved to us in a Report, from the short-hand notes of Mr. Gurney, which was for some time in the possession of the late Duke of Norfolk, but was afterwards restored to Mr. Sheridan, and is now in my hands.

In order to enable the reader fully to understand the extracts from this Report which I am about to give, it will be necessary to detail briefly the history of the transaction, on which the charge brought forward in the Speech was founded.

Among the native Princes who, on the transfer of the sceptre of Tamerlane to the East India Company, became tributaries or rather slaves to that Honourable body, none seems to have been treated with more capricious cruelty than Cheyte Sing, the Rajah of Benares. In defiance of a solemn treaty, entered into between him and the government of Mr. Hastings, by which it was stipulated that, besides his fixed tribute, no further demands, of any kind, should be made upon him, new exactions were every year enforced; — while the humble remonstrances of the Rajah against such gross injustice were not only treated with slight, but punished by arbitrary and enormous fines. Even the proffer of a bribe succeeded only in being accepted * — the exactions which it was intended to avert being continued as rigorously as before. At length, in the year 1781, Mr. Hastings, who invariably, among the objects of his government, placed the interests of Leadenhall Street first on the list, and those of justice and humanity *longo intervallo* after, — finding the treasury of the Company in a very exhausted state, resolved to sacrifice this unlucky Rajah to their replenishment; and having, as a preliminary step, imposed upon him a mulct of 500,000*l.*, set out immediately for his capital, Benares, to compel the payment of it. Here, after rejecting with insult the suppliant advances of the Prince, he put him under arrest, and imprisoned him in his own palace. This violation of the rights and the roof of their sovereign drove the people of the whole province into a sudden burst of rebellion, of which Mr. Hastings himself was near being the victim. The usual triumph, however, of

* This was the transaction that formed one of the principal grounds of the Seventh Charge brought forward in the House of Commons by Mr. Sheridan. The suspicious circumstances attending this present are thus summed up by Mr. Mill:—" At first, perfect concealment of the transaction — such measures, however, taken as may, if afterwards necessary, appear to imply a design of future disclosure; — when concealment becomes difficult and hazardous, then disclosure made." — *History of British India.*

might over right ensued; the Rajah's castle was plundered of all its treasures, and his mother, who had taken refuge in the fort, and only surrendered it on the express stipulation that she and the other Princesses should pass out safe from the dishonour of search, was, in violation of this condition, and at the base suggestion of Mr. Hastings himself*, rudely examined and despoiled of all her effects. The Governor-General, however, in this one instance, incurred the full odium of iniquity without reaping any of its reward. The treasures found in the castle of the Rajah were inconsiderable, and the soldiers, who had shown themselves so docile in receiving the lessons of plunder, were found inflexibly obstinate in refusing to admit their instructor to a share. Disappointed, therefore, in the primary object of his expedition, the Governor-General looked round for some richer harvest of rapine, and the Begums of Oude presented them-

---

* In his letter to the Commanding Officer at Bidgegur. The following are the terms in which he conveys the hint:—
" I apprehend that she will contrive to defraud the captors of a considerable part of the booty, by being suffered to retire *without examination*. But this is your consideration, and not mine. I should be very sorry that your officers and soldiers lost any part of the reward to which they are so well entitled; but I cannot make any objection, as you must be the best judge of the expediency of the *promised* indulgence to the Rannee."

selves as the most convenient victims. These
Princesses, the mother and grandmother of the
reigning Nabob of Oude, had been left by the
late Sovereign in possession of certain govern-
ment-estates or jaghires, as well as of all the treasure that was in his hands at the time of his
death, and which the orientalized imaginations
of the English exaggerated to an enormous sum.
The present Nabob had evidently looked with
an eye of cupidity on this wealth, and had been
guilty of some acts of extortion towards his
female relatives, in consequence of which the
English government had interfered between
them, — and had even guaranteed to the mother
of the Nabob the safe possession of her property,
without any further encroachment whatever.
Guarantees and treaties, however, were but cob-
webs in the way of Mr. Hastings; and on his
failure at Benares, he lost no time in concluding
an agreement with the Nabob, by which (in
consideration of certain measures of relief to his
dominions) this Prince was bound to plunder his
mother and grandmother of all their property,
and place it at the disposal of the Governor-
General. In order to give a colour of justice
to this proceeding, it was * pretended that these

* " It was the practice of Mr. Hastings (says Burke, in his
fine Speech on Mr. Pitt's India Bill, March 22. 1786,) to ex-

I I 3

Princesses had taken advantage of the late insurrection at Benares, to excite a similar spirit
of revolt in Oude against the reigning Nabob
and the English government. As Law is but
too often, in such cases, the ready accomplice
of Tyranny, the services of the Chief Justice,
Sir Elijah Impey, were called in to sustain the
accusations ; and the wretched mockery was exhibited of a Judge travelling about in search of
evidence *, for the express purpose of proving
a charge, upon which judgment had been pronounced and punishment decreed already.

---

amine the country, and wherever he found money to affix
guilt. A more dreadful fault could not be alleged against a
native than that he was rich."

* This journey of the Chief Justice in search of evidence
is thus happily described by Sheridan in the Speech :—
" When, on the 28th of November, he was busied at Lucknow on that honourable business, and when, three days after,
he was found at Chunar, at the distance of 200 miles, still
searching for affidavits, and, like Hamlet's ghost, exclaiming,
' Swear !' his progress on that occasion was so whimsically
rapid, compared with the gravity of his employ, that an observer would be tempted to quote again from the same scene,
' Ha! Old Truepenny, canst thou mole so fast i' the ground?'
Here, however, the comparison ceased; for, when Sir Elijah
made his visit to Lucknow ' to whet the almost blunted purpose' of the Nabob, his language was wholly different from
that of the poet, — for it would have been totally against
his purpose to have said,

" ' Taint not thy mind, nor let thy soul contrive
        Against thy *mother* aught.' "

The Nabob himself, though sufficiently ready to make the wealth of those venerable ladies occasionally minister to his wants, yet shrunk back, with natural reluctance, from the summary task now imposed upon him ; and it was not till after repeated and peremptory remonstrances from Mr. Hastings, that he could be induced to put himself at the head of a body of English troops, and take possession, by unresisted force, of the town and palace of these Princesses. As the treasure, however, was still secure in the apartments of the women, — that circle within which even the spirit of English rapine did not venture, — an expedient was adopted to get over this inconvenient delicacy. Two aged eunuchs of high rank and distinction, the confidential agents of the Begums, were thrown into prison, and subjected to a course of starvation and torture, by which it was hoped that the feelings of their mistresses might be worked upon, and a more speedy surrender of their treasure wrung from them. The plan succeeded : — upwards of 500,000*l.* was procured to recruit the finances of the Company ; and thus, according to the usual course of British power in India, rapacity but levied its contributions in one quarter, to enable war to pursue its desolating career in another.

To crown all, one of the chief articles of the

treaty, by which the Nabob was reluctantly induced to concur in these atrocious measures,
was, as soon as the object had been gained, in-
fringed by Mr. Hastings, who, in a letter to his
colleagues in the government, honestly confesses
that the concession of that article was only frau-
dulent artifice of diplomacy, and never intended
to be carried into effect.

Such is an outline of the case, which, with all
its aggravating details, Mr. Sheridan had to state
in these two memorable Speeches; and it was
certainly most fortunate for the display of his
peculiar powers, that this should be the Charge
confided to his management. For, not only was
it the strongest, and susceptible of the highest
charge of colouring, but it had also the advantage of grouping together all the principal de-
linquents of the trial, and affording a gradation
of hue, from the showy and prominent enormities of the Governor-General and Sir Elijah
Impey in the front of the picture, to the subordinate and half-tint iniquity of the Middletons
and Bristows in the back-ground.

Mr. Burke, it appears, had at first reserved
this grand part in the drama of the Impeachment for himself; but, finding that Sheridan had
also fixed his mind upon it, he, without hesitation, resigned it into his hands; thus proving the

sincerity of his zeal in the cause *, by sacrificing even the vanity of talent to its success.

The following letters from him relative to the Impeachment, will be read with interest. The first is addressed to Mrs. Sheridan, and was written, I think, early in the proceedings ; the second is to Sheridan himself.

" MADAM,

" I am sure you will have the goodness to excuse the liberty I take with you, when you consider the interest which I have and which the Public have (the said Public being, at least, half an inch a taller person than I am,) in the use of Mr. Sheridan's abilities. I know that his mind is seldom unemployed ; but then, like all such great and vigorous minds, it takes an eagle flight by itself, and we can hardly bring it to rustle along the ground, with us birds of meaner wing, in coveys. I only beg that you will prevail on Mr. Sheridan to be with us *this day*, at half after three, in the Committee. Mr. Wombell, the

* Of the lengths to which this zeal could sometimes carry his fancy and language, rather, perhaps, than his actual feelings, the following anecdote is a remarkable proof. On one of the days of the trial, Lord ——, who was then a boy, having been introduced by a relative into the Manager's box, Burke said to him, " I am glad to see you here — I shall be still gladder to see you there — (pointing to the Peers' seats) I hope you will be *in at the death* — I should like to *blood* you."

Paymaster of Oude, is to be examined there *to-day*. Oude is Mr. Sheridan's particular province; and I do most seriously ask that he would favour us with his assistance. What will come of the examination I know not; but, without him, I do not expect a great deal from it; with him, I fancy we may get out something material. Once more let me intreat your interest with Mr. Sheridan and your forgiveness for being troublesome to you, and to do me the justice to believe me, with the most sincere respect,

" Madam, your most obedient
" and faithful humble Servant,

" Thursday, 9 o'clock.   EDM. BURKE."

" MY DEAR SIR,

" You have only to wish to be excused to succeed in your wishes; — for indeed, he must be a great enemy to himself who can consent, on account of a momentary ill-humour, to keep himself at a distance from you.

" Well, all will turn out right, — and half of you, or a quarter, is worth five other men. I think that this cause, which was originally yours, will be recognized by you, and that you will again possess yourself of it. The owner's mark is on it, and all our docking and cropping cannot hinder its being known and cherished by its original master. My most humble respects to

Mrs. Sheridan. I ~~am happy to find that she~~
takes in good part the liberty I presumed to
take with her. Grey has done much and will
do every thing. It is a pity that he is not always
toned to the full extent of his talents.

" Most truly yours,

" Monday. EDM. BURKE.

" I feel a little sickish at the approaching day.
I have read much — too much, perhaps, — and,
in truth, am but poorly prepared. Many things,
too, have broken in upon me." *

Though a Report, however accurate, must
always do injustice to that effective kind of
oratory which is intended rather to be heard than
read, and, though frequently, the passages, that
most roused and interested the hearer, are those
that seem afterwards the tritest and least animat-
ing to the reader†, yet, with all this disadvantage, the celebrated oration in question so well
sustains its reputation in the perusal, that it

* For this letter, as well as some other valuable com-
munications, I am indebted to the kindness of Mr. Burgess,
the Solicitor and friend of Sheridan during the last thirty
years of his life.

† The converse assertion is almost equally true. Mr. Fox
used to ask of a printed speech, " Does it read well?" and,
if answered in the affirmative said, " Then it was a bad
speech."

would be injustice, having an authentic Report in my possession, not to produce some specimens of its style and spirit.

In the course of his exordium, after dwelling upon the great importance of the enquiry in which they were engaged, and disclaiming for himself and his brother-managers any feeling of personal malice against the defendant, or any motive but that of retrieving the honour of the British name in India, and bringing down punishment upon those whose inhumanity and injustice had disgraced it, — he thus proceeds to conciliate the Court by a warm tribute to the purity of English justice : —

" However, when I have said this, I trust Your Lordships will not believe that, because something is necessary to retrieve the British character, we call for an example to be made, without due and solid proof of the guilt of the person whom we pursue : — no, my Lords, we know well that it is the glory of this Constitution, that not the general fame or character of any man — not the weight or power of any prosecutor — no plea of moral or political expediency — not even the secret consciousness of guilt, which may live in the bosom of the Judge, can justify any British Court in passing any sentence, to touch a hair of the head, or an atom, in any respect, of the property, of the fame, of the liberty of the poorest or meanest subject that breathes the air of this just and free land. We know, my Lords, that there can be no legal guilt without legal proof, and that the rule which defines the evidence is as much the law of the land as that which creates the crime. It is upon that ground we mean to stand."

Among those ready equivocations and disavowals, to which Mr. Hastings had recourse upon every emergency, and in which practice seems to have rendered him as shameless as expert, the step which he took with regard to his own defence during the trial was not the least remarkable for promptness and audacity. He had, at the commencement of the prosecution, delivered at the bar of the House of Commons, as his own, a written refutation of the charges then pending against him in that House, declaring, at the same time, that "if truth could tend to convict him, he was content to be, himself, the channel to convey it." Afterwards, however, on finding that he had committed himself rather imprudently in this defence, he came forward to disclaim it at the bar of the House of Lords, and brought his friend Major Scott to prove that it had been drawn up by Messrs. Shore, Middleton, &c. &c. — that he himself had not even seen it, and therefore ought not to be held accountable for its contents. In adverting to this extraordinary evasion, Mr. Sheridan thus shrewdly and playfully exposes all the persons concerned in it : —

" Major Scott comes to your bar — describes the short-
ness of time — represents Mr. Hastings as it were *contracting for* a character — putting his memory *into commission* — making *departments* for his conscience.   A
number of friends meet together, and he, knowing (no
doubt) that the accusation of the Commons had been
drawn up by a Committee, thought it necessary, as a
point of punctilio, to answer it by a Committee also.
One furnishes the raw material of fact, the second spins
the argument, and the third twines up the conclusion,
while Mr. Hastings, with a master's eye, is cheering
and looking over this loom.   He says to one, ' You
have got my good faith in your hands — *you*, my veracity
to manage. Mr. Shore, I hope, you will make me a good
financier — Mr. Middleton, you have my humanity in
commission.' — When it is done, he brings it to the
House of Commons, and says, ' I was equal to the task.
I knew the difficulties, but I scorn them : here is the
truth, and if the truth will convict me, I am content
myself to be the channel of it.'   His friends hold up
their heads, and say, ' What noble magnanimity ! This
must be the effect of conscious and real innocence.'
Well, it is so received, it is so argued upon — but it fails
of its effect.

" Then says Mr. Hastings, — ' That my defence !
no, mere journeyman-work, — good enough for the
Commons, but not fit for Your Lordships' consideration.'
He then calls upon his Counsel to save him : — ' I fear
none of my accusers' witnesses — I know some of them
well — I know the weakness of their memory, and the
strength of their attachment — I fear no testimony but
my own — save me from the peril of my own panegyric
— preserve me from that, and I shall be safe.'   Then is

this plea brought to Your Lordships' bar, and Major Scott gravely asserts, — that Mr. Hastings did, at the bar of the House of Commons, vouch for facts of which he was ignorant, and for arguments which he had never read.

" After such an attempt, we certainly are left in doubt to decide, to *which* set of his friends Mr. Hastings is the least obliged, those who assisted him in making his defence, or those who advised him to deny it."

He thus describes the feelings of the people of the East with respect to the unapproachable sanctity of their Zenanas : —

" It is too much, I am afraid, the case, that persons, used to European manners, do not take up these sort of considerations at first with the seriousness that is necessary. For Your Lordships cannot even learn the right nature of those people's feelings and prejudices from any history of other Mahometan countries, — not even from that of the Turks, for they are a mean and degraded race in comparison with many of these great families, who, inheriting from their Persian ancestors, preserve a purer style of prejudice and a loftier superstition. Women there are not as in Turkey — they neither go to the mosque nor to the bath — it is not the thin veil alone that hides them — but the inmost recesses of their Zenana they are kept from public view by those reverenced and protected walls, which, as Mr. Hastings and Sir Elijah Impey admit, are held sacred even by the ruffian hand of war or by the more uncourteous hand of the law. But, in this situation, they are not confined from a mean and selfish policy of man — not from a coarse

and sensual jealousy — enshrined, rather than im‐
mured, their habitation and retreat is a sanctuary, not
a prison — their jealousy is their own — a jealousy of
their own honour, that leads them to regard liberty as
a degradation, and the gaze of even admiring eyes as
inexpiable pollution to the purity of their fame and the
sanctity of their honour.

" Such being the general opinion, (or prejudices, let
them be called,) of this country, Your Lordships will
find, that whatever treasures were given or lodged in a
Zenana of this description must, upon the evidence of
the thing itself, be placed beyond the reach of resump‐
tion.   To dispute with the Counsel about the original
right to those treasures — to talk of a title to them by
the Mahometan law ! — their title to them is the title of
a Saint to the relics upon an altar, placed there by
Piety *, guarded by holy Superstition, and to be snatched
from thence only by Sacrilege."

In showing that the Nabob was driven to this
robbery of his relatives by other considerations
than those of the pretended rebellion, which was

---

* This metaphor was rather roughly handled afterwards
(1794) by Mr. Law, one of the adverse Counsel, who asked,
how could the Begum be considered as " a Saint," or how
were the camels, which formed part of the treasure to be
" placed upon the altar ?" Sheridan, in reply, said, " It was
the first time in his life he had ever heard of *special pleading*
on a *metaphor*, or a *bill of indictment* against a trope.   But
such was the turn of the Learned Counsel's mind, that,
when he attempted to be humorous, no jest could be found,
and, when serious, no fact was visible."

afterwards conjured up by Mr. Hastings to justify it, he says, —

" The fact is, that through all his defences — through all his various false suggestions — through all these various rebellions and disaffections, Mr. Hastings never once lets go this plea — of unextinguishable right in the Nabob. He constantly represents the seizing the treasures as a resumption of a right which he could not part with ; — as if there were literally something in the Koran, that made it criminal in a true Mussulman to keep his engagements with his relations, and impious in a son to abstain from plundering his mother. I do gravely assure Your Lordships that there is no such doctrine in the Koran, and no such principle makes a part in the civil or municipal jurisprudence of that country. Even after these Princesses had been endeavouring to dethrone the Nabob and to extirpate the English, the only plea the Nabob ever makes, is his right under the Mahometan law; and the truth is, he appears never to have heard any other reason, and I pledge myself to make it appear to Your Lordships, however extraordinary it may be, that not only had the Nabob never heard of the rebellion till the moment of seizing the palace, but, still further, that he never heard of it at all ; — that this extraordinary rebellion, which was as notorious as the Rebellion of 1745 in London, was carefully concealed from those two parties — the Begums who plotted it, and the Nabob who was to be the victim of it.

" The existence of this rebellion was not the secret, but the notoriety of it was the secret; — it was a rebellion which had for its object the destruction of no human creature but those who planned it ; — it was a rebellion which, according to Mr. Middleton's expression, no man, either horse or foot, ever marched to quell. The Chief Justice was the only man who took the field against it, — the force against which it was raised, instantly withdrew to give it elbow-room, — and, even then, it was a rebellion which perversely showed itself in acts of hospitality to the Nabob whom it was to dethrone and to the English whom it was to extirpate ; — it was a rebellion plotted by two feeble old women, headed by two eunuchs, and suppressed by an affidavit."

The acceptance, or rather exaction, of the private present of 100,000*l.* is thus animadverted upon : —

" My Lords, such was the distressed situation of the Nabob about a twelvemonth before Mr. Hastings met him at Chunar. It was a twelvemonth, I say, after this miserable scene — a mighty period in the progress of British rapacity — it was (if the Counsel will) after some natural calamities had aided the superior vigour of British violence and rapacity — it was after the country had felt other calamities besides the English — it was after the angry dispensations of Providence had, with a progressive severity of chastisement, visited the land with a famine one year, and with a Col. Hannay the next — it was after he, this Hannay, had returned to retrace the steps of his former ravages — it was after he and his voracious crew had come to plunder ruins which himself had made, and to glean from desolation the little that famine had spared, or rapine overlooked : — *then* it was that this miserable, bankrupt Prince, march-

ing through his country, besieged by the clamours of
his starving subjects, who cried to him for protection
through their cages — meeting the curses of some of his
subjects, and the prayers of others — with famine at his
heels, and reproach following him, — then it was that
this Prince is represented as exercising this act of pro-
digal bounty to the very man whom he here reproaches
— to the very man whose policy had extinguished his
power, and whose creatures had desolated his country.
To talk of a free-will gift! it is audacious and ridiculous
to name the supposition. It was *not* a free-will gift.
What was it then? was it a bribe? or was it extortion?
I shall prove it was both — it was an act of gross bribery
and of rank extortion."

Again he thus adverts to this present : —

" The first thing he does is, to leave Calcutta, in
order to go to the relief of the distressed Nabob. The
second thing, is to take 100,000*l.* from that distressed
Nabob on account of the distressed Company. And the
third thing is to ask of the distressed Company this very
same sum on account of the distresses of Mr. Hastings.
There never were three distresses that seemed so little
reconcileable with one another."

Anticipating the plea of state-necessity, which
might possibly be set up in defence of the measures of the Governor-General, he breaks out into
the following rhetorical passage : —

" State-necessity! no, my Lords; that imperial tyrant, *State-Necessity*, is yet a generous despot, — bold is

his demeanour, rapid his decisions, and terrible his grasp. But what he does, my Lords, he dares avow, and, avowing, scorns any other justification, than the great motives that placed the iron sceptre in his hand. But a quibbling, pilfering, prevaricating State-Necessity, that tries to skulk behind the skirts of Justice; — a State-Necessity that tries to steal a pitiful justification from whispered accusations and fabricated rumours. — No, my Lords, that is no State-Necessity; — tear off the mask, and you see coarse, vulgar avarice, — you see peculation lurking under the gaudy disguise, and adding the guilt of libelling the public honour to its own private fraud.

"My Lords, I say this, because I am sure the Managers would make every allowance that state-necessity could claim upon any great emergency. If any great man in bearing the arms of this country; — if any Admiral, bearing the vengeance and the glory of Britain to distant coasts, should be compelled to some rash acts of violence, in order, perhaps, to give food to those who are shedding their blood for Britain; — if any great General, defending some fortress, barren itself, perhaps, but a pledge of the pride, and, with the pride, of the power of Britain; if such a man were to *   *   * while he himself was   *   * at the top, like an eagle besieged in its imperial nest †; — would the Commons of England come to accuse or to arraign such acts of state-necessity? No."

In describing that swarm of English pensioners and placemen, who were still, in violation of

† The Reporter, at many of these passages, seems to have thrown aside his pen in despair.

the late purchased treaty, left to prey on the finances of the Nabob, he says, —

" Here we find they were left, as heavy a weight upon the Nabob as ever, — left there with as keen an appetite, though not so clamorous. They were reclining on the roots and shades of that spacious tree, which their predecessors had stripped branch and bough — watching with eager eyes the first budding of a future prosperity, and of the opening harvest which they considered as the prey of their perseverance and rapacity."

We have, in the close of the following passage, a specimen of that lofty style, in which, as if under the influence of Eastern associations, almost all the Managers of this Trial occasionally indulged * : —

* Much of this, however, is to be set down to the gratuitous bombast of the Reporter. Mr. Fox, for instance, is made to say, " Yes, my Lords, happy is it for the world, that the penetrating gaze of Providence searches after man, and in the dark den where he has stifled the remonstrances of conscience darts his compulsatory ray, that, bursting the secrecy of guilt, drives the criminal frantic to confession and expiation." — *History of the Trial.* Even one of the Counsel, Mr. Dallas, is represented as having caught this Oriental contagion, to such a degree as to express himself in the following manner : — " We are now, however, (said the Counsel,) advancing from the star-light of Circumstance to the day-light of Discovery ; the sun of Certainty is melting the darkness, and — we are arrived at facts admitted by both parties ! "

"I do not mean to say that Mr. Middleton had *direct* instructions from Mr. Hastings, — that he told him to go, and give that fallacious assurance to the Nabob, — that he had that order *under his hand*. No — but in looking attentively over Mr. Middleton's correspondence, you will find him say, upon a more important occasion, ' I don't expect your public authority for this; — it is enough if you but *hint* your pleasure.' He knew him well; he could interpret every nod and motion of that head; he understood the glances of that eye which sealed the perdition of nations, and at whose throne Princes waited, in pale expectation, for their fortune or their doom."

The following is one of those laboured passages, of which the orator himself was perhaps most proud, but in which the effort to be eloquent is too visible, and the effect, accordingly, falls short of the pretension : —

"You see how Truth — empowered by that will which gives a giant's nerve to an infant's arm — has burst the monstrous mass of fraud that has endeavoured to suppress it. — It calls now to Your Lordships, in the weak but clear tone of that Cherub, Innocence, whose voice is more persuasive than eloquence, more convincing than argument, whose look is supplication, whose tone is conviction, it calls upon you for redress, it calls upon you for vengeance upon the oppressor, and points its heaven-directed hand to the detested, but unrepenting author of its wrongs !"

His description of the desolation brought upon some provinces of Oude by the misgovernment of Colonel Hannay, and of the insurrection at Goruckpore against that officer in consequence, is, perhaps, the most masterly portion of the whole speech : —

" If we could suppose a person to have come suddenly into the country, unacquainted with any circumstances that had passed since the days of Sujah ul Dowlah, he would naturally ask — what cruel hand has wrought this wide desolation, what barbarian foe has invaded the country, has desolated its fields, depopulated its villages ? He would ask, what disputed succession, civil rage, or frenzy of the inhabitants, had induced them to act in hostility to the words of God, and the· beauteous works of man? He would ask, what religious zeal or frenzy had added to the mad despair and horrors of war ? — The ruin is unlike any thing that appears recorded in any age; it looks like neither the barbarities of men, nor the judgments of vindictive heaven. There is a waste of desolation, as if caused by fell destroyers, never meaning to return and making but a short period of their rapacity. It looks as if some fabled monster had made its passage through the country, whose pestiferous breath had blasted more than its voracious appetite could devour.

" If there had been any men in the country, who had not their hearts and souls so subdued by fear, as to refuse to speak the truth at all upon such a subject, they would have told him, there had been no war since the time of Sujah ul Dowlah, — tyrant, indeed, as he was, but then deeply regretted by his subjects — that no hostile blow of any enemy had been struck in that land — that there had been no disputed succession — no civil war — no religious frenzy. But that these were the tokens of British friendship, the marks left by the embraces of British allies — more dreadful than the blows of the bitterest enemy. They would tell him that these allies had converted a prince into a slave, to make him the principal in the extortion upon his subjects ; — that their rapacity increased in proportion as the means of supplying their avarice diminished ; that they made the sovereign pay as if they had a right to an increased price, because the labour of extortion and plunder increased. To such causes, they would tell him, these calamities were owing.

" Need I refer Your Lordships to the strong testimony of Major Naylor when he rescued Colonel Hannay from their hands — where you see that this people, born to submission and bent to most abject subjection — that even they, in whose meek hearts injury had never yet begot resentment, nor even despair bred courage — that *their* hatred, *their* abhorrence of Colonel Hannay was such that they clung round him by thousands and thousands ; — that when Major Naylor rescued him, they refused life from the hand that could rescue Hannay ; — that they nourished this desperate consolation, that by their death they should at least thin the number of wretches who suffered by his devastation and extortion. He says that, when he crossed the river, he found the poor wretches quivering upon the parched banks of the polluted river, encouraging their blood to flow, and consoling themselves with the thought, that it would not sink into the earth, but rise to the common God of humanity, and cry aloud for vengeance on their destroyers ! — This warm description — which is no declamation of mine, but founded in actual fact, and in fair, clear proof before Your Lordships — speaks powerfully what

the cause of these oppressions were, and the perfect just-
ness of those feelings that were occasioned by them.
And yet, my Lords, I am asked to prove *why* these people
arose in such concert: — 'there must have been machinations, forsooth, and the Begums' machinations, to produce all this!' — Why did they rise! — Because they
were people in human shape; because patience under
the detested tyranny of man is rebellion to the sovereignty
of God; because allegiance to that Power that gives us
the *forms* of men commands us to maintain the *rights*
of men. And never yet was this truth dismissed from
the human heart — never in any time, in any age —
never in any clime, where rude man ever had any social
feeling, or where corrupt refinement had subdued all
feelings, — never was this one unextinguishable truth
destroyed from the heart of man, placed, as it is, in the
core and centre of it by his Maker, that man was not
made the property of man; that human power is a trust
for human benefit; and that when it is abused, revenge
becomes justice, if not the bounden duty of the injured.
These, my Lords, were the causes why these people
rose."

Another passage in the second day's Speech
is remarkable, as exhibiting a sort of tourney
of intellect between Sheridan and Burke, and
in that field of abstract speculation, which was
the favourite arena of the latter. Mr. Burke
had, in opening the prosecution, remarked, that
prudence is a quality incompatible with vice,
and can never be effectively enlisted in its cause:
— " I never (he said) knew a man who was

bad, fit for *service* that was good. There *is*
always some disqualifying ingredient, mixing
and spoiling the compound. The man seems
paralytic on that side, his muscles there have
lost their very tone and character — they cannot move. In short, the accomplishment of any
thing good is a physical impossibility for such a
man. There is decrepitude as well as distortion:
he could not, if he would, is not more certain
than that he would not, if he could." To this
sentiment the allusions in the following passage
refer : —

"I am perfectly convinced that there is one idea,
which must arise in Your Lordships' minds as a subject
of wonder, — how a person of Mr. Hastings's reputed
abilities can furnish such matter of accusation against
himself. For, it must be admitted that never was there
a person who seems to go so rashly to work, with such
an arrogant appearance of contempt for all conclusions,
that may be deduced from what he advances upon the
subject. When he seems most earnest and laborious to
defend himself, it appears as if he had but one idea uppermost in his mind — a determination not to care what
he says, provided he keeps clear of fact. He knows
that truth must convict him, and concludes, *à converso,*
that falsehood will acquit him; forgetting that there must
be some connection, some system, some co-operation,
or, otherwise, his host of falsities fall without an enemy,
self-discomfited and destroyed. But of this he never
seems to have had the slightest apprehension. He falls
to work, an artificer of fraud, against all the rules of

architecture ; — he lays his ornamental work first, and his massy foundation at the top of it ; and thus his whole building tumbles upon his head. Other people look well to their ground, choose their position, and watch whether they are likely to be surprised there ; but he, as if in the ostentation of his heart, builds upon a precipice, and encamps upon a mine, from choice. He seems to have no one actuating principle, but a steady, persevering resolution not to speak the truth or to tell the fact.

" It is impossible almost to treat conduct of this kind with perfect seriousness ; yet I am aware that it ought to be more seriously accounted for — because I am sure it has been a sort of paradox, which must have struck Your Lordships, how any person having so many motives to conceal — having so many reasons to dread detection — should yet go to work so clumsily upon the subject. It is possible, indeed, that it may raise this doubt—whether such a person is of sound mind enough to be a proper object of punishment ; or at least it may give a kind of confused notion, that the guilt cannot be of so deep and black a grain, over which such a thin veil was thrown, and so little trouble taken to avoid detection. I am aware that, to account for this seeming paradox, historians, poets, and even philosophers — at least of ancient times — have adopted the superstitious solution of the vulgar, and said that the gods deprive men of reason whom they devote to destruction or to punishment. But to unassuming or unprejudiced reason, there is no need to resort to any supposed supernatural interference ; for the solution will be found in the eternal rules that formed the mind of man, and gave a quality and nature to every passion that inhabits in it.

" An Honourable friend of mine, who is now, I believe, near me, — a gentleman, to whom I never can on
any occasion refer without feelings of respect, and, on
this subject, without feelings of the most grateful homage;
— a gentleman, whose abilities upon this occasion, as
upon some former ones, happily for the glory of the age
in which we live, are not entrusted merely to the perishable eloquence of the day, but will live to be the admiration of that hour when all of us are mute, and most of
us forgotten; — that Honourable gentleman has told
you that Prudence, the first of virtues, never can be used
in the cause of vice. If, reluctant and diffident, I might
take such a liberty, I should express a doubt, whether
experience, observation, or history, will warrant us in
fully assenting to this observation. It is a noble and a
lovely sentiment, my Lords, worthy the mind of him who
uttered it, worthy that proud disdain, that generous scorn
of the means and instruments of vice, which virtue and
genius must ever feel. But I should doubt whether we
can read the history of a Philip of Macedon, a Cæsar, or
a Cromwell, without confessing, that there have been evil
purposes, baneful to the peace and to the rights of men,
conducted — if I may not say, with prudence or with
wisdom — yet with awful craft and most successful and
commanding subtlety. If, however, I might make a
distinction, I should say that it is the proud attempt to
mix a *variety* of lordly crimes, that unsettles the prudence
of the mind, and breeds this distraction of the brain. *One*
master-passion, domineering in the breast, may win the
faculties of the understanding to advance its purpose, and
to direct to that object every thing that thought or human
knowledge can effect; but, to succeed, it must maintain
a solitary despotism in the mind — each rival profligacy
must stand aloof, or wait in abject vassalage upon its

throne. For, the Power, that has not forbad the entrance of evil passions into man's mind, has, at least, forbad their union ; — if they meet they defeat their object, and their conquest, or their attempt at it, is tumult. Turn to the Virtues — how different the decree ! Formed to connect, to blend, to associate, and to co-operate; bearing the same course, with kindred energies and harmonious sympathy, each perfect in its own lovely sphere, each moving in its wider or more contracted orbit, with different, but concentering, powers, guided by the same influence of reason, and endeavouring at the same blessed end — the happiness of the individual, the harmony of the species, and the glory of the Creator. In the Vices, on the other hand, it is the discord that insures the defeat — each clamours to be heard in its own barbarous language; each claims the exclusive cunning of the brain ; each thwarts and reproaches the other ; and even while their fell rage assails with common hate the peace and virtue of the world, the civil war among their own tumultuous legions defeats the purpose of the foul conspiracy. These are the Furies of the mind, my Lords, that unsettle the understanding ; these are the Furies, that destroy the virtue, Prudence, — while the distracted brain and shivered intellect proclaim the tumult that is within, and bear their testimonies, from the mouth of God himself to the foul condition of the heart."

The part of the Speech which occupied the Third Day (and which was interrupted by the sudden indisposition of Mr. Sheridan) consists chiefly of comments upon the affidavits taken before Sir Elijah Impey, — in which the irrelevance and inconsistency of these documents is shrewdly exposed, and the dryness of detail, inseparable from such a task, enlivened by those light touches of conversational humour, and all that by-play of eloquence of which Mr. Sheridan was such a consummate master. But it was on the Fourth Day of the oration that he rose into his most ambitious flights, and produced some of those dazzling bursts of declamation, of which the traditional fame is most vividly preserved. Among the audience of that day was Gibbon, and the mention of his name in the following passage not only produced its effect at the moment, but, as connected with literary anecdote, will make the passage itself long memorable. Politics are of the day, but Literature is of all time — and, though it was in the power of the orator, in his brief moment of triumph, to throw a lustre over the historian by a passing epithet *, the name of the latter will, at the long run, pay back the honour with interest. Having repro- bated the violence and perfidy of the Governor-

* Gibbon himself thought it an event worthy of record in his Memoirs. " Before my departure from England (he says), I was present at the august spectacle of Mr. Hastings's Trial in Westminster Hall. It is not my province to absolve or condemn the Governor of India ; but Mr. Sheridan's elo- quence demanded my applause ; nor could I hear without emotion the personal compliment which he paid me in the presence of the British nation. From this display of genius, which blazed four successive days," &c. &c.

General, in forcing the Nabob to plunder his
own relatives and friends, he adds ; —

> " I do say, that if you search the history of the world,
> you will not find an act of tyranny and fraud to surpass
> this; if you read all past histories, peruse the Annals of
> Tacitus, read the luminous page of Gibbon, and all the
> ancient or modern writers, that have searched into the
> depravity of former ages to draw a lesson for the present,
> you will not find an act of treacherous, deliberate, cool
> cruelty that could exceed this."

On being asked by some honest brother Whig,
at the conclusion of the Speech, how he came
to compliment Gibbon with the epithet " luminous," Sheridan answered, in a half whisper,
" I said ' *voluminous.*' "

It is well known that the simile of the vulture
and the lamb, which occurs in the address of
Rolla to the Peruvians, had been previously employed by Mr. Sheridan, in this Speech ; and it
showed a degree of indifference to criticism, —
which criticism, it must be owned, not unfre-
quently deserves, — to reproduce before the
public an image, so notorious both from its application and its success.   But, called upon, as
he was, to levy, for the use of that Drama, a
hasty conscription of phrases and images, all of
a certain altitude and pomp, this veteran simile,
he thought, might be pressed into the service

among the rest. The passage of the Speech in which it occurs is left imperfect in the Report: —

" This is the character of all the protection ever afforded to the allies of Britain under the government of Mr. Hastings. They send their troops to drain the produce of industry, to seize all the treasures, wealth, and prosperity of the country, and then they call it Protection ! — it is the protection of the vulture to the lamb. •   •   • "

The following is his celebrated delineation of Filial Affection, to which reference is more frequently made than to any other part of the Speech ; — though the gross inaccuracy of the printed Report has done its utmost to belie the reputation of the original passage, or rather has substituted a changeling to inherit its fame.

" When I see in many of these letters the infirmities of age made a subject of mockery and ridicule ; when I see the feelings of a son treated by Mr. Middleton as puerile and contemptible ; when I see an order given from Mr. Hastings to harden that son's heart; to choke the struggling nature in his bosom ; when I see them pointing to the son's name and to his standard, while marching to oppress the mother, as to a banner that gives dignity, that gives a holy sanction and a reverence to their enterprise ; when I see and hear these things done — when I hear them brought into three deliberate Defences set up against the Charges of the Commons — my Lords, I own I grow puzzled and confounded, and almost begin to doubt whether, where such a defence can be offered, it may not be tolerated.

" And yet, my Lords, how can I support the claim of filial love by argument — much less the affection of a son to a mother — where love loses its awe, and veneration is mixed with tenderness ? What can I say upon such a subject ? what can I do but repeat the ready truths which, with the quick impulse of the mind, must spring to the lips of every man on such a theme ? Filial Love ! the morality of instinct, the sacrament of nature and duty — or rather let me say, it is miscalled a duty, for it flows from the heart without effort, and is its delight, its indulgence, its enjoyment. It is guided, not by the slow dictates of reason ; it awaits not encouragement from reflection or from thought ; it asks no aid of memory ; it is an innate, but active, consciousness of having been the object of a thousand tender solicitudes, a thousand waking watchful cares, of meek anxiety and patient sacrifices, unremarked and unrequited by the object. It is a gratitude founded upon a conviction of obligations, not remembered, but the more binding because not remembered — because conferred before the tender reason could acknowledge, or the infant memory record them — a gratitude and affection, which no circumstances should subdue, and which few can strengthen ; a gratitude, in which even injury from the object, though it may blend regret, should never breed resentment ; an affection which can be increased only by the decay of those to whom we owe it, and which is then most fervent when the tremulous voice of age, resistless in its feebleness, enquires for the natural protector of its cold decline.

" If these are the general sentiments of man, what must be their depravity, what must be their degeneracy, who can blot out and erase from the bosom the virtue that is deepest rooted in the human heart, and twined within the cords of life itself — aliens from nature, apostates from humanity!   And yet, if there is a crime more fell, more foul — if there is any thing worse than a wilful persecutor of his mother — it is to see a deliberate, reasoning instigator and abettor to the deed : — this it is that shocks, disgusts, and appals the mind more than the other — to view, not a wilful parricide, but a parricide by compulsion, a miserable wretch, not actuated by the stubborn evils of his own worthless heart, not driven by the fury of his own distracted brain, but lending his sacrilegious hand, without any malice of his own, to answer the abandoned purposes of the human fiends that have subdued his will! — To condemn crimes like these, we need not talk of laws or of human rules — their foulness, their deformity does not depend upon local constitutions, upon human institutes or religious creeds : — they are crimes — and the persons who perpetuate them are monsters who violate the primitive condition, upon which the earth was given to man — they are guilty by the general verdict of human kind."

In some of the sarcasms we are reminded of the quaint contrasts of his dramatic style. Thus :—

" I must also do credit to them whenever I see any thing like lenity in Mr. Middleton or his agent : — they do seem to admit here, that it was not worth while to commit a massacre for the discount of a small note of hand, and to put two thousand women and children to death, in order to procure prompt payment."

Of the length to which the language of crimination was carried, as well by Mr. Sheridan as by Mr. Burke, one example, out of many, will suffice. It cannot fail, however, to be remarked that, while the denunciations and invectives of Burke are filled throughout with a passionate earnestness, which leaves no doubt as to the sincerity of the hate and anger professed by him, — in Sheridan, whose nature was of a much gentler cast, the vehemence is evidently more in the words than in the feeling, the tone of indignation is theatrical and assumed, and the brightness of the flash seems to be more considered than the destructiveness of the fire : —

" It is this circumstance of deliberation and consciousness of his guilt — it is this that inflames the minds of those who watch his transactions, and roots out all pity for a person who could act under such an influence. We conceive of such tyrants as Caligula and Nero, bred up to tyranny and oppression, having had no equals to controul them — no moment for reflection — we conceive that, if it could have been possible to seize the guilty profligates for a moment, you might bring conviction to their hearts and repentance to their minds. But when you see a cool, reasoning, deliberate tyrant — one who was not born and bred to arrogance, — who has been nursed in a mercantile line — who has been used to look round among his fellow-subjects — to transact business with his equals — to account for conduct to his master, and, by that wise system of the Company, to detail all his transactions — who never could fly one moment from himself, but must be obliged every night to sit down and hold up a glass to his own soul — who could never be blind to his deformity, and who must have brought his conscience not only to connive at but to approve of it — *this* it is that distinguishes it from the worst cruelties, the worst enormities of those, who, born to tyranny, and finding no superior, no adviser, have gone to the last presumption that there were none above to controul them hereafter. This is a circumstance that aggravates the whole of the guilt of the unfortunate gentleman we are now arraigning at your bar."

We now come to the Peroration, in which, skilfully and without appearance of design, it is contrived that the same sort of appeal to the purity of British justice, with which the oration opened, should, like the repetition of a solemn strain of music, recur at its close, — leaving in the minds of the Judges a composed and concentrated feeling of the great public duty they had to perform, in deciding upon the arraignment of guilt brought before them. The Court of Directors, it appeared, had ordered an enquiry into the conduct of the Begums, with a view to the restitution of their property, if it should appear that the charges against them were unfounded; but to this proceeding Mr. Hastings objected, on the ground that the Begums themselves had not called for such interference in their favour, and that it was inconsistent with the " Majesty of Justice" to condescend to volunteer her services. The pompous and jesuitical style in which this singular doctrine † is expressed, in a letter addressed by the Governor-General to Mr. Macpherson, is thus ingeniously turned to account by the orator, in winding up his masterly statement to a close : —

" And now before I come to the last magnificent paragraph, let me call the attention of those who, possibly, think themselves capable of judging of the dignity and character of justice in this country ; — let me call the attention of those who, arrogantly perhaps, presume that they understand what the features, what the duties of justice are here and in India ; — let them learn a lesson from this great statesman, this enlarged, this liberal philosopher : — ' I hope I shall not depart from the simplicity of official language in saying, that the Majesty of Justice ought to be approached with solicitation, not descend to provoke or invite it, much less to debase itself by the suggestion of wrongs and the promise of redress, with the denunciation of punishment before trial, and even before accusation.' This is the exhortation which Mr. Hastings makes to his Counsel. This is the character which he gives of British justice.

* * * * * *

† " If nothing (says Mr. Mill) remained to stain the reputation of Mr. Hastings but the principles avowed in this singular pleading, his character, among the friends of justice, would be sufficiently determined."

" But I will ask Your Lordships, do you approve this representation ? Do you feel that this is the true image of Justice ? Is this the character of British Justice ? Are these her features ? Is this her countenance ? Is this her gait or her mien ? No, I think even now I hear you calling upon me to turn from this vile libel, this base caricature, this Indian pagod, formed by the hand of guilty and knavish tyranny, to dupe the heart of ignorance, — to turn from this deformed idol to the true Majesty of Justice here. *Here*, indeed, I see a different form, enthroned by the sovereign hand of Freedom, — awful without severity — commanding without pride — vigilant and active without restlessness or suspicion — searching and inquisitive without meanness or debasement — not arrogantly scorning to stoop to the voice of afflicted innocence, and in its loveliest attitude when bending to uplift the suppliant at its feet.

" It is by the majesty, by the form of that Justice, that I do conjure and implore Your Lordships to give your minds to this great business ; that I exhort you to look, not so much to words which may be denied or quibbled away, but to the plain facts, — to weigh and consider the testimony in your own minds : we know the result must be inevitable. Let the truth appear and our cause is gained. It is this, I conjure Your Lordships, for your own honour, for the honour of the nation, for the honour of human nature, now entrusted to your care, — it is this duty that the Commons of England, speaking through us, claims at your hands.

" They exhort you to it by every thing that calls sublimely upon the heart of man, by the Majesty of that Justice which this bold man has libelled, by the wide fame of your own tribunal, by the sacred pledge by which you swear in the solemn hour of decision, knowing

that that decision will then bring you the highest-reward
that ever blessed the heart of man, the consciousness of
having done the greatest act of mercy for the world, that
the earth has ever yet received from any hand but Heaven. — My Lords, I have done."

Though I have selected some of the most remarkable passages of this Speech *, it would be
unfair to judge of it even from these specimens.
A Report, *verbatim*, of any effective speech
must always appear diffuse and ungraceful in
the perusal. The very repetitions, the redun-

---

* I had selected many more, but must confess that they
appeared to me, when in print, so little worthy of the reputation of the Speech, that I thought it would be on the
whole, more prudent to omit them. Even of the passages,
here cited, I speak rather from my imagination of what they
must have been, than from my actual feeling of what they
are. The character, given of such Reports by Lord Lough-
borough, is, no doubt, but too just. On a motion made by
Lord Stanhope, (April 29. 1794,) that the short-hand writers, employed on Hastings's trial, should be summoned to
the bar of the House, to read their minutes, Lord Lough-
borough, in the course of his observations on the motion,
said, " God forbid that ever Their Lordships should call on
the short-hand writers to publish their notes ; — for, of all
people, short-hand writers were ever the farthest from correctness, and there were no man's words they ever heard
that they again returned. They were in general ignorant,
as acting mechanically ; and by not considering the antece-
dent, and catching the sound, and not the sense, they per-
verted the sense of the speaker, and made him appear as
ignorant as themselves."

dancy, the accumulation of epithets, which gave
force and momentum in the career of delivery,
but weaken and encumber the march of the
style, when read. There is, indeed, the same
sort of difference between a faithful short-hand
Report, and those abridged and polished records which Burke has left us of his speeches,
a3 there is between a cast taken directly from
the face, (where every line is accurately preserved but all the blemishes and excrescences
are in rigid preservation also,) and a model, over
which the correcting hand has passed, and all
that was minute or superfluous is generalised
and softened away.

Neither was it in such rhetorical passages as
abound, perhaps, rather lavishly, in this Speech,
that the chief strength of Mr. Sheridan's talent
lay. Good sense and wit were the great weapons of his oratory — shrewdness in detecting
the weak points of an adversary, and infinite
powers of raillery in exposing it. These were
faculties which he possessed in a greater degree
than any of his contemporaries; and so well did
he himself know the strong hold of his powers,
that it was but rarely, after this display in Westminster Hall, that he was tempted to leave it for
the higher flights of oratory, or to wander after
Sense into that region of metaphor, where too
often, like Angelica in the enchanted palace of

Atlante, she is sought for in vain. * His attempts, indeed, at the florid or figurative style,
whether in his speeches or his writings, were
seldom very successful.   That luxuriance of
fancy, which in Burke was natural and indi-
genous, was in him rather a forced and exotic
growth.   It is a remarkable proof of this difference between them, that while, in the memorandums of speeches left behind by Burke, we
find, that the points of argument and business
were those which he prepared, trusting to the
ever ready wardrobe of his fancy for their adorn-
ment, — in Mr. Sheridan's notes it is chiefly the
decorative passages, that are worked up before-
hand to their full polish ; while on the resources
of his good sense, ingenuity, and temper, he
seems to have relied for the management of his
reasonings and facts.   Hence naturally it arises
that the images of Burke, being called up on the
instant, like spirits, to perform the bidding of his
argument, minister to it throughout, with an
almost co-ordinate agency ; while the figurative
fancies of Sheridan, already prepared for the
occasion, and brought forth to adorn, not assist,
the business of the discourse, resemble rather
those sprites which the magicians used to keep

* Curran used to say laughingly, " When I can't talk
sense, I talk metaphor."

inclosed in phials, to be produced for a momentary enchantment, and then shut up again.

In truth, the similes and illustrations of Burke form such an intimate, and often essential, part of his reasoning, that if the whole strength of the Samson does not lie in these luxuriant locks, it would at least be considerably diminished by their loss. Whereas, in the Speech of Mr. Sheridan, which we have just been considering, there is hardly one of the rhetorical ornaments that might not be detached, without, in any great degree, injuring the force of the general statement. Another consequence of this difference between them is observable in their respective modes of transition, from what may be called the *business* of a speech to its more generalised and rhetorical parts. When Sheridan rises, his elevation is not sufficiently prepared; he starts abruptly and at once from the level of his statement, and sinks down into it again with the same suddenness. But Burke, whose imagination never allows even business to subside into mere prose, sustains a pitch throughout which accustoms the mind to wonder, and, while it prepares us to accompany him in his boldest flights, makes us, even when he walks, still feel that he has wings:—

" *Même quand l'oiseau marche, on sent qu'il a des ailes.*"

The sincerity of the praises bestowed by Burke on the Speech of his brother Manager has some-

times been questioned, but upon no sufficient
grounds.   His zeal for the success of the Impeachment, no doubt, had a considerable share
in the enthusiasm, with which this great effort
in its favour filled him.   It may be granted, too,
that in admiring the apostrophes that variegate
this speech, he was, in some degree, enamoured
of a reflection of himself;

" *Cunctaque miratur, quibus est mirabilis ipse.*"

He sees reflected there, in fainter light,
All that combines to make himself so bright.

But whatever mixture of other motives there
may have been in the feeling, it is certain that
his admiration of the Speech was real and unbounded.   He is said to have exclaimed to Mr.
Fox, during the delivery of some passages of it,
" There, — that is the true style ; — something
between poetry and prose, and better than
either."   The severer taste of Mr. Fox dis-
sented, as might be expected, from this remark.
He replied, that " he thought such a mixture
was for the advantage of neither — as producing
poetic prose, or, still worse, prosaic poetry."   It
was, indeed, the opinion of Mr. Fox, that the
impression made upon Burke by these somewhat
too theatrical tirades is observable in the change
that subsequently took place in his own style of

writing; and that the florid and less chastened taste, which some persons discover in his later productions, may all be traced to the example of this speech. However this may be, or whether there is really much difference, as to taste, between the youthful and sparkling vision of the Queen of France in 1792, and the interview between the Angel and Lord Bathurst in 1775, it is surely a most unjust disparagement of the eloquence of Burke, to apply to it, at any time of his life, the epithet " flowery,"— a designation only applicable to that ordinary ambition of style, whose chief display, by necessity, consists of ornament without thought, and pomp without substance. A succession of bright images, clothed in simple, transparent language, — even when, as in Burke, they " crowd upon the aching sense" too dazzlingly, — should never be confounded with that mere verbal opulence of style, which mistakes the glare of words for the glitter of ideas, and, like the Helen of the sculptor Lysippus, makes finery supply the place of beauty. The figurative definition of eloquence in the Book of Proverbs — " Apples of gold in a network of silver" — is peculiarly applicable to that enshrinement of rich, solid thoughts in clear and shining language, which is the triumph of the imaginative class of writers and orators; —while, perhaps, the net-work, *without* the gold inclosed, is a type equally significant of what is called "flowery" eloquence.

It is also, I think, a mistake, however flattering to my country, to call the School of Oratory, to which Burke belongs, *Irish*. That Irishmen are naturally more gifted with those stores of fancy, from which the illumination of this high order of the art must be supplied, the names of Burke, Grattan, Sheridan, Curran, Canning, and Plunkett, abundantly testify. Yet had Lord Chatham, before any of these great speakers were heard, led the way, in the same animated and figured strain of oratory * ; while another Englishman, Lord Bacon, by making Fancy the handmaid of Philosophy, had long since set an example of that union of the imaginative and the solid, which, both in writing and in speaking, forms the characteristic distinction of this school.

* His few noble sentences on the privilege of the poor man's cottage are universally known. There is also his fanciful allusion to the confluence of the Saone and the Rhone, the traditional reports of which vary, both as to the exact terms in which it was expressed, and the persons to whom he applied it. Even Lord Orford does not seem to have ascertained the latter point. To these may be added the following specimen : — " I don't inquire from what quarter the wind cometh   ut whither it goeth ; and if any measure that comes from the Right Honourable Gentleman tends to the public good, my bark is ready." Of a different kind is that grand passage, — " America, they tell me, has resisted — I rejoice to hear it," — which Mr. Grattan used to pronounce finer than any thing in Demosthenes.

The Speech of Mr. Sheridan in Westminster Hall, though so much inferior, in the opinion of Mr. Fox and others, to that which he had delivered on the same subject in the House of Commons, seems to have produced, at the time, even a more lively and general sensation; — possibly from the nature and numerousness of the assembly before which it was spoken, and which counted among its multitude a number of that sex, whose lips are in general found to be the most rapid conductors of fame. But there was *one* of this sex, more immediately interested in his glory, who seems to have felt it, as women alone can feel. " I have delayed writing," says Mrs. Sheridan, in a letter to her sister-in-law, dated four days after the termination of the Speech, " till I could gratify myself and you by sending you the news of our dear Dick's triumph — of *our* triumph I may call it; for, surely, no one, in the slightest degree connected with him, but must feel proud and happy. It is impossible, my dear woman, to convey to you the delight, the astonishment, the adoration, he has excited in the breasts of every class of people! Every party-prejudice has been overcome by a display of genius, eloquence, and goodness, which no one, with any thing like a heart about them, could have listened to, without being the wiser and the better for the rest of their lives. What must *my* feelings be ! — you only can imagine. To tell you the truth, it is with some difficulty that I can ' let down my mind,' as Mr. Burke said afterwards, to talk or think on any other subject. But pleasure, too exquisite, becomes pain, and I am at this moment suffering for the delightful anxieties of last week."

It is a most happy combination when the wife of a man of genius unites intellect enough to appreciate the talents of her husband, with the quick, feminine sensibility that can thus passionately feel his success. Pliny tells us, that his Calpurnia, whenever he pleaded an important cause, had messengers ready to report to her every murmur of applause that he received ; and the poet Statius, in alluding to his own victories at the Albanian Games, mentions the ·· breathless kisses " with which his wife, Claudia, used to cover the triumphal garlands he brought home. Mrs. Sheridan may well take her place beside these Roman wives ; — and she had another resemblance to one of them, which was no less womanly and attractive. Not only did Calpurnia sympathise with the glory of her husband abroad, but she could also, like Mrs. Sheridan, add a charm to his talents at home, by setting his verses to music and singing them to her harp, — " with no instructor," adds Pliny, " but Love, who is, after all, the best master."

This letter of Mrs. Sheridan thus proceeds : —
" You were perhaps alarmed by the accounts of
S.'s illness in the papers ; but I have the pleasure to assure you he is now perfectly well, and
I hope by next week we shall be quietly settled
in the country, and suffered to repose, in every
sense of the word ; for indeed we have, both of
us, been in a constant state of agitation, of one
kind or another, for some time back.

" I am very glad to hear your father continues so well. Surely he must feel happy and
proud of such a son. I take it for granted you
see the newspapers : I assure you the accounts
in them are not exaggerated, and only echo the
exclamation of admiration that is in every body's
mouth. I make no excuse for dwelling on this
subject : I know you will not find it tedious.
God bless you : — I am an invalid at present,
and not able to write long letters."

The agitation and want of repose, which Mrs.
Sheridan here complains of, arose not only from
the anxiety which she so deeply felt, for the
success of this great public effort of her husband,
but from the share which she herself had taken,
in the labour and attention necessary to prepare
him for it. The mind of Sheridan being, from
the circumstances of his education and life, but
scantily informed upon all subjects for which
reading is necessary, required, of course, con-

siderable training and feeding, before it could venture to grapple with any new or important task. He has been known to say frankly to his political friends, when invited to take part in some question that depended upon authorities, " You know I'm an ignoramus — but here I am — instruct me, and I'll do my best." It is said, that the stock of numerical lore, upon which he ventured to set up as the Aristarchus of Mr. Pitt's financial plans, was the result of three weeks' hard study of arithmetic, to which he doomed himself, in the early part of his Parliamentary career, on the chance of being appointed, some time or other, Chancellor of the Exchequer. For financial display it must be owned that this was rather a crude preparation. But there are other subjects of oratory, on which the outpourings of information, newly acquired, may have a freshness and vivacity which it would be vain to expect in the communication of knowledge that has lain long in the mind, and lost in circumstantial spirit what it has gained in general mellowness. They, indeed, who have been regularly disciplined in learning, may be not only too familiar with what they know to communicate it with much liveliness to others, but too apt also to rely upon the resources of the memory, and upon those cold outlines which it retains of knowledge whose details are faded.

The natural consequence of all this is that
persons, the best furnished with general information, are often the most vague and unim-
pressive on particular subjects ; while, on the
contrary, an uninstructed man of genius, like
Sheridan, who approaches a topic of importance
for the first time, has not only the stimulus of
ambition and curiosity to aid him in mastering
its details, but the novelty of first impressions to
brighten his general views of it — and, with a
fancy thus freshly excited, himself, is most sure
to touch and rouse the imaginations of others.

This was particularly the situation of Mr.
Sheridan with respect to the history of Indian
affairs ; and there remain among his papers numerous proofs of the labour, which his preparation for this arduous task cost not only himself
but Mrs. Sheridan. Among others, there is a
large pamphlet of Mr. Hastings, consisting of
more than two hundred pages, copied out neatly
in her writing, with some assistance from another
female hand. The industry, indeed, of all
around him was put in requisition for this great
occasion — some, busy with the pen and scissors,
making extracts — some, pasting and stitching
his scattered memorandums in their places. So
that there was hardly a single member of the
family that could not boast of having contributed
his share, to the mechanical construction of this

speech. The pride of its success was, of course, equally participated; and Edwards, a favourite servant of Mr. Sheridan, was long celebrated for his professed imitation of the manner in which his master delivered (what seems to have struck Edwards as the finest part of the speech) his closing words, " My Lords, I have done! "

The Impeachment of Warren Hastings is one of those pageants in the drama of public life, which show how fleeting are the labours and triumphs of politicians — " what shadows they are, and what shadows they pursue." When we consider the importance which the great actors in that scene attached to it, — the grandeur with which their eloquence invested the cause, as one in which the liberties and rights of the whole human race were interested, — and then think how all that splendid array of Law and of talent has dwindled away, in the view of most persons at present, into an unworthy and harassing persecution of a meritorious and successful statesman, — how those passionate appeals to justice, those vehement denunciations of crime, which made the halls of Westminster and St. Stephen's ring with their echoes, are now coldly judged, through the medium of disfiguring Reports, and regarded, at the best, but as rhetorical effusions, indebted to temper for their warmth, and to fancy for their details; — while so little was the reputation of the delinquent himself even scorched by the bolts of eloquence thus launched at him, that a subsequent House of Commons thought themselves honoured by his presence, and welcomed him with such cheers * as should reward only the friends and benefactors of freedom ; — when we reflect on this thankless result of so much labour and talent, it seems wonderful that there should still be found high and gifted spirits, to waste themselves away in such temporary struggles, and, like that spendthrift of genius, Sheridan, to *discount* their immortality, for the payment of fame in hand which these triumphs of the day secure to them.

For this direction, however, which the current of opinion has taken, with regard to Mr. Hastings and his eloquent accusers, there are many very obvious reasons to be assigned. Success, as I have already remarked, was the dazzling talisman, which he waved in the eyes of his adversaries from the first, and which his friends have made use of to throw a splendour over his tyranny and injustice ever since. † Too often,

* When called as a witness before the House, in 1813, on the subject of the renewal of the East India Company's Charter.

† In the important article of Finance, however, for which he made so many sacrifices of humanity, even the justification

in the moral logic of this world, it matters but CHAP.
little what the premises of conduct may be, so XI.
the conclusion but turns out showy and prosperous.   There is also, it must be owned, among
the English, (as perhaps, among all free people,)
a strong taste for the arbitrary, when they themselves are not to be the victims of it, which invariably secures to such accomplished despo-
tisms, as that of Lord Strafford in Ireland, and
Hastings in India, even a larger share of their
admiration than they are, themselves, always
willing to allow.

The rhetorical exaggerations, in which the
Managers of the prosecution indulged, — Mr.
Sheridan, from imagination, luxuriating in its
own display, and Burke from the same cause,
added to his overpowering autocracy of temper
— were but too much calculated to throw suspicion on the cause in which they were employed,

---

of success was wanting to his measures.   The following is
the account given by the Select Committee of the House of
Commons in 1810, of the state in which India was left by his
administration : — " The revenues had been absorbed ; the
pay and allowances of both the civil and military branches
of the service were greatly in arrear ; the credit of the Company was extremely depressed ; and, added to all, the whole
system had fallen into such irregularity and confusion, that
the real state of affairs could not be *ascertained* till the conclusion of the year 1785-6." — *Third Report.*

and to produce a re-action in favour of the person whom they were meant to overwhelm. " *Rogo vos, Judices,*"— Mr. Hastings might well have said, — " *si iste disertus est, ideo me damnari oportet ?* " *

There are also, without doubt, considerable allowances to be made, for the difficult situations in which Mr. Hastings was placed, and those impulses to wrong which acted upon him from all sides — allowances which will have more or less weight with the judgment, according as it may be more or less fastidiously disposed, in letting excuses for rapine and oppression pass muster. The incessant and urgent demands of the Directors upon him for money may palliate, perhaps, the violence of those methods which he took to procure it for them ; and the obstruction to his policy which would have arisen from a strict observance of Treaties, may be admitted, by the same gentle casuistry, as an apology for his frequent infractions of them.

Another consideration to be taken into account, in our estimate of the character of Mr. Hastings as a ruler, is that strong light of publicity, which the practice in India of carrying on the business of government by written documents threw on all the machinery of his measures, deliberative as well as executive. These

* Seneca, Controvers. lib. iii. c. 19.

Minutes, it is true, form a record of fluctuation CHAP.
and inconsistency — not only on the part of the XI.
Governor-General, but of all the members of the
government — a sort of weather-cock diary of
opinions and principles, shifting with the interests or convenience of the moment*, which
entirely takes away our respect even for success,
when issuing out of such a chaos of self-contra-
diction and shuffling. It cannot be denied, however, that such a system of exposure — submitted, as it was in this case, to still further scrutiny, under the bold, denuding hands of a Burke
and a Sheridan — was a test to which the coun-

---

* Instances of this, on the part of Mr. Hastings, are numberless. In remarking upon his corrupt transfer of the
management of the Nabob's household in 1778, the Directors
say, " It is with equal surprise and concern that we observe
this request introduced, and the Nabob's ostensible rights so
solemnly asserted at this period by our Governor-General;
because, on a late occasion, to serve a very different purpose, he has not scrupled to declare it as visible as the light
of the sun, that the Nabob is a mere pageant, and without
even the shadow of authority." On another transaction in
1781, Mr. Mill remarks: " It is a curious moral spectacle to
compare the minutes and letters of the Governor-General,
when, at the beginning of the year 1780, maintaining the
propriety of condemning the Nabob to sustain the whole of
the burden imposed upon him, and his minutes and letters
maintaining the propriety of relieving him from those bur-
thens in 1781. The arguments and facts adduced on the
one occasion, as well as the conclusion, are a flat contradiction to those exhibited on the other."

cils of few rulers could with impunity be brought.
Where, indeed, is the statesman that could bear
to have his obliquities thus chronicled? or where
is the Cabinet that would not shrink from such
an inroad of light into its recesses?

The undefined nature, too, of that power which
the Company exercised in India, and the uncertain state of the Law, vibrating between the
English and Hindoo codes, left such tempting
openings for injustice as it was hardly possible
to resist. With no public opinion to warn off
authority from encroachment, and with the precedents set up by former rulers all pointing the
wrong way, it would have been difficult, perhaps,
for even more moderate men than Hastings, not
occasionally to break bounds and go continually
astray.

To all these considerations in his favour is to
be added the apparently triumphant fact, that
his government was popular among the natives
of India, and that his name is still remembered
by them with gratitude and respect.

Allowing Mr. Hastings, however, the full advantage of these and other strong pleas in his
defence, it is yet impossible, for any real lover of
justice and humanity, to read the plainest and
least exaggerated history of his government*,

* Nothing can be more partial and misleading than the
colouring given to these transactions by Mr. Nicholls and

without feeling deep indignation excited at almost every page of it. His predecessors had, it
is true, been guilty of wrongs as glaring — the
treachery of Lord Clive to Omichund in 1757,
and the abandonment of Ramnarain to Meer
Causim under the administration of Mr. Van-
sittart, are stains upon the British character
which no talents or glory can do away. There
are precedents to be found, through the annals
of our Indian empire, for the formation of the
most perfect code of tyranny, in every department, legislative, judicial, and executive, that
ever entered into the dreams of intoxicated
power. But, while the practice of Mr. Hastings was, at least, as tyrannical as that of his predecessors, the principles upon which he founded

---

other apologists of Hastings. For the view which I have
myself taken of the whole case I am chiefly indebted to the
able History of British India by Mr. Mill, — whose industrious research and clear analytical statements make him the
most valuable authority that can be consulted on the subject.

The mood of mind in which Mr. Nicholls listened to the
proceedings of the Impeachment may be judged from the
following declaration, which he has had the courage to promulgate to the public: — " On this Charge (the Begum
Charge) Mr. Sheridan made a speech, which both sides of the
House professed greatly to admire — for Mr. Pitt now
openly approved of the Impeachment. *I will acknowledge,
that I did not admire this speech of Mr. Sheridan.*"

that practice were still more odious and unpardonable. In his manner, indeed, of defending himself he is his own worst accuser — as there is no outrage of power, no violation of faith, that might not be justified by the versatile and ambidextrous doctrines, the lessons of deceit and rules of rapine, which he so ably illustrated by his measures, and has so shamelessly recorded with his pen.

Nothing but an early and deep initiation in the corrupting school of Indian politics could have produced the facility with which, as occasion required, he could belie his own recorded assertions, turn hostilely round upon his own expressed opinions, disclaim the proxies which he himself had delegated, and, in short, get rid of all the inconveniences of personal identity, by never acknowledging himself to be bound by any engagement or opinion which himself had formed. To select the worst features of his Administration is no very easy task; but the calculating cruelty with which he abetted the extermination of the Rohillas — his unjust and precipitate execution of Nuncomar, who had stood forth as his accuser, and, therefore, became his victim, — his violent aggression upon the Raja of Benares, and that combination of public and private rapacity, which is exhibited in the details of his conduct to the Royal family of Oude, — these are acts, proved by the testimony of himself and his accomplices, from the disgrace of which no formal acquittal upon points of law can absolve him, and whose guilt the allowances of charity may extenuate, but never can remove. That the perpetrator of such deeds should have been popular among the natives of India only proves how low was the standard of justice, to which the entire tenor of our policy had accustomed them ; — but that a ruler of this character should be held up to admiration in England, is one of those anomalies with which England, more than any other nation, abounds, and only inclines us to wonder that the true worship of Liberty should so long have continued to flourish in a country, where such heresies to her sacred cause are found.

I have dwelt so long upon the circumstances and nature of this Trial, not only on account of the conspicuous place which it occupies in the fore-ground of Mr. Sheridan's life, but because of that general interest which an observer of our Institutions must take in it, from the clearness with which it brought into view some of their best and worst features. While, on one side, we perceive the weight of the popular scale, in the lead taken, upon an occasion of such solemnity and importance, by two persons brought forward from the middle ranks of society into the very van of political distinction and influence, on the other hand, in the sympathy and favour extended by the Court to the practical assertor of despotic principles, we trace the prevalence of that feeling, which, since the commencement of the late King's reign, has made the Throne the rallying point of all that are unfriendly to the cause of freedom. Again, in considering the conduct of the Crown Lawyers during the Trial — the narrow and irrational rules of evidence which they sought to establish — the unconstitutional control assumed by the Judges, over the decisions of the tribunal before which the cause was tried, and the refusal to communicate the reasons upon which those decisions were fo unded — above all, too, the legal opinions expressed on the great question relative to the abatement of an Impeachment by Dissolution, in which almost the whole body of lawyers * took the wrong, the pedantic, and the unstatesman-like side of the question ; — while in all these indications of the spirit of that profession, and of its propensity to tie down the giant, Truth, with its small threads of technicality and precedent, we perceive the danger to

* Among the rest, Lord Erskine, who allowed his profession, on this occasion, to stand in the light of his judgment. " As to a Nisi-prius lawyer (said Burke) giving an opinion on the duration of an Impeachment — as well might a rabbit, that breeds six times a year, pretend to know any thing of the gestation of an elephant ! "

be apprehended from the interference of such a
spirit in politics, on the other side, arrayed against
these petty tactics of the Forum, we see the
broad banner of Constitutional Law, upheld
alike by a Fox and a Pitt, a Sheridan and a Dundas, and find truth and good sense taking refuge
from the equivocations of lawyers, in such consoling documents as the Report upon the Abuses
of the Trial by Burke — a document which, if
ever a reform of the English Law should be
attempted, will stand as a great guiding light to
the adventurers in that heroic enterprise.

It has been frequently asserted, that on the
evening of Mr. Sheridan's grand display in the
House of Commons, The School for Scandal and
The Duenna were acted at Covent Garden and
Drury Lane, and thus three great audiences
were at the same moment amused, agitated, and,
as it were, wielded by the intellect of one man.
As this triple triumph of talent — this manifest-
ation of the power of Genius to multiply itself,
like an Indian god — was, in the instance of Sheridan, not only possible, but within the scope of
a very easy arrangement, it is to be lamented
that no such coincidence did actually take place,
and that the ability to have achieved the miracle
is all that can be with truth attributed to him.
From a careful examination of the play-bills of
the different theatres during this period, I have

ascertained, with regret, that neither on the evening of the speech in the House of Commons, nor on any of the days of the oration in Westminster Hall, was there either at Covent Garden, Drury Lane, or Haymarket theatres, any piece whatever of Mr. Sheridan's acted.

The following passages of a letter from Miss Sheridan to her sister in Ireland, written while on a visit with her brother in London, though referring to a later period of the Trial, may without impropriety be inserted here : —

" Just as I received your letter yesterday, I was setting out for the trial with Mrs Crewe and Mrs. Dixon. I was fortunate in my day, as I heard all the principal speakers — Mr. Burke I admired the least — Mr. Fox very much indeed. The subject, in itself, was not particularly interesting, as the debate turned merely on a point of law, but the earnestness of his manner and the amazing precision with which he conveys his ideas is truly delightful. And last, not least, I heard my brother ! I cannot express to you the sensation of pleasure and pride that filled my heart at the moment he rose. Had I never seen him or heard his name before, I should have conceived him the first man among them at once. There is a dignity and grace in his countenance and deportment, very striking — at the same time that one cannot trace the smallest degree of conscious superiority in his manner. His voice, too, appeared to me extremely fine. The speech itself was not much calculated to display the talents of an orator, as of course it related only to dry matter. You may suppose I am not so lavish of praises before indifferent persons, but I am sure you will acquit me of partiality in what I have said. When they left the Hall we walked about some time, and were joined by several of the managers — among the rest by Mr. Burke, whom we set down at his own house. They seem now to have better hopes of the business than they have had for some time; as the point urged with so much force and apparent success relates to very material evidence which the Lords have refused to hear, but which, once produced, must prove strongly against Mr. Hastings; and from what passed yesterday they think Their Lordships must yield. — We sat in the King's box," &c.

END OF THE FIRST VOLUME.

London:
Printed by A. & R. Spottiswoode,
New-Street-Square.

GS
SS
SM

Check Out More Titles From HardPress Classics Series In this collection we are offering thousands of classic and hard to find books. This series spans a vast array of subjects – so you are bound to find something of interest to enjoy reading and learning about.

Subjects:
Architecture
Art
Biography & Autobiography
Body, Mind &Spirit
Children & Young Adult
Dramas
Education
Fiction
History
Language Arts & Disciplines
Law
Literary Collections
Music
Poetry
Psychology
Science
…and many more.

Visit us at www.hardpress.net